DATE DUE

			1 0 2008

Demco, Inc. 38-293

NUKAK

PUBLICATIONS OF THE INSTITUTE OF ARCHAEOLOGY, UNIVERSITY COLLEGE LONDON

Director of the Institute: Stephen Shennan
Publications Series Editor: Peter J. Ucko

The Institute of Archaeology of University College London is one of the oldest, largest, and most prestigious archaeology research facilities in the world. Its extensive publications program includes the best theory, research, pedagogy, and reference materials in archaeology and cognate disciplines, through publishing exemplary work of scholars worldwide. Through its publications, the Institute brings together key areas of theoretical and substantive knowledge, improves archaeological practice, and brings archaeological findings to the general public, researchers, and practitioners. It also publishes staff research projects, site and survey reports, and conference proceedings. The publications program, formerly developed inhouse or in conjunction with UCL Press, is now produced in partnership with Left Coast Press, Inc. The Institute can be accessed online at www.ucl.ac.uk/archaeology.

ENCOUNTERS WITH ANCIENT EGYPT Subseries, Peter J. Ucko, (ed.)

Jean-Marcel Humbert and Clifford Price (eds.), *Imhotep Today* (2003)

David Jeffreys (ed.), *Views of Ancient Egypt since Napoleon Bonaparte: Imperialism, Colonialism, and Modern Appropriations* (2003)

Sally MacDonald and Michael Rice (eds.), *Consuming Ancient Egypt* (2003)

Roger Matthews and Cornelia Roemer (eds.), *Ancient Perspectives on Egypt* (2003)

David O'Connor and Andrew Reid (eds.), *Ancient Egypt in Africa* (2003)

John Tait (ed.), *¿Never Had the Like Occurredî: Egyptís View of its Past* (2003)

David O'Connor and Stephen Quirke (eds.), *Mysterious Lands* (2003)

Peter Ucko and Timothy Champion (eds.), *The Wisdom of Egypt: Changing Visions Through the Ages* (2003)

Andrew Gardner (ed.), *Agency Uncovered: Archaeological Perspectives* (2004)

Okasha El-Daly, Egyptology, *The Missing Millennium: Ancient Egypt in Medieval Arabic Writing* (2005)

Ruth Mace, Clare J. Holden, and Stephen Shennan (eds.), *Evolution of Cultural Diversity: A Phylogenetic Approach* (2005)

Arkadiusz Marciniak, *Placing Animals in the Neolithic: Social Zooarchaeology of Prehistoric Farming* (2005)

Robert Layton, Stephen Shennan, and Peter Stone (eds.), *A Future for Archaeology* (2006)

Joost Fontein, *The Silence of Great Zimbabwe: Contested Landscapes and the Power of Heritage* (2006)

Gabriele Puschnigg, *Ceramics of the Merv Oasis: Recycling the City* (2006)

James Graham-Campbell and Gareth Williams (eds.), *Silver Economy in the Viking Age* (2007)

Barbara Bender, Sue Hamilton, and Chris Tilley, *Stone Worlds: Narrative and Reflexivity in Landscape Archaeology* (2007)

Andrew Gardner, *An Archaeology of Identity: Soldiers and Society in Late Roman Britain* (2007)

Sue Hamilton, Ruth Whitehouse, and Katherine I. Wright (eds.) *Archaeology and Women* (2007)

Gustavo Politis, *Nukak: Ethnoarchaeology of an Amazonian People* (2007)

Janet Picton, Stephen Quirke, and Paul C. Roberts (eds.), *Living Images: Egyptian Funerary Portraits in the Petrie Museum* (2007)

Eleni Asouti and Dorian Q. Fuller, *Trees and Woodlands of South India: Archaeological Perspectives* (2007)

Timothy Clack and Marcus Brittain, *Archaeology and the Media* (2007)

Sue College and James Conolly, *The Origins and Spread of Domestic Plants in Southwest Asia and Europe* (2007)

NUKAK

Ethnoarchaeology of an Amazonian People

Gustavo G. Politis
translated by Benjamin Alberti

Left
Coast
Press
inc.

Walnut Creek, CA
University College London Institute of Archaeology Publications

Left Coast Press, Inc.
1630 North Main Street, #400
Walnut Creek, California 94596
http://www.Lcoastpress.com

Library of Congress Cataloging-In-Publication Data

Politis, Gustavo G.
   [Nukak. English]
   Nukak: ethnoarchaeology of an Amazonian people/Gustavo Politis;
translated by Benjamin Alberti.
      p. cm.
   Includes bibliographical references and index.
   ISBN 978-1-59874-229-9 (hardback: alk. paper)
   1. Nukak Indians—Social life and customs. I. Title.
   F2270.2.N8P65 2007   981'.13—dc22   2006102358

07 08 09 5 4 3 2 1

Printed in the United States of America

The paper used in this publication meets the minimum requirements of American National Standard for Information Sciences—Permanence of Paper for Printed Library Materials, ANSI/NISO Z39.48—1992.

g green press
INITIATIVE

Left Coast Press Inc. is committed to preserving ancient forests and natural resources. We elected to print *Nukak: Ethnoarchaeology Of An Amazonian People* on 30% post consumer recycled paper, processed chlorine free. As a result, for this printing, we have saved:

   3 Trees (40' tall and 6-8" diameter)
   1,444 Gallons of Wastewater
   581 Kilowatt Hours of Electricity
   159 Pounds of Solid Waste
   313 Pounds of Greenhouse Gases

Left Coast Press Inc. made this paper choice because our printer, Thomson-Shore, Inc., is a member of Green Press Initiative, a nonprofit program dedicated to supporting authors, publishers, and suppliers in their efforts to reduce their use of fiber obtained from endangered forests.

For more information, visit www.greenpressinitiative.org

Cover design by Andrew Brozyna

To Iannis, Theo, and Amparo

CONTENTS

Preface

This book presents and explains the results of ethnoarchaeological research carried out among the Nukak since 1990. It is the final report on a project that, sad to say, I could not continue owing to the extreme violence in the region. Through this book I hope to contribute both to knowledge of the Nukak and to the creation of a methodological and conceptual corpus that will improve the interpretation and explanation of the archaeological record of hunter-gatherers.

The Nukak are at an extremely fragile point in their history, embedded as they are in a complex and hazardous sociopolitical context. They probably represent one of the last opportunities to observe a hunter-gatherer society that still lives in a traditional way. The data that form the core of this book were recorded prior to massive changes brought about by consistent contact between the Nukak and Westerners. Now the Nukak situation is significantly different. Many bands have dramatically changed their traditional lifestyles and are partially settled near the Colombian colonist ranches. Unfortunately, I have not been able to follow these changes up close. In 1996, at the beginning of our eighth fieldwork season, we encountered a column of FARC guerillas (Revolutionary Armed Forces of Colombia), as we had on other occasions. However, this time we were made to leave the area and were told not to return until the violence had calmed. The violence has yet to subside.

The research project from which this book derives was established in 1990 jointly with Gerardo Ardila (Professor at the Universidad Nacional, Santafé de Bogotá) (see Ardila 1992; Ardila & Politis 1992). Subsequently, the project split as a result of differing scientific interests, and I continued the research under the financial and institutional support of the Wenner Grenn Foundation for Anthropological Research and the Instituto Amazónico de Investigaciones Científicas (SINCHI), Colombia. With the support of these institutions I was able to complete the seven fieldwork seasons that gave origin to this book.

By means of this book I aim to expand knowledge of the variability in modes of life, social patterns, and ideational orders among forager societies. I also explore causal factors that are not usually considered in archaeological studies (that is, factors other than the technoeconomic), both for human behavior and its material derivatives. My principal case study consists of the Nukak as they were found when I carried out my fieldwork (the so-called ethnographic present). However, I do not mean to imply that they have always been this way, even in the recent past. I further wish to stress that I do not use the Nukak case inferentially to claim that all past hunters-gatherers behaved in the same way; neither do I attempt to make universal generalizations based on one particular sample.

I began writing this book in 2001 thanks to a generous invitation by Ian Hodder to take up a position as Visiting Professor in the Department of Social Anthropology, University of Stanford. During the seven months I was there I made significant advances, drafting a number of chapters and especially making intensive use of the library resources. This enabled me to gain information on other South American hunter-gatherers that I would not have had access to in Argentina. Moreover, the intellectual environment of Stanford University, including frequent chats with Ian Hodder and the other professors in the department, was stimulating and enriching. A large part of the originality of this book is due to this positive input.

Although this book is an original piece of work, preliminary versions of some chapters have been published as articles, principally in Spanish. Chapters 1, 2, 3, and 10 and Appendices I and II are original, having not been published elsewhere. Chapter 8 is based on two previous publications with other members of the research team (Cárdenas & Politis 2000; Politis, Martínez, & Rodríguez 1997); Chapter 9 also has two antecedent publications (Politis & Martínez 1996; Politis & Saunders 2002). Throughout the book I have made an effort to incorporate information on other Makú and Amazonian indigenous groups, with the goal of making the finished product useful to the ethnoarchaeology of tropical hunter-gatherers. As such, I attempt both to place the Nukak within a broader sociopolitical context and to analyze the information generated from a regional perspective.

Acknowledgments

This book was made possible with the help of many people and institutions.

Foremost, I would like to express my gratitude to Julián Rodríguez Pavón, who was an outstanding fieldwork companion from 1992 onward. Most of the data presented in this book were collected with his invaluable assistance. Moreover, Julián was an astute observer and a person with whom I was able to discuss and analyze most of the ideas presented here. I owe him a large debt of gratitude. Dairon Cárdenas (Director of SINCHI's Amazonian Herbarium, Colombia) and Gustavo Martínez (Researcher for CONICET, Argentina) also accompanied me into the field, in 1995–1996 and 1992, respectively, and made all kinds of valuable contributions. Dairon carried out all the floral identifications and studies of plant distributions. Gustavo analyzed the faunal remains recovered, and made substantial contributions especially to questions concerning faunal exploitation and subsistence (see Appendix II). My debt to both Dairon and Gustavo is considerable.

The consistent support of Darío Fajardo Montaña, colleague and friend, was fundamental to the successful development of the investigation. In his position as Director of the Instituto Amazónico de Investigaciones Científicas SINCHI, he supported my research from the start, providing resources, equipment, and advice that made possible fieldwork in an area as fraught with complications as Colombia's Guaviare Department. Rosario Piñeres Vergara of the same institution always offered invaluable assistance.

Several colleagues and friends in Colombia provided support at various points during my research. Gerardo Ardila and I designed the first project together, which we initiated from the Department of Anthropology of the Universidad Nacional, Bogotá, Colombia, where he holds the position of professor. Our research interests later diverged. On two occasions Ardila and I visited Dr. Reichel-Dolmatoff, who advised us on how to make initial contact with the Nukak. During this first stage of research Professor Jaime Arocha, Universidad Nacional, Bogotá, Colombia, also provided us with words of wisdom. Alicia Eugenia Silva, Director of the Museo de la Casa de Marquéz de San Jorge and the Fondo de Promoción de la Cultura of the Banco Popular collaborated in the initial stages of the project, giving not only help but also friendship. Blanca Diaz and Pedro Lamus from the same Institution assisted me in every way possible. The various directors of the Office of Indigenous Affairs of the Ministerio del Gobierno (the Colombian State Department) were always extremely cooperative; I would like to make special mention of Luis Azcárate and Martín Von Hildebrand. The missionaries of the Asociación Nuevas Tribus de Colombia, Israel Gualteros, Andrés Jiménez, and Kenneth Conduff, generously shared with me the rich information that they had collected through many years of contact with the Nukak. Finally, Colombian colleagues and friends—Cristóbal Gnecco, Hector Mondragón, Carl Langebaeck, Carlos López, José Octavio López, Leonardo Reina, Roberto Pineda Camacho, and Ivan Yunnis—in one way or another provided continuous support for the project, lending a hand when necessary. The Argentinian anthropologist Juan Manuel Alegre—living at that time in San José del Guaviare—gave me great advice and warm friendship.

Two institutions provided the bulk of the financial backing for this project: the Wenner Gren Foundation for Anthropological Research, which awarded the project two grants (5882 and 5707), and the Amazonian Institute for Scientific Research, SINCHI, Colombia. Thanks to these two institutions I was able to conduct my fieldwork and carry out all stages of the research. In Argentina, the National Council of Scientific Research (CONICET), the Universidad Nacional del Centro de la Provincia de Buenos Aires (UNCPBA), and the Universidad Nacional de La Plata (UNLP) provided additional support.

Most of this book was written in the Center for Archaeological Research at Stanford University, thanks to a generous invitation by Dr. Ian Hodder. On both this occasion and several others Ian was a true promoter of this project, and he has given me help, advice, and friendship in recent years. I owe him a large debt of gratitude. In Stanford I also received the friendship and support of John and Rosa Rick, and my entertaining office companion (and, fortunately, fellow football fan) "Stringy" Carter.

Over the last few years I have discussed many of the ideas and opinions that I summarize in this book with a number of colleagues, who have undoubtedly enriched the final product in addition to improving earlier, possibly confused, versions. I would especially like to highlight the contributions of Peter Ucko, Clive Gamble, Nick Saunders, Almudena Hernando, Lewis Binford, Luis Borrero, María Gutiérrez, Rafael Curtoni, and Michael Shott. Diego Gobbo gave me an extraordinary help with the maps and figures; Clara Scabuzzo with the bibliography and the tables; and Violeta Di Prado with the index.

Without a doubt, this book would not have been possible without the help of Benjamin Alberti, who not only completed the English translation but also made innumerable suggestions and did a good deal of editorial work.

Finally, I would like to thank Carolina for her unconditional support throughout these years.

ILLUSTRATIONS

Chapter 1

Chapter 4

Chapter 5

Chapter 6

Chapter 7

Chapter 8

Chapter 9

Appendix II

TABLES

Appendix II

Chapter 1

Introduction

This book brings together the results of six years research of the Nukak, a hunter-gatherer group from the Colombian Amazon. These results are based on information collected during seven fieldwork seasons carried out between 1990 and 1996, as well as on interviews with two Nukak boys with a good command of the Spanish language and three Nukak women who were hospitalized in Santafé de Bogotá. In the mid-1990s the Nukak population was estimated at approximately 500 known people, a figure arrived at from several different sources of information and by correlating data from researchers in the area. Of this population I have had contact with 223 individuals from nine different bands (or band segments) in their habitat in the tropical rainforest, as well as the three women in Santafé de Bogotá mentioned above (they had been taken there temporarily for medical treatment) and three children who lived in *colonos* (settlers'[1]) houses in Guaviare. This gives a total of 229 people with whom I have had face-to-face contact, and from whom I have gained knowledge of the various aspects of Nukak culture.

In addition to the information I collected personally, I have incorporated into my discussion the results published by other researchers who have studied different aspects of the Nukak culture, especially Gabriel Cabrera, Carlos Franky, and Dany Mahecha (Cabrera, Franky, & Mahecha 1994, 1999; Franky, Cabrera, & Mahecha 1995), Hector Mondragón (Ms, 2000), and Ivan Yunis, Marion Piñeros, and Juan Pablo Rueda (Ms). I have also included in my arguments data collected by the missionaries of the New Tribes Mission Association of Columbia (Asociación Nuevas Tribus de Colombia), which I obtained through interviews with Kenneth Conduff, Israel Gualteros, Andrés Jiménez, and Joaquín Foster, and from several of their unpublished reports, which are available in the Division of Indigenous Affairs of the Government Ministry of Colombia (División de Asuntos Indígenas del Ministerio de Gobierno de Colombia). These reports have been used widely by other researchers, especially in the initial phase of the scientific study of the Nukak. Finally, I have incorporated information and commentary from the *colonos* who have had contact with the Nukak and other indigenous groups in the region (especially the Tukano, the Kurripaco, and the Puinave). As such, I have attempted to present my observations, interpretations, and ideas within a broad context in which the perspectives of other researchers and people on different aspects of Nukak culture are included. The center around which the book develops is rooted in the idea that, by presenting several perspectives, interpretative horizons can be widened and discussions opened up, despite the fact that our ethnographic narratives derive from the categories of Western capitalist urban society. By so doing, I intend to reduce the effect of what has been called the "my people" syndrome—meaning the interpretation of another culture through the categories generated between the researcher and his or her informants, resulting in unwarranted generalizations.

In terms of theory, the research on which this book is based has three layers of influence. First, Lewis Binford's impressive work on hunter-gatherer archaeology and ethnoarchaeology has produced powerful tools with which to examine and interpret the archaeological record, design ethnoarchaeological research projects, and set a series of questions. His work has been a constant source of inspiration. Binfordian processual archaeology, much more than other processual currents, is one of the pillars on which I have built my archaeological and ethnoarchaeological research, and I mention or discuss his ideas in virtually every chapter of this book. Although two other theoretical approaches have covered this foundational theoretical layer, I believe that it is still easily recognizable in the theoretical/methodological structure of my ethnoarchaeological research.

However, and in spite of the use of an array of processual conceptual tools, I have always been suspicious of the way in which ecological-materialist approaches, which dominated the archaeology of such societies during the 1980s and 1990s, have presented hunter-gatherers. These approaches put too much weight on ecological factors and how these have supposedly shaped and determined hunter-gatherer behavior (Thomas 2000). The majority of such studies have produced reductionist and generalist models. There is nothing inherently wrong with this; in scientific research the number of variables must be reduced to make them manageable and analyzable. Generalizations from a handful of examples are a valid resource in allowing one to arrive at broader and more comprehensive conclusions. Nonetheless, in the case of hunter-gatherer models and their archaeological applications such reductionism has mislead the process of inquiry, and the generalizations have erased the significant variation in the category labeled "hunter-gatherer" or "forager" (*latu sensu*, not that in Binford 1982). My doubts became stronger when I began my research among the Nukak and understood the influence of social and ideational aspects on daily life. At this point, and after I had been encouraged by a stay of several months at Cambridge University, the second layer of theoretical contributions to this book began to form. This layer would be located within postprocessualism and influenced principally by Ian Hodder (1982, 1986, 1987, 1990). Within this area the insightful review papers by Whitley (1992, 1998) and the analysis of the ethical and moral implication of the practice of archaeology developed by Peter Ucko (1983, 1985) were also enlightening.

The third, and probably less visible, layer of influence comes from the work of William Balée (1994, 1998a, 1998b) and other authors engaged with the historical ecology approach (that is, Crumley 1994; Posey 1994). These studies reinforced and delimited two ideas that gestated during the process of investigation. First, that the historical process of events is responsible for the major transformations in the relationships between people and environment (Balée 1998a); and second, that the relationship between human beings and the environment should be conceived of as dialectical rather than the process of adaptation of people to the environment (Balée 1998a:14; Ingerson 1994:65). As such, this complimentary perspective enabled gaps to be bridged to a degree between the first two sets of contributions. In some way my research can be considered part of a broader change from the view of Amazonian people as isolated in an adaptive, one-to-one dialogue with nature, toward a fundamentally historical conception of human ecology (Balée 1998a, 1998b; Viveiros de Castro 1996).

Owing to my background in archaeology, when I started this project I was familiar with the research and adaptive models emerging from cultural ecology put forward for the Amazon (that is, Brochado 1984; Lathrap 1970; Meggers 1971; Meggers & Evans 1957; Moran 1993; Roosevelt 1980; Ross 1978; Steward 1948). Many of these models, furthermore, had been formulated from within archaeology. Nonetheless, I knew little about Amazonian ethnography, and especially the social and cosmological aspects of the indigenous peoples of the region. The gateway to tackling these subjects was several works by Reichel-Dolmatoff (1971, 1976, 1985, 1991), especially his research among the Desana (1968, 1978, 1996), in which he referred to the Makú numerous times. Subsequently, other authors working from different perspectives achieved a more integrated view of Amazonian cultures, not only of their adaptive processes but also their cosmology and religion (that is, Århem 1990; Descola 1994; Hugh-Jones 1979; Reichel-Dussan 1989; Viveiros de Castro 1992, 1996). This work opened my mind to subject matter usually overlooked in the archaeology of hunter-gatherers and gave me a less adaptationist view of Amazonian societies. These studies enabled me to compare and contextualize my case study.

The goal of the research that led to this book was to develop a series of models of different degrees of resolution and hierarchy to contribute to the interpretation of the archaeological record of hunter-gatherers specifically and material culture in general. To date, most interpretations of hunter-gatherer archaeological sites have consistently adopted cost-benefit materialist approaches, thereby denying the potential of ideational imperatives in shaping the archaeological record and informing our views of the past. Previously, the latter was often avoided on the grounds that cosmology, or beliefs are difficult to identify or control in the archaeological record, especially those produced by simple societies such as hunter-gatherers. I admit these difficulties but believe that it is possible to take an initial step toward overcoming them. I propose to demonstrate in this book that even though ecological factors always play a role, the behavior and decisions taken by the Nukak—and I imagine many other hunter-gatherers as well—are neither shaped by the environment nor based on the search for an optimal cost-benefit relationship. In other words, I agree that the external environmental must be incorporated in our explanations/interpretations of the behavior of hunter-gatherers. But, it is by no means only through these variables that we will be able to understand and explain their behavior or the archaeological record left by them. Therefore, I believe that the study of hunter-gatherers through narrow ecological models leaves aside important causal factors that shape their behavior and go beyond adaptation to the physical and social environments. This is not intended to be an antiecological manifesto. Neither do I intend to use this case study to criticize popular approaches within the archaeology of hunter-gatherers, such as behavioral ecology (Kelly 1995; Winterhalder 1987, 2001), evolutionary archaeology, or selectionism (Dunnell 1980; O'Brien 1996; O'Brien and Holland 1995). Such critiques have already been done (that is, Hodder 1982; Ingold 2000; Leach 1973; Shanks & Tilley 1987a, 1987b; Thomas 2000; Whitley 1998) and have generated an active exchange of opinions. Although processual archaeology has already abandoned the pretension of generating laws or lawlike prepositions (with the exception, perhaps, of behavioral archaeology and Darwinian approaches), it still retains an aftertaste of ecological functionalism, especially in hunter-gatherer studies. Therefore, this book attempts to locate the debate on a wider plain, one that does not consider ecological factors to be the only principle variables that structure hunter-gatherer behavior, and to place social and ideational aspects in the same order of importance and magnitude. It also aims to generate interpretative tools that enable these factors to be identified in the archaeological record; that is, to construct a set of methods and models that are context-specific, strategically engaged, and designed to draw out particular information from particular contexts (Thomas 2000:3). Finally, I aim to add a new kind of data that is relevant to the interpretation of the archaeological record of tropical rainforests, a kind of record with its own distinctive characteristics.

The goal of the project was to study the Nukak from an ethnoarchaeological perspective, based on a methodology that would enable relevant information to be collected from the start of the investigation, despite my lack of knowledge of the language (at the commencement of fieldwork all the Nukak were monolingual). Above all, it was clear to me that gaining such knowledge would be a long and complex process. However, it is far more complex to translate beyond words and phrases and to transfer the experience of fieldwork and different cultural categories. Nonetheless, I believed it was possible to obtain relevant quantitative information from the beginning of the investigation and then properly contextualize and interpret the information gathered in the exploratory phase later as I advanced in the language and general understanding of this ethnic group.

The study of hunter-gatherers has always been a key area in social anthropology and archaeology, and its status has been the subject of intense debate. Although some have postulated that the category of "hunter-gatherers" is an absurd and obsolete derivation of evolutionary theory, others see it as firmly anchored in empirical reality (Bird-David 1992; Lee 1992; Lee & Daly 1999). In spite of the strong revisionary current that contests the actual existence of such a category (Arcand 1981; Myers 1988; Price & Brown 1985; Stiles 1992; Wilmsen 1983, 1989) and assumes that "pure" hunter-gatherers do not exist, it is still possible to identify groups whose economy and sociopolitical organization are located within the broader meaning of the concept of hunter-gatherers or foragers (Bird-David 1990, 1992; Burch 1994; Lee 1992). The Nukak are found within this category, and, unlike the majority of present-day hunter-gatherer groups, a part of their population still maintains (or maintained during our fieldwork) traditional cultural patterns and independence from other Indian groups and Western society.

Within Western society tradition has a clear meaning, "tradition is the illusion of permanence" (Allen 1998). However, the adjective "traditional" has a completely different meaning when used in this book and within the context of Nukak culture. I will start with a series of negations in order to be clear. In referring to traditional Nukak bands I am not implying any of the following ideas: that they are encapsulated in a "pure" or "pristine" state; that they are living representatives of prehistory; that they are a fossilized society; or that they have remained unchanged for generations. The Nukak have their own history and assuredly have changed through time within the processes of the cultural dynamics of American indigenous societies. Amazonian archaeology and Amazonian ethnohistory provide abundant evidence in this regard (that is, Heckenberger, Neves, & Petersen 1998; Heckenberger, Peterson, & Neves 1999; McEwan, Barreto, & Neves 2001; Meggers 1971; Meggers & Evans 1957; Neves 1999; Roosevelt 1991). This process of change developed within an Amazonian cultural context in which the Nukak related in particular ways with their indigenous neighbors and endured as best they could the invasions of European and Western cultures (the rubber industry boom, the *tigrillada* or jaguar craze, and so on). The linguistic information collected by Reina (1990), Mondragón (Ms 2000) and Cabrera, Franky, and Mahecha (1999) stands as witness of the numerous words of diverse origin (that is, Cubeo, Puinave, Tukano, and so on) in the Nukak language that testify to contact with nearby indigenous groups or perhaps a common ancestor. Nukak mythology also mentions their origin lying to the southeast of their present territory, which implies migrations and old interethnic relations with groups that are today distant, especially the other Makú peoples. Before the 1980s the Nukak certainly had indirect and possibly direct but sporadic contact with Western society, probably for quite some time, through the complex supraregional systems of exchange in the Amazon and the Llanos. Friedemann and Arocha's synthesis (1982:43–50) testifies to the complexity and magnitude of these networks for the circulation of information, ideas, objects, and slaves. Throughout this period, Nukak culture changed and transformed, but remained firmly entrenched within, an indigenous Amazonian context. In other words, these changes and adjustments took place with the rhythm and dynamic proper to these societies. In the 1980s this rhythm of change and the magnitude of the impact were altered by regular and growing contact with the increased colonization of Guaviare (Acosta 1993; Molano 1987). Within some bands cultural patterns began to transform rapidly with a new dynamic and an asymmetrical relationship generated by the colonization. This different rhythm was imposed on them by their position of subordination to Western society. For some bands the impact has not been as great, and although they have started to use metal axes and machetes and even items of clothing, their culture by and large maintains its traditional patterns. Hence, their way of life still preserves a type of mobility, subsistence patterns, social organization, and cosmology, among other things, that have not been significantly altered by contact with the colonos.

THE NUKAK AND THE MAKÚ

The Nukak are hunter-gatherers who inhabit the Colombian Amazon and are affiliated with the Makú. The foragers of the northwest Amazon have been grouped under the generic name Makú (Correa 1987; Jackson 1983:148–63; Koch-Grünberg 1906; Metraux 1948; Münzel 1969–1972; Tastevin 1923). This is not a self-denomination, since none of the indigenous groups call themselves by this name. *Makú* is considered a word of Arawak or Tukano origin that is used to designate some of the interfluvial hunter-gatherer groups of the northwest Amazon, and it generally has a pejorative connotation when used by other indigenous peoples (especially the Tukanos, for who the term *Makú* means servant or slave). For some researchers the word *Makú* simply means "Indian of another group" (G. Taylor in Henley, Mattei-Müller, & Reid 1994–1996:4), used to "designate nothing more precise than the 'wild' Indian in a given region" (Jackson 1983:149), or "a word in the Arawak language from the Rio Negro that means speechless" (following Taylor in Cabrera, Franky, & Mahecha 1999:34). According to Giacone (1955) the word *Makú* is used to refer to entirely different indigenous groups from Colombia, Brazil, and Venezuela. For the Spanish-speaking *colonos* of Colombia, *Makú* is used as a synonym of "wild Indian," and for the Portuguese-speaking Brazilian *caboclos*, *Makú* is synonymous of *indios do mato* ("Indians of the forest"). Therefore, a first point to bear in mind when undertaking an anthropological analysis of any of these groups is that the term *Makú* is vague and imprecise. Despite affinities in certain aspects of their lifeways, and the fact that they belong to the same language trunk, distinct linguistic/ethnic groups are encompassed by this term. Each has its own historical trajectory and has suffered the effects of Western society in variable and significantly different ways at different times.

Between the seventeenth and nineteenth centuries the word *maco* was used by historical sources from the Orinoco to designate indigenous people "subjected to servitude" (Useche 1987:164). In the nineteenth century several travelers and scientists mentioned the word *Makú* in designating hunter-gatherers who had usually been taken into slavery by other groups that inhabited the Rio Negro region. In 1820 Martius collected reports on the Makú in the area of the Japurá River and some of its tributaries (Münzel 1969–1972:143). Also in 1820 the Austrian explorer Natterer navigated the Rio Negro and collected a list of words that he indicated as Anodocete-Makú from the Teyá River (Biocca 1965:435). Herndon (1851:253, 279) heard Makú spoken on the Japurá River and in Magú (described as Makú), in the area of the Cuiuni, the Urubaxi, and the Japurá rivers. In 1853 Spruce mentioned that the "Macú" were "one of the few wandering tribes with no fixed residence who existed in the Amazon forest and are met with along nearly the entire length of the Rio Negro, but principally westward of it, basically between this river and the Japurá" (Spruce 1908:344, 477). In 1882, in a Franciscan missionary document, the Tukanos from the Upper Tiquié River are prohibited for all eternity from capturing and selling *macús* (Makú) to whites (Giacone 1955:3). Whiffen (1915:60) mentioned the nomadic nature of the Makú, whom he characterized as "a tribe of small, dark people, universally regarded and treated as slaves." Since these early accounts the Makú have generally been considered as "miserable specimens of humanity" (Spruce 1908:344), a view that persisted into the twentieth century (McGovern 1927:147).

The word spread in the ethnographic literature following the work of Koch-Grünberg (1906, 1995 [1909]), who recognized the existence of several groups in the area of the Negro, the Tiquié-Vaupés, and the Japurá rivers. He considered these groups to be ethnically distinct but with some shared traits. Subsequently, Rivet and Testevin (1920) examined Kock-Grünberg's work and arrived at the conclusion that all the languages of the groups generically denominated Makú—the majority of which are mutually unintelligible— were dialects of a single mother tongue. As such, they proposed the existence of the Makú-Puinave linguistic family, which included not only the groups mentioned but also the Puinave. Metraux (1948) caused a degree of confusion concerning the Makú in his paper published in the well-known *Handbook of South American Indians*. Metraux (1948:864) proposed the existence of "three different tribes of Indian who are linguistically unrelated," which, as well as the classic Makú from the Rio Negro-Japurá, included two other distinct groups: the "Macu of the Uraricoera Basin" (in Brazilian Guiana) and the "Macu-Piaroa," a subgroup of the latter who live on the lower Ventuari and Orinoco rivers. These last two are not now considered part of the groups generically known as Makú. Furthermore, in the second half of the twentieth century several authors referred to the Makú, drawing attention to their linguistic differences and distinct ways of life (Biocca 1965; Giacone 1955; Schultz 1959; Terribilini & Terribilini 1961; and so on).

There are currently six recognized ethnic/linguistic Makú groups (Pozzobon 1992) geographically distributed between Brazil and Colombia, principally on the eastern side of the Rio Negro between the Guaviare and the Caquetá-Japurá rivers (Figure 1.1). The six groups are the Hupdu, Yuhup, Dow or Kamaa, Nadöb or Kabori-Nadöb, Kakwa or Bará, and Nukak. Some of these have been relatively well studied. Articles and monographs are available on

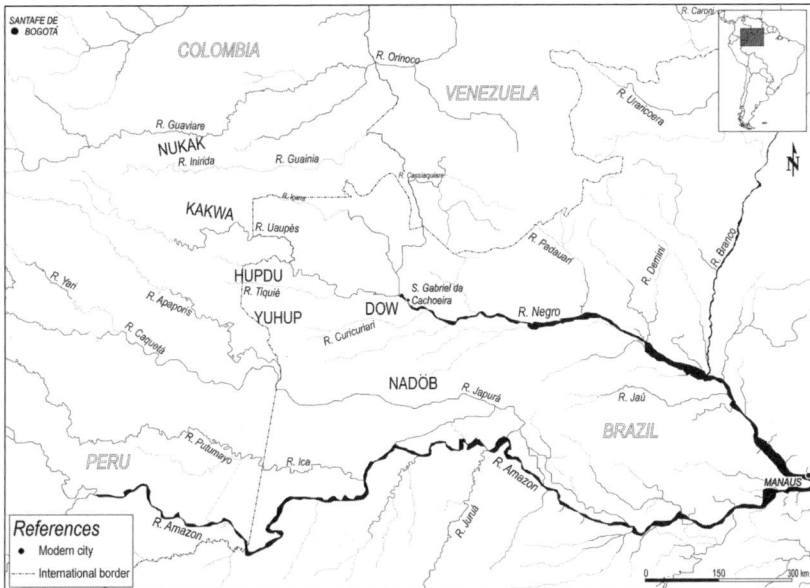

Figure 1.1   Approximate locations of the six recognized ethnic/linguistic Makú groups

the Hupdu (Athias 1995; Giacone 1955; Pozzobon 1983, 1992; Reid 1979; Terribilini & Terribilini 1961), Yuhup (Pozzobon 1983, 1992; Reina 1986), Kakwa (Silverwood-Cope 1990), and Nukak (Cabrera, Franky, & Mahecha 1999; Politis 1996a, 1996b). There are fewer scientific references for the other two, the Kabori-Nadöb being the least well known (Münzel 1969–1972[2]; Schultz 1959).

The Hupdu are the most numerous and live in the interfluvial zone of the Tiquié, the Uaupes, and the Papurí rivers. Around 1989 their population was estimated at 1,144 (Pozzobon 1992), divided into three dialectical groups. The westernmost group is located between the Upper Tiquié and the Upper Papurí rivers; the central group between the middle reaches of both rivers; and the eastern group in the forest to the southeast of the Iauareté River and Japú Creek (a tributary of the Uaupes). The Yuhup live along the tributaries south of the Tiquié Apaporis River and a tributary of the latter, the Trairá River. Their population has been estimated at 370 (Pozzobon 1992). According to Pozzobon), there are three dialects: to the west around the Castanha and Veneno creeks; to the east along the Samaúma, the Cunuri, and the Ira creeks and southward; and at the mouth of the Apaporis River. The Nadöb inhabit the most southeasterly sector of Makú land, and their population has been estimated at between 300 and 400 (Pozzobon 1992). Four dialects have been identified, corresponding to the Jurubaxi, the Uneiuxi, the Paraná Boá Boá, and the Téa rivers. The Kamaa are probably the least numerous—recently numbered at only 70 people (Pozzobon 1992)—and the most acculturated, as they live in the vicinity of the city of São Gabriel de Cachoeira.

The six known Makú groups had all incorporated some elements of horticultural practice by the time they were studied. Nonetheless, in the case of the Nukak (the most traditional) horticultural products still represented only a small proportion of their annual diet at the time fieldwork was carried out. In other cases, such as the Hupdu and Kakwa, horticulture contributes significantly to their subsistence, and its impact goes beyond diet with a notable influence on mobility patterns (Biocca 1965; Pozzobon 1992; Reid 1979; Silverwood-Cope 1972; Terribilini & Terribilini 1961). The Kakwa, Hupdu, Yuhup, and the Nadöb are considered hunter-gatherers because until a few generations ago their subsistence was based almost exclusively on the hunting and gathering of wild products (Giacone 1955; Koch-Grünberg 1906:879, 1909; Martius 1867:247; McGovern 1927; Whiffen 1915), although this was not the case when they were studied or visited after mid-twentieth century.[3] However, they have been presented as "pure hunter-gatherers" on numerous occasions. For example, Sponsel (1986:73), referring to the work of Silverwood-Cope, stated that the Makú [Kakwa] ". . . subsist exclusively by foraging without recourse to agriculture," in spite of the fact that a single Kakwa family consumes on average 100 kilos of manioc per week, which they harvest from their own gardens, where they also cultivate other domesticated species (Silverwood-Cope 1990). Similarly, the Hupdu spend some six months in their residential base, during which time "carbo-hydrate [is the] base of the diet, more than 80 percent of which is derived from manioc . . ." (Reid 1979:93). In the late 1950s manioc was the main food source for the Nadöb (Schultz 1959:119), and in the 1960s labor related to the production of manioc occupied more time in men's daily lives than did hunting and gathering combined (Münzel 1969–1972). The Yuhup were also in a similar state when studied by Pozzobon (1983).

Linguistically the Nukak belong to the Makú-Puinave family (Mondragón Ms; Reina Ms, 1990), as stated above. Within this family the Kakwa is the ethnic group most closely related to the Nukak in terms of linguistic affinity. Actually, the two languages appear to be largely mutually intelligible and may be considered as dialects (Cabrera, Franky, & Mahecha 1999; Henley, Mattei-Muller, & Reid 1994–1996; Mondragón Ms). The other mutually intelligible Makú groups are the Hupdu and Yuhup (Pozzobon 1992). Henley, Mattei-Müller, and Reid (1994–1996) offer a new perspective, proposing that the language spoken by the Hotï (a group that inhabit the Sierra de la Maigualida and its neighboring region in the Orinoco River Basin, Venezuela) is closely related to Makú, and that both could have derived from a hypothetical Proto-Makú/Puinave family. Furthermore, a series of similarities between Hotï and Nukak/Kakwa stand out in regard to lifeways and material culture that could support a common origin for these groups. In contrast, Zent and Zent (2002) reaffirm the genetic connection between the Hotï and Piaroa languages of Sáliva affiliation previously argued for by several authors (Guarisma 1974; Jangoux 1971; Vilera-Diaz 1985). The work of Henley, Mattei-Müller, and Reid (1994–1996) has at least called attention to the various cultural similarities between the Makú and the Hotï. These similarities are fairly significant judging by the data presented in Coppens (1983), but there are also notable differences in the modes of life of these peoples (Politis & Jaimes Ms; Zent & Zent Ms; Zent, Zent, & Martius 2001). Recently, Mondragón (2000) has also proposed a slender linguistic connection between the Nukak and Hotï, arguing, furthermore, that they both belong to the same family as Makú and Puinave. Based on a comparative study of these languages and eastern Tukano (especially as spoken by the Tatuyo), he has proposed the existence of a Tukano-Makú linguistic family.

The land inhabited nowadays by the Nukak is the interfluvial area between the Guaviare and the Inírida rivers. The Trocha Central (a dirt road that joins San José del Guaviare with Calamar) and the Cerro de las Cerbatanas (the Blowpipe Hills) mark the limits of their territory to the west and east respectively (Figure 1.2). Some researchers argue that until recently Nukak territory was far more extensive, the southern edge reaching the Papunaua River and the Aceite Creek, while to the west it included the headwaters of the Inilla, the Utilla, and the Ajajú rivers (see Mondragón Ms; Torres 1994). The creation of the "Nukak National Park" to the south of the Inírida River is due to a belief at first that the group also occupied this region. However, all the research has been concentrated in the region between the Guaviare and the Inírida rivers, and it appears that at present no Nukak bands live south of this area.

The Nukak had maintained a traditional way of life until just a few years ago, distinguishing them from other Makú who substantially reduced their mobility and spend a large part of the year in the vicinity of their cultivated plots. Obviously, they have had direct and indirect contact with riparian indigenous groups (Puinaves, Kurripacos, Guayaberos, Tukanos, and so on) and with the *colonos* and missionaries, but such contact has not substantially modified the Nukak way of life. During fieldwork, Nukak bands were found in various degrees of acculturation. Some, especially the northwestern bands, became semisedentary in the early 1990s, living alongside *colono* settlements.

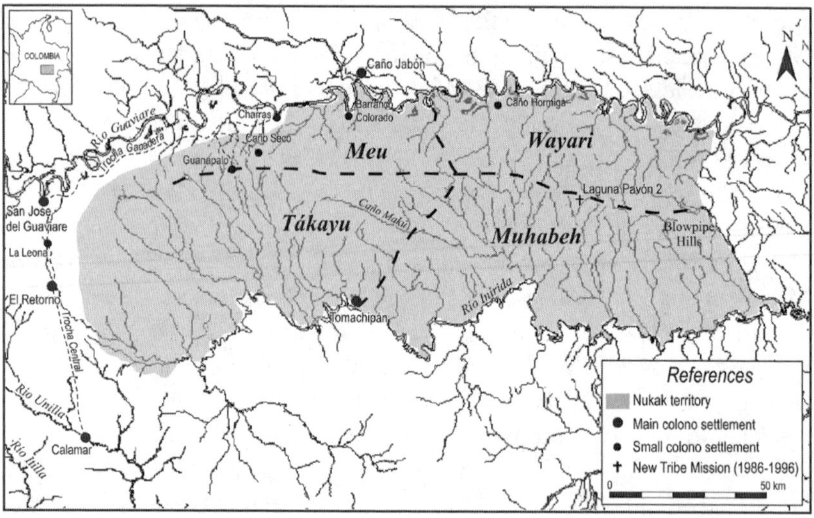

Figure 1.2 Map of the Nukak territory (including the *colonos* settlements)

Their members speak few words in Spanish and have begun to be incorporated into the labor system of the estates that temporarily hire them as *raspadores*.[4] Such bands rapidly lose their traditional mobility and settlement and technology patterns, and they become integrated into a foreign and different society. Other bands maintain a level of low contact with the *colonos* and with the New Tribes Mission but have not substantially changed their way of life. Consequently, it is to these latter bands that I refer when I use the adjective "traditional."

RECENT HISTORY OF THE NUKAK

We know little about the history of the Nukak prior to contact. Moreover, it seems that the Nukak do not keep detailed records more than three or four generations back. Nonetheless, dispersed historical, ethnohistorical, and ethnographic accounts are available and prove useful in outlining historical reconstructions. An important clue in tracing the history of the Nukak in recent centuries is the observed distribution of the Makú in the northwestern Amazon, and the relative isolation of the Nukak, the most northwestern group. Between the Nukak and their closest Makú neighbors, the Kakwa, there are several other groups (Tukano, Karapana, Uanana, and so on), one of which is the Cubeo (a Tukano-speaking tribe), who live between the Vaupés and the Cuduiarí rivers. Among the Cubeo there are several sibs—the *Bahúkiwa*—that acknowledge Makú ancestry. As Koch-Grünberg noted, they might be one of the groups that were assimilated with the Makú in the past (Goldman 1966:7). The author assigns the same origin to the Huhúteni (now within the Arawakan linguistic family) of the Lower Aiarí River and to the Catapolítani of the Middle Içana River (see Metraux 1948). Furthermore, Mondragón (2000) explains the linguistic affinity of the Nukak and Tatuyo on the basis that the latter originated from a "Tukanized" Makú. If this were the case then the distance between the Nukak and the closest Makú, the Kakwa, can be partially explained by the assimilation of Makú groups into neighboring Cubeo or Arawak, or by the "Tukanization" of Makú groups such as the Tatuyo.

A further possibility was proposed by Henley, Mattei-Müller, and Reid (1994–1996), who, based on the linguistic similarities between the Hotï and the Nukak/Kakwa, suggested a possible common origin. One piece of evidence they relied on is the existence in the colonial period of a group called the Quaqua that inhabited the zone around the junction of the Cuchivero and the Orinoco rivers. According to the Jesuit missionary Gilij (1965), this group spoke a different language to their Carib-speaking Tamanakú neighbors, and it proved impossible to subjugate them or make them settle at the missions. Henley, Mattei-Müller, and Reid (1994–1996:26) suggest, therefore, a possible genetic connection between the Quaqua (whose ethnonym sounds similar to the Kakwa), the Hotï and Kakwa, further supporting their argument with the latter group's contention that their ancestors came from the northeast. Given that the Nukak/Kakwa dialects are not mutually intelligible with the Hupdu/Yuhup/Kamaa (which are inter-intelligible), it is possible to postulate an important boundary at the middle course of the Vaupés River, where the early separation of the most significant Makú linguistic groups could have occurred. As far as we know the Kabori-Nadöb constitute a third Makú group, its language unintelligible to the other two (Henley, Mattei-Müller, & Reid 1994–1996). However, the doubts cast on the supposed linguistic links between the Hotï and Nukak/Kakwa make this a highly speculative model.

Another factor that must be borne in mind is the general southeast-northwest orientation of the Makú along the Upper Rio Negro and its principle tributaries, especially the Içana and the Tiquié rivers (Figure 1.1). If one considers that the Nukak are the most northwesterly group, and that they claim their origin to be in the southeast, a second possibility can be argued for a general dispersal of the Makú from this quadrant toward the northwest, the axis being formed by the meeting of the Upper Rio Negro-Vaupés and the Upper Japurá-Apaporis.

Finally, considering that the most important linguistic separation among the Makú clusters the Nukak with the Kakwa, and the Yuhup and Hupdu with the Kamaa, it is possible to speculate a third alternative that contemplates a common origin for both linguistic groups in the area that separates them. This area is now found in the confluence of the Tiquié and the Vaupés rivers. Of course, the location of the Makú ethno/linguistic groups will have changed, but they at least appear to have maintained a more or less clear territorial separation between the Nukak/Kakwa speakers and the Yuhup/Hupdu/Kamaa speakers. Nonetheless, the three proposals are still highly speculative, and there is no historical, linguistic, or archaeological evidence as yet to reject or accept them. Within these three fields a great deal more work must be done to understand the origin and dispersal of the Makú in the northeast Amazon.

HISTORY OF CONTACT

Until the late 1980s the Nukak were practically unknown to anthropologists; only Gerardo Reichel-Dolmatoff (1967) had made a brief reference to them and a demographic estimate of the Makú groups in the Guaviare-Inírida and the Inírida-Papunaua interfluvial areas, which he placed at 3,000 people. In the face of the arrival of the *colonos* in Guaviare in the 1960s the Nukak proved to be evasive and escaped deep into the rainforest as the felling of the forest advanced. There were reports of hostile encounters in the area of Charras in the late 1960s, which caused a degree of commotion and were widely covered in the news media. The most talked about event occurred when a group of indigenous people were murdered in late 1963 by a gang of *colonos* from La Charra (today Charras), a *colono* village on the Guaviare River (Figure 1.2), while supposedly defending themselves from an attack by "500 Makú Indian braves" (*El Espectador*, 29 December 1963). Obviously, these must have been the western bands of the Nukak. Two prisoners were taken—a man with several shotgun wounds and his wife who stayed to help him. Their fates are unknown. Other Nukak were killed by the *colonos*, and their bodies were probably buried. The event was later referred to as the "Charras massacre" (Mondragón Ms), and it most likely prompted the interest of the New Tribes Mission in contacting the Nukak. Some time later, in the mid 1970s, the missionaries began a phase of initial contact through the installation of Laguna Pavón 1, some 100 km directly east to Charras.[5] A few years later, in 1966, the parish priest of San José del Guaviare, Tulio A. Gómez, made an expedition into the forest in search of the "Macús" who had recently appeared in Charras. In a newspaper article the priest mentioned the existence of cultivated fields and "sixteen provisional houses . . . and a network of forest paths towards the 'pepeo' places [sites where *pepas* (fruits) were consumed], or [made while] searching for wild fruit, the principle means of Macú subsistence" (*El Espectador*, 20 May 1966).

Toward the end of the 1980s there were virtually no news reports on the "Makú of the Guaviare," even though the New Tribes missionaries had already made contact with the Nukak during this period and were learning their language. Therefore, when forty-three Nukak appeared in Calamar in 1988, the *colonos* were taken aback. An unclothed group of Nukak made up of women, youths, and children, with barely a single item of Western culture and not speaking a word of Spanish, had arrived at the outskirts of the village. Calamar was on their path toward ancestral territory that lay along the Unilla and the Itilla rivers. Leonardo Reina, the Colombian linguist and an expert in Yuhup, was the first on the scene. He confirmed the linguistic proximity of these people with the other Makú groups. But it was only on the arrival of Kenneth Conduff, a New Tribes missionary, that anything was found out about the group that called themselves Nukak, and whose language was closely related to that of the Kakwa. Their appearance attracted the attention of the media, and the event was widely covered by newspapers, magazines, and television (see Córdova 1988; Wirpsa 1988; and so on). Some members of the band continued westward, between the Inilla and the Utilla rivers. The trail of this group was lost. Another segment of the band was later moved to Mitú.[6] They subsequently returned to their territory from Laguna Pavón 2, a seat of the New Tribes Mission, to which they had been transported by air. Luis Azcárate (Ms), in an unpublished report, traced the journey of this first band during their incursion into the colonized zone and their assisted return to the forest. Chaves and Wirpsa (1988), Wirpsa and Mondragón (1988), Reina (1990), and Zambrano (1992, 1994) have also published detailed accounts of this "first encounter." Juan Manuel Alegre (pers. comm.:1990) provided additional information.

The reasons for this band's journey to Calamar and its subsequent relocation toward the confluence of the Inilla and the Utilla rivers are intriguing and have been subject to debate. Hector Mondragón (pers. comm.:1990) has attributed the arrival in Calamar of this band—composed, curiously, of women, children and, some young men but no adult males—to a massacre of Nukak in the Guaviare area, on the edge of the Savanna de la Fuga. Apparently, the *colonos* in the region had organized a raid into Nukak territory to recover a *colono* child who had been abducted by the indigenous group. During the raid the *colonos* killed many adult men with shotguns and forced the rest of the band to flee. Later, before their arrival in Calamar, other people—probably from southern bands—joined the group. I have not been able to corroborate these events through my own investigations, but I have been told the story of the abduction of the child and the subsequent rescue party sent to the Caño Seco and the Guanapalo zones. Among the many *colonos* who told me of the event only one admitted that he had actually taken part in the rescue attempt, although he obviously did not mention having fired on the Nukak.

Even though there was knowledge of the existence of the Nukak before 1988, and the New Tribes mission had already relocated to Laguna Pavón 2, it was in that year that the Nukak began to appear regularly at the points of colonization and to interact in a more sustained fashion with Western culture. For some unknown reason, between 1988 and 1989 the Nukak went beyond the sporadic contacts that until that moment they had had with the *colonos* and began to appear in centers of *colono* population such as Calamar, Tomachipán, and Guanapalo. It is possible that two external factors had accelerated the contact process. The first was the activity of the missionaries, who treated the Nukak entirely differently than did the hostile *colonos*. This activity also generated a demand for Western products, which were unknown or scarce before the arrival of the missionaries. The second factor was the coca rush that brought thousands of *colonos* to Nukak land and produced a notable shrinkage of their territory from the late 1980s. The advance of logging began to affect the bands' territories and consequently made contact far more frequent. As such, it was not so much that the Nukak "emerged" from the rainforest but rather that the *colonos* reduced the size of the forest, and with it Nukak territory.

On some occasions in the late 1980s the Nukak were taken to the villages on the left bank of the Guaviare River, such as Caño Jabón and Mapiripán, by the same *colonos* with whom they had recently initiated frequent and peaceful contact (Figure 1.3). After the contact in Calamar anthropologists and the Colombian government became aware of the ethnic group and began to take the necessary steps to protect and study them. In the following years various national and local institutions (from Guaviare Department), and national and regional indigenous organizations, developed partial-aid programs, particularly focused on sanitary attention for the Nukak when they entered populated areas (usually San José del Guaviare). These programs arose from the high rate of mortality among the Nukak population after contact caused by the introduction of diseases (primarily bronchial-pulmonary illnesses and measles). An international aid campaign also arose to defend Nukak territory led by the NGO Cultural Survival.

Following the communication initiated by Conduff, anthropologists discovered that the New Tribe missionaries had established the Mission Laguna Pavón 1 in 1975, on the right bank of the Guaviare River, and that in the mid-1980s they had moved it into the heart of Nukak land (Figure 1.2).

Figure 1.3 Picture of a Nukak family in Caño Jabón in 1989 (taken by a *colono* when Nukak appeared at this village for the first time)

The new Mission was called Laguna Pavón 2, from where the missionaries had begun more fluid and permanent contact with the Nukak, who regularly appeared at the Mission seeking medical attention and to exchange some of their handicrafts for metal pots, machetes, and matches. The Nukak generally stayed only a few days, usually leaving once they had been cured. During the period when the Nukak visited Calamar for the first time the missionaries estimated their total population to be between 700 and 1,000 (Azcárate Ms), of which they had had direct contact with 350. Several reports presented by the missionaries (IANTC 1990a, 1990b, 1992a, 1992b, 1993) to the Dirección de Asuntos Indígenas (Department of Indigenous Affairs) of the Colombian Government bear witness to the abundant information gathered based on a good knowledge of the language and daily contact with different bands. Through this contact the missionaries introduced new cultigens and promoted horticultural practices. Several chagras (small, multistrata cultivated plots) were located in the area around Laguna Pavón 2, which belonged to the bands with adjoining territories or those that had relocated there after the establishment of the Mission so that a greater number of bands could have access to it.

From the 1990s onward contact was far more frequent, especially when the Nukak identified colonos who treated them well and gave them food, clothing, and tools. At some of these points of contact, such as Caño Hormiga (Figure 1.4), Laguna Barajas, Caño Makú (Finca Roballos), La Rompida, and Tomachipán, the visits were regular but lasted only a few hours. The Nukak usually traveled from a camp in the area but did not sleep at the farms. Between 1991 and 1995 in the northeastern sector of the territory, bands neighboring the farms near Guanapalo, Caño Seco, La Charrasquera, Caño Mosco, and Barranco Colorado established semipermanent settlements around these points. It became a common sight to see the Nukak wandering through the villages, drinking soft drinks or beer in the bars, or setting up camps in the nearby farms. From the late 1980s Nukak women began to be abducted or taken as wives, or occasionally partners, by some colonos. Furthermore, several children were adopted by colono families and remained in their villages. The vast majority of these children lost most of the Nukak cultural traits (Sánchez Botero 1998).

Among the most important legislative actions in relation to the defense of the Nukak ethnic group was the creation of a 634,160-hectare indigenous reserve exclusively for the Nukak (Resolution Number 136, 23 November 1993, Instituto Colombiano de Reforma Agraria-Colombian Institute for Agrarian Reform), which was later extended to a total of almost 1 million

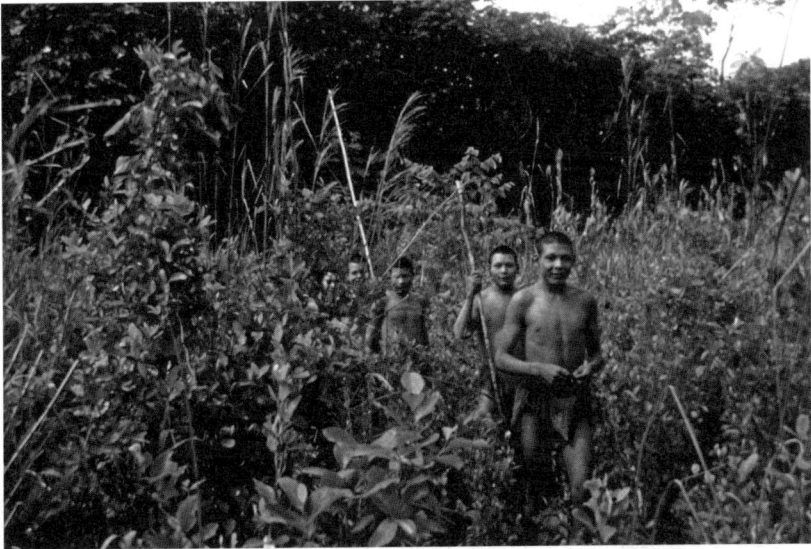

Figure 1.4 Group of young Nukak crossing a recently abandoned coca field; they are the segment of a band visiting the *colonos* of the small settlement known as Caño Hormiga.

hectares in 1997. In spite of the fact that the creation of the reserve legally protects the greater part of Nukak territory, in practice this has had no effect, because year after year thousands of hectares of forest are devastated for the planting of illicit crops (basically coca), which constitute the economic motor of the *colonos* of the Guaviare Department. The Colombian state does not have effective control over this part of the Department, and it is therefore difficult to prevent the colonization of Nukak lands. Another important landmark event was the judicial ruling in favor of the Nukak in a suit initiated by the Organización Nacional de Indígenas de Colombia (ONIC; National Organization of Indigenous People of Colombia) against a petroleum company, which resulted in the suspension of petroleum exploration in the territory.

PREVIOUS STUDIES

Several linguistic and anthropological studies were initiated shortly after the appearance of the Nukak in Calamar. Later, research was conducted in the fields of medicine and demography. This series of investigations enabled us to begin to understand the characteristics of Nukak culture, health, and relationship to the *colonos* and missionaries. Current demographic data indicate that the Nukak population is considerably smaller than the missionaries had thought or that existed during the 1980s. Cabrera, Franky, and Mahecha (1994: 472) counted 218 people affiliated to the seven local groups with which they carried out fieldwork, and another 165 for whom they had references, totaling 383 people. Detailed studies carried out by Iván Yunis, Marion Piñeros, and Juan Pablo Rueda (Ms) confirm this count and indicate that population during the mid-1990s fluctuated at around 400 people.

A significant proportion of these studies remains in the form of unpublished reports. Luis Azcárate (Ms) related how the first Nukak group that appeared in Calamar was taken to the New Tribes Mission. He also completed one of the first outlines of Nukak cultural characteristics. Leonardo Reina undertook the first linguistic study, assigning the Nukak language to the Makú-Puinave linguistic family, as well as producing the first ethnographic account (Reina Ms, 1990, 1992). Reina stayed with the group that appeared at Calamar for a short field season and was able to collect first-hand information on the Nukak way of life in their environment. An analysis of the circumstances that led to this group's arrival at Calamar and the moment of contact was done by Wirpsa (1988) and Zambrano (1992, 1994). In late 1990 and early 1991 William Torres (1994) explored the limits of Nukak territory at that time and studied the relationship between the indigenous population and the *colonos*. He proposed an extensive region within the Guaviare Department as the "nomadic territory" of this ethnic group, and although their territory appears to be smaller now (see Chapter 3), the map produced by Torres was the first attempt to determine the limits of Nukak mobility, previously unknown to anthropologists (although the New Tribe missionaries probably already had an idea of Nukak territorial boundaries).

In 1991 Héctor Mondragón (Ms) produced a report (as yet unpublished) in which he analyzed linguistic and territorial aspects of the Nukak while also presenting information related to social organization and annual subsistence. Mondragón based his work on data provided by Hupdu and Kakwa informants, who translated interviews with the Nukak. Using this information he prepared a map in which the Nukak territory appears smaller than in Torres's map and approaches what we currently believe to be the extent of their area. Furthermore, Mondragón was the first to identify regional affiliation groups, propose an annual subsistence cycle, and determined some of the plant species consumed by the Nukak. This report delineated aspects of their culture that had not previously been studied (that is, social organization and band territories) and served as the basis for the design of subsequent research projects. After this first report Mondragón (Ms) continued to study the Nukak language in depth (Mondragón 2000), a field in which he made significant advances. He was also involved in intense and sustained political activity in defense of Nukak rights.

Other published work from the early 1990s includes a study by Jean Jackson (1991) in which he examined the relationship between the Nukak and other indigenous groups within the Makú-Tukano symbiotic model. At that time the first results of the project from which the present book originated were published (Ardila & Politis 1992; Politis 1992). In 1992, under the auspices of the Sixth National Anthropology Congress in Colombia, Gerardo Ardila organized the symposium "Past and Present of American Hunter-Gatherers," in which several papers were presented on the Nukak research (Ardila 1992a; Politis & Martínez 1992; Rodríguez & Rodríguez 1992). Concurrently, Ardila (1992b) published a vivid narrative about his first experiences in the field among the Nukak. Shortly afterward, Caycedo Turriago (1993) published a lengthy article in which he analyzed the relationship between the Nukak and other ethnic groups from an historical perspective and within a micro- and macroregional context. Simultaneously, the results of preliminary medical studies carried out by researchers from the Expedición Humana were published (Salazar Gómez et al. 1993; Zarante & Salazar Gómez 1993).

In 1993 the English researcher Howard Reid visited Nukak territory for a brief fieldwork season among the western bands (Howard Reid pers. comm.:1993). Reid compared the Nukak linguistically to the Kakwa and the Hotï of Venezuela (Henley, Mattei-Müller, & Reid 1994–1996), proposing strong affinities. I know of no other publications resulting from this visit, although in Henley, Mattei-Müller, and Reid (1994–1996:18) a paper is cited as "Reid 1992" but is not found in the bibliography.

Gabriel Cabrera, Carlos Franky, and Danny Mahecha's undergraduate dissertation—presented in 1994 and subsequently revised and published in 1999 (Cabrera, Franky, & Mahecha 1999)—has undoubtedly been an important contribution to knowledge of the Nukak ethnic group. It details the results of research they carried out between 1991 and 1995, including several fieldwork seasons for relatively long periods (two or three months) among different bands, especially from the western sector. The authors collected an abundance of information, and their work addresses the most important aspects of Nukak culture, covering language, territory and mobility, shelter, material culture, subsistence, kinship and social organization, and interethnic relations. The only subject deliberately not included as a specific goal was the religious world, because, as they state, ". . . one needs to have linguistic and cultural competence to arrive at an understanding of the symbolic world as such" (Cabrera, Franky, & Mahecha 1994:20). Nonetheless, they did present and analyze some ideological and cosmological subject matter, based partially on the numerous unpublished reports (sixteen in total) of the New Tribes Mission, archived in the Department of Indigenous Affairs, Government of Colombia, to which they had access. Furthermore, one of the authors had the opportunity to spend a fieldwork season in the seat of Misión de Laguna Pavón 2 and was in direct contact with the missionaries.

To summarize and analyze every one of the subjects addressed in Cabrera, Franky, and Mahecha 1994 would exceed the objective of this brief summary of previous work on the Nukak. On the one hand their study is one of the most complete sources of information on the Nukak and without a doubt a compulsory reference for any work on this group. The information is abundant and varied. Throughout the present book the many contributions of Cabrera, Franky, and Mahecha are tested and discussed. In some areas their advances are significant: For linguistics, they put forward a proposal for a segmental phonology and investigate certain suprasegmental aspects while also contributing to the knowledge of the Makú-Puinave linguistic family. With respect to social organization, they made important contributions to knowledge of kinship, the composition and dynamic of local groups, and the existence of a patrilineal affiliation structure. They furthermore examined the possible existence of clans and discussed their characteristics. I believe the most significant contributions of this research lie in both these subject areas, language and kinship and social organization. Subsistence and mobility are also significant contributions. On the other hand, their work contains two main shortcomings: (1) previous work and authors who had worked with the Nukak are ignored; and (2) a certain amount of conceptual confusion exists in some themes (especially in the 1994 monograph). As well as the undergraduate dissertation and its updated version published in 1999, Cabrera, Franky, and Mahecha published several articles in which they presented complementary aspects of their work on the Nukak, such as questions of demography (Franky, Cabrera, & Mahecha 1995), subsistence and nutrition (Sotomayor et al. 1998), and palm management (Morcote-Rios et al. 1996, 1998).

In 1993 a research and health-care project was initiated among the Nukak under the direction of Drs. Iván Yunis and Marion Piñeros (Ms). This project has achieved success in the diagnosis and vaccination of the Nukak and produced a health-care plan that has been in effect since 1995. The plan provided medical care not only for the Nukak but also for the *colono* population and the other indigenous groups of the riverine areas of the Guaviare and the Inírida (Guahibos, Guayabero, Tukano, Puinave, and Kurripaco). In conjuncture with their research Iván Yunis and Pablo Rueda generated a complete database on the Nukak population and the composition of the bands and their territories. Regrettably, the greater part of this work remains unpublished (Yunis & Rueda Ms; Yunis, Piñeros, & Rueda Ms).

Other researchers have carried out work among the Nukak. Jorge Restrepo (Fundación Apincunay) presented several unpublished reports on the unstable state of Nukak territory and the frontier of the colonization. Savine Groux (Cambridge University) has studied ethnographic aspects of the northwestern bands and has discussed issues related to Nukak body art. Werner Diehl (1993, 1994) studied the health of the bands that periodically visit Laguna Pavón 2. In 1995 Ruth Gutiérrez Herrera (Universidad Nacional de Colombia) completed studies oriented toward the exploitation of natural resources by some bands in the north of the Nukak territory, basing her undergraduate dissertation on this work (Gutiérrez Herrera 1996).

Since 1996 it has been impossible to continue anthropological work among the Nukak owing to violence in the area, since many bands are found within zones controlled by FARC (Fuerzas Armadas Revolucionarias de Colombia, Revolutionary Armed Forces of Colombia) guerillas. The continuous confrontations between FARC and the Colombian Army—and more recently paramilitary groups—mean that the area is out of bounds for any type of scientific research.

Environment

The region in which the Nukak territory is currently found is a relatively high-altitude zone (Figure 1.5). Here the waters divide and head toward the Orinoco and the Amazon river basins. Although the Guaviare and the Inírida rivers flow into the Orinoco this part of the tropical rainforest is considered the Colombian Amazon owing to its geographical continuity with the Amazon Basin, and it is essentially the same tropical forest environment.

In the Amazon rainforest the minimum annual volume of precipitation fluctuates between 1,500 mm and 2,500 mm. The study area is located in the northwestern Amazon—strictly speaking the Colombian Eastern Rainforest—where precipitation reaches 2,500 mm to 3,000 mm annually (Domínguez 1985). Following Koeppen's classification, the climactic characterization for the zone between the Guaviare and the Inírida rivers corresponds to a rainy tropical forest climate with a short dry period (Domínguez 1985). This climate is characterized by strong pluviosity but is tempered by the existence of a dry

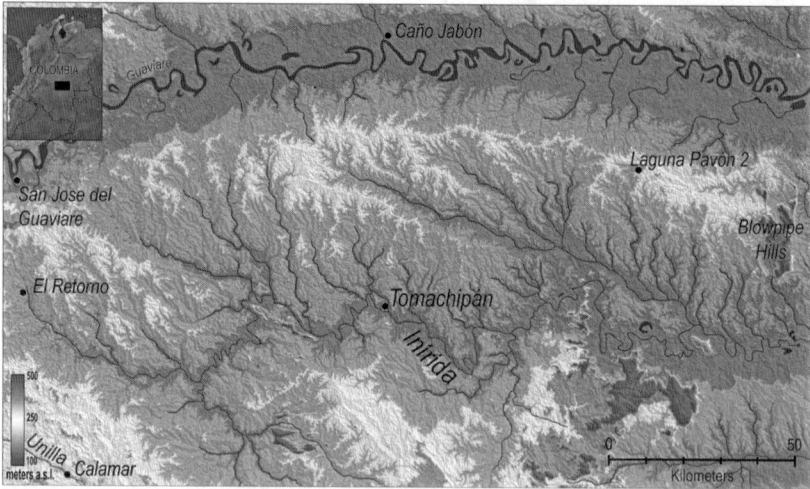

Figure 1.5 Elevation map of Nukak territory

period that, together with a relatively high average temperature (25–27°C), has obvious effects on the plant morphology of the zone; the type of rainforest that results is low and with narrow trunks. Vegetation is sparse and thin, which allows more light to penetrate to the forest floor. This effect creates a lower forest (thicket forest), far denser than that which exists on the floor of the rainforests with continuous rainfall.

The dry periods occur in opposite seasons north and south of the equator. At two degrees north, where the Guaviare and the Inírida rivers are found, the dry period (or summer) takes place from the second half of November through March, during which time not only are rainy days scarce but the pluviometric volume is also notably reduced (between 50 mm and 100 mm monthly) (Domínguez 1985). The remainder of the year is characterized by abundant precipitation (approximately 400 mm of rainfall per month), creating a rainy season (or winter) between April and the middle of November that reaches its apogee in June, July, and August. This compensates for the dry season and enables the development of the low forest.

Physiography and Soils

Although the Nukak territory appears to be a homogeneous tropical rainforest, detailed physiographic studies carried out by Dairon Cárdenas and the author (Cárdenas & Politis 2000) revealed that the following physiographic formations exist. The greater part of Nukak territory is found within the physiographic province of the Pericratonic structural plain of the Guaviare, Vaupés and

Caquetá salient, where a wide expanse of structural plains predominates (EE), covered with fluvio-deltic, fluvial, and riverine (ES) sediments with local outcrops of Paleozoic and Precambrian (EM) rocks, marked by the alluvial flatlands of the Guaviare (SN) and the Inírida (EV) rivers (Figure 1.6).

The structural plains are slightly undulating to level and terraced. They are made up of terraces and low slopes (EE1); terraced hills with gently undulating to level slopes associated with shelves that are combined with Paleozoic relief (EE2); slopes, ridged and undulating slopes, and taluses (EE3); extensive and lightly undulating hills in the vicinity of structural relief (EE4); and layers of undulating and ridged ground (EE5). The structural-errosional, mountainous-hilly topography is represented by mountain ranges, mesas, hills, and undulations skirted by escarpments and taluses of variable heights (100–400 m above-base-level) (EM1 and EM3). Surrounding the mountainous topography is a landscape dominated by the meeting of the Amazonian plains with the high plains and craton—undulating, level landscapes that constitute transitional zones for climate, vegetation, soils, and lithology.

The errosional alluvial flatlands of meandering dark-water Amazonian rivers (EV) constitute the predominant landscape for the length of the Inírida, the Caño Makú, and the Caño Caparroal rivers. These are characterized by a floodplain and several levels of terraces, flat topography, boxing of channels, erosion, and the dark color of their waters. In contrast to the alluvial flatlands mentioned above the northern extent of the territory is represented by the alluvial flatlands of the Guaviare River (SN), with several flood levels (fertile plains, higher fertile plains, and low terraces) and nonflood levels (low, medium, and high terraces). The terraces are separated by short errosional and/or structural taluses that create slight differences in height.

The soils are moderately deep, with imperfect to poor drainage, low organic material content, and a clay horizon that in some cases impedes the radial development of vegetation. Chemically their fertility is low, with a low cationic exchange capacity and a pH between 4.5 and 6.5, characteristics that condition their productivity. The zones with greatest potential are the alluvial flatlands, which can be utilized for semi-intensive agriculture in accordance with the flood seasons (EV, SN). They are classified as Paleudult, Kandiudult, Paleaquult, Plinthaquult, Tropopsamment, Dystropept, and Tropaquet.

Plant Physiognomy of the Environments in Nukak Territory

Plant physiognomy for structural and representative floral elements was estimated by field observation in the principal environments of the eastern sector of Nukak territory (Figure 1.6).

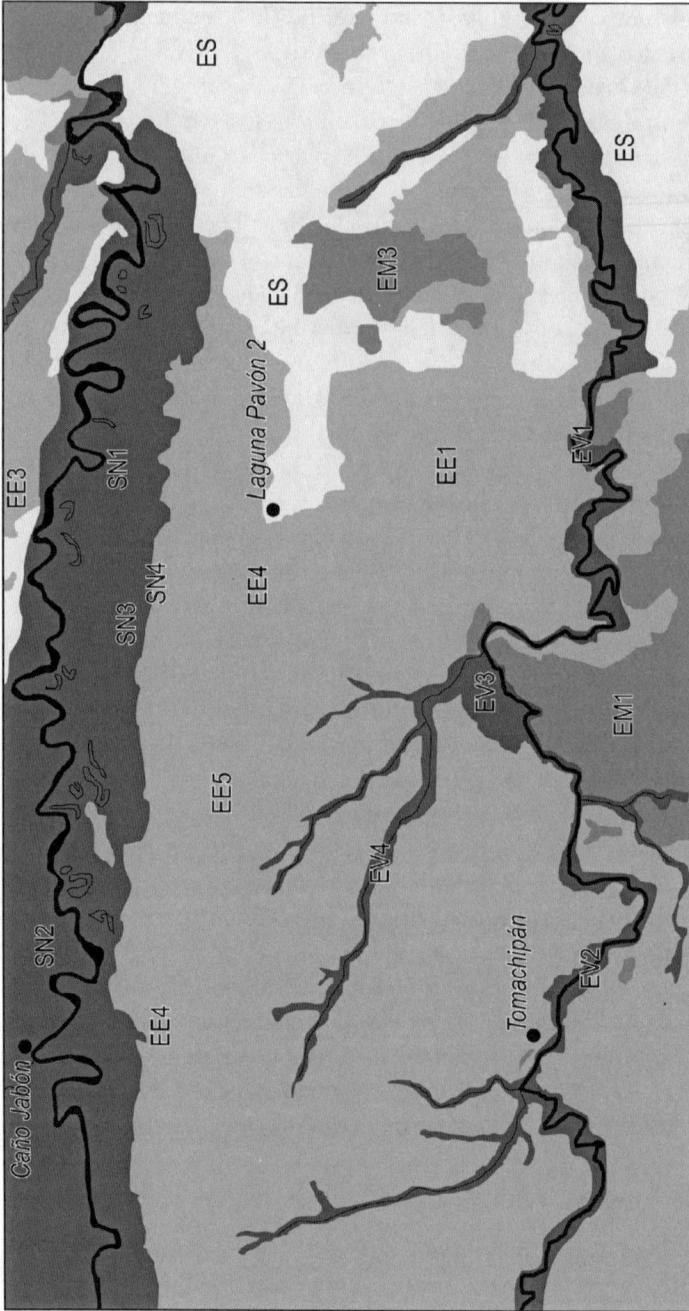

EE1: Lower terraces - EE2: Terraced slopes - EE3: Drainage basins, hillsides, and taluses - EE4: Extensive slopes - EE5: Undulating topography with some flat surfaces - EM1: Tabular hills - EM3: Residual hills - EV1: Floodplain - EV2: Lower and middle terraces - EV3: Upper terraces - EV4: Lower alluvial plains - SN1: Modern alluvial plain - SN2: Lower to middle alluvial terrace - SN3: Upper to middle alluvial terrace - SN4: Upper terrace - ES: Fluvio-deltic, fluvial and riverine sediment

Figure 1.6 Physiographic map of Nukak territory (adapted from Cárdenas & Politis 2000)

***EE*. Structured plains covered by fluvial and lake quaternary to tertiary sediments, with local outcrops of Paleozoic and Precambrian rock** The surfaces are gently undulating or flat, the product of ancient structural shelves composed of Paleozoic sediments. These environments sheltered marshes, lakes, and permanent lagoons that formed deposits of fine sediments enriched by organic material when they dried out. The forest in this environment is low to medium in height, at 15–20 m (with some emergents of 25 m) and is semidense to open with a heterogeneous canopy (cover). There are a high number of individuals with DAP (diameter at chest height) between 10 cm and 40 cm, and few individuals with DAPs greater than 60 cm. This undergrowth regenerates slowly and is dense and extremely diverse. The genera *Aechmea, Heliconia, Calathea, Miconia, Scleria, Piper*, and some ferns dominate. The floor has dense leaf coverage, low epiphytism, and few lianas.

The most abundant species in the arboreal strata are *Couma macrocarpa, Parkia* sp., *Virola* sp. (sangretoro), *Naucleopsis* spp., *Brosimum utile* (mirapiranga), *Clathrotropis macrocarpa, Caryocar glabrum* (castañita), *Goupia glabra* (chaquiro), *Dialium guianense* (pepa agria), *Aniba* sp. (amarillo), *Cedrelinga cateniformis*; and palms such as *Oenocarpus bataua* (seje), *Oenocarpus bacaba* (patabá), *Astrocaryum aculeatum, Iriartea deltoidea* (bombona), and *Socratea exorrhiza* (zancona). It is common to find patches of *Phenakospermum guyanense* (platanillo).

***EM*. Mountainous topography, eroded structural hills of sandy quartz, and granite with sandy savannas and rocky outcrops** This environment consists of a vegetation complex over irregular topography with gradients of 1–50%. Herbaceous-shrubby vegetation with low (6–10 m), open forests and a high number of individuals with narrow stems. The herbaceous vegetation that grows on rocks is dominated by *Vellozia lithophylla, Paspalum tillettii, Navia garcia-barrigae, Aechmea* sp., *Syngonanthus* sp., and *Drosera capillaris*. The shrub strata are composed of *Byrsonima crassifolia* (chaparro manteca), *Curatella americana* (chaparro), *Senefelderopsis chiribiquetensis, Acanthella sprucei, Bonnetia martiana, Clusia chiribiquetensis, Parahancornia surrogata* (juansoquillo), *Xylopia aromatica*, and *Ouratea* sp., among others. The level of epiphytism is low.

The Cerro de las Cerbatanas (Blowpipe Hills), Cerro Cocuy, Cerro Machete, and other small elevations belong to this formation, which is found the length of the Inírida River. These constitute places of vital importance within the Nukak territory because they are the natural habitat of the canes used for blowpipes and the plants from which their preferred curares are obtained.

EV. **Eroded alluvial plain of meandering dark-water Amazonian rivers (Inírida River)** This consists of a floodplain and one or several levels of alluvial terraces of structural errosional character, traversed by rivers that have their sources in the Pericratonic surface. The topography is nearly flat to undulating, with gradients of up to 5% (Botero 1997). They are characterized by low, open forests, 10–15 m in height, with emergents of 20 m. There are few individuals with DAPs greater than 10 cm and maximum trunk sizes of 70 cm. The dominant species are *Euterpe precatoria (*açaí*), Tapirira guianensis*, and *Pouteria* sp. (caimo). Toward the sector of Golondrinas torrents there is a marked abundance of *Attalea insignis* (wine palm). The undergrowth is dense, with abundant regeneration and presence of lianas belonging to *Bauhinia guianensis* (bejuco cadena), *Hippocratea* sp., *Desmoncus* sp., and *Smilax* sp. This description corresponds to the low terraces between Tomachipán and Golondrinas torrents on the banks of the Inírida River, which flood three months of the year.

On the locally poorly drained low terraces located along the Caño Makú, a tall, dense forest has developed, attaining a height of 20–25 m and composed of trunks between 20 cm and 80 cm DAP. The degree of epiphytism is low. The dominant species are *Oenocarpus bataua, Astrocaryum aculeatum, Iriartea deltoidea* (bombona), *Couma macrocarpa, Theobroma* sp. (cacao de monte), *Parkia* sp., *Hevea sp.*, and *Clathrotropis macrocarpa.* The undergrowth consists of poor, scarce herbaceous vegetation with dense leaf coverage and little regeneration.

ES. **Association of Amazonian plains with high plains and the craton** This area is characterized by the dominance of timbered natural savannas, consisting of individuals of *Curatella americana, Byrsonima crassifolia*, and *Xylopia aromatica.* The pulses of the genera *Andropogon, Axonopus, Leptocoriphium, Panicum, Paspalum,* and *Trachypogon* stand out, as well as several cypresses of the genus *Bulbostylis.* There are marked abundance and diversity of sufrutices and small shrubs: *Byrsonima verbascifolia* (Malpighiaceae), *Macroptilium* sp. and other fabaceae, *Calea montana* (Asteraceae) and several species of *Palicourea* (Rubiaceae), and *Melochia* sp. (Sterculiaceae). There are horizontal differentiation in level of diversity and specific composition depending principally on two factors: the drainage and the fertility characteristics of the soils linked to extrinsic factors such as occasional burnings and pasturing.

In some places, enclaves of low and sparse forests develop, which grow on moderately undulating land with gradients of 3–10%. These areas correspond to the western boundaries of Nukak territory in the Fuga savanna, although they are also present in the eastern part of the Colombian Amazon.

***SN*. Alluvial plain of the Guaviare River**   This consists of level ground subject to periodic flooding and is characterized by an open forest lower than 10 m with some 15-m emergents. The dominant species are *Phenakospermum guyanense*, *Caryocar glabrum*, and a marked occurrence of copses of *Mauritia flexuosa*. Undergrowth includes an abundance of lianas that make up a closed stratum. A feature that stands out is the presence of abundant exposed roots.

To conclude, a summary of the floral and structural composition of the forests in the eastern Nukak territory indicates a continuum of different successive stages that range from open land (chagras), through impoverished areas, to mature forests where slow-growing, well-developed trees dominate. In the mature forests one finds individuals up to 1 m in diameter, among which are recorded species such as *Couma macrocarpa*, *Pachira nukakii*, *Hymenaea oblongifolia*, *Parinari montana*, *Couratari guianensis*, and *Aspidosperma excelsum*. There is diverse undergrowth, including the species *Geonoma*, *Calathea*, *Miconia*, and *Piper*, and large lianas. In the impoverished areas or those that constitute late secondary forests the species *Theobroma glaucum*, *Tapirira guianensis*, *Phenakospermum guyanense*, *Cecropia* spp., and *Siparuna decipiens*, among others, are common, with dense undergrowth and a high degree of competition from invasive bush and arboreal species. Finally, alongside the cultivated species in gardens, primary herbaceous colonizers initiate regrowth.

Final Considerations

Based on the preceding information, one can conclude that the Nukak are effectively a Makú-affiliated ethnic/linguistic group. Within this generic group, the Nukak are the last with whom contact has been made; the most traditional (at least during the 1990–1996 fieldwork) have the least relations with other indigenous groups and inhabit the extreme northwest of the Makú limits of dispersion. Their strongest linguistic affinity is with the Kakwa, to such a degree that Henly, Mattei-Müller, and Reid (1994–1996) argue that differences between the two are at the dialectical level.

Given the state in which the Nukak were encountered in the early 1990s they provided a unique opportunity to develop an ethnoarchaeological project. This project took place over the course of six years and was interrupted for reasons beyond my control. Nonetheless, during the seven fieldwork seasons completed I was able to collect original information on several aspects of Nukak culture. This information has been used to develop models that have contributed to the interpretation of the archaeological record of hunter-gatherers in the past. Similarly, because of the absence of previous ethnographic information, my research also recorded other aspects of Nukak culture, therefore constituting a form of "rescue ethnography."

The goals of this study were ambitious owing to its three layers of theoretical influence; not only was the identification of ecological causes attempted (and therefore their material derivatives) but also the identification of intervening social and ideational causes. The conclusions reached and models developed—based on both my own research and incorporating and discussing data collected by other authors—are integrative in character and contribute to the identification of the multiple factors involved in the formation of hunter-gatherer archaeological assemblages.

Notes

1. The *colonos* are generally Colombian peasants from other regions of Colombia who have recently arrived in the area. In some cases these are people who have been displaced owing to the violence in their places of origin. In other cases they are poor peasants who arrive in the area searching for a future in the "virgin lands of the Guaviare," as they phrase it.
2. Münzel uses the name *Kaborí* ("man" in the Kabori language) as the preferred self-designation of the Makú from the Uneiuxi River, and the term *Nadöb* ("people" in the Kabori language) as the name they give to neighboring Makú who had not had contact with the West.
3. 1968–1970 the Bará; 1974–1976 the Hupdu; the 1960s the Kabori-Nadöb; and during the 1980s the Yuhup.
4. A term used in the region to designate those temporary workers whose principle job is to cut (or "scrape" [*raspar*]) the coca leaves and transport them to the local laboratories where they are processed.
5. The mission consisted of a pond in Laguna Pavón, a meandering body of water in the floodplain of the Guaviare River. From this pond the phase of contact began that lasted several years. The principal contact with the Western world of the few families that lived in the mission was carried out predominantly by hydroplane.
6. Monicaro and Boori, two Nukak young men I met in my early fieldwork, followed this route and were taken to Mitú.

Chapter 2

THEORY AND METHODS: ETHICS AND TECHNIQUES

In this chapter I summarize particular conceptual and methodological aspects of ethnoarchaeology that framed the research that led to this book. During the last thirty years archaeologists have carried out fieldwork in traditional societies to help answer certain questions regarding the interpretation of the archaeological record, and to develop and examine analogies (see recent reviews in David & Kramer 2001; González Ruibal 2003). Within the framework of ethnoarchaeology the key concept is that of analogy, which can be broadly defined as the transferal of information from one object or phenomenon to another based on certain relations of compatibility between them. In the words of Wylie (1985:92), "analogical inference consists of the selective transportation of information from source to subject on the basis of a comparison that, fully developed, specifies how the 'terms' compared are similar, different, or of unknown likeness."

Ethnoarchaeology has been looked upon with a degree of mistrust by some archaeologists owing to the difficulties that exist in extrapolating from actualistic information to past societies, starting with the fact that the epistemological bases of how to conduct such extrapolations are not sufficiently developed. This has generated doubts and criticism of analogical reasoning. I will not delve into the large and intricate discussion on the use of ethnographic analogy, a discussion that has fueled archaeological debate for at least the last forty years (for example, Ascher 1961; Fernández Martínez 1994; Freeman 1968; Gándara 1990; Hodder 1986; Kuznar 2001a; Ravn 1993; Wylie 1982, 1985; Yacobaccio 1995). I will, however, mention some key concepts in order to clarify my position and to present the theoretical and methodological framework within which my ethnoarchaeological research was carried out.

Many archaeologists have cast doubt on the use of analogies to bridge the gap between the present and past, whether at the level of a tool, a set of behaviors involved in butchering an animal, or the form of society as a whole

(Gosden 1999). These critiques have had a long history, peaking some twenty years ago (Gould 1980; Gould & Watson 1982; Wobst 1978). Freeman (1968:262), for example, rejected the use of ethnographic analogy, treating this line of reasoning as unscientific, fundamentally because of the fact that he considered it impossible to discover "the parameters of sociocultural structure unique to prehistoric time periods" (see also Gould 1980; Wobst 1978). Schrire (1984) disapproved of the use of the !Kung San as representative of Paleolithic lifeways, stressing that these societies are the result of their long-term interaction with nonforager peoples, and that they should by no means be considered isolated hunter-gatherers (see also Wilmsen 1989). Currently, and especially after the epistemological analyses by Wylie (1982, 1985), and despite certain inherent and difficult-to-resolve problems (see Hodder 1986; Layton 1992), the great majority of archaeologists recognize the usefulness of analogical arguments in the process of interpretation or explanation of the archaeological record and consider them as indispensable tools (for example, Hernando Gonzalo 1995:20; Johnson 1999:48; Sillar 2000a:8). I subscribe to this point of view and believe that the argument for analogy is a central element in archaeological interpretation. I believe analogical reasoning is necessary in every step of the investigation, especially in the formulation of hypotheses and the interpretation of data; it is even part of the process of the (always provisional) verification of hypotheses.

Another point that has generated mistrust is that to a greater or lesser degree present-day indigenous societies—the source of analogies—have all had contact with Western society and are integrated in one form or another into the process of "globalization" (see, for example, discussion in Burch & Ellana 1994; Solway & Lee 1990; Stahl 1993; Wilmsen 1989). In most cases this is an entirely accurate description, and it has been proposed, consequently, that present-day societies can not serve as analogical references for past hunter-gatherers. This criticism, however, is unjustified. Ethnoarchaeological research operates under the principles of analogical reasoning, and therefore the two elements of analogy (the source and the subject) need not be the same (in the contrary case analogical reasoning would not be necessary), but rather there should be certain conditions of comparability between terms. Analogy's strength does not lie in the degree of similarity between source (in this case, the present-day society) and subject (the past society as perceived through the archaeological record) but rather in the logical structure of the argument and the similarity between the terms of the relation (Wylie 1982). Obviously, the greater the similarity between source and subject the greater the potential of the analogical argument, but the degree of similarity alone in no way guarantees the strength of the argument or the veracity of the statements.

The interaction between present or historically known hunter-gatherer populations with others does not nullify the usefulness of ethnographic analogy in archaeology. Usually both present-day and past foragers have had contact with other, distinct societies. During the Pleistocene these other populations were merely other hunter-gatherers, and eventually fishers; but in the Holocene many were already in contact with food-producer societies with varied degrees of sociopolitical complexity. Therefore, the state of isolation or the degree of integration on a regional or macro-regional level is not a valid criterion with which to reject or accept any particular analogical argument. Moreover, it is widely recognized that the power of a given analogy does not depend on the delimitation of which traditional or "pristine" group is the source of the analogy but rather on its logical structure and the conditions of comparability (Borrero 1994:248; Wylie 1982).

A major problem still subject to debate is what the necessary conditions are for analogical and uniformitarianist arguments (this has been discussed extensively by Binford 1977a; Hodder 1987:424; Wylie 1982, 1985). Among the many possible solutions is the so-called "relational analogy" (Wylie 1985:95) that attempts to strictly control the variables of the ethnographic case in question, as well as take into consideration the structuring principles behind the observed case. This approach also calls for rich contextual archaeological information that ensures the comparability of terms. Nonetheless, for many (for example, Gronnow 1993) the requisites for the application of this type of analogy are removed from the actual situation and therefore "will always stay an unattainable ideal" (Gronnow 1993:79). Essentially, there is no single formula for the application of analogy; this will always depend on the kind of analogy, the source, and the subject. In this sense analogical argumentation is a construction that depends on the researcher, and hence there are unavoidable subjective components. Context, theoretical background, and personal preferences are always present in the process of analogical reasoning. Obviously, there must be constant vigilance to assure the greatest degree of objectivity possible and to identify clearly the relevance of the terms being compared in analogical arguments, but this by no means corresponds to the application of fixed formulas of reasoning.

Nonetheless, numerous questions have been raised concerning the use of present-day societies as analogical models for understanding past societies. How far can observations of contemporary groups shed light on the understanding of the behavior of extinct societies? The answer is simple: the construction of a model can be derived from any class of information, including one's own intuition (Burch 1994:446). The crucial point does not concern the basis for a particular model but rather the manner in which this expands our understanding and comprehension of the subject in question. Ethnographic studies of hunter-gatherers have demonstrated that they significantly expand knowledge of such societies, both in the present and the past.

On Ethnoarchaeology

There are various definitions of the subdiscipline of ethnoarchaeology (see David & Kramer 2001:12 for a review of the many different definitions), but it can simply and basically be summarized as the acquisition of ethnographic data to assist archaeological interpretation. It can also be defined as the study of the relationship between human behavior and its archaeological consequences in the present (O'Connell 1995). Ethnoarchaeology is differentiated from other actualistic studies in that it includes the systematic observation of living societies, and from other types of ethnography through its explicit focus on the intention to identify the archaeological—material—implications of human behavior. Among the variety of definitions and characteristics of ethnoarchaeology one of my favorites, which comes closest to my conception of the subdiscipline, is one that states that ethnoarchaeology is "the study of how material culture is produced, used, and deposited by contemporary societies in relation to the wider social, ideological, economic, environmental, and/or technical aspects of the society concerned, and with specific reference to the problems of interpreting archaeological material" (Sillar 2000a:6).

The immediate objectives of ethnoarchaeology are to identify and explain the pattern of relationships between behavior and its material derivatives and to establish the processes and the causal factors that determine this pattern. The final goal is to expand the range of inferences possible from the archaeological record concerning past behavior and to improve the conditions of accuracy and verification (O'Connell 1995). As such, the subdiscipline attempts to formulate models that permit the better understanding of the cultural patterns of human societies, both in the present and the past. Essentially, ethnoarchaeology is a form of ethnography that takes into consideration aspects and relationships not approached in detail by traditional ethnographies.

One must recognize that the attempt to use ethnographic information to interpret the archaeological record is neither new nor the exclusive domain of ethnoarchaeology (see summaries in David & Kramer 2001; Fernández Martínez 1994; Oswalt 1974). What is new is that ethnoarchaeological information has been obtained by archaeologists with the central objective of aiding comprehension of the archaeological record. On the advent of processual archaeology Binford (1967) became interested in ethnographic analogy in a systematic way in his pioneering work, *Smudge Pits and Hide Smoking: The Use of Analogy in Archaeological Reasoning*. He subsequently developed his ethnoarchaeological approach theoretically and conceptually in *Nunamiut Ethnoarchaeology* (Binford 1978a). These contributions, together with Yellen (1977) and Gould (1978a, 1980), established the foundations of ethnoarchaeology within the processual paradigm and transformed the subdiscipline into one of the most important producers of the models that feed "middle range theory."

Contemporary ethnoarchaeology emerged as a direct result of the testing of actualistic studies and of the optimism of the potential for such studies to explain the archaeological record. Consequently, from the late 1970s, and especially the 1980s, specific studies of living societies by archaeologists were initiated (for example, Kent 1984; Roux 1985; Watson 1979; Wiessner 1983; see recent reviews in David & Kramer 2001 and González Ruibal 2003). As such, a new approach was born—the search for general principles that connected human behavior to material culture, and the obtaining of conclusions that did not depend exclusively on sociocultural anthropological theory. The initial optimism of processual archaeology in the belief that human behavior was subject to laws (more or less similar to those of biology) pervaded ethnoarchaeology and oriented its conceptual development in the 1970s. During these early years of the subdiscipline there was also an underlying conviction that universal laws could be generated that related human behavior to material remains (Yellen 1977). In fact, it was presumed that, together with experimental archaeology, ethnoarchaeology would be the principal source for the production of these laws (Schiffer 1978).

In the early 1980s ethnoarchaeology broadened its focus and began to be included within a postprocessual agenda as well, although in a different form (for example, David, Sterner, & Gavua 1988; Hodder 1982, 1986). In part, these new developments had already been anticipated by Gould (1978b). From within postprocessualism the range of interests that ethnoarchaeology incorporated was expanded, especially as it widened its focus beyond techno-economic aspects to understanding greater levels of complexity, attempting to discern material correlates of the social and ideational. Principally, this new current reconceptualized material culture, seeking to determine the multiple dimensions in which it operates. Within this new conceptual framework ethnoarchaeology does not try to "explain" (in the processual sense of the word) material culture but rather endeavors to interpret its meaning for the society that produced it. In this sense, certain aspects are emphasized that were barely touched on in previous research, such as symbolism and the study of nonutilitarian dimensions of material culture within society (for example, see the collection of papers in Hodder 1982). A new generation of critiques was also produced from this perspective; one such states that, "ethnoarchaeological studies are of interest in their own right, but they cannot contribute directly to our understanding of the past since the meaning of settlement organization and discard can be derived only from the context (present or past) within which settlement use and artifact discard take place" (Hodder 1987:424).

Already by the 1990s ethnoarchaeological studies had multiplied and encompassed the analysis of all types of societies (see summary in David & Kramer 2001). The questions diversified (for example, David & Sterner 1999; Haber 2001; Hernando Gonzalo 1999; Kuznar 2001b), and in all the major regions of the world long-term ethnoarchaeological projects were initiated. In recent years many ethnoarchaeological studies have been carried out among all kinds of societies in the Americas, Africa, Asia, Europe, and Oceania. Furthermore, these studies have not been limited to indigenous groups but have also included creole peoples, peasants, and Western urban societies.

Hunter-gatherers have been an important focus from the beginning of systematic ethnoarchaeological research, so much so that it has been said that "archaeologists are now arguably the largest 'consumers' (and producers) of research on hunting and gathering people . . ." (Lee & Daly 1999:11). Within this area important fieldwork has been carried out that has noticeably increased knowledge of hunter-gatherer societies (for example, Binford 1978a, 1978b, 1981; Gould 1968, 1969, 1978a; Hawkes, Hill, & O'Connell 1982; Lupo 1994, 1995; O'Connell, Hawkes, & Blurton-Jones 1988a, 1988b, 1990, 1992; Yellen 1977, 1991a, 1991b). Paradoxically, as interest grows in these studies and their contributions are valued as means of archaeological inference, "traditional" societies are diminishing, especially and dramatically hunter-gatherers, and the range of variation of analogous referents is consequently reduced. As I stated initially, the strength of analogical reasoning does not lie in the degree of isolation of the source society. However, the potential of ethnoarchaeology lies in its grasp of variations in the cultural conditions (technoeconomic, social, and ideational) of material production in such a way as to be able to identify this variation in the archaeological record. Consequently, the Westernization of indigenous societies notably diminishes the availability of contemporary analogous referents that reflect some of the conditions of past societies or that are comparable in some way.

Moving beyond the more common applications ethnoarchaeology has broadened its horizons, above all within the last decade. Traditionally, the subdiscipline had emphasized the search for recurrent relationships between human behavior and material culture (Binford 1978a; Longacre 1981). This is the most common meaning of contemporary ethnoarchaeology and the vast majority of current projects probably ascribe to this approach. This search is directly related to the construction of middle range theory, in the meaning intended by Binford (1983a:14), "to establish non-ambiguous relations of cause-effect between the dynamic causes and static derivatives." Research on use and discard of artifacts; kill, transport and consumption of prey; construction and abandonment of shelters; or the sequence of object fabrication; and so on are incorporated within this field (for example, Fisher & Strickland 1989; García 2001; Jones 1993; Williams 1994; Yacobaccio 2001).

Within the past decade ethnoarchaeology has developed a more ambitious agenda, to generate models and postulate material derivatives within ideational and social contexts, and therefore address more complex systems. The possibility of such an approach was already being criticized during the height of processual archaeology. For example, Gould (1980) stated that Clark's argument that emic categories and cognitive codes exist as a black box for the archaeologist is well suited to living archaeology. Although some archaeologists have at times argued for the discovery of a "mental template" or "the man behind the artifact" (Spaulding 1953), the conviction has grown that such efforts at reconstructing prehistoric categories of thought lie beyond any means of effective testing (Gould 1980:118). However, recently ethnoarchaeologists have increasingly understood that the social and ideational spheres are inseparable from techno-utilitarian aspects (Dobres 2000; Hodder 1986; Pfaffenberger 1992) and have developed research projects that seek to capture the intersection of several cultural dimensions (for example, Sillar 2000a, 2000b). Within this area ethnoarchaeology studies both the relationship between human behavior and its material derivatives in situations in which there is a certain degree of control over the variables, as well as attempting to do so at more complex societal levels where the material dimension is less direct and its detection less obvious. The current research project is framed by this approach, and consequently, as will be seen in the following chapters, the contributions of the social and ideational dimensions to the formation of the archaeological record are explored. Nonetheless, it is necessary to clarify that analyzing such dimensions is always a difficult task; moreover, it requires either an extremely complete knowledge of the language of the group under study or highly skilled translators, conditions that are rarely met in many investigations. Without a doubt this was a problem in our Nukak research, restricting the full exploitation of the immense informative potential of this ethnic group. As a consequence, despite our intention to penetrate emic categories, this book maintains a strong technofunctional component in the interpretation of many aspects of Nukak behavior.

Finally, the subdiscipline has been active in the more general anthropological goal of understanding and exploring other forms of thought or cosmologies, which is of great importance also to archaeology. Within this field, patterns of rationality and ontologies are looked for that differ from Western patterns. In this use of ethnoarchaeology the correlation with material culture is secondary to the attempt to understand alternative cosmovisions and different rationalities independently of their material correlates (Hernando Gonzalo 1995). Obviously, one is not attempting to understand in depth extinct norms of thought but rather to detect keys to its functioning and discern how and which ideational and social factors (as well as technoeconomic factors) acted on the configuration of the material record, where this is possible. These goals have motivated my research, as well as that of various other archaeologists (for example, David, Sterner, & Gauva 1988; Dillehay 1998; Haber 2001; Hernando Gonzalo 1995; Hodder 1982; Sillar 2000a; Silva 2000).

It is obvious that as we ascend through the levels of complexity and abstraction the capacity to control the variables in play and the strength of the relationship between behavior and its material derivatives diminish. However, this should not be an obstacle to an attempt to systematically approach the study of social and belief systems in order to identify in living societies generative principles and generalizations that can be tested against archaeological data. Such an approach has become commonplace in the archaeology of South American complex societies (see González 1977, 1992; Reichel-Dolmatoff 1972); it is now assumed, for example, that the production of objects with a symbolic character—icons—and the construction of monuments are inherent to social complexity, and consequently an archaeological record in which this is manifested is to be expected. However, egalitarian societies not only produce objects but also consume food or construct living spaces exclusively as a consequence of adaptation to the natural and social environment. There is no doubt that foragers as well as herders and villagers maintain highly developed belief structures and complex social rules that infuse all their activities, as ethnography and ethnohistory show us. Such structures determine, for example, which animals and which parts of animals will be eaten, where the encampment will be erected, or from which place the rocks used to manufacture artifacts will be collected. These causal factors should not be considered epiphenomenal or secondary derivations from the material conditions of life. Certainly they are largely responsible for the configuration of the archaeological record. Social and ideational aspects have been gravely overlooked in the archaeology and ethnoarchaeology of South America, and information universally recorded in ethnographic studies of hunter-gatherer societies, such as food taboos, the existence of sacred places, and the symbolic context and the social meaning of ordinary artifacts, have rarely been considered as possible causes that contribute to the formation and distribution of the archaeological record in South America. In this book, I endeavor to contribute both data concerning the socioideational dimension (and explore methodological means of interpreting them) and information directly related to techno-utilitarian aspects of material culture. Information on the former is the least obvious, the most difficult to record, and the least well represented in this book. Nonetheless, I believe the information that we were able to gather on the socioideational realm opens small windows on the wealth and variety of causal factors that contribute to the formation of the archaeological record.

I conclude this section with a clarification. In this book, when I refer to "archaeological visibility" I refer exclusively to what is left after an activity or an event has taken place—in other words, the way in which one "sees" a given behavior in the landscape after it has been performed. Of course, the possibilities of survival for any material remains and their context, as well as the multiple transformations they undergo, vary a great deal depending on the natural conditions of each region. It is not my intention to examine here the possibilities for preservation in tropical rainforest environments of the different classes of material items or to study their possible taphonomic histories. For such an examination, which exceeds the objectives of this book, regional taphonomic information would need to be obtained through continuous and systematic studies, which have yet to be carried out.

Ethnoarchaeology in South America

The research project that formed the basis for this book is part of an incipient South American tradition of ethnoarchaeology. Unfortunately, most of the achievements of this new trend have been ignored in books and review papers on ethnoarchaeology (for exceptions see González Ruibal 2003), the recent book by David and Kramer (2001) being the most flagrant example. In their book, probably the most complete and comprehensive text on ethnoarchaeology ever written, the authors stated: "It is curious that with rare exceptions (for example, Williams 1994, 1995) Latin Americans have not been attracted to ethnoarchaeology" (2001:28). As I hope to demonstrate in this section, Latin American researchers have been active participants in ethnoarchaeology in the region for more than ten years and have produced significant results.

Ethnoarchaeology arrived relatively early in the region but has not been fully utilized or explored in spite of the wealth and variety of indigenous societies on the continent who could provide inspiration and a valuable resource for up-to-date studies. Among the earliest antecedents are studies of agropastoral societies in the Andes (for instance, Miller 1977), as well as the work of Deboer and Lathrap (1979) and Zeidler (1984) among the Shipibo and Ashuar of eastern Ecuador. Other early work was carried out by Lyon (1970), who observed the action of dogs on bones discarded by humans in a Peruvian Amazonian village, and Carneiro (1979), who has done some specific research related to the use of stone axes among the Yanomamö of Venezuela. In addition to these North Americans some local archaeologists initiated ethnoarchaeological studies early on. Among these, Wüst 1975 stands out (an article rarely mentioned in the literature). It is one of the earliest studies of pottery manufacture, carried out, moreover, within the framework of a regional archaeological project (Schmitz 1975). The Brazilian archaeologist T. Miller, Jr. conducted interesting studies on lithic production among the last of the Xetá in Paraná State, Brazil (Miller, Jr. 1975, 1979). This author also made some early reflections on ethnoarchaeology and brought attention to the potential of South American indigenous societies (Miller, Jr. 1981–1982). A. Laming-Emperaire later published more complete observations of the Xetá together with her Brazilian colleagues, M. J. Menezes and M. D. Andreatta (Laming-Emperaire et al. 1978).

In the last decade or so, far-reaching and systematic research programs have followed these pioneer works, focusing on two main areas: Andean herders (for example, Caracotche 2001; Delfino 2001; Haber 2001; Kuznar 1995, 2001b; Nasti 1993; Nielsen 1998, 2001; Reigadas 2001; Tomka 1993, 2001; Yacobaccio 1995; Yacobaccio & Madero 1994, 2001; Yacobaccio, Madero, & Malmierca 1998) and tropical lowland horticulturists (for example, Assis 1995–1996; Frias 1993; Heckenberger, Petersen, & Neves 1999; Wüst 1998). Other areas of research include the Pumé of the tropical savannas (Greaves 1996; 1997), the Mapuche of the southern Andes (Dillehay 1998), as well as my own work among the Nukak (Politis 1996a, 1996b, 1998, 1999a, b). The subjects concentrated on vary from the technology of ceramic production (Cremonte 1988–1989; García 1988, 2001) and its function as a vehicle of social expression (Hosler 1996; Sillar 2000a, 2000b; Silva 2000) to technological organization and its relation to subsistence (Greaves 1997), bone and artifactual refuse in agropastoralist sites (Tomka 1993; Yacobaccio, Madero, & Malmierca 1998), the settlement patterns and residential huts of lowland villagers (Assis 1995–1996; Wüst 1998; Wüst & Barreto 1999), the relationship between floor area and demography, the study of the material consequences of food taboos (Politis & Martínez 1996; Politis & Saunders 2002), and the symbolic significance of the jaguar (Dillehay 1998).

At least three tendencies can be identified in ethnoarchaeological studies in the region. The first restricts case studies to the physical effects of behavior defined within systems by variables that can in principle be well controlled, as with, for example, ceramic production (Garcia 1993; Williams 1994) or the spatial distribution of discarded bones (Borrero & Yacobaccio 1989; Jones 1993). Scholars working from this perspective argue that effort should be directed toward particular cases within general theoretical models (Yacobaccio 1995). This group of investigations emphasizes the technoeconomic function of material culture. The second tendency is orientated toward the study of more complex systems whose variables are harder to control but that take into account more diverse phenomena and attempt to discern the non-technoeconomic meaning of objects through ethnographic case studies (for example, Hosler 1996; Sillar 2000a; Silva 2000). In the second approach archaeological artifacts are considered as the representation of ideas (Leach 1977:16) and polysemic in character. Of course, both tendencies are tied to the material effects of behavior and their respective properties (that is, density, variability, and so on), but while the first attempts to establish nonambiguous relationships and strong cross-cultural regularities, the second is directed toward understanding under what conditions (social and ideological as well as material) one can expect certain kinds of archaeological records. This second tendency valorizes the usefulness of context-specific cultural particularities and explores the continuity of cosmovisions and meanings attached to specific symbols and icons (see discussion in Saunders 1998). The ethnoarchaeological study of symbolic and religious issues has been incorporated into this line of research through the medium of material derivatives in egalitarian societies such as Amazonian hunter-gatherers (Politis & Saunders 2002), or societies with low levels of social hierarchy, such as the pastoralists of the Central Andes (Haber 2001; Kuznar 2001a; Nielsen 1998), lowland villagers (Frias 1993; Silva 2000), and the Mapuche of the southern Andes (Dillehay 1998). The research from which this book originated can be placed within this latter trend.

The third tendency is represented by a group of research projects—notably from Brazil—that focus on collecting ethnoarchaeological data to reconstruct the historical processes of present-day Indians (Heckenberger 1996; Heckenberger, Petersen, & Neves 1999; Wüst 1975, 1998; Wüst & Barreto 1999). This is closely allied with what has been called "indigenous history" (in the sense of Eremites de Oliveira 2001). In this approach emphasis is on understanding the process of cultural continuity using both ethnographic and archaeological data obtained from the same area, where a genetic connection between contemporary people and the people who produced the archaeological deposit under investigation can be proven. It is argued that the cultural continuity of the chronological sequence from pre-Hispanic periods to the present, based on a "marked conservatism" not only in the spatial organization of the villages but also on ceramic technology, subsistence, and the placement of settlements, "permits fairly detailed direct historical comparisons" (Heckenberger, Petersen, & Neves 1999). Although the results obtained by this kind of research could be considered historically restricted, the potential for understanding general cultural patterns, such as village configuration and size, village occupation and abandonment, formation of black soils, and so on in past Amazonian societies is enormous.

FIELDWORK

I will explain in detail my fieldwork, because I believe it is important to be able to make a critical evaluation of the information that gave rise to this book. Although this type of exposition may seem tedious or irrelevant, we must still contextualize the recording of data and compare and evaluate the results obtained.

Since the first season the objective of the proposed fieldwork has been to collect original in situ information concerning the way of life of the Nukak within their habitat, the tropical rainforest between the Guaviare and Inírida rivers. Those Nukak living next to *colonos* or who travel across the neighboring savannas, such as the Sabana de La Fuga, are not, therefore, included in the study. As such, the research was orientated toward the study of bands that have experienced (or had at the time of our fieldwork) a low level of western influence. This selection does not mean that some bands are "more Nukak" than others or that the more Westernized bands provide lesser quality information. The selection of the more traditional groups was based simply on the fact that they maintained behavior that had changed less—behavior relevant to the objectives of the planned research.

The information presented in this book was gathered during seven fieldwork seasons among the Nukak between 1990 and 1996. The first season took place from 21 September to 2 October 1990. In this short period of time I made contact with two bands; one had left the Trocha Central and was found in a wild area known as La Leona (Figure 1.2, p. 36), and the other was camped in the forest approximately three-and-a-half km southeast of Caño Seco.

The band at La Leona consisted of sixteen individuals, and the camp in the forest was made up of twenty-three people.

I and Gustavo Martínez carried out the second fieldwork season from 3 July to 2 August 1991. We entered the forest at Caño Seco and stayed with two different bands; one was found to the southeast of this location and the other to the south of Barranco Colorado. The first group (Band-1991a) consisted of ten to fifteen people pertaining to two families and was probably only a segment of a band. The second band (recorded as Band-1991b) was larger and made up of four nuclear families; its membership fluctuated between twenty-two and twenty-six individuals. During most of this season Luis, an indigenous Tikuna who was working as a *raspador* in Caño Seco, accompanied us.

Julián Rodríguez accompanied me for the third season, from 20 August to 21 September 1992. On this occasion we entered by Caño Hormiga, and contact was made with a band (Band-1992) to the south of this region in the northern part of Nukak territory. This band was made up of five families and varied in number from nineteen to twenty-four people. During this season Javier Cruz, a *colono* from La Tigrera, accompanied us as a guide and collaborator.

The fourth fieldwork season was again carried out with Julián Rodríguez, from 15 January to 12 February 1994. We visited the same band as the previous year (they had moved to the south of Caño Hormiga). This group consisted of the same people and several newborn babies, totaling twenty-seven individuals; they were recorded as Band-1994. During this trip we made contact with a young Nukak, fourteen or fifteen years old, called Monicaro, who was with us almost the entire time. Owing to Monicaro's fluency in Spanish he contributed important data on various aspects of Nukak culture and further enabled us to better interpret the observations made in previous years. Monicaro had been orphaned and taken by a *colono* to Caño Jabón. He had later returned to the forest, entering at Barranco Colorado and Caño Cumare. During the two previous years he had been entering and leaving the forest where he lived with what was left of Band-1991b. During this season's fieldwork we also visited this latter band for a few days. As in the previous year Javier Cruz collaborated with us.

The fifth fieldwork season took place between 16 January and 18 February and was conducted by Julián Rodríguez, accompanied for a few days by Ruth Gutiérrez Herrera, at that time a biology student at the Universidad Nacional de Santafé de Bogotá. Rodríguez again entered by way of Caño Hormiga and established contact with a segment of the same band as in the two previous years. This group varied from fourteen to sixteen members and contained the two youngest families. It was recorded as Band-1995a. On this occasion this segment joined the rest of the band on 6 February and also combined with another segment of a different band of fourteen people that consisted of two nuclear families.

The sixth season took place from 21 August to 18 September 1995. The party consisted of Julian Rodriguez, Dairon Cárdenas (a botanist from the Instituto Amazónico de Investigaciones Científicas SINCHI), Jorge Octavio López (an anthropologist from the Department of Indigenous Affairs, Colombian Government), and I. At the beginning of the expedition I had the opportunity to visit the Laguna Pavón 2 Mission for the first time thanks to an invitation from the Department of Indigenous Affairs of the Colombian Government. There I was able to observe briefly the situation in the Mission in whose environs a band of twenty-five people had camped. In this season we explored the Inírida River and its principle tributaries from Tomachipán to Santa Rosa. We also traveled for a week down a Nukak trail that headed from the middle course of the Caño Makú (Finca Roballos) in a northeasterly direction. During this journey we successfully delimited the southern and eastern borders of the territory occupied by the Nukak and gathered information about them from the neighboring Kurripako and Puinave Indians. Contact with the Nukak during this period was limited to one band of six people that had camped 3.1 km north of Tomachipán, on the Inírida River.

The seventh period of fieldwork took place from 13 January to 2 February 1996, and the team was the same as the previous year. The young Nukak Yorena accompanied us for the duration. We started at Laguna Pavón 2 from where we moved northward until reaching the edge of the Guaviare River floodplain. During this expedition an important botanical collection was made and deposited in the Amazonian Herbarium in the SINCHI Institute. We visited two bands to the south and north of Laguna Pavón 2. The first was composed initially of eleven individuals who were later joined by two families, making a total of twenty-six people in the coresidential group. The second band was a large band of thirty-nine individuals who slept in two separate camps close to each other, and constituted distinct coresident groups when relocating.

In September 1996, Rodriguez, Cárdenas, and I returned to Guaviare for the eighth fieldwork season. We decided to start our trip from Caño Hormiga, because the missionary settlement of Laguna Pavón 2 had already been abandoned. Unfortunately, on our arrival by motor launch at Mocuare we met with a FARC column, the regional commander of which prevented us from continuing our journey, alluding to problems with security. From this date on I have been able to interview only a few Nukak who were removed to Santafé de Bogotá for medical attention.

As well as the seven field seasons, we conducted several interviews in 1995 and 1996 with Yorena, a young Nukak man approximately fifteen years old, who was subsequently given the Spanish name Manuel García. Yorena also accompanied us during the 1996 field season, partly because he wanted to visit an older brother who was living in the eastern part of their land. This young man, who was at the time ten or eleven years old, was a member of the group that left for La Leona in 1990. When this band returned to the forest at Trocha Ganadera, Yorena stayed with a *colono* who took responsibility for him. Yorena's cousin Maube (Spanish name Belisario) also remained behind on an estate nearby. At the time, Yorena was attending the San José del Guaviare school and spoke Spanish extremely well (he was perhaps the most fluent Nukak Spanish-speaker). He also remembers the Nukak language perfectly, which he speaks often with his cousin and with other Nukak who pass through San José del Guaviare. His help as translator and sometimes informant was extremely beneficial to us, and he was able to clarify some doubts that we had had concerning the interpretation of data obtained in the field. I also interviewed three Nukak women who were hospitalized in Santafé de Bogotá. These interviews were carried out with two members of the Asociación Nuevas Tribus de Colombia, Kenneth Conduff and Israel Gualteros, who helped me with translation. These sets of interviews took place over several occasions in the house of Kenneth Conduff and in the Casa Indígena in Santafé de Bogotá.

Finally, on several occasions I was able to interview the New Tribe (currently Asociación Nuevas Tribus de Colombia) missionaries Kenneth Conduff, Israel Gualteros, Andrés Jiménez, and Joaquín Foster, who kindly shared with me part of the wealth of information they had managed to collect through an excellent facility for the language and many years of permanent contact with the Nukak. They contributed valuable information concerning the period in which they had first contacted the Nukak from Mission Laguna Pavón 1, and they also shared with me information recorded by the missionaries over more than ten years of close relations with the Nukak. Moreover, they summarized for us their knowledge of the cosmology of the Nukak, one of the least-known aspects of this ethnic group.

DATA COLLECTION: METHODS, TECHNIQUES, AND PROBLEMS

In spite of having delineated precise objectives, from the commencement of fieldwork I realized it was necessary to record other, unconsidered factors owing to the lack of an ethnographic database on the Nukak. In this case, more so perhaps than in any other ethnoarchaeological study, there was no previous research that could serve as a foundation for the proposed study. There were also very few Nukak who spoke any Spanish (or even other indigenous languages), since they are basically monolingual. During the first two three seasons we had no help with translation other than our own efforts to learn the basics of Nukak language. As a result, we carried out a broader and more general first stage of data collection than had been foreseen, with the aim of discussing in greater detail the archaeological implications. In some ways the structure of this book reflects this particular dynamic of the investigation, which intersected the various degrees of proximity between us and the Nukak as well as the consequences for scientific knowledge (Marcus & Fisher 1986:31).

In Harris's terms (1985:46), in this initial phase the investigation sketched out "behavioral" phenomena and their external effects expressed through material culture and the environment. The "mental" phenomena were not taken into consideration at this stage, since we would need to "employ operations capable of unraveling the thoughts of the people" (Harris 1985:46). In any case, we considered that either one or the other type of phenomena should be analyzed, thereby satisfying the demands of testability and the making explicit of methods and techniques.

One of our major problems was obviously the lack of an in-depth knowledge of the Nukak language. This was partially solved by some basic learning, the interaction and translations by Monicaro and Yorena, and the translations by Kenneth Conduff and Israel Gualteros. Another problem was how to interpret nonacoustic (vocal and paralinguistic) modes of communication, which included facial expressions, gestures, touching (tactility), posture and gait, chemical (smells, tastes, scents, and so on), and proxemics (the use of space) (Schiffer 1999:32). In this case, the emission (the effect, ultimately the "message") is inferred or interpreted, and therefore is subject to misinterpretation. A profound understanding of these modes of communication would require long periods of contact with the Nukak, and I doubt that any non-Nukak people would be able to achieve such knowledge. Unfortunately, these are some of the undeniable limitations of this type of study, and they need to be clearly stated.

As with all ethnographic and ethnoarchaeological work there are a series of procedures to be carried. These are summarized in the following section. During fieldwork we designed a strategy that enabled us to observe directly the relationship between behavior and material culture. To this end we recorded the place, the contextual situation, and the material results of certain observed behavior, and we recorded not only technological or economy-related behavior but also other types of activities, such as rituals, burials, games, and so forth. Furthermore, we collected information on the composition of the bands, kinship relations, and affiliations with other bands. We emphasized the collection of quantitative data and designed special procedures in each case. For the estimation of subsistence all the food products that entered the camp on a daily basis were weighed over a period of several weeks in both seasons. Based on this information, and the consumption that we recorded during the daily foraging trips, we made an estimation of annual diet (see Chapter 8). One of us accompanied a party each day and recorded distance traveled, products obtained, time taken, tools used, techniques employed, and other data of interest. The other team member remained at the camp to record systematically the entry and exit of people, what each person carried, the method of carrying products, the composition of the parties, the time at which they left and returned, the production of artifacts, and the techniques and place of food preparation. Distances were measured with electronic pedometers, and, because each of us carried one, we averaged out the readings when possible to reduce the margin of error.

A substantial photographic record was made, to the extent that the Nukak allowed us to take photographs. In the vast majority of cases they did not object, nor did it appear to bother them; eventually they pulled faces and asked us to take photographs in particular situations (after a successful hunt, for example). On the occasions that we had the assistance of Monicaro and Yorena the investigation was far more complete and the level of understanding more profound. The Nukak frequently asked us for the camera to examine it (a task that cost us several pictures), and they took photographs of us on several occasions. Many Nukak had become familiar with this piece of equipment owing to their visits to Laguna Pavón 2 and the visits of other anthropologists.

The Nukak only infrequently did not allow us to take photographs. In particular circumstances (fights between couples, accidents, and so on) they made it evident that they were annoyed by any intervention on our part including the taking of photographs. In other cases, for example a ritual nighttime meeting (*baak-wáadn*), the first flash photographs we took upset them and we took no more as a result, neither in ritual situations nor in the camps (except for a few expressly authorized exceptions).

During our stays in the camps we tried hard to advance in our learning of their language. Progress was slow and below our expectations in spite of the fact that after a time we developed mutual means of communication. Currently, my understanding of the Nukak language is at an elementary level.

ETHICS

A certain amount of resistance to ethnoarchaeology exists because it is questioned from an ethical point of view by both archaeologists and anthropologists. Since the origin of ethnoarchaeology doubts have arisen not only about its usefulness but also about the competence of archaeologists to take on the study of living societies, and of the ethical aspects of this practice. By the mid-1970s when "processual archaeology" was at its peak of optimism, and the discovering of "covering laws" or "lawlike prepositions" was one of the main goals of theoretical archaeologists, ethnoarchaeology was considered a "respectable research activity" (Schiffer 1976:31). Here, a subtle moral connotation, in a positive sense, is manifested.

Behavioral archaeology is considered to have stimulated the growth of ethnoarchaeology as a nomothetic research strategy (Schiffer 1995:ix). Correspondingly, some social anthropologists questioned—generally verbally rather than in writing—the use that archaeologists made of living societies, as if they were laboratory samples. For example, on one occasion in 1991 a professor of anthropology at the Universidad Nacional de Bogotá stated in a departmental meeting his rejection of ethnoarchaeology, arguing that he knew little about the subdiscipline but that it did not seem a good thing to him to, "go and trouble the living Indians in order to understand what had happened to the dead Indians." Along the same lines of thought, Gosden (1999:9) has stated strong ethical objections more recently and in a more formal manner: "I feel that ethnoarchaeology is immoral, in that we have no justification for using the present of one society simply to interpret the past of another. . . . Societies ought to be studied as interesting in their own right or not at all." These extreme positions are incorrect and misleading. Archaeology, in the same way as ethnography or any other branch of the anthropological sciences, holds as principle goals the study of the variability of human societies and the understanding of cultural processes and different forms of behavior; to which end it is entirely permissible to study present-day societies, whether contributing directly or indirectly to these goals through the identification of analogous referents, and to approach them with temporal depth from archaeology.

Ethnoarchaeological research should, however, abide by the ethical rules that apply to any kind of ethnographic work (see David & Kramer 2001: 63–90). Like ethnography, ethnoarchaeology is plagued with ethical dilemmas the resolution of which depends on the context and the situation, on the good faith of the researchers, and above all on the principle of respect for the decisions taken by the indigenous group in question. In our case, the Nukak's implicit acceptance of our presence and the consistent cooperation and help, in spite of their lack of a clear understanding of what we were doing and why we were doing it, was a constant characteristic.

The Nukak's attitude toward us was always open and friendly from the time of first contact in 1990. Obviously, we caused them some minor annoyances, such as walking slower on a hunting or gathering trip, or inadvertently stepping on a pet that was roaming around the camp. In every case the Nukak were highly amused by our limitations in the forest and our clumsiness, and we quickly became the brunt of jokes. For the first few days the young hunters were always patient with us, and even invited us to go out with them on trips, as we were still a novelty to the band. After approximately ten days (this varied in every case) we noted that some of the young hunters suddenly "disappeared" from the camp in the morning without us having realized. Subsequently we understood this to be a strategy to avoid our accompanying them, since we undoubtedly slowed them down in the forest. During the final days of our stay we gathered with the women (we held their babies while they carried out their tasks in greater comfort) or with the older men, who in absolutely every case had infinite patience with us and excellent dispositions.[1]

I should clarify our position concerning gift giving and the Nukak, not because ours is the only correct attitude to take but because it is the one I consider most appropriate. The only occasion on which I gave presents— two pieces of raw sugar and a box of fishhooks—was during the first visit in 1990, on the recommendation of Dr. Gerardo Reichel-Dolmatoff, who kindly advised me and Gerardo Ardila about how to approach possible isolated Makú. He recommended that it was convenient to carry objects for gifts because at times the first encounters were unfriendly, and presents would mitigate doubts generated by this first contact. Apart from this one occasion we did not arrive with gifts. If our presence had bothered the Nukak, we would have left and not used bribes of products that had a high value to them but to which they had no access (until some Nukak began to work as coca harvesters) in order to be allowed to stay. I believe the indiscriminate use of gifts generates increased dependency and empowers the patronizing attitude of Westerners. To date we have always been well received and accepted without problem into the various bands with which we have lived.

However, we did engage in exchanges before our departure at the end of each season. In every case the Western elements exchanged were only those that the band already possessed and that formed part of their daily technology. We gave them the things we were no longer going to use: salt, spoons, a lighter, our camping pot, and eventually a machete or a knife. We received in exchange—after prolonged negotiations—baskets, spears, and earthenware pots. On no occasion did we leave in the camp or give to members of the bands clothes or objects that might replace the traditional artifacts they still possessed (net hammocks, packs, and so forth).

We also did not depend on the Nukak for food at any point during the seven fieldwork seasons. We carried our own food and we accepted food from them only when it was offered to us; our sustenance depended almost exclusively on what we had brought with us and the little we could collect or fish. It is fairly clear that the Nukak are extremely mutually supportive, and the band as a whole undertakes the feeding of all its members including guests. However, on the one hand, we feared we could become a burden to the group, who could feel an obligation to feed us. The food that we would have been able to contribute to the band in our roles as adult men if we had tried to participate in its maintenance would have been insignificant. On the other hand, we believe that one of the objectives of the project was to portray Nukak subsistence quantitatively as adequately as possible, and the margin of error each day would have increased had the band been feeding us.

Except during the visit to the band in the rainforest in 1991, and during a few days with Band-1991a, we always hung our hammocks and built our fires outside the Nukak camp. This was for two fundamental reasons. First, we felt that sleeping within the Nukak encampment would be invading a space that at night was charged with intimacy. Second, the space we needed to occupy to hang the hammocks would have changed the footprint and the surface area of the camp, which we wanted to record as accurately as possible.

Finally, because the Nukak are included within a regional context that involves diverse social actors—other indigenous groups, *colonos*, the guerilla group FARC, and government functionaries—the duration and objectives of the work had to be discussed with them for each season. The requirements of Colombian legislation for this type of research were fulfilled, and during the project the Colombian Department of Indigenous Affairs was aware of the stage of the investigation and received annual reports with the results of each season's work. This was of great help in the design of protection policies for the Nukak ethnic group and in the delimitation of their territory.

CONCLUDING REMARKS

In summary, the study of present-day societies is indeed an important analogical resource for understanding the behavior of hunter-gatherers, and for understanding the significant elements of these societies. Present-day hunter-gatherers are not the same as those in the past, but they do provide information that can be used to examine similar behavior and to model the conditions of the relationship between such behavior and its material derivatives. I am certainly not searching for lawlike prepositions or systematic cross-cultural connections. Relationships are culturally specific, and conditions for analogical arguments have to be carefully examined in order to use present-day information to contribute to the interpretation of the archaeological record and ultimately to better understand human behavior, evolution, and history.

I believe it is possible to stress cultural meaning and context specifics, a legacy of the so-called interpretive or contextual archaeology, and at the same time retain processual archaeology's emphasis on process and variability (Hodder 1987:446). Through the combination of quali-quantitative methods and a variety of other methodological resources I hope to generate material for the better understanding of past societies. With this new case study I expect to broaden the range of variability of hunter-gatherer societies and to explore the multiple factors that contribute to the generation of the archaeological record.

Note

1. In spite of this I often had the sensation that if we had lived long enough with the same band we would have ended up being the nannies of the group, or merely accompanying the children to collect water from the nearby water hole.

Chapter 3

SOCIOPOLITICAL ORGANIZATION AND COSMOLOGY

The data on sociopolitical organization are based on my fieldwork complemented by research conducted by Cabrera, Franky, and Mahecha (1999), Yunis and Piñeros (Ms), and Mondragón (Ms). Moreover, both my research and that of the aforementioned authors have benefited from a complete register of people, births, deaths, and kinship that the New Tribes missionaries have maintained since the establishment of Laguna Pavón 2. This list has been the basis of the majority of studies on Nukak kinship.

Nukak ideology and cosmovision have not been approached in detail in our research, fundamentally because of idiomatic limitations and the original research project's principal objectives of collecting other types of data. However, as the research has progressed, understanding of these aspects has turned out to be the key to interpretation and discussion of the information obtained. Our data relating to ideology, beliefs, and cosmovision are based on the accounts of the Nukak informants who collaborated with us (Monicaro and Yorena). More important, it is based on their translations of information related by other Nukak during our field trips.

The New Tribe missionaries have collected a great deal of material in this regard, part of which has been presented in the reports that they periodically write for the Colombian Government Ministry and to which I have had access. Other data were passed on to me personally by Kenneth Conduff, Israel Gualteros, Andrés Jiménez, and Joaquin Foster during the course of numerous interviews; some I gleaned from their translations of information from the Nukak who remained in Santafé de Bogotá (see Chapter 1). The following summary is based on my own data as well as the preceding references.

SOCIOPOLITICAL ORGANIZATION

The Nukak are organized sociopolitically into autonomous bands linked to larger affiliation groups called *munu*. The band is the Nukak unit of political and social organization. Bands are composed of agnates and affines and are made up of several nuclear families (usually no more than 5 although 11 in one exceptional case). The maximum size of a band recorded during our fieldwork was 63 individuals (the eastern band of the *Wayari* people), and the minimum was 12 (from the western *Meu* people), although the latter figure probably represents a band segment. The median range was 20 to 30 individuals per band. Yunis and Piñeros (Ms) recorded a total of 256 people in a sample of bands (including some small ones that were probably segments) and attained an average of 18.28 persons per band (min = 3; max = 38; $n = 14$). On certain occasions two or three bands (or segments of bands) may camp together for several days. Such groupings do not constitute a new band, but rather should be considered sporadic congregations for particular and specific purposes (that is, ritual gatherings, harvest feasts, and so on). These gatherings do not imply changes in kinship ties between individuals of different bands (unless they form new couples), nor do they involve transformations in political and economic relations. In other words, the membership of an individual to a band is not defined by temporary residency of one or several nights in a residential camp but rather by long-term residence and kinship ties.

Based on this information, I make a distinction between the number of members of a band and the number of people that inhabit a camp, or, in other words, the coresident group. As well as being flexible, the number of members of a band is difficult to ascertain, because in a particular camp there may be visiting members of other bands or temporary members (orphans, for example), and members of the home band might be away from the camp. In contrast, the coresident group is easy to quantify and is directly observable. Based on my fieldwork, the average number of coresidents is 22.07 (min = 6; max = 46; $n = 26$). Other authors have given ranges of 12 to 35 (Mondragón Ms) and 6 to 30 (Torres 1994). In general, band members coreside for most of the year (this is one of the characteristics that allows them to be identified as a sociopolitical unit), but in some cases—such as one band with 63 people (recorded in 1995)—the segments of the band camp separately, although close together, within the band territory. The combination of families is dynamic; the segments that camp together are not always made up of the same nuclear families. As such, the band mentioned above (the largest yet recorded) spends most of the year split into two or three coresident groups that camp close to one another.

During fieldwork I had contact with nine coresident groups belonging to nine different bands. I also gathered information on other bands, especially those from the southeastern part of the territory, but my figures on the total number of bands are speculative. I estimate that prior to the main period of

Western contact (in the late 1980s) there were around 20 bands. Cabrera, Franky, and Mahecha (1999) arrived at a figure of 13 "local groups" in the mid 1990s. Yunis and Piñeros (Ms) mention 14 bands in only one portion of Nukak territory. Given the flexibility of band composition, the difficulties in measuring the exact number of people per band and the extensive demographic changes of the last years make it probable that the number of bands in this recent period ranged between 13 and 20.

Two of the properties of bands as a form of sociopolitical organization are fusion and fission. In the case of the Nukak, fission (permanent or temporary) is witnessed when two or more families decide no longer to live together. In this case kinship ties may remain unmodified, but residential and economic relations change substantially. The fission or fragmentation of bands is understood to occur only when those family groups that constitute the kinship units that make up the band are involved. The immigration or incorporation of members without their nuclear family group (for example, orphans or single youths) should be considered as a modification of the band with the loss or gain of individual members and not as a process of fusion or fission. These processes of people moving between bands occur frequently owing to a variety of causes, and they modify slightly the number of people in the co-resident group. We did not observe the process of periodic fission in bands for long periods (that is, a season), as occurs, for example, among the Cuiva of the neighboring Colombian Llanos Orientales (Arcand 1972). Generalized seasonal and systematic fusion and fission events have led to a proposed differentiation between "maximum" bands (during periods of fusion) and "minimum" bands (during phases of fission) (Gamble 1986:32).[1] Such differentiation does not appear to exist among the Nukak.

Cabrera, Franky, and Mahecha (1999) present a different interpretation of the social organization of the Nukak, arguing that the domestic group (the nuclear family) and not the band is the basic unit of production and consumption. The "local group" is considered to consist of a social aggregation, which, based on the description provided (Cabrera, Franky, & Mahecha 1999:101–08), appears to be intermediate between the so-called band and the larger affiliation group. The authors discuss and analyze the regrouping and transference of people and families between bands and local groups using the concept of "social mobility" (see Franky, Cabrera, & Mahecha 1995).

From my perspective, the band must be considered the basic Nukak sociopolitical entity, since it is the unit of procurement, production, distribution, and consumption of food, as well as the first level of social aggregation. My view is supported by the continuous cooperation of the different domestic groups that make up the band in its hunting, collecting, and fishing tasks, as well as in all activities associated with horticulture. This includes the systematic distribution of production that results in the consumption of many of the products hunted or collected by different domestic groups. Several rituals also required the participation of members from different nuclear families. Furthermore, some economic activities require the participation of more than one domestic group (in general including at least one participant from every group), such as, for example, the communal hunting of the white-lipped peccary. This does not imply that a domestic group is not self-sufficient, which is the central argument of Cabrera, Franky, and Mahecha (1999) in postulating the family as a sociopolitical unit; rather, it emphasizes the fact that the mutually cooperative, regular relationships that link the domestic groups within a band are the relevant organizational features, not only in techno-economical terms but also in the social and the ideational spheres. Thus, I believe the band must be considered the basic unit of Nukak procurement, production, distribution, and consumption.

In terms of social aggregation and organization, each band functions as a political unit with a leader, generally an adult man who is head of one of the nuclear families. Leadership is not marked, being based on the prestige of the individual leader, who is generally a good hunter and a well-balanced person who attends to the general well-being of the group. The leader makes certain decisions, such as when to relocate to a new campsite, where gathering takes place, when a celebration occurs, and so forth, but these decisions must be agreed on by the heads of the other families. He may also adjudicate in the resolution of conflicts, although he rarely interferes in marital disputes. Some adult women hold significant weight in decision making. The problems that can occur between the leader of a band and another head of a family may result in the temporary or permanent fragmentation of the band. In practical terms, leaders have few advantages or privileges. When a band establishes itself in a new location to set up camp, the leader or his wife is always the first to hang the couple's hammock, after which the other families follow suit. As such, the layout of the camp depends to some degree on the location of the leader's dwelling. At the ritual gatherings between bands (baak-wáadn), the leaders, followed by the other adult men, are the first to begin the dance.

The composition of the bands is relatively stable. They utilize a particular territory, although with lax limits (see Chapter 6). This situation has been modified in various ways by contact with Western colonization. The northwestern bands (Meu-munu) have segmented to a greater extent (Figure 1.2, p. 36). Owing to the influence of the colonization, especially in the Trocha Ganadera area, the processes of fission and the relocation of members appear more intense. There is a greater number of orphans in these bands, some of whom end up living with the *colonos* (we have recorded at least seven cases, and Yunis and Piñeros [Ms] cite 26 minors living in farmers' houses, see also Sánchez Botero 1998). Moreover, some Nukak women have been taken as wives by *colonos* and live on their farms. The northeastern group (*Wayari*) appears to be the most stable, maintaining the same three bands during the 1990s with little modification in their membership. In one of these bands, which occupies the western part (*meuri*) of the *Wayari munu*, the same five families were observed living together for at least three years, between 1992 and 1995.

The bands share a territory within which reorganizations, exchange of partners, visits, ritual gatherings, and feasts occur frequently although not exclusively within this area. The domains of these greater affiliation groups to which the members of the bands ascribe have particular names that make reference to the band's location within the territory and are connoted with the suffix *munu*, which indicates something like "people of." The best known *munu* are *Wayari* (northeast), *Tákayu* (center-southwest), *Muhabeh* or *Mipah* (south or southeast), and *Meu* (northwest) (Figure 1.2). Cabrera, Franky, and Mahecha (1999:160–61) propose an alternative concept, essentially arguing for the existence of only two principle subgroups, one of which includes the "local groups," whose territories are in the watershed of the Inírida river (*Mipah*), the other subgroup being on the Guaviare (*Wayari*). Mondragón (Ms) identified six affiliation groups and named them "endogamous regional territorial groups"; Yunis and Piñeros (Ms) call these "affiliation groups." The suffix *munu* also serves to connote bands, and its usage along with the name of the band leader is common (Cabrera, Franky, & Mahecha 1999). I found that it was most frequently used with reference to regional groups, but we occasionally recorded its use restricted to a single band, suffixed to the leader's name.

In general, couples are monogamous, although some men have two partners. There were seven cases of polygamy recorded during our fieldwork (*n* = 30 couples), a rate of 23.3. In three of these cases the two wives were sisters. In a more representative sample (*n* = 90 couples), Yunis and Piñeros (MS) recorded 77 men with one wife, 12 with two wives, and 1 with three wives, giving a polygamy rate of 14.4. Cabrera, Franky, and Mahecha (1999:157) arrived at a figure close to this, with a rate of 15.0 (*n* = 73 couples). We did not record a single case of polyandry; neither do such cases seem to be recorded in the studies carried out by Cabrera, Franky, and Mahecha (1999:157) or by other authors. The exception is the work of Yunis and Piñeros (Ms), who mention 84 women with a single husband, 5 with two husbands, and one case of a woman with three husbands. These data must be treated cautiously, as all others investigators, including some who worked with the same bands, have not recorded them.

Cabrera, Franky, and Mahecha (1999:149) concluded that the ideal norm appears to be viri-patrilocal residence. Nonetheless, there are situations in which it is expected that a daughter remain in her family's band with her husband (a situation we observed in one of the *Wayari* bands). Furthermore, in 1991 one of the *Meu munu* bands had formed around four sisters and their brother, the leader of the band. Israel Gualteros (pers. comm.:1995) notes that in some cases men that join the band must demonstrate their skill at obtaining food. It is common that some men will go and live with their wife's band at the beginning of their relationship. Given the range of variation observed and the situational factors that affect postmarital residence, "virilocal" may not be the most appropriate characterization. Even if it is usually the case that patrilineal societies are virilocal, a smaller proportion, in spite of its patrilineality, is bilocal or neolocal (Ember 1975; Van der Berhge 1977:111). In conclusion, it would be more accurate to characterize the Nukak postmarital residence pattern as bilocal.

According to Conduff and Jiménez (pers. comm.:1995), the first choice of partner among the Nukak is a cross-cousin; the union of parallel cousins is prohibited. Cabrera, Franky, and Mahecha (1999:155) suggest that the "ideal model to be followed in attaining a spouse is that of the prescribed marriage with a bilateral cross-cousin." The authors propose that the clans are the exogamous units, and the clan segments that live in the same local group are units of exchange. Conduff and Jiménez (pers. comm.:1995) knew of only one case in which parallel cousins formed a couple. In this situation the permission of the families was required, to which they finally acceded after a lengthy discussion. It also transpired that the couple had not been raised together.

One of the most important Nukak collective rituals is the *baak wáadn*, which generally takes place between bands or band segments from the same *munu*. This ritual, which occurs in the residential camp of one of the bands, consists of a succession of activities that develop more or less in the following sequence: (1) a song and dance by the men from the host camp; (2) the entrance of the men from the visiting band who join the dance; (3) the violence increases among the dancing men; (4) when the violence reaches a peak the women rush in and calm the men, who continue to dance, occasionally returning to controlled peaks of violence; (5) the men sit down in groups of two or three and, embracing one another, begin to cry and sing a mournful song while the women begin to dance; (6) the women join the lamenting groups, whose members reassemble in different subgroups. This ritual is associated with the dead relatives of the participants. The grouping of people during the prayer-lament is related to the degree of kinship they have with the dead for whom the ritual takes place. Other less frequent rituals occur at the harvesting of certain fruit, such as the chontaduro (*Bactris gascipaes*) and the *kupé* (*Dacryodes chimantensis*) feasts.

Mondragón (pers. comm.:1995) has recently identified the existence of paternally affiliated lineages (*nüwayi*), noting that people from different lineages coexist in a single band or territorial group. He further suggests that the term *nüwa* or *nüw* is used to refer to ancestors from the paternal line. Cabrera, Franky, and Mahecha (1999) argue that the Nukak have patrilineal descent groups; in other words, every person is ascribed permanently and uniquely during his or her entire lifetime to the descent group of his or her father. Since each of these groups has a name, and shared agnatic descent cannot be proven (genealogical memory goes back only a few generations), they are designated as clans (Cabrera, Franky, & Mahecha 1999:146). The authors further hypothesize that "local groups" are formed by people of different clans and that each clan, in turn, is associated with a specific territory. The New Tribes missionaries made reference to the existence of a clan system in several of their unpublished reports. Two terms are recognized to refer to these Nukak clans: *diwaji* and *etaji*. Significantly, the names of the *diwaji* and *etaji* recorded by Cabrera, Franky, and Mahecha (1999:147) refer to animals with powerful symbolic connotations, such as jaguar, tapir, deer, and peccary. Reptiles, caiman, birds, plants, colors, and objects have also been mentioned. The affiliation of clans with certain animals that make up the "house of the tapir" (see below) has been confirmed by my research. Although the paternal descent group is the most important, the maternal descent group is also present and may acquire importance in some ritual contexts or during affiliation events (Cabrera, Franky, & Mahecha 1999:147).

Finally, one of the Nukak's commonest means of representing gender and social identity is through facial and body painting. Body painting occurs frequently among the Nukak and is considered a type of "clothing." There are numerous occasions when they will paint themselves entirely red with achiote (*Bixa orellana*) and a preparation of leaves known as *éóro* (*Arrabidaea chica*; see discussion in Chapter 8). The most common of such events is when another band is visited, or during menstruation. Every band has its own designs, and there is a marked difference between men's and women's motifs. Unfortunately, we do not yet understand body painting's symbolic and ritual complex or how it functions in the social realm.

Ideology and Cosmology

Although concepts such as "ideology," "ideational," and "cosmology" are widely used in anthropology, there is no consensus on their meanings and distinctions. For the purposes of this book, I follow a simple yet clear and practical definition provided by Silverwood-Cope (1990:133–34) in relation to the Kakwa: "[F]or 'cosmology' I employ a lengthy definition which, in terms of our own culture, is understood as a cultural system to conceive of space, time, energy and life phenomena" (translated from the Portuguese by the author). Furthermore, the difficulty of dissecting the ideational dimension from other aspects of behavior is acknowledged throughout this book.

As will be seen in the following chapters, the Nukak cosmological order is not an abstract concept used to cope with inexplicable phenomena and satisfy existential angst. It is far more than this, being a series of beliefs and ideas that influences the daily lives of the Nukak and that provides practical rules for everyday behavior. Silverwood-Cope (1990:133), in regard to the Kakwa, formed the same impression, stating that, "I want to show that [Bara] Makú cosmology is a very real institution of constant and immediate importance for every Makú." Steven Hugh-Jones's narrative, captured on camera in Barasana land, not far from Nukak territory, is telling and nicely portrays the difficulties in decoding Amazonian categories into our own thought: "Every single mountain, river, technical process, plant, and animal *is* the religion. When we said we were studying [Barasana] religion, that is rubbish . . . there isn't a religion, everything is religion" (Moser 1971). This body of beliefs permeates every aspect of Amazonian societies and cannot be separated from any one of them.

The Nukak conceive of the world in three levels: the "world-of-below"; the land where they live, or the "intermediate world"; and the upper level, or the "world-of-above." Although these worlds have mythical origins and traverse time and space, they are envisioned as real and tangible. The world-of-above is like an inverted plate over the Earth, which it touches at its outer edges. According to the Nukak one can reach the edge of the intermediate world and ascend to the sky in the east. In the world-of-above one lives a better life; there are large shelters and gardens, and food abounds and is not subject to taboos. The shelters have zinc roofs, the same as the *colonos* houses, and are so big that they have subdivisions within. They are positioned around a central square that is devoid of grass and rubbish, containing just a little sand. Many objects in this world, such as spears and flutes, are made of metal, and the hammocks are cotton, identical to those of the *colonos*. Moreover, there is no anger, and the spirit-ancestors no longer die, although the existence of a being called *Choubjumka*, who is able to kill and eat the spirits in the sky, is admitted to. In this world the spirit-ancestors sing, dance, and play metal flutes. They sleep little because there is no night, only a time with less light, and they never get sick. These spirits cast spells on the people of the Earth, sometimes killing them. There are no taboos whatsoever; men, women, and children may eat any animal on any occasion.

Poles in the four cardinal points support the world-of-above. Earthquakes occur when the spirits of the "old ones" shake the poles vigorously. The landscape of this world is clearly defined as a space antithetical to the rainforest that predominates in the intermediate world. Principally, in the world-of-above the rainforest with its animals and plants occupies a peripheral position, existing only on the edges, where this world touches the Earth. Toward one side there are large orchards (some 300 m to 400 m in diameter) with abundant crops of yucca, yam, banana, tobacco, chontaduro, and so on. As it never rains, they must be irrigated with river water using gourds. A single, large *kupé* tree, inhabited by birds and monkeys, occupies the center of this world. There are also palms with edible fruit, among which seje (*Oenocarpus bataua*) stands out. Birds, monkeys, and other animals are present, as well as snakes and insects, but the sacred animals (tapir, deer and jaguar) are not, because their spirits are not able to ascend to the sky. Neither are there limpets, mollusks whose sacred status is not yet clear, although it appears that in the recent past gathering and consuming them was prohibited. There are also rivers and lagoons in this world, from which many caiman and fish (*yamú* [*Brycon siebenthalae*], catfish, and so on) are taken. One of these rivers is so large that the far bank cannot be seen. There are no mountains, but rocks are present on the edges, where the rainforest lies.

"East" and "west" are cardinal points with mythic significance for the Nukak. The spirits travel to the east to obtain the "truth drug" (*éóro baká*). Also toward the east, along one of the paths that lead to the world-of-above, there is a camp from where the sun rises. The sun is conceived of as a Nukak with many wives. Beings represented by the sun, the moon, and several large stars (considered brothers-in-law of the sun) live in this camp, which lies beyond a lagoon close to the hole through which the Nukak reached the Earth. Many stars are thought to be glowworms that live in the caves in the rocks of this world. Because the world-of-above is visualized as flat, the sun is conceptualized as a man who sets out in the morning to distribute food (the animals that are hunted) and, at midday, returns toward the east from where he came. After approximately one o'clock in the afternoon (Kenneth Conduff, pers. comm.:1995), what one sees is not the sun but its reflection returning to the camp in the east in order that it may return in the same direction the following morning. The reflection is made possible by the fact that Sun-Nukak possesses a mirror that refracts light.[2] When Sun-Nukak arrives in the extreme east he paints himself red to enter the camp, hence producing the reddish reflection at dusk. This idea of a Sun-Nukak who returns from the middle of the sky is related to the idea that the Earth is not spherical but flat. Consequently, if Sun-Nukak were to continue traveling toward the west he would not be able to appear the following day in the east. For this to happen Sun-Nukak must return before nightfall to the east. Informants indicated to us several times that the world-of-above was full of mirrors, which is certainly connected to the reflection of Sun-Nukak and probably also with the reflection of the moon.

The intermediate world is where the present-day life of the Nukak takes place. This world is populated by people and many kinds of spirits who live in trees and take the forms of animals (see below). The Earth and the trees have always existed, as have some animals. An ancestral mythical hero called *Mauroijumját*, who probably has the appearance of a monkey, was the creator of many animals and trees. He is the motive for a great many stories and myths, such as the origin of curare being his wife's urine (see Chapter 7). It also appears that a howler monkey (probably embodying *Mauroijumját* himself) created the Cerro de las Cerbatanas (Blowpipe Hill).

There is an underground level, or an underworld, below the level where people live. Other Nukak live there, as well as animals such as the tapir and deer, which inhabit villages and shelters. The tapir is the most powerful animal-spirit in this level. So powerful, in fact, according to one of our informants, that in the "house of the tapir" the jaguar is kept as a pet. In Nukak mythology there are other "houses" in this level, including the house for animals of the floodplains, harboring animals that are perceived as "crowded" and over-abundant. The nature of this house is poorly understood, but it appears to differ from the "house of the tapir," since the animals that live there are not considered spirit-animals in the same sense. Caiman, capybara, and various kinds of fish are associated with this house. Caiman were Nukak in ancestral times, but when the floods came they dove into the waters and turned into their current form. It is important to reiterate that this underground level is considered to exist close to the surface of the intermediate world. A story told by Israel Gualteros conveys this sense. The missionaries were digging a hole to extract water. When they reached a depth of approximately 5 or 6 meters, gravel and sand began to emerge. This was identified by the Nukak as the shore of one of the large rivers from the underworld. When water began to gush up quickly, the Nukak, in a state of alarm, said that this was the water of the river from below that the missionaries had undoubtedly reached.

The world-of-below is the deepest and most dangerous. It lies below the intermediate world at a depth of 100 to 150 meters. Extremely powerful spirits live there, and it is a place only rarely visited in dreams by the strongest Nukak. During these visits the weak spirits may be captured by the powerful forces of the world-of-below and remain there trapped (see below).

The Nukak origin myth is relatively well known, with minor variations occurring on each occasion it is narrated. In essence, it is said that long ago many Nukak left the world-of-below through a hole in the Earth. This hole was excavated by a woman, *Mainako'jemjat*, with her long fingernails. She had been living for some time on Earth and had heard noises from below.[3] In one variation I recorded, this woman was cooking maize and yucca. The hole she made was not very large or deep (some 3 meters in diameter). It is located in the east, and still exists, but no Nukak has traveled to see it. The hollow was covered, but someone later removed the cover and caused a flood. Water simultaneously poured down from above. This hole was later blocked off by the waters of a river (*Wayari* or Guaviare) and by the flood. Those who could not reach the Earth remained below, while those who were already there saved themselves by climbing the Cerro de las Cerbatanas. When the Nukak arrived they first slept; then they rolled themselves in ash to remove a layer of skin that was making them ill. Some survived and buried those that had died. Subsequently, they began to populate the Earth, following an easterly direction. The Nukak already possessed sexual organs and were naked. However, the men were embarrassed and dressed themselves in loincloths. Other Nukak returned to the world below and remained there. In Nukak mythology these events occurred only a few generations ago. For example, they say that an old man who died recently (in the late 1980s or early 1990s) was the son of one of the Nukak who had come through the hole (Kenneth Conduff pers. comm.:1995).

The Earth, or the intermediate world, "has always been, nobody made it," but was very different before the Nukak arrived. The things that have always existed are the rivers (although with much less water), the fish, some birds, the sun, moon, stars, clouds, and so on. But there were no other human beings; neither were there mountains nor many of the animals, such as deer, jaguar, tapir, anteaters, *paujil* (a bird, *Nothocrax urumutum*), and so forth. In regard to the trees, it appears that some were already there but others arrived after the Nukak or were brought by them, including *kupé* (the first to be brought), platanillo (*Phenakospermun guyanensis*), and chontaduro. It did not rain during this time because the sky was low. One textual narrative concerning the time of creation was recorded and translated by Andrés Jiménez (Ms):

> What was the time of woolly monkey like? The woolly monkey, he comes from *nemep*. In the rows of *macanilla* he came and went. He normally looked for this type of fruit; he climbed up and collected them. This is their normal food; they eat this type of fruit and they are changed. In rows of *macanilla* they sat and later they also went. He saw fruit from this tree, he climbed and collected them all together, they say. He was usually eating. They, upon eating, were changed; from *nemep* comes the *choruco*. What was the brown capuchin monkey like? The brown capuchin monkey comes from the red jaguar as well. It was created by *Mauroijumját*, he was the creator. *Mauroijumját* was the creator of this brown capuchin monkey and of the *ninewa* monkey. What was the howler monkey like? The howler monkey was made also, he comes from the Nukak. The howler monkey is what was created. This is all. What was the time of the honey like? That kind of small honey, *Maúroijumját* used that kind of reed, he used that junk. Why is that? He did it. It was the time of the spines, the spines of the seje palm he took off and shot with them, that's how it was. What were these floodplain trees like? These floodplain trees are only tall poles, they exist by themselves, these poles exist by themselves. These kinds of poles from the floodplain exist by themselves.

There is a continuous and dynamic connection among the three worlds, with a degree of subordination of the intermediate world to the other two. The world-of-above holds a position of dominance, since many things that happen there have direct consequences in the intermediate world and affect people's daily lives. For example, there are rivers and lagoons in the world-of-above from which the spirit-ancestors may drop water on the intermediate world when they wash, play, or make dams with branches. Heat and cold in the intermediate world are the product of an enormous cigar that the beings in the upper world smoke, especially one called *Chuu'jumka*. When the cigar is smoked profusely it is hot, and when it is put out in the river it is cold. Powerful men from the intermediate world, or their spirits (this is not sufficiently clear), may also ascend and smoke this cigar in order to call into effect the summer season. Another version of the origins of heat in the intermediate world suggests that summer is caused by the heat of the Nukak-sun's body when he travels though his territory, and that the cold is created by birds called *widíwidipwun*. The spirit-ancestors of the world-of-above also wish for the death of the people of the intermediate world, as the latter can then ascend to the upper world where life is so much better. The yield of edible fruit is related to how much the spirit-ancestors of the world-of-above eat. If they eat a great deal, the trees of the intermediate world produce in abundance. In the case of *koró-paanját* (*Iryanthera ulei*), the abundance of fruit directly derives from sexual activity in the world-of-above. This is related to the fact that many trees contain ancestral tree-spirits in the world-of-above with which they have a continuous relationship of dependence.

The connection between the different worlds is also created by the journeys of spirit-ancestors, which take one of the two paths that connect the intermediate world with the world-of-above. Or they may adopt the form of a bird, *waák*, to ascend to this world. The spirit-ancestors also have pet animals that are brought from the intermediate world. An interesting feature of Nukak cosmology is their attitude toward *salados* ("salt licks"). While for many Amazonian groups these salt licks are preferred locations for hunting large mammals, Nukak regard them as "doors" that communicate with the "house of the tapir." In other words, they connect the two levels of the intermediate world. The Nukak believe that the tapir, jaguar, deer, and other animals whose tracks can be seen in the *salados* use these locations to emerge from the underworld at night. In this sense, *salados* are sacred places and are rarely visited by the Nukak. Other, probably less important, animals that inhabit the "house of the tapir" and emerge at night are paca (Agouti paca), anteater (*Myrmecophaga tridactyla*), and freshwater otter ("*perro de agua*," *Lutra longicaudis*)

According to the Nukak, everybody fundamentally has three spirits. However, some Nukak mention the existence of four or even five personal spirits. These spirits leave the body in different directions when a person dies. The main spirit is the image of a person in the mirror. This spirit travels toward the world-of-above, where the spirits of the ancestors reside, and lives there forever. This spirit exists within a person when he or she is alive, departing and returning to the body through the medium of dreams. If the spirit does not return before the person wakes up, the person dies. For the Nukak, dreams are actual events that happen to their spirits when they leave their bodies. Journeys to the clouds and to distant places take place during dreams. The principal spirits of the extremely powerful Nukak, who have shamanic powers, can travel in their dreams to the world below, where dangerous "forces" exist that can capture souls traveling during their dreams. Whatever takes place during a dream is considered to have been an actual event, or is a message that must be interpreted. For example, dreaming of an animal means that a person from that clan is dying or that someone from another clan will visit.

The second spirit is called *yorehat*, which means "whiteness." This spirit makes its way to the underground level in the intermediate world, to the "house of the tapir," where it remains, going out only at night to eat the fruit from trees. In an IANTC (1992a) report one informant explained that two spirits with similar characteristics actually existed, both of which go to the "house of the tapir." This second spirit's journey appears to be linked to burial since it heads directly toward its dwelling place in the underworld from the bottom of the grave pit. It dons the skin of a deer, tapir, or jaguar for its nocturnal trips. When it returns it removes them and hangs them on a pole. It appears that each of the spirits owns three shirts to use. It is possible eventually to kill one but never all three; otherwise, the people who belong to the clan of this spirit-animal would be killed off. As such, it appears that all the tapir, deer, and spirits of the underworld are disguised as these animals, and therefore it is prohibited to hunt them and especially to eat their meat (see Chapter 9). These spirits take animals for their wives and maintain sexual relations with them. The children of such unions look like their fathers, but have flat faces.

The jaguar is apparently a case apart. Sometimes it is considered a spirit of the world-of-below dressed in the feline's skin, and at others it is merely an animal that contains no spirit. Hunting jaguar is not strongly restricted when it is solely an animal. There have been cases when jaguar have been hunted and their canines removed, but their meat was left uneaten.

The third spirit is the *nemep*, which means "the dark" or "the black." While a person is alive this spirit manifests itself in his or her shadow. When a person dies it remains in the forests of the intermediate world, living in certain places such as the hollows of trees.[4] It is essentially a malignant spirit, but its evil is tempered because the *nemep* is conceived of as a foolish and unintelligent being. In appearance it is like a large, clumsy hairy monkey with enormous feet. At times it takes the appearance of an anteater when searching for food. At night it travels in search of nourishment and molests the Nukak, causing them harm. Fundamentally, this spirit's anger is directed toward the people with whom it had problems in life. It is said to eat the eggs of guinea fowl and to drink the blood and eat the flesh of humans. Using a particular type of witchcraft (*naa* and *ébep*) it can even kill those who speak badly of another person. This spirit can fly or walk, but not run. It does not laugh, cry, play the flute, or speak Nukak; it wears neither clothes nor body paint. There are many stories concerning the kinds of mischief caused by the *nemep*, all of which are generally disagreeable and filthy. One of the most frequently told is when the *nemep* enters camp stealthily at night and "puts its dirty buttocks on the faces of the sleeping people." *Nemep* are also said to be full of worms. When its presence is felt, palm wreaths and leaves are placed around the camp perimeter for protection. In general, the Nukak are wary of *nemep* when they camp near the graves of certain powerful persons or persons with whom they have had disputes. On such occasions they are more alert and take precautions to neutralize the spirit's evil actions.

Besides these three spirits, there are others called *takwe'yi* (roughly translatable as "chest spirits"), whose origin is unclear. They are strong spirits who have taken the "truth drug" (*óóro baká*). They exist in immediate proximity to people and are akin to them, except smaller. In this sense, they are not personal spirits but rather "associated" or "related" to some (or all, this is unclear) people. Neither is it clear if all *takwe'yi* are related to a particular Nukak, or whether, to the contrary, there are those that exist independently of a Nukak ancestor. Whichever the case, some have said that these *takwe'yi* go to the "house of the tapir" when a person dies. There they take particular kinds of fish as wives and produce children similar to themselves. It would appear that the *takwe'yi* have an existence related to men and that they are masculine in gender. They sleep during the day and at night go out in search of food, adopting the appearance of tapir, peccary, and birds. It is also said that there is only one type of tree, called *din*, that contains *takwe'yi*. These spirits reside in this tree, and when a Nukak takes an ax to the tree the *takwe'yi* are unhurt, as "the ax passes through them without causing them harm." When this happens the *takwe'yi* moves, using another tree as its dwelling. The *takwe'yi* are always traveling eastward in search of the "truth drug" (*óóro baká*). On their return they share the drug with the other spirits who dwell in the "house of the tapir," who ask for it singing and extending their hands. The *takwe'yi* distribute it among them. They also give *óóro baká* to the living, and when people take this drug it lodges itself in their heads (in the form of a red substance), and they can "see the shadow of that which cannot be seen."

In some ways the *takwe'yi* have the opposite characteristics of the *nemep*. They do not fly but walk and run a great deal. During the day they watch over people, but not during the night while they are out looking for food. They are extremely clean and bathe often with special water from the underworld. They laugh, they paint themselves with *óóro*, and they stick feathers to their bodies as decoration. They speak the language of the world-of-below (*jeén náu*); they play metal flutes and generally enjoy themselves; they possess magic darts; and so on and so forth. These spirits also help people search for food, and they provide the important substance *óóro baká*.

The *takwe'yi* are considered to be the cause of many events, including, frequently, a person's death. Some Nukak have shamanic abilities and can see these spirits and detect their scent, as well as talk to them to persuade them to end storms and thunder. These spirits can cause all sorts of evil, including dispersing poison through the air or in rainfall; shooting invisible poison darts and killing people; and sending deluges to flood the Nukak; and so on. One of the Nukak's great fears is that people with shamanic powers may, upon dying, negotiate the death of the Nukak-sun with the *takwe'yi*, which would lead to total darkness. Through communication with and control of their *takwe'yi*, Nukak may cause harm to people of another clan or an enemy.

The actions of the *takwe'yi* cause most climatic phenomena, such as the strong wind that they are said to provoke by making giant birds flap their wings, or by dropping large palm leaves. The shouts of the *takwe'yi* are responsible for thunder: when someone is angered, the *takwe'yi* related to him or her are also angry and make thunder. These spirits possess shotguns and may kill *takwe'yi* from another clan and eat them. Thunder is also caused by the gunshots of the *takwe'yi*. They make clouds: when they shout they produce a smokelike vapor over the land that then forms into clouds. To make it rain the *takwe'yi* ascend skyward in the form of a bird whose wings are full of water, which they hurl down from above as rain. These spirits also produce lightening when they make fire with two sticks. An alternative explanation of lightening is that it is a form of witchcraft used by the *takwe'yi* to kill people.

Finally, there are more beings and spirits with ambiguous characteristics. For example, certain trees have spirits that dwell in the world-of-above. There are also red beings, such as those that live far off in the west, who have "long tails and a gaze made of fire that kills." They cannot be visited, and no Nukak would dare go in search of them. Other beings of indeterminate sex, the *chák ´naugú*, live on the banks of the rivers; their dregs are the clay that women collect to fabricate ceramic pots (see Chapter 7).

FINAL CONSIDERATIONS

Based on the preceding material, one can conclude that the Nukak sociopolitical unit is the exogamous band, usually consisting of three to five families and formed by agnates and affines from members of different clans. Bands have a postmarital, bilocal residence pattern. They generally comprised coresident groups of 20 to 30 people, although not exclusively. These values are within the range of variation recorded in comparative studies of numerous hunter-gatherer groups; that is, 25 to 50 individuals (Lee & De Vore 1968) or 15 to 50 individuals, with an average of 25 individuals (Hassan 1981:51). For the Nukak, the maximum recorded number of coresidents (46 people) would appear to indicate that when this figure approaches 50, groups tend to fragment and camp apart.

The Nukak kinship system is similar to the closest Makú group, the Kakwa (based on Silverwood-Cope 1990), a further factor that supports the hypothesis of a Nukak-Kakwa common trunk and of their relatively recent separation (Mondragón 2000). The Kakwa are organized into a system comprising groups of patrilineal descent, or clans, and they cannot demonstrate common agnatic descent. (Their genealogical memory goes back no further than two generations.) During Silverwood-Cope's fieldwork, of 11 local groups made up of two or more domestic groups, only two were patrilineal and patrilocal extended families; the remainder were bilateral and bilocal extended families. The Nukak demonstrate a similar pattern, although the proportions appear to be different. In the case of the Kakwa, the suffix *muna*[5] ("people") is also used, both when referring to a band (local group) and a conjunction of local autonomous groups. Furthermore, these *muna* tend toward endogamy and are named, in a fashion similar to the Nukak, based on their location in relation to the rivers of the region. Among the Kakwa, if a person marries a sibling, a parallel cousin, or a member of the same clan it is considered comparable to marrying oneself, which has connotations similar to incest (Silverwood-Cope 1990:134). In regional terms, the Nukak and the Kakwa cases point to the significance of supralocal arrangements of politico-matrimonial alliances in regional systems, as has been proposed for the northwestern Amazon (Jackson 1983).

Nukak patrilocality versus bilocality deserves comment. There has been a change of perception concerning the postmarital residence patterns of hunter-gatherers, from the early view that they were typically patrilocal to the belief that they are bilocal (Ember 1978). Recent work indicates that patrilocality (Kelly 1995) is more frequent, although bilocality is common among small-band hunter-gatherers such as the Ju/'hoansi/!Kung and the Mbuti (Ember 1975). This category could also include the Nukak. It is possible that the Nukak may traditionally have been patrilocal and that the tendency toward bilocality observed during the 1990s was influenced by the drastic population decline in the late 1980s. This transformation from unilocal to bilocal has already been noted in other hunter-gatherer populations submitted to severe processes of depopulation (Ember 1975; Service 1962).

The most common characteristics of foragers are exogamous bands, patrilineality, and limited polygamy (Ember 1978; Van der Berghe 1977). Further examples support these tendencies. Among the Cuiva, Coppens (1975) recorded an 8.3 ($n = 24$) polygamy rate, and Hewlett (1995) recorded rates between 3.0 and 19.5 among the most conspicuous African tropical rainforest hunter-gatherers (that is, Mbuti, Efe, and so on). Although most of the Makú groups are patrilineal-patrilocal, the matrilineal and matrilocal Kaborí-Nadöb (Münzel 1969–1972:158) are a notable exception.

Nukak cosmology is firmly rooted in the Amazonian cosmology more broadly, in regard to both its content and its structural and superstructural aspects, as well as its symbolic referents (that is, the tapir, the jaguar, and so on). As such, it includes the characteristic components of shamanism, a religious phenomenon that is formally delineated and differentiated from other religions and is present in most hunter-gatherer societies (Guenther 1999:426). Cosmogenic themes, such as cataclysmic events like great floods, that played a major role in shaping the Earth as it is now known are among the most common motifs in Amazonian mythologies (Wilbert & Simoneau 1992:27). Such themes are also frequent among other South American hunter-gatherers such as the Guayaki (Clastres 1998) and the Cuiva (Wilbert & Simoneau 1991: 45–61). Furthermore, the idea of a human origin of many animals (caiman, capybaras, peccaries, and so forth), some of whom fell into the waters during the great flood, is common among indigenous South Americans. This is fundamental to a typical shamanic element, the transformation, which contrass with creation *ex nihilo* of the biblical kind (Furst 1973/1974:48). An integrating component is the conception of the world and the universe as existing in the form of superimposed planes. These planes are where the several spirits of each individual go after death, and consequently are where ancestral spirits live. The Hupdu and the Kakwa (Reid 1979; Silverwood-Cope 1990) also believe in the existence of distinct terrestrial and cosmic planes placed one above the other. The belief in the existence of stratified worlds is also shared by the Puinave (Triana 1987), the Huaorani (Rival 1996), the Hotï (Storrie 1999), and many other Amazonian groups, as well as hunter-gatherers worldwide (Guenther 1999:429). Moreover, the connection between worlds via holes—real and concrete in their existence, and identifiable in the territory—through which the first peoples emerged is a common element among South American groups (for example, the Cuiva; Wilbert & Simmoneau 1992:75–81).

Among the Nukak, events in the world-of-above are directly mirrored by occurrences on Earth. Among the Huaorani the situation seems to be the reverse, the intermediate world being where acts and things are produced that are reflected in the world or worlds above (Rival 1996:92). In general terms, the hierarchical organization of the several worlds, in which the Earth is conceived of as just another layer in an intermediate position, and the recurrent and somewhat unforced connection between humans and otherworldly beings/spirits are shared characteristics of many South American indigenous peoples (Wilbert & Simoneau 1992:24). The world-of-above has a double status among the Nukak. On the one hand, it is a place of abundance and well-being where all the principal spirits of the Nukak go when they die. On the other hand, it is a place where powerful spirits reside, both ancestral and *takwe'yi*, who may harm the living Nukak. This double status confers on the world-of-above a special status similar to other supernatural elements. It is simultaneously a place of well-being and pleasure and a place where powerful spirits reside who must be feared and worshiped if one does not want to fall victim to their ire.

The existence of evil spirits associated with shadows resembles other Makú and Amazonian groups' beliefs. In the case of the Kakwa, the similarity is striking. They are even called by the same word, *nemep*, which in Kakwa also means "shadow." They refer to spirits that wander the forests, feeding on human flesh and blood (Silverwood-Cope 1990:165). Among the Huaorani, people's evil spirit-shadows—the *huene*—also inhabit the forest, visiting people in order to cause them harm, to drink their blood and eat their flesh (Rival 1996:116). As in the case of the *nemep*, the *huene* attack the people with whom they had problems in life. This spirit symbolizes the revenge of the dead on the living, an image that is exacerbated by their blood-drinking, cannibalistic behavior.

In the case of the Nukak, as with other Amazonian groups, it is profoundly difficult to translate into our categories the concept of "spirit" or related concepts such as "supernatural forces" owing, above all, to ontological differences between Amazonian and Occidental cosmovisions that encompass this idea. In Western discourse the notion of spirit is opposed to that of the material, and spiritual existence is understood as a bodiless or extracorporeal animating principle (Valeri 2000). For the Nukak, spirits, whether of ancestors, *takwe'yi*, or trees, possess varying degrees of materiality. When a person is alive their *nemep* actually has a bidimensional materiality that bestows on it the status of shadow. Likewise, the spirit-ancestors of the tapir and the jaguar are not immaterial forces that invade the bodies of these animals; on the contrary, they have a corporeal existence that is "dressed" in the animal's skin. Therefore, in this book the terms "spirit" and "spirit-ancestor" are used to express supernatural entities that are significantly different from their homologues in Western thought (see Valeri 2000:24–25 for discussion of a similar problem).

A further characteristic of Nukak cosmology is its incorporation of Western objects and attitudes as a metaphor for a better, more pleasurable life. Hence, the world-of-above is rich with many artifacts that until recently were extremely difficult for the Nukak to obtain (zinc roofs, metal spears, lanterns, and so on). In this world of abundance the Nukak know how to read and write. They no longer paint themselves because they no longer resemble the inhabitants of the intermediate world, so they wear clothing like the *colonos* do. The Kabori-Nadöb have a similar conceptualization, but it is projected toward the world-of-below, which is conceived of as a more "evolved" place than is the intermediate world (for example, there are electric lighting, roads, and transit of trucks) (Münzel 1969–1972:166).

Although all are rooted in Amazonian cosmologies, the bodies of belief of the six Makú groups are not the same. Their differences are manifested in their origin myths, their "cultural heroes," food taboos, and other cosmological aspects. Nonetheless, these differences are no less significant than those among the northeastern Amazonian groups, such as the Puinave, the Tukano, and the Desano, and even with groups beyond the Amazon, such as the Cuiva. In some cases they are less apparent than are those among the other Makú, such as the differences between the Kakwa and the Tukano. This observation has two consequences. First, it reinforces the idea of the heterogeneity of the Makú, because the absence of a unified body of beliefs can be added to other known differences (linguistic, kinship systems, modes of interaction with neighboring groups, and so forth). Second, the dividing line between these groups in terms of cosmology and bodies of belief does not correspond to the (always diffuse) line that separates types of subsistence. In other words, in terms of religion and cosmology Amazonian groups are segregated along different limit to the separation based on modes of subsistence.

Like other lowland Amazonian societies, the Nukak do not regard the natural world as a discrete domain, separate from the social and supernatural realms. The overwhelming ideational importance assigned to some animals (jaguar, tapir, deer) is also significant, a characteristic that the Nukak share with many other Amazonian societies and that reinforces the idea that these societies are organized around some central cosmological elements. This integrated, holistic, and fundamentally shamanic worldview—called *ecosophy* by Århem (1990)—endows animals with a range of humanlike attitudes, motives, and behavior for a variety of mythological and cosmological reasons. Along with plants and "inanimate" objects, animals are integrated into several hierarchical levels, their use mediated by a mythic system in which some animals play a significant role as "owners" of places and "managers" of situations (Descola 1994; Reichel-Dolmatoff 1971; Reichel-Dussan 1995; Van der Hammen 1992; Wilbert & Simoneau 1992).

Notes

1. Alternative concepts of maximum and minimum bands have been proposed by Wobst, who sees maximum bands as the most extensive exchange networks in the marriage system.
2. The Nukak word for mirror is *kenari*, and, according to what we were told by *Yorena*, before they had access to glass mirrors the Nukak made them from

fragments of ceramic. One of the surfaces of the sherd was covered with resin or wax and was rubbed until a polished surface was obtained that reflected light. Conduff had also heard a similar explanation but had never seen one of these traditional mirrors.

3. Another version recorded by the New Tribe missionaries states that the woman lived in the world-of-below and from there dug the hole through to the intermediate world.

4. This association of shadow with spirits that detach themselves from the individual after death is observable also in other Amazonian groups such as the Achuar, for whom the brocket deer (*Mazama americana*) is the transformed shadow of a deceased person (Descola 1994:92)

5. Among the Kakwa, this suffix is also used after the name of the leader of the local group in designating that band.

Chapter 4

SHELTERS AND CAMPS

This chapter synthesizes observations of Nukak architecture and camps. These aspects of Nukak culture have not suffered substantial change through the effects of contact with Western society, and so they provide a unique opportunity to scrutinize the multiple dimensions of domestic architecture, "public" and "sacred" architecture, and the arrangement of camps among hunter-gatherers. First I examine aspects of residential-camp family shelters. Formal properties such as shape, size, and construction materials will be characterized, as well as the basic construction process. Second I discuss the rectangular dwelling called the "house of tapir," as well as transitory structures, in order to present a complete picture of the variety of the architectural forms created by the Nukak. As such, an understanding is reached of how the Nukak dwell in their forest environment and how they have developed different settlement types. Similarly, information provided by the Nukak contributes to understanding the way in which human societies globally have modified their settings to create protected and habitable spaces.

Architectural studies within anthropology, and specifically within archaeology, have taken three basic directions. These include an evolutionary perspective, related to the empirical study of energy as a universal attribute of architecture that is considered cross culturally valid, verifiable, and valuable for comparative analysis (McGuire & Schiffer 1983, see review in Abrams 1989); a behavioral approach (Kent 1990; Schiffer 1987); and a consideration of architecture's role in communicating kinship relationships, as well as a means of symbolic expression and connection with the supernatural (Hodder 1982, 1986, Joyce & Gillespie 2000). Architecture and its metaphoric use in standing for principles of social order have been widely examined of late (Carsten & Hugh-Jones 1995; Parker-Pearson & Richardson 1992). Among others, Bourdieu has persuasively emphasized the role of the house in providing a consistent language with which to arrange reality (Tilley 1999). Because of its visibility and relative durability architecture has frequently been a means of political, social, symbolic, and ideational expression (Abrams 1989). The use of the house as a metaphor, as a replica and a model of the structure of the cosmos, or as a symbolic expression of the kinship system, has a long tradition among sedentary and seminomadic Amazonian horticulturist-fishers (Hugh-Jones 1979; Reichel-Dolmatoff 1971).

In the case of the Nukak the symbolic dimension of the shelter and its metaphorical value are not established with the depth achieved by other Amazonian groups. One reason is that the shelter and the camps do not seem to be as charged with symbolism related to social organization or ideational order as are the "malocas." This does not mean that they have no social-symbolic connotation, or that they have no relation to the supernatural. However, the facts that these aspects are neither obvious nor evident and that our knowledge of the language and of the ideational world is partial mean that we are unable to capture in depth such symbolism. Nonetheless, it has been possible to uncover some social and ideational components of Nukak architecture, especially the "house of the tapir," which are summarized below.

The residential camps are by far the major architectural structures produced by the Nukak, and, given the Nukak's high rate of residential mobility, they occur frequently in the Nukak territory. Based on my fieldwork, I calculated that each coresident group constructs between 70 and 80 camps per year (see Chapter 5). Most other camps are fewer and smaller. Therefore, this chapter is largely based on information from the residential camps, which is also the type that has been scrutinized in the greatest depth in the archaeology and ethnoarchaeology of foragers. Other archaeological approaches to the study of hunter-gatherer residential camps have concentrated on the use of space and on the identification and the interpretation of activity areas (for example, Binford 1978b; Gamble & Boismier 1991; Kent 1990; Yellen 1977). These issues—of great signification for archaeology—are only touched on here; they receive a more in-depth treatment in the following chapter.

ARCHITECTURE OF THE SHELTERS

As has already been mentioned, an essential characteristic of the Nukak is their high residential mobility. This is expressed in the frequent movement of the entire band from one place to another, which implies the complete abandonment of one camp and the construction of a new one. This situation undoubtedly conditions the type of shelter that is constructed, both in terms of the materials used and the structure, as well as the relative positioning of the habitation units in the formation of the camp.

The basis of Nukak architecture is the functional units that are grouped together to form the residential camp. These units, called *wopyii*,[1] fall within the category of domestic or household unit. A nuclear family and occasionally one or two close relatives occupy each of these. They include at least one central hearth, around which the members' hammocks are hung (Figures 4.1 and 4.2). In cases in which other relatives without partners (single youths, widows, and so on) live in the unit with the couple and their children, or if there is a second wife with or without progeny, there may also be one or two further lateral hearths. These units are functional from an architectonic perspective and are conceived of as domestic units both in the spatial dimension (a physical place where one sleeps, cooks, and carries out multiple tasks)

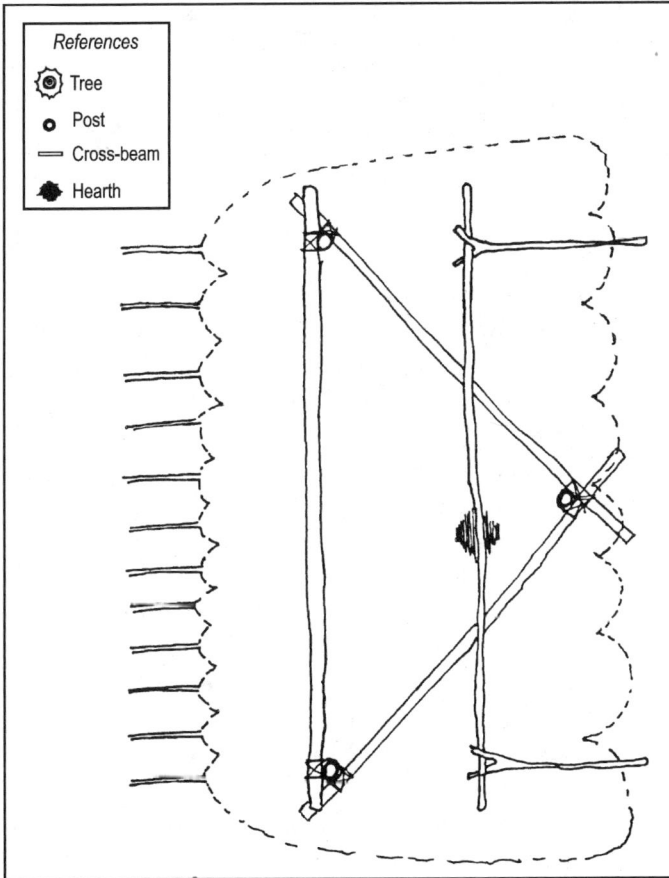

Figure 4.1 Layout of a lean-to

Figure 4.2 Rainy-season lean-to

and the familiar and social dimensions (where one lives with one's closest relatives and performs a variety of social activities).

Shelters differ according to rainy and dry seasons. In the former they are more elaborate, the most significant difference being the inclusion of a roof. The camps with this kind of shelter (lean-to) are also far more abundant than are those made during the latter season, owing to the fact that in Nukak territory the dry season is short. However, in both seasons essentially two elements are used in the construction of the functional units: (1) the trunks of medium-sized and large trees to secure the crosspieces and to hang the hammocks; (2) strips of bark and reeds to fasten the structure. In the rainy season a third important element is added: the platanillo (*Phenakospermun guyanense*) and seje (*Oenocarpus bataua*) leaves used to construct the roof.

Four basic components make up the structure of the rainy-season camps formed by lean-tos (Figure 4.3): (1) preexisting trees that were left standing and that provide the "anchors" for the system of posts and crosspieces; (2) posts that are positioned in relation to the trees and that are fastened to them by means of crosspieces, constituting the secondary rigid structural element; (3) central and secondary crosspieces or rafters that connect trees and posts and that support the rows of leaves of the roof to avoid the drip line being too close to the hearths and to increase the dry area of the unit; and (4) long, thin stakes forked at one end, inclined between 80 and 60 degrees, that hold up the "floating" crosspieces. As such, the structure that supports each unit consists of two types of element: the posts and the crosspieces, which lend rigidity to the structure and support the roof, and the floating crosspieces and the long, forked stakes, which provide plasticity and movement.

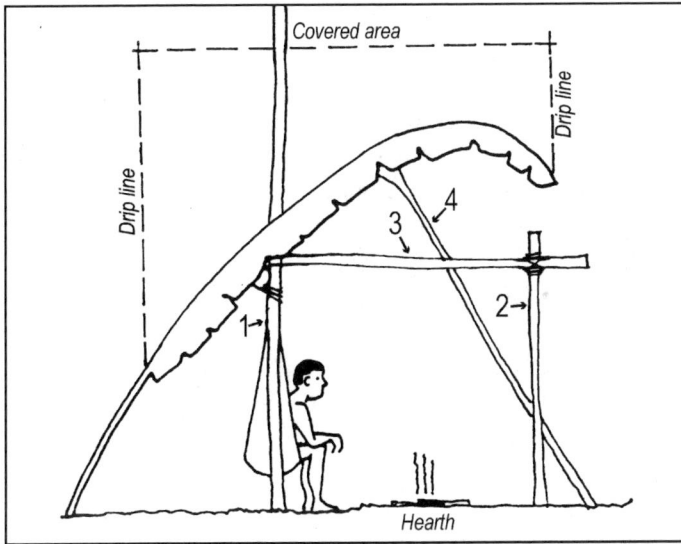

Figure 4.3   Structural components of a rainy-season lean-to

The form of these functional units is fairly well defined, and no substantial differences have been observed in the construction techniques or structure within the camps studied of the bands living within the rainforest. Furthermore, these observations are in agreement with those of other researchers who have been in the field (Ardila 1992b; Cabrera, Franky, & Mahecha 1994, 1999; Mondragón Ms; Reina 1990). Each unit is made up of a central beam at a height between 1.60 and 1.95 m. This is supported by posts and trees over which between one and three rows of plantain leaves are arranged obliquely. Occasionally these rest on a row of seje leaves to reinforce and maintain the gradient of the plantain leaves. In this way, a roof of some 5 to 7 m in length and 2.5 to 4.3 m wide is created, according to the number of rows of plantain leaves used. This constitutes the covered area of each unit, with two well-defined drip lines. One line is located over the foundation of platanillo leaves that face the outer part of the camp, toward the "back" of the shelter; the other runs from the tip of the leaves toward the "front," over the edge that faces the other units. As can be observed in Figure 4.3, the design of the roof allows for the best possible drainage of water, whether toward the back or the front of the camp. To this end, the strongest part of the leaves—the stem— is angled between 55 and 70 degrees and collects the greatest percentage of water that falls on the domestic unit (approximately 80%).

In both the dry- and the rainy-season camps the domestic unit is organized around the beam. The couple's hammocks are hung below this beam, the man's hammock above and the woman's below, and one or two secondary crosspieces attached to posts positioned in an *ad hoc* fashion are frequently placed at its ends (Figure 4.2). The secondary crosspieces are positioned at sharp angles (almost always between 40 to 50 degrees) in relation to the central beam, and when there are two they frequently form a triangular plan.

One of the most interesting functional aspects of the rainy-season shelter is its design in function of the circulation of air and, consequently, of smoke. As such, it has been observed that the shape and openings of the rainy-season shelters in the camps allow floor-level ventilation, which helps keep the hearth lit (at times a difficult task, because when the wind does not blow the humidity is extremely high and firewood is frequently damp). As the platanillo and/or seje leaves are supported by their stems, the lateral cover begins between 0.90 and 1.10 m above ground level, below which there is only a window of stems that allows the air to circulate freely (Figure 4.2). Simultaneously, the arched form of the roofs that converge in the open central space creates a smoky atmosphere which, although not thick enough to irritate human beings, succeeds in keeping insects away (Figure 4.4). Similarly, because the floor- level ventilation is not strong and the arched ceilings prevent a significant back draft or the rapid dissipation of heat, the temperature in the camp is slightly higher within the shelters than outside. As a result, during the night when the weather is cool the Nukak are able to maintain a temperature appro- priate for sleeping by keeping the fire stoked. This effect is not produced during the dry season, since the absence of a roof does not allow the creation of a smoky atmosphere, and the dissipation of heat occurs more rapidly. If a camp in the vicinity of the Guaviare River floodplain has been occupied for several days, insects become abundant in the shelters at night (in part attracted by the accumulated refuse), so the inhabitants of the camp hang their hammocks outside, close to the camp, and sleep by a hearth that they keep smoking.

Figure 4.4 Rainy-season camp consisting of four lean-tos (note the hearth smoke ventilating through the center of the roof)

The Residential Camp

The form and structure of the camp are dictated by the quantity of shelters of which it is constituted. Forty-one camps in use in the rainforest[2] were recorded during the course of our fieldwork, giving an average of 3.9 shelters or architectural units per camp (min = 2; max = 8). A further approximately 130 abandoned camps were observed in various stages of deterioration. These abandoned camps were identical to the occupied ones in terms of shape, structure, and dimensions. In our sample, the maximum number of shelters in a camp occupied by a single band was 6. In 1995, when a band and the segment of another cohabited for several days, camps of 7 and 8 shelters were observed.

The number of shelters constituting the camps is directly related to the number of nuclear families occupying the camps and not to the total number of people present. The number of people occupying a shelter varies from 2 to 12. As shown in Table 4.1, almost the same number of people occupied camps with 2 to 5 shelters, the difference resulting from people belonging to different numbers of families and therefore to distinct domestic units. As Table 4.1 indicates, the larger the surface area the greater the number of architectural units. This correlation is maintained both in the rainy-season and

Table 4.1 Residential Camp Surface Areas

Construction Date	Number of Domestic Units	Number of Individuals	Surface Area (in m²)
Rainy season			
24-10-90	–	16	–
29-10-90	2	23	–
25-6-91	2	10	32.5
10-7-91	2	10	43.5
14-7-91	2	10	42.6
15-7-91	2	12	37.6
16-7-91	2	12	47.2
17-7-91	2	12	–
19-7-91	2	12	33.7
21-7-91	2	12	36.3
17-7-91	4	26	85
27-7-91	4	22+16*	170
28-8-91	2	16	
28-8-92	5	24	114
10-9-92	5	24	105
13-9-92	4	18	104

(Table 4.1 continued)

(*Table 4.1 continued*)

Construction Date	Number of Domestic Units	Number of Individuals	Surface Area (in m²)
24-8-95	3	20	–
17-9-95	2	6	–
Dry season			
21-1-94	5	27	129.9
24-1-94	5	27	108.6
26-1-94	5	27	111.5
29-1-94	5	27	103.8
1-2-94	5	27	114
8-2-94	3	16	–
19-1-95	4	14	60
21-1-95	3	14	78
24-1-95	4	14	–
26-1-95	4	14	68
4-1-95	4	16	–
5-2-95	4	16	45
6-2-95	8	46	130
8-2-95	7	46	112
10-2-95	6	41	99
16-2-95	6	41	–
12-1-96	3	11	38.8
17-1-96	5	23	66.4
19-1-96	5	26	80.6
19-1-96	2	9	49.6
20-1-96	6	41	178.9
24-1-96	6	38	122.3
25-1-96	3	21	–
26-1-96	5	34	141
28-1-96	3	18	74.9

★Camp where a *baak-wáadn* took place. Two bands get together for one night.

the dry-season camps. In the former the average surface area per person is 3.89 m² (*n* = 11, min. = 2.8 m², max. = 5.77 m²). In the dry-season camps, the surface area per person is slightly greater at 4.46 m² (*n* = 8, min. = 3.84 m², max. = 5.57 m²). When the camp is composed of two distinct bands (observed in the *Wayari munu* bands in February 1995), the surface area per person decreases notably, to 2.61 m² (*n* = 4), which indicates that the tendency is that the more people join together, the more compact the camps become.

Some abandoned camps included only one shelter. Such shelters are constructed by small groups of men traveling from one camp to another or by a single family moving between camps or journeying to the mission to seek medical attention. Such camps are uncommon; during our fieldwork we saw none under occupation, and they are rarely mentioned in reports from other researchers.

The quantity of shelters in a camp is related to the number of couples or nuclear families that make up the coresident group. Eventually, orphans, single youths whose parents have died or are temporarily in other coresident groups, and widows generally occupy a couple's functional unit. They at times have their own hearth, although these are placed in unfavorable places, often near the internal drip line or in areas that are not entirely protected from the rain. On several occasions we saw that on nights with heavy rain these occupants had to take down their hammocks and wait until the rain had passed, huddled by the fire, sitting or lying on the floor in a dry section close to the hammocks of the couple to whom the shelter belonged. On some occasions the orphans circulated among the shelters, sleeping on the floor on platanillo leaves close to the edge of the drip line.

Occasionally the domestic unit is not occupied by a couple; for example, a partnerless, mature widow lived with her children in her own shelter, although one child was already an adolescent who hunted and performed all the tasks of an adult man. Another situation involved a wife who remained alone for several days while her husband traveled with his other wife. In this case the woman lived with her young son and built a shelter them both when the band changed camp.

The footprint of the camps varies noticeably between the rainy and the dry seasons. During the winter the footprint is polygonal in shape, with the front of every shelter facing a central space. This space is an area around which the domestic units are positioned (Figure 4.5). In summer the distributional pattern of the shelters is irregular, since the lack of roofs makes it impossible to clearly distinguish between "back" and "front." The hammocks are hung side by side according to the available posts and trees, and crosspieces are frequently not placed above the couples' hammocks. The edges of the summer shelters are far less precise and are basically marked only by the difference between areas that have been frequently walked over (which leaves the ground almost bare) and others not so denuded. In this season the hammocks and hearths are more scattered, and there is no central space (Figure 4.6). Consequently, in spite of the differences in the forms of the camps, the surface area they occupy is approximately the same in both seasons (see Table 4.1).

The form of the rainy-season camps varies according to the number of units that make them up. In camps of two shelters these face each other, and the ends of the plantain leaves touch or are close together. The central crosspieces are positioned in a subparallel form, in such a way that the plan of the

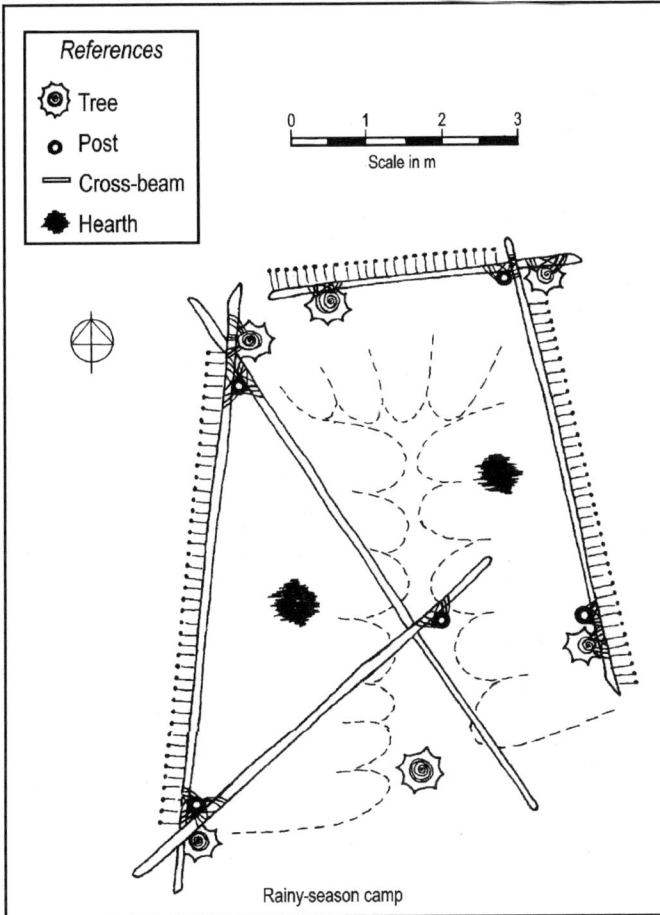

Figure 4.5 Layout of a rainy-season camp formed by three
domestic units

camp describes a trapezoid or an uneven triangle. What would correspond to
the base of the triangle faces the "front" of the camp and an open area where
various activities are carried out. When there is prolonged occupation (longer
than a week), this area is left almost devoid of vegetation owing to constant
traffic. The opposite side, the base of the trapezoid, faces toward the "back,"
a sector where refuse accumulates and onto which one of the entrances opens.
Sometimes the two shelters facing each other give the appearance of a single
communal domed "house." Nonetheless, the central beams and the hearths
allow one to recognize that there are in fact two opposed architectural and
domestic units. Furthermore, an opening for the hearth smoke is always present in the roof between the two units.

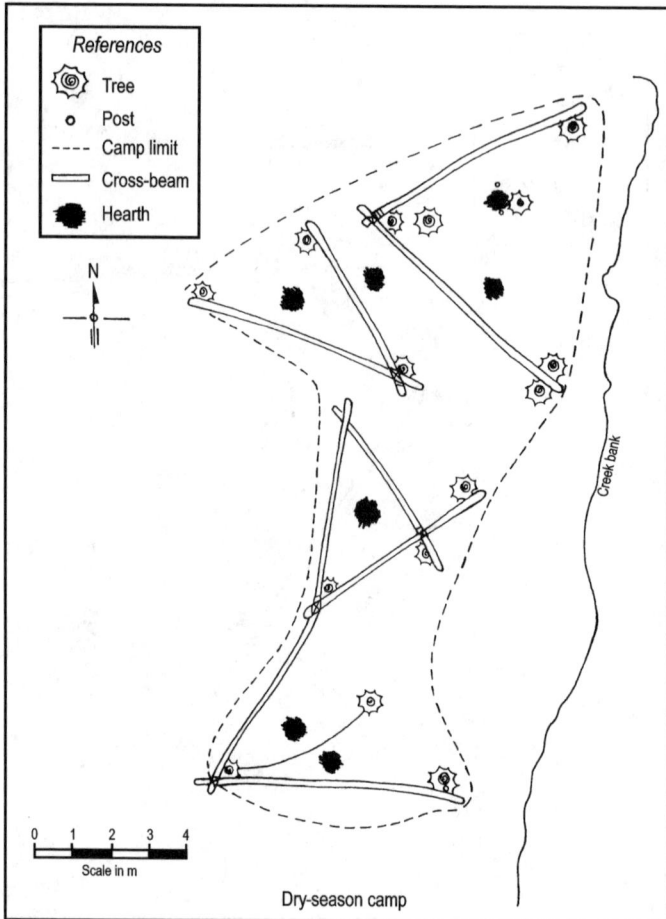

Figure 4.6 Layout of a dry-season camp formed by four domestic units

In 1991 three winter camps of four shelters were recorded that corresponded to four couples, three of which were monogamous with children and a fourth was composed of a man with two wives but no children. The four shelters were positioned around an open central space, three of which were fairly close together and faced one another, completing three sides of a rectangle, while the fourth (belonging to the man with two wives) also faced the central space but lay some meters back. In this area, delimited by the functional units, various socialization activities took place at night, such as children's games and friendly "fights" between youths. Also, some communally used elements, such as axes and firewood, were stored here. It is interesting to note that this band constructed a camp on 27 July, arranging their shelters in a more spread-out fashion than is common, which produced a central space considerably larger than usual (see Table 4.1). The same night that the camp was erected a ritual gathering (*baak-wáadn*) occurred in this central space in which all the members of two bands took part (38 people in total).

In 1992 another rainy-season camp with four shelters was also observed after some members of the coresident group (one nuclear family and part of another) had temporarily abandoned the site to collect medicine from the Mission (Figure 4.7). When the larger group moved camp they positioned the four shelters in the form of a pentagon, maintaining the previous footprint but leaving one side open. In this way the surface area of the camp was about the same, 105 m² with 5 units and 104 m² with 4 units (Figures 4.8 and 4.9).

In the 1992 season two 5-shelter winter camps were recorded, built by the same band. The functional units made up a pentagonal footprint around a central place. Furthermore, in the neighboring areas 5 more abandoned camps were located with 5 shelters that demonstrated the same structural pattern, suggesting that the pentagonal footprint is the trend for coresident groups composed of 5 nuclear families. The central place of these camps was not intensely used for communal activities. People generally circulated around

Figure 4.7   Rainy-season camp formed by four lean-tos (1992)

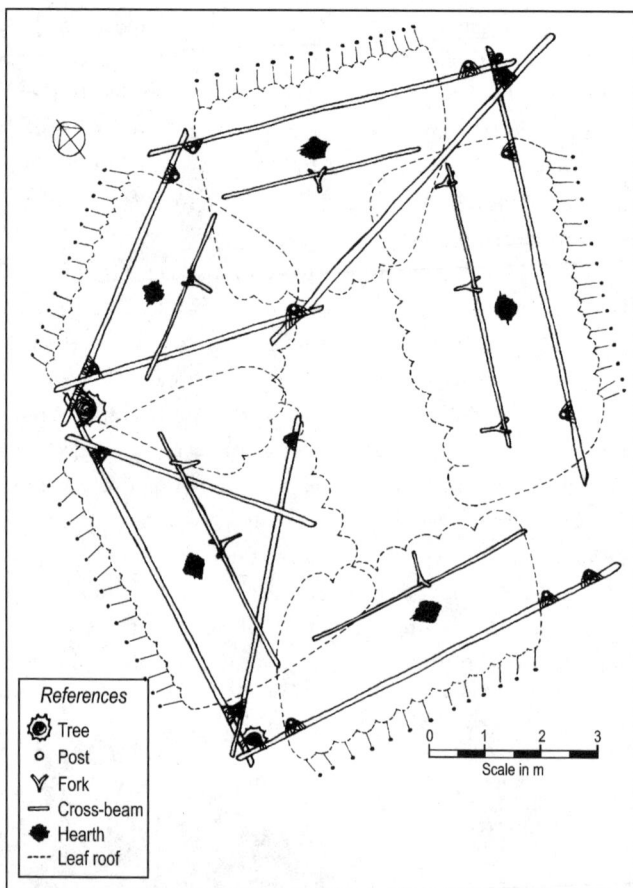

Figure 4.8 Layout of a rainy-season camp formed by five lean-tos (1992)

the outskirts of the space, and in the center there remained uncut plants, an accumulation of firewood, and a little rubbish (Figure 4.10), although this area was eventually used by the children in their games.

During the dry seasons of 1994 and 1996, camps of 3 to 8 domestic units were observed. These did not demonstrate a marked pattern, and their footprints were irregular. In one case in 1994 the band installed itself on the banks of a river, and as a consequence the camp acquired an elongated form, because all the units bordered the bank. The grouping of summer shelters does not leave a central space, the circulation between them occurring through the units themselves or around the edge of the camp (Figure 4.11).

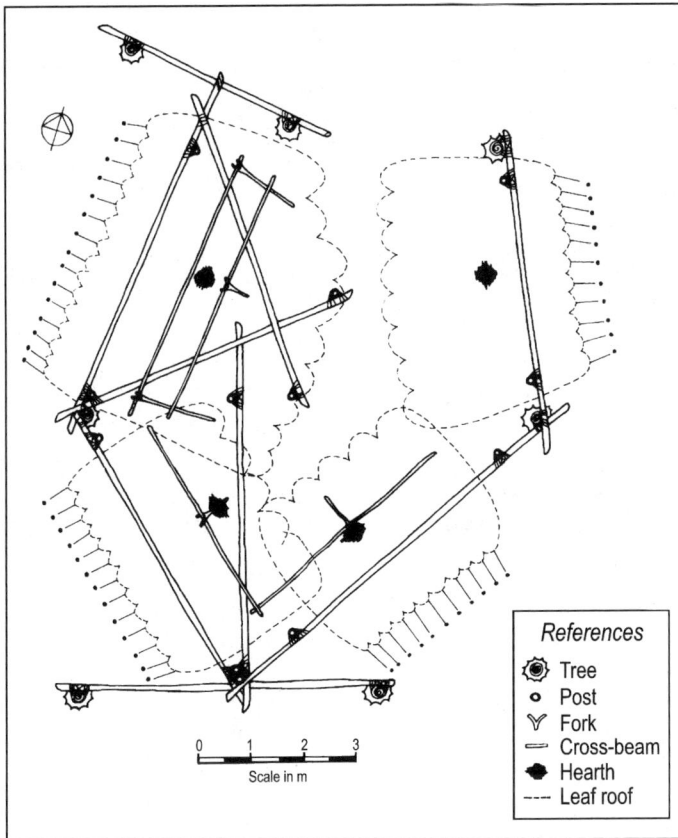

Figure 4.9 Layout of a rainy-season camp formed by four lean-tos (1992)

An interesting characteristic of dry-season camp occupation was observed when the camps were located close to the floodplain of the Guaviare River, a zone with extended areas of swamps produced by the low-level water. After a few days the camps became infected with insects attracted by the garbage, especially the large amount of fish waste (which is extremely smelly). When the numbers of insects reached extremely bothersome levels, the families lit a fire outside the camp, approximately 15–30 m away. They cleared the leaf coverage and plants a little and hung their hammocks from the preexisting trees. There they spent the night, beside a continually smoking fire.[3] They generally abandoned the camp the following day and moved to a new location, following their usual mobility pattern.

Figure 4.10   The central place of a five-lean-to residential camp

The Construction of Residential Camps

The Nukak have a highly defined modality for constructing their camps in the rainy season, as has been seen, with minimum variation among the bands studied. Once it has been decided to move to a new site the Nukak collect all their things, usually midmorning, and begin walking along well-known paths (see below). There was no case observed in which the band explored the area or opened a trail before constructing a new camp. The direction and route to follow are decided beforehand, and articulated by the leader of the band. There are two basic relocation scenarios. The most frequent involves a walk of a few hours in one day and the installation at a place not far from the previous camp, at a distance that varies from 0.9 km to 10 km. In such cases, the new camp is constructed slowly, beginning at midday or in the early afternoon and finishing before nightfall. The second situation is when the coresident group moves fairly quickly, with the goal of arriving at a particular place soon. In such cases, they walk throughout the day, traveling up to a maximum of 18.1 km, although the stops to collect fruit, hunt, or eat are frequent. In this case, they arrive at the new campsite at 4:00 or 5:00 p.m. and construct the new camp in approximately one to two hours. (While constructing the camp they also do other things; that is, the time spent from beginning to end is not the net construction time.)

Figure 4.11   Dry-season residential camp

The bands studied almost never reoccupied an abandoned camp, even when it was in good condition. On only two occasions (camps 2 and 3 of 1992) did they construct camps in clearings that had probably been left after the total deterioration of old camps. In only one case (camp 5 of 1994) did a band reoccupy an abandoned camp that still had its structure intact and dry roof leaves. Moreover, in the three cases the reoccupation was of a former camp or campsite of the same band. The percentage of reoccupations is 10 ($n = 30$). In all other cases a new sector is cleared in which they construct their shelters, although these can be close to preexisting clearings resulting from abandoned camps. Some bands that have settled close to the frontier of the colonization or who visit the rural populations occasionally reoccupy a campsite (as was seen in the area around Tomachipán and Caño Seco). However, this is a recently acquired behavior that appears to be motivated by the frequent visits and longer stays close to certain *colono* ranches. The figures provided by Cabrera, Franky, and Mahecha (1999:117) record higher percentages of reoccupied camps (18.81%; $n = 101$), but this could be due to a significant part of their fieldwork being carried out among the northeastern bands (see Cabrera, Franky, & Mahecha 1999:21), who were more attracted to the *colonos* and in some ways were more affected during the early 1990s. The majority of the researchers who have worked in the area (for example, H. Mondragon, I. Yunis, and so on) also concur that the reoccupation of an abandoned camp is exceptional.

There appear to be several reasons for not reoccupying camps. An important reason, which is closely related to the way the Nukak manage the forest, relates to the transformation of abandoned sites into areas of high concentration of useful plants. This occurs through the presence of thousands of seeds of the fruit consumed by the Nukak during their stay, favoring the growth of patches of such fruit in much higher densities than is normal in such rainforest environments (see the in-depth discussion in Chapter 8). Consequently, the construction of a new camp over an old site would imply the destruction of the productive potential of the latter.

There are reasons other than economic ones that lead to camps not being reoccupied, for example, burial in the abandoned camp. The Nukak believe that one of the spirits (the *nemep*) of a buried person stays in the immediate area and can cause trouble or harm to people during the night. Usually this happens when the deceased is an adult person, and if that person was important—a leader or somebody with shamanistic power—the fear is greater. Cabrera, Franky, and Mahecha (1994:153) further mention that the Nukak do not inhabit the abandoned camps of other bands, because they believe that they may contract illnesses.

In almost every case the construction sequence of the rainy-season camps is similar, independent of the time employed or the foreseen duration of the camp's occupation. The steps are as follows:

1. Clear the area chosen for the shelters. Plants and some bushes are uprooted. The small and medium-sized trees are felled.
2. Place the first crossbeam (at first using a preexisting tree), below which the hammocks of the band leader couple are hung.
3. From this structure arrange the other principle crosspieces and posts of each shelter, conforming to the camp footprint. The hammocks of the other couples are hung, and the process of lighting the hearths begins.
4. Position secondary posts and crosspieces.
5. In some cases hang hammocks from the secondary crosspieces.

At this point construction of the dry-season camp is completed. The construction of rainy-season camps continues with the following steps:

6. Place leaves above the principle beams to form the roof. If the camp is to be occupied for one night only platanillo leaves are used, but if the expected occupation is longer, the structure is reinforced with a row of seje leaves (Figure 4.12).

Figure 4.12 Construction of a rainy-season residential camp; note the leaves of seje that reinforce the roof.

7. Put the floating crosspieces and the long posts (forks) in place to reinforce the roof structure (especially if there are two or three overlapping rows of plantain leaves). Simultaneously, some of the crosspieces and secondary posts are reinforced, and the rest of the hammocks are hung.

The construction of the camp is an eminently masculine task. The men cut the branches and plant the posts. While the women may at times help, they habitually carry out other activities or simply sit in their hammocks and watch. The men also collect the leaves for the roof. In one case an adult widow along with her adolescent son constructed shelters in at least two camps (camps 2 and 3 of 1992), and in another example a woman whose husband had gone with his second wife for a few days constructed her own shelter (in camp 3 of 1992) in which she lived until the return of her partner (Figure 4.13)

Figure 4.13 Woman attaching platanillo leaves to a lean-to

An important characteristic of camp construction is the camp's proximity to water. In general, the Nukak do not usually camp by main watercourses or lagoons. They obtain water from holes that they dig in low ground near the camp. These holes have a maximum depth of approximately 1 m, beyond which it is difficult to reach with one's arm from the surface. In this way they obtain purified, good-quality water from the groundwater table rather than from the surface. In the dry season, the camps are usually located by ponds or creeks, some of which are dry. The Nukak dig water holes in the beds.

Occasionally residential camps or temporary camps are surrounded by a sort of "fence" of stalks and leaves between 0.5 and 1.2 m high, which protects residents from harmful spirits, such as those of the jaguar (*híu*), which may enter the camp during the night. Within the camp we also observed the construction of small circular structures made of seje leaves. These arrangements form a domed shape, with a diameter of 1.5 to 2 m and have only one entrance, which usually remains covered. These structures were occupied briefly—almost always for less than a day—by menstruating girls. They provide a space isolated from the rest of the coresidents and are probably places where female rituals are carried out.

Furthermore, within the residential camps or on their periphery there are two types of constructions made by children. One is the small open area where the children hang hammocks and light a fire during the day. Generally, these constructions consist of a few flimsy posts and crosspieces, occasionally with plantain leaves. These camps are not used to sleep in; their function is to replicate in miniature the residential camps and facilitate the mimicking of adult activities (Figure 4.14). The other type is the replication of single shelters on a smaller scale, constructed inside the camps by the children. This second type of structure might also have socioideational meaning, as yet unidentified, since on occasion heavily painted children remain there quietly for some time (Figure 4.15).

OTHER TYPES OF CAMPS

In addition to residential camps the Nukak build other structures, although these are usually occupied far less frequently and by a few people only. These other sites are found distributed throughout Nukak territory and are connected by paths and form part of the Nukak settlement system. The following types have been identified.

Figure 4.14 Small camps made by children on the periphery of the residential camps

Figure 4.15 Small lean-tos made for children inside the residential camp

Transitory Camps

These constructions are smaller than the typical residential camps, and they have a less elaborate structure, although they have roughly the same layout. They are generally made when small groups (less than 10 people) move quickly through the forest with a specific objective in mind, as on journeys between residential camps (if the distance is greater than one day's travel), to Laguna Pavón 2, or to the Cerro de las Cerbatanas.

Small Shelters Peripheral to Residential Camps

These shelters are constructed by young people when they visit another band. They generally consist of a small structure built of plantain leaves that serve as a wall and form a low, arched roof below which there is a dry area and a hearth. The structure is less than 10 m² and is occupied by two or three young men who visit the residential camp and participate in various tasks (communal hunts, gathering, and so on) with members of the band during the day but who at night sleep on the floor of the shelter on plantain leaves. This precarious shelter is generally found close to the residential camp and is where the young people sleep after several days of performing the various ritual stages with the guest band. After a few days, when all the required performances and social tasks are completed, the young visitors sleep inside the camp of the guest band.

Small Shelters between Camps

These shelters are similar to the shelters peripheral to the residential camps but are found alone in the forest, with no relation to residential camps. In our fieldwork we recorded only two such structures, one of which was surrounded by a "fence" of seje leaves to protect against jaguars. Although precise and clear information about the function of these small shelters could not be obtained some indirect evidence suggests that they might be related to ritual activities.

Rectangular Constructions in Chagras, or the "House of the Tapir"

These "houses" consist of wall-less rectangular structures with flat roofs of one or two pitches; they are located on the edges of chagras, (orchards or garden areas) (Figure 4.16). In our fieldwork we recorded five of these with

Figure 4.16 House of the tapir

variable dimensions. They are usually isolated. The two examples measured had footprints of 17 m by 7 m and 3 m by 3.5 m and were found together. The height of the exterior crosspieces was 1.9 m.

The shape and function of these structures differ substantially from those in the residential camps. They are not occupied by people but, significantly, are better constructed than residential dwellings are. Cabrera, Franky, and Mahecha (1994:155–56) have observed in detail their construction, which takes two to three days and uses about 30 seje palm trunks and 10 *kurá* (*Attalea maripa*) trunks. These authors recorded four of these "houses," the largest being 6 m by 4 m. Their function would appear to be essentially symbolic, since they are said to be similar in form to the "house of the tapir" of the underworld, of which they appear to be replicas created in the intermediate world. Nukak believe that by building an earthly house the tapir will have somewhere to go as it roams the surface-world forest during the night and therefore will not become angry with humans. It seems that while wondering around the tapir drinks water and eats. Therefore, the fact that the "house" is built close to a cultivated plot suggests its use in feeding this animal-spirit.

As well as fulfilling their symbolic role, these structures appear also to function as stores for tools, including axes and machetes; occasionally we saw large quantities of *puiú* stored (wild cotton, which is obtained from the flowers of the ceiba trees, *Ceiba pentranda* or *Pachira nukakica*). During the day the Nukak at times rest under the roofs of these structures to eat the produce from the chagra. On several occasions members of the band chewed sugar cane inside these constructions.

Although at present these "houses" are built next to the chagras (consisting of recently introduced domesticated plants, see Chapter 8), in the past it seems that the Nukak planted nondomesticated trees such as seje, *kurá, juiup (Attalea* sp.*)* around them. Cabrera, Franky, and Mahecha (1999:124) mention that achiote (*Bixa orellana*), a plant with a high symbolic significance, is also planted in the vicinity.

Bridges

A characteristic of Nukak architecture that is related to their high residential mobility is the creation of bridges. These are constructed by felling a palm on one bank of a river or creek so that its far end lands on the other bank. Palm trunks are long and free of branches, so they naturally offer a clean and even surface to walk on. In the majority of cases a vine is attached and used as a railing, or tall posts are driven into the trunk along its length to serve as support (Figure 4.17). These bridges are commonplace in Nukak territory; each band constructs several, especially along the main paths.

Discussion

Nukak architectural units and residential camps present many features in common with structures built by other foragers. In general, the aggregation

Figure 4.17 Man crossing a bridge during a daily foraging trip

of shelters during the rainy season generates a sort of domed structure, which seems to be the one most likely to be constructed by more mobile societies (McGuire & Schiffer 1983:284). Moreover, in general terms the values obtained from the Nukak confirm those from studies carried out to understand the relationship between habitat and density of shelters in hunter-gatherer camps (Whitelaw 1989). As such, the Nukak camps support the expectation that in tropical forest regions shelters tend to be close together, camps are compact, and the average square meterage of space occupied per inhabitant is among the lowest for hunter-gatherer groups. The Efe from the Ituri forest have a similar occupational density (Fisher & Strickland 1991), although their camps show a higher minimum (44 m^2) and a much higher maximum (532 m^2). The Nukak case also supports positive correlations between level of social complexity and the segmentation of dwellings. It has been observed that among noncomplex hunter-gatherers there is an absence of segmentation in architectural structures and few specific activity areas (Kent 1990), which is basically the case in Nukak residential camps. However, these two basic characteristics have their own peculiarities, and their causal factors should be discussed. In the first case, in spite of the constructional and energy advantages that evidently exist (McGuire & Schiffer 1983:284–25), the domed rainy residential camps appear also to come about because of one significant attribute: each shelter faces toward the others, which means that while inside the camp everyone can see everyone, resulting in a total lack of intimacy. This seems to answer, in part, the need for close contact (tactile, visual, and auditory) in dense forested environments, reflected in the architectonic patterning. Since the dry-season shelters do not have lean-to roofs, there are no partitions that interfere with this contact; neither is there a "front" or a "back" to each shelter. Consequently, because there are no roofs a domed camp is not formed. Nonetheless, it seems that the need for close contact is stronger at night, associated with fear of the *takwe'yi*, the *nemep* and other malevolent spirits. This notably reduces intimacy such that couples habitually carry out sexual relations outside the camp during the day while on foraging trips (see Chapter 7).

The several factors that could cause the integration and layout observed in residential camps have been discussed. It has further been proposed that the fear of predators or predator pressure would be a determinant for household spacing (Gould & Yellen 1987:100). In relation to the Nukak this appears not to be the case. Nukak camps have no defensive structure and thus protection. We have neither experienced nor heard of cases of jaguars or other carnivores entering camps and attacking people or taking meat. The only protection—the fence of seje leaves—is entirely insufficient as a solid material barrier against jaguars. Therefore, it is obvious that this fence must be interpreted as defense against what the jaguar embodies: a powerful and dangerous spirit. I argue, then, that one of the overriding causal factors that influence the residential camp design is this need to be close together to provide mutual protection against supranatural spirits. This is crucial at night, when there are many more spirits roaming the intermediate world. The grouping together of people improves defense against malevolent spirits,.

Other causal factors that could be involved in the creation of such compact camps include psychological reasons, individual preferences, interpersonal relationships, and so forth. Also, an important factor is the high degree of sharing, not only of food but also water, firewood, and objects that have a positive correlation to the distance between shelters, as has already been noted among other foragers (see Fisher & Strickland 1991; Whitelaw 1991). The distance that must be traversed by people for communication, food, water, and objects is notably reduced in compact camps, and the Nukak have taken full advantage of this. Of course, this trait is also supported by the close kinship ties that enable this fluid circulation. In other words, close relationships between the level of spatial organization and the social patterns of interaction, communication, and coresident group integration are observed, as has been previously anticipated from cross-cultural analysis (Whitelaw 1991:140–41).

Based on the data presented, some archaeological implications can be drawn. First, the structural patterns of the residential shelters and the basic construction materials are similar in the rainy and the dry seasons, the major differences lying in the overall form of the camps and the lack of leaf roofs in the dry season. This means that the seasonal differences in the camp layouts produce distinctive archaeological signatures. In both seasons, the surface area of a residential camp correlates weakly with the number of inhabitants, but strongly with the number of shelters. This is in agreement with patterns detected among other rainforest foragers such as the Mbuti (Fisher & Strickland 1989). Second, it must be emphasized that to solve the problem of high mobility the Nukak have combined the abundant and relatively homogeneously distributed elements provided by the tropical rainforest with simple, but ingenious, construction techniques. The Nukak shelters are constructed rapidly and maintain dry sectors even in the middle of the rainy season, and it is always possible to keep a fire burning within them. Furthermore, the camps abandoned by the Nukak are converted into areas of high concentration of vegetable resources; they become "wild orchards" to which the Nukak will return (see Chapter 8).

Nukak architecture contributes a number of aspects to the understanding of more complex aggregation phenomena. Within Nukak groups, which maintain one of the simplest forms of architectonic organization, we see that the hierarchy of some of their members has a direct correlation to the way in which the camps are designed. The leader of the band hangs his and his partner's hammocks first, after which the other hammocks are arranged. In other words, individual and familial status, however lax or unmarked, grants prerogatives in the choice of the location of a shelter within the camp, which in turn has varied implications for other aspects of life (social, symbolic, and so on). In this respect, I agree that the decision to include particular architectural features and the way they are arranged into settlements does not passively mirror or symbolize power relationships and the practice of social interaction but rather incorporates active elements of social agency (Parckington & Mills 1991).

Even so, when the aggregation of winter shelters is greater than two, the concept of a "central place" arises, a space within the camp delimited by domestic units that is used for diverse community purposes (see Chapter 5). It is also the space in which a part of Nukak ritual and religion unfolds. As can be observed in Table 4.1, in the only camp measured in which a *baak wáadn* took place the central space was larger, having a relationship of 7.72 m² per person ($n = 22$, only the inhabitants of the camp) or 4.47 m² per person ($n = 38$, including all the participants of the *baak wáadn*). These values allow a double interpretation: on one side, if all the participants of the ritual are included, the square meterage per person approaches the general average; that is, in some fashion the size of a camp designated for a ritual retains a relationship of square meterage per person similar to a usual residential camp. However, this camp has a fundamental distinction: the size of the "central place" is far greater than normal. Consequently, this feature has the potential to enable identification of the distinctive characteristic of the site—ritual— in relation to other sites.

There are some peculiarities in the way the Nukak build their residential camps. Among these, it is clear that shape of the shelters and camps is not conditioned by the length of their occupation. Whether used for one night or several weeks, the camps maintain the same structure, the only slight difference observable being the reinforcement of the lean-to roof with seje leaves during prolonged occupations. The archaeological implication of this particular observation is that the form and the structure of these residential camps do not reflect the length of occupation. This fact contradicts other studies, which have proposed that the expected time of occupation conditions the construction characteristics of the residential camps of hunter-gatherers (that is, the case of the Basarwa; see Kent & Vierich 1989:124–26). In other words, among foragers the anticipated use life can not be regarded as a general causal factor that influences the design of architectural structures, as some previous research suggested (McGuire & Schiffer 1983).

A comparative study of Nukak settlements and those of other Makú groups reveals some differences. It seems clear that the Nukak shelters differ from the semipermanent camps (village settlements) of the Hupdu and the Kakwa (Silverwood-Cope 1972:50–3), although there are many similarities with the transitory forest hunting camps of the latter group (Silverwood-Cope 1972:58–62). It seems that the basic structure and shape of the architectural units of the Nukak residential camps are similar to the forest transitory camps of many groups, including the Kawka and the Hupdu. Also, this kind of shelter has been depicted in numerous drawings made of Amazonian Indians since the sixteenth century, and it has been recorded in a variety of groups (that is, the Sirionó, Rydén 1941:41–4; the Hotï, Politis, & Jaimes Ms), including non-hunter-gatherers. It would seem, therefore, that these lean-to structures serve as "functional units" that can be aggregated in camps of different types and sizes, and probably have a long tradition in the Amazon. Unfortunately, the archeology of the hunter-gatherers of the region has yet to recover evidence of the form and characteristics of camps of pre-European foragers. Nonetheless, their broad distribution and chronicling during early periods of the European conquest suggest a certain antiquity.

FINAL REMARKS

This chapter summarized the principal characteristics of the architecture of the Nukak residential camps. We have learned some information, first, about architectural structures and settlement arrangements among mobile foragers and, second, about archeological expectations related to such structures and arrangements. The lack of visual and auditory division or segmentation in the shelters and residential camps as a whole is an active component in social practices that characterize the Nukak, practices such as the need for proximity among band members, the strong pattern of sharing, kinship ties, and blind solidarity. Although in-camp intimacy is sacrificed in favor of face-to-face interaction, alternative places and times are found to perform intimate acts.

The easy correlation between energy expenditure and benefit return in the way the Nukak build and maintain their camps does not match energy-based models neatly. Although residential camps are built in a highly efficient way, quickly and using entirely local, ubiquitous materials, there are three significant characteristics that prevent a direct correlation. One is that the work invested in the residential camps does not correlate with the expected time of occupancy. The manner of construction varies independently of the predicted use life. The second characteristic is the "house of the tapir," which, although far less common than the residential camp, manifests the highest energy investment per architectural unit of all the architectural structures built by the Nukak. As has been shown, the tapir is not only the subject of Nukak food proscriptions but also an important ancestor-spirit animal in Nukak beliefs (see Chapter 3). Nevertheless, it might be thought unlikely to see it play a part in the potential settlement archaeology of a Nukak site area, that is, leaving a unique archaeological signature of a specific tabooed animal. Significantly for archaeology, the floor of the "house of the tapir" is kept scrupulously clean and would yield little or no evidence suggestive of its use. Thus, the most elaborate, time-consuming, and substantial Nukak structure does not relate to chiefly or shamanic occupancy (as might be expected) but to a powerful spirit-animal whose natural prototype is a tabooed food resource and, consequently, is archaeologically invisible. The "house of the tapir" illustrates the problems faced by archaeologists dealing with nonhierarchical societies in which the most energy-expensive structure has no "obvious" real-time material benefit and is consecrated to an animal that is excluded from the human food chain (Politis & Saunders 2002). The third unexpected architectural feature is that the only protective structure produced by the Nukak— the fence of seje leaves—is not for predators or other humans but for defense against powerful spirit-ancestors embodied by the jaguar.

Another interesting feature of Nukak camps is the presence of structures such as the menstruating girls' small shelters and the children's replica shelters, which are the architectural reflection of the agency of children and youths. Other tropical hunter-gatherers show strong similarities; for example, among the Efe of the Ituri Forest the children construct miniature play huts and fires (Fisher 1987:86). When Fisher (1987:86) mentioned this fact, he timidly stated, "I am not arguing that these sorts of events occur frequently. I simply raise these points as matters about what archaeologists should be aware. . . ." However, in recent years the contribution that children make to the archaeological record has become increasingly clear (Park 1998; Politis 1998, 1999; Sofaer-Derevenki 1994, 2000), a contribution that should not be underestimated in terms of architectural features.

In regard to the menstruating girls' small shelters, such architectural traits are the materialization of "rites of passage" through which members of a society change their status, rights, and obligations. The reflection in the archaeological record of such ritual practices that involve children and adolescents has been poorly explored in the discipline (see, for an exception, Owens & Hayden 1997).

In sum, this chapter demonstrates that the ways in which hunter-gatherers organize their living space is linked both to ecological and material factors and to cosmology and the tapestry of social life. In this sense, the architecture of residential camps is another of the ways in which the connections among human beings, and between human beings and the different supernatural levels, are materialized.

Notes

1. This word, or a word with a very similar sound, is also used when referring to other spaces modified by human and supernatural intervention, such as chagras or the areas inhabited by the *nemep*.
2. There are 43 camps in Table 4.1. However, the camp of 24 October 1990 involved the occupation of an abandoned *colono* ranch in the savannah. The other case not considered is the camp of 8 February 1994, which was permanently installed in the neighborhood of a *colono* farm on a chagra south of Barranco Colorado. There were two shelters, one of traditional form in which a family lived and the other rectangular, with a gable roof and loft similar to those constructed by riverine indigenes in the region.
3. The same behavior has been recorded among other tropical hunter-gatherers such as the Cuiva, who place their camps close to rivers or creeks during the dry season (Coppens 1975). This has also been recorded among the Efe of the Ituri forest, who burn a "sleeping fire" next to where they lie (Fisher 1987:85).

Chapter 5

THE USE OF SPACE AND DISCARD PATTERNS

This chapter discusses the use of space in residential camps and the discard processes of the Nukak, as well as archaeological expectations for sites formed under similar conditions. Both subjects are intrinsically co-nected in archaeological research because there has always been an interest in identifying the function of sites and the activities carried out at them from the material record via the by-products of these activities. The ethnoarchaeological information on discard patterns in hunter-gatherer societies essentially refers to the analysis of activity areas within the camps and how to recognize them in archaeological sites (Bartram 1993; Binford 1978b, 1987; Fisher 1993; Gould 1968; Kent 1987; O'Connell 1987; Yellen 1977). This information derives from the third phase of intrasite spatial analysis, which emerged partly as a reaction to the models generated from visual and statistical approaches (see review in Kent 1987) that had been used to analyze spatial data (Kroll & Price 1991). In general, such ethnoarchaeological studies aimed to identify the spatial correlation between primary residues and the activities that had produced them in order to contribute to the identification of activity areas in archaeological sites and to discuss intrasite variability (Kent 1987; O'Connell, Hawkes, & Blurton-Jones 1991).

This kind of analysis was also included in the archaeological literature under the concept of "cultural formation process" (Tani 1995), a prime derivation of behavioral archaeology (Schiffer 1976, 1987). During the heyday of behavioral archaeology, (Schiffer 1976), it was thought that there were already available "a respectable number of quantitative archaeological laws" (Schiffer 1976;58), some of which concerned the relationship between human behavior and discarded waste products. These were based on the idea that cultural processes responsible for the configuration of the archaeological record (the result of the primary location and distorting effects) are regular, that there is a systematic (indirect) relationship between material remains and past human behavior (Schiffer 1976:12).

A contrary view has been advanced by Hodder (1987), who perceives that settlement activity organization and discard have to be understood on their own terms; therefore, there is no universal method for measuring and interpreting them. Hodder (1982) also focused attention on the meaning of garbage, rejecting the idea that it is an unintentional derivative of human behavior by proposing that garbage is a vehicle for agency within society and must be seen as an active means of communication and social resistance.

Although the literature on activity area and related discarded products in hunter-gatherer societies is relatively abundant, only a few studies have recorded in any detail the treatment of waste and refuse and how these are displaced from the moment of their production until a camp is abandoned (for example, Fisher 1987; Fisher & Strickland 1991). This is precisely the part of the discard process I address—the period between the generation of the waste and the abandonment of the camp. During this interface, several events affect the spatial distribution of the discarded items, some of which produce rearrangement trends. Above all, I explore how residues are produced and displaced and what remains when a camp is abandoned. In South America, ethno-archaeological information on these subjects is scarce and mainly concerned with the formation of waste in sedentary horticultural societies (for example, Stahl & Zeidler 1990; Zeidler 1984), Andean herders (Yacobaccio, Madero, & Malmierca 1998), and, to a far lesser degree, hunter-gatherers (Borrero & Yacobaccio 1989; Jones 1993).

Although this chapter presents a gradation of the disintegration of camps, I do not examine here the possibilities of preservation of settlements in tropical rainforest environments. This would require further taphonomic studies not contemplated in this research project (see Chapter 1).

RESIDENTIAL CAMP ACTIVITY AREAS

The main activity areas in the camps are the areas around the hearths, where hammocks are hung (Chapter 4). Basically, adults and children sit in the hammocks when they are processing food and eating (Figure 5.1). Therefore, residues that are produced are dropped and tossed (in the sense of Binford 1978b) to both sides, and then bones and the nonedible parts of the fruit (shells, seeds, fruit peels, and so on) are discarded. This area is also heavily used for a myriad of technological tasks. Women's technological activities most frequently carried out from the hammock include weaving of bracelets (*kdn'yii*), spinning of plant fibers, weaving of baskets, perforation of teeth for necklaces, and hollowing out of palm tree trunks to make mortars. The technological tasks most frequently carried out by men from the hammocks or around the hearth are fabrication of blowpipe darts, smoking the poison off the tips of darts, elaboration and securing of bone points for harpoons, retouch and termination of the ends of the blowpipes (mouthpieces and exit holes), fabrication of breech cloths (a type of loincloth used by men, called *dú*) (Figure 5.2), fabrication of *balay* (flat baskets of open weave that are used as sieves or for macerating fruit), fire-hardening of points, (partial) smoothing of the surfaces of spears, and preparation of curare (the final, boiling stage). Moreover, children essentially perform all these activities by imitating the adults. All members of the family also participate in body and facial painting. All these manufacturing activities produce material derivatives that build up on the floor of the campsite.

Debris falls to the floor in this area in basically two ways. First, when people are seated in front of the fire the residue of food or production technology falls to the floor in the area surrounding the hearth. Second, some residues are tossed toward the rear either by being thrown over the person's shoulder or, at times, by the person's twisting his or her body over the hammock. In the rainy-season camp this second action produces an accumulation of debris between the hammock and the line of seje leaves, which forms a type of backward- or side-toss area.

Figure 5.1 Two women peeling and eating fruits of *koró-paanját* in a dry-season residential camp

Figure 5.2 Man making a breechcloth (*dú*) in a rainy-season residential camp

Other than the vicinity of the hearth, the next activity area, in order of importance in use intensity, is the remainder of the surface area of the camp. This is the interior of the residential camp, excluding the hearths and their close surroundings. In this area any of the activities carried out around the hearth might take place, with the exception of those that require fire (that is, cooking, hardening spear points, and so on). Activities that are usually performed sitting down rarely occur here, and few exclusive tasks are carried out in this loosely defined area. One such task, however, is the grinding of plantain seeds in deep palm-trunk mortars. These mortars are positioned between the hearth and the central place, and women stand and grind the seeds with long pestles (Figure 5.3). Owing to the repeated grinding, the mortars sink up to a maximum depth of about 0.30 m, at which point the women change the position of the mortar, since it becomes uncomfortable to use. This leaves a hollow in the floor that gradually fills with garbage. Occasionally the mortar may be located "outside" the camp, thus leaving a hole in that location.

The children use this inside area heavily for playing. Here children perform all sorts of activities that leave material residues, such as the making of tools or toys (see Chapter 7). Basically, these areas are used by adults for a smaller range of activities and are used less intensely than is the area surrounding the hearth. In contrast, this space is used more frequently and for a greater number of activities by children.

Figure 5.3 Woman grinding in a rainy-season residential camp

In the rainy-season residential camps there is a third area with some degree of distinctiveness, the "central place" (Figure 4.10, p. 114). Frequently, this "central place" is where the children's games, the processing of some foods, and tasks involving members of several families are carried out. It is an area frequently used for storage of firewood. It is also the scene of dances, games, and other intraband social activities, and of interband meetings (such as the *baak wáadn*). As stated in Chapter 4, when a *baak waádn* is anticipated the "central place" is larger. In the rainy-season camps with two or three lean-tos the space "in front" of the camp (but outside the roofed area) functions as a communal "central place." On one occasion, a hearth for cooking a peccary was recorded in this area—peccary are prohibited to women and children and, therefore, cannot be cooked in the domestic hearth (see Chapter 9). Tortoise may also be butchered in this communal area.

The fourth distinct activity area within the camps consists of the entrance/exit paths (see Chapter 4). This area is defined by the daily transit of people and leaves no residue. It can be visualized by the absence of rubbish, which is displaced or disintegrates under the continuous traffic. Logically, these areas are recognizable only from the zone immediately adjacent to the camp and beyond. The most marked is the path that leads to the water-collection site.

The fifth distinct activity area is the immediate vicinity of the camp, usually within a radius of 10 to 15 m. This area is only sporadically used, and children are responsible for most of the activities carried out (largely games) (Figure 5.4). This is basically a children's playground; what remains are a few broken or complete infantile artifacts.

Hearths are eventually built in this area for specific tasks, such as straightening canes for blowpipes or cooking and smoking. In the latter case, men sit around the hearth to eat peccary and toss bones, so various material

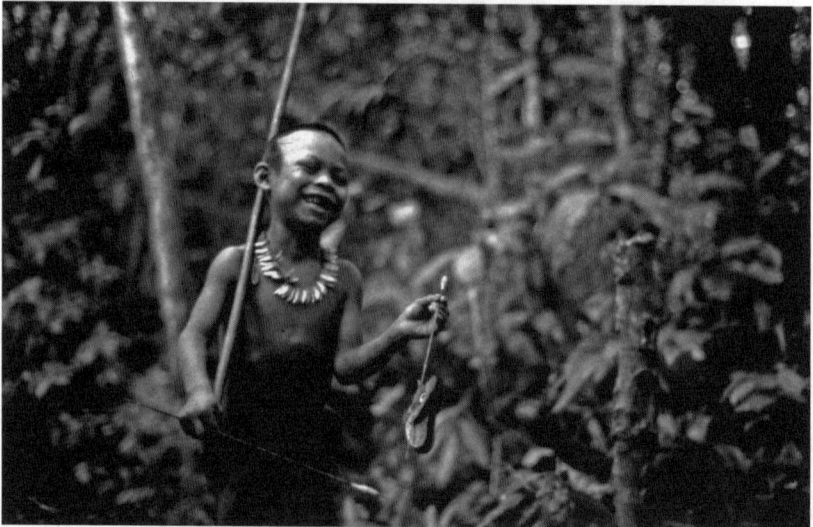

Figure 5.4 Child playing with a blowpipe and darts in the immediate vicinity of a camp

residue products of this activity remain in the area (see Chapter 9). Beyond this outer radius virtually nothing is left of activities related to the residential camps. The only exception is the water holes that are found at a slightly greater distance from the camps.

DISCARD PATTERNS DURING RESIDENTIAL CAMP OCCUPATION

There are significant differences regarding waste discard and management between the two seasons. The rainy-season residential camps are the most frequently built (see Chapter 4); during their occupation distinctive patterns are generated that have strong archaeological implications. During the occupation of these camps multiple material residues are produced that accumulate in different zones. These zones occur in the following places (Figure 5.5):

1. Within the lean-to in the vicinity of the hearths (1 in Figure 5.5).
2. Between the hammocks and the course of leaves that is laid over the central crossbeam and forms the roof (2 in Figure 5.5).
3. On both sides of the entrance/exit paths of the camp (3 in Figure 5.5).

The first two concentration zones consist of primary residue (in the sense of Schiffer 1985:24) and occur owing to the many activities that are carried

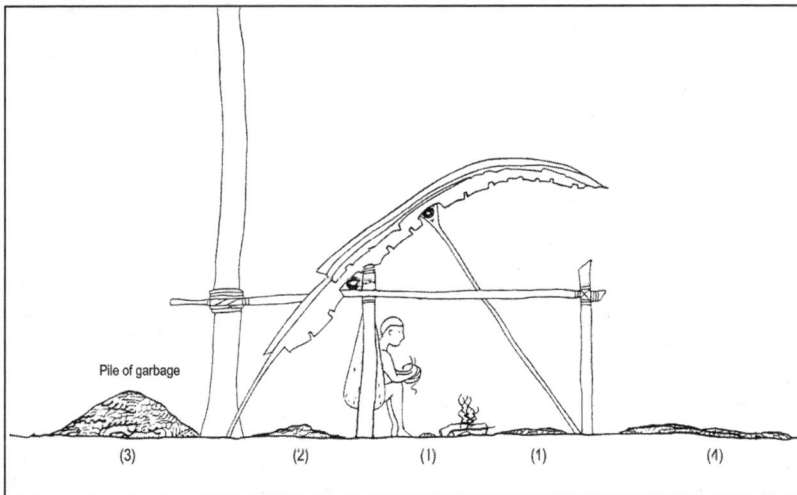

Figure 5.5 Schematic representation of the discard areas in a rainy-season residential camp

out from the hammock facing the hearth, or in its close vicinity (Figure 5.6). However, the second zone is basically formed by three actions: dropping, tossing from hammocks, and sweeping/raking from around the hearth. The first action clearly produces primary residues; the second produces a kind of refuse that could be considered primary or secondary, since for some authors tossing represents "the most casual form of activity area maintenance" (Tani 1995:234); the third unmistakably produces secondary refuses.

Figure 5.6   Man and woman eating *guaná* while sitting in their hammocks around the hearth

The third concentration zone is a discrete secondary refuse accumulation (in the sense of Schiffer 1985), a sort of "door dump" (Binford 1983a:165) (Figure 5.7), and is formed by two main types of residue. First, some larger pieces of waste (racemes that no longer have fruit, *búrup*, broken baskets, and so on) are dumped daily directly onto trash heaps outside the lean-tos on both sides of the entrance/exit paths. More voluminous residue also collects in the same place, such as hundreds of seje, *popere*, and *guaná* seeds from when the fruit are macerated to make *chicha*. Second, this concentration grows owing to the cleaning activity within the camp, because refuse is dumped there.

Every few days during the rainy season, depending on a number of factors, the women clean sectors of the camp and collect together the refuse in specific places where waste has already been collected (Figure 5.8). These areas are between the hammock and the row of leaves in the lean-to, and on both sides of the camp entrance/exit paths. The former sector increases in density and

Figure 5.7 Pile of secondary refuse in a rainy-season residential camp

Figure 5.8 Woman sweeping the floor inside a lean-to

eventually forms an accumulation of refuse some 6 or 7 m long and approximately 1 m wide, which is approximately 10 to 15 cm higher than the level of the floor (2 in Figure 5.5; Figure 5.9). The latter sector becomes a formal waste structure and increases in size regularly during the occupation of the camp. In this way, trash heaps are generated on the edges of the camp, close to the entrances/exits, which reach a diameter of up to 2 m and heights close to 1 m. These secondary accumulations are the deposits that have a high positive

Figure 5.9 Refuse in the area between the hammock and the row of leaves in the lean-to (2 in Figure 5.5)

correlation with the duration of occupation, because the majority of the waste produced in the camp passes through this area. In other words, the longer the occupation, the larger the refuse piles. Trash heaps reach their maximum number when every entrance/exit path has a heap on both sides, and heaps have even been recorded between paths.

The frequency of the cleaning events—performed by the women—is in direct relation to the type and the quantity of refuse produced in the days prior to the cleaning and the predicted abandonment date of the camp. If the activities carried out at the site and the food consumed do not generate a large quantity of refuse, cleaning takes place every five or six days. If the opposite is the case, the cleaning is more frequent, usually every three to four days. The predicted abandonment of the camp is taken into account when cleaning—if the camp is close to being abandoned, there is a greater accumulation of primary refuse observable on the surface. This implies that the lean-tos are cleaned not only when there is a predetermined quantity of refuse on the floor but also when the plan is to remain in that camp for a few more days. This has an important consequence for the formation of the site, because camps are almost never abandoned with clean floors.

There are also more restricted sweeping episodes, which occur most frequently around the hearths, although this does not imply that the hearth is emptied.[1] During these minor events refuse is not deposited on the piles but rather is displaced a short distance, preferably toward one of two places: (1) the line of waste that lies between the hammocks and the course of leaves (2 in Figure 5.5); or (2) the "central place" between the lean-tos (4 in Figure 5.5) (Figure 5.10).

When undertaking the more extensive cleaning of the floor women collect the larger pieces of waste by hand, whereas they sweep or rake the medium- and small-sized pieces with a raceme or reused branches in the form of a brush. The branches most frequently used for this function are rachises of the infrutescence of *yúbudi* (*Euterpe preacatoria*). As such, the women carry the refuse by hand toward the entrance/exit paths and, once they are outside the camp, deposit it on both sides, hence forming the piles.

In some cases during the rainy season the "central place" in the camp becomes a transitional place for secondary deposition. When small-scale cleaning events occur, that is, when only the vicinity of the hearth is swept, some of the displaced refuse is moved toward this space between the lean-tos (Figure 5.11). This type of refuse is similar to what Nielsen (1994:15) calls "displaced waste." Afterward, during a more extensive cleaning event

Figure 5.10 Recently cleaned area around the hearth; note the waste displaced to the "central place."

Figure 5.11 Woman holding a baby and displacing refuse toward the space between the lean-tos

when virtually the entire floor of the camp is cleaned, the refuse collected in the "central place" is deposited on the piles to the sides of the entrance/exit paths.

The only animals that alter the distribution of the primary deposits during the occupation of the camp are dogs.[2] Their activity is exclusively focused on bones and produces a random distribution pattern, which involves only some osseous elements, above all of monkey and peccary. The dogs chew the remains, destroying or reducing the bone assemblage. No cases have been recorded of Nukak dogs bringing bones into the camps. In the analysis of marks on bones collected at several Nukak camps it was detected that those bones from camps with dogs had significant percentages of tooth marks, indicating the intense activity of these animals (see Appendix II). The action of carnivores other than dogs has not been observed, neither on the outskirts of the camps during occupation nor after their abandonment. A low large carnivore biomass and the intense consumption of the carcasses are the primary reasons for the lack of scavenging activity. In Nukak sites the bone assemblage seems to be created entirely by human activity, and dogs produce the only postconsumption carnivore modifications. However, it cannot be totally ruled out that small carnivores, rodents, and other wild scavengers probably eliminate some bones after camps are abandoned.

The trampling action of the inhabitants of the camp causes limited horizontal displacement of the remains that accumulate on the surface. Owing to the relatively compact surface of the floor, human trampling does not cause burial of the material. Strikingly, the most important action is that of children, who habitually play with their own artifacts or occasionally those of the adults. This produces an intensive displacement of broken artifacts and waste since children spend the most amount of time in the camp (see Chapter 7).

During the dry season the pattern of production, distribution, and accumulation of refuse changes, because the camps and the occupation characteristics are different. The boundaries of summer settlements are difficult to determine, since the shelters do not offer marked edges owing to the lack of a wall of leaves and the irregularity of the footprint (Figure 4.6, p. 110). A diffuse line that separates two sectors provides the observable limit (Figure 5.12). The first sector is around the hammocks and hearths where there is no vegetation, part of the leaf coverage has been removed and patches of bare ground are visible. The second is the area around the camp where there has been far less trampling, plants are still standing, the leaf coverage has not been removed, and there are no bare pieces of ground. The former corresponds to the domestic space and the latter to the periphery. Because there is almost never a course of roof leaves,[3] there is no line of refuse generated to the sides of the hammocks. The waste that is produced from the hammocks is not aligned in a parallel pile in the wet season. Rather, it is tossed toward the "outside" of the camp (Figure 5.13). The piles of rubbish on both sides of the entrance/exit paths are consistently produced, but they are smaller and flatter than those in the winter camps and have diffuse borders. These are the only secondary refuse accumulations during occupation of dry season camps.[4]

Figure 5.12 Border of a dry-season residential camp

Figure 5.13 Dispersed refuse generated from the hammock and hearth area in a dry-season residential camp

ABANDONMENT REFUSE

The second point examined was the state in which the refuse remained—both in the primary and secondary deposits—once the camp was abandoned. In other words, an attempt was made to analyze in what condition the residue is found at the moment in which, in a given space, the human production and displacement of waste is interrupted. While the camp is occupied refuse is produced that circulates within the domestic environment. When the camp is abandoned the dynamic of production and distribution of residue stops, and multiple natural agents begin to operate (this has been the subject of extensive discussions, see Binford 1981; Gifford 1978; Kent 1993; Schiffer 1976, 1985, 1987). Therefore, it is important to understand in what condition the material waste is found at the moment that these changes occur during the formation of the archaeological site. This does not imply that natural factors do not act during the production of the residue, or that once the camp is abandoned a human agent will not modify the remains. In fact both situations occur, but it is clear that during the occupation of the camp human agents contribute most to the formation of the site and the distribution of materials, and once the site is abandoned natural agents predominate.

With the preceding issues in mind I examined the distribution of the refuse in camps after they had been abandoned. Initially, there are two points to be emphasized: (1) There are differences between camps during the same season; (2) there are consistent differences between the summer and winter camps. With respect to the variations between the camps in the same season there are two principle causes for the accumulation and distribution of residue: (1) the duration of occupation; and (2) the frequency of cleaning events. As far as the first point is concerned there is a directly proportional relationship between the quantity of refuse produced and the length of occupation.

The majority of the food debris that can be seen on the floor of the residential camp when it is abandoned is food remains, such as seeds, nuts, shells, fruit peel, and a few complete and broken bones (Figure 5.14). The sub-products of artifact production, including bark string, plant fibers and wood flakes, are found to a lesser degree. Finally, and in far lesser proportion, a few complete or broken artifacts—generally less then ten and almost always less that five[5]—are found scattered on the camp floor. These artifacts consist of baskets and balayes, wood pestles, ax shafts, metal pans, spears, calabashes, sticks for beating or stirring (*dúri*), mixing sticks (*teu*), pot sherds, broken darts and blowpipes, hardwood artifacts with a small central depression that are used to break open hard fruit (similar to the so-called coconut breakers), and so forth (see Chapter 7 for a description of each of these artifacts). The expedient baskets (*búrup*) are treated differently. First, they are far more abundant than the other artifacts; a band can fabricate five or six per day. This means that at the moment of abandonment there may be dozens of discarded *búrup* in the camp. Second, they are discarded in several loci: the floor of the lean-to, the central place between the lean-tos, the refuse piles, and the outskirts of the camp.

Figure 5.14   Floor of a rainy-season residential camp just after abandonment

Artifacts are discarded for various reasons. First, some are abandoned at the end of their use life when they can no longer be repaired or recycled. In this group are included blowpipes,[6] baskets, balayes, metal pans, calabashes, and ax handles (*pewe-na* or *chak naát*). In general, when these artifacts are left on the floor of the abandoned camps they are found in a deteriorated condition: the baskets have loose and cut fibers, the metal pans have holes and/or are rusted, the ax handles are broken, the calabashes are dried out (with one or several cuts along the edges), and the blowpipes are broken lengthways. Artifacts that break by accident (that is, through involuntary falls), although these seems to be extremely scarce, can also be included within this group.

Second, there are expedient artifacts that still have use life but have reached a point at which it is more economical and/or better to make new ones (the "*de facto* residues," in Schiffer's terms [1985]). In making these decisions the

Nukak might consider the calculation of transport costs and comfort versus the fabrication of a new item. This category basically consists of the *búrup*, the pestles, the stirrers, the mixing sticks, and the "coconut breakers."

Third, there are artifacts that have been intentionally broken and abandoned in the camp. We have observed the intentional breakage of ceramic pots, blowpipes, and darts during situations generated by problems between couples or members of a family (Figure 5.15). The only two cases of breakage of pottery recorded in our fieldwork were due to family conflicts.[7] Other elements destroyed *ad hoc* in family fights included mirrors, bags of salt, baskets, clothing, and hammocks. Within the group of intentionally broken artifacts are also found the belongings of the dead, which are destroyed immediately after the person's death. This includes, for men, blowpipes and darts, curare, hammocks, and axes; for women, hammocks, pots, baskets, and calabashes. Furthermore, in both cases some of the crops planted by the dead person are cut.

Figure 5.15 Floor of a recently abandoned rainy-season residential camp with pottery sherds left after a marital argument; note the *búrup* in the upper right, a wooden pestle in the upper left, and a gourd container in the lower left.

Fourth, on rare occasions artifacts with a long remaining use life, such as mortars and unfinished artifacts, canes for blowpipes, and raw material to make specific artifacts such as *puiú* (wild cotton used on the blowpipe darts), were observed abandoned in rainy-season camps. In the first case, the mortars were resting on *ad hoc* platforms located within the camp to prevent them rotting by coming into contact with the ground. In the second case, the unfinished blowpipes had their ends covered with leaves to prevent insects entering them, and they were placed on the central beam of the lean-to, under the leaf roof. In the third case, the *puiú* was kept in a *búrup* hanging from the central beam of the lean-to, again, protected by the leaf roof. As has been stated, the reoccupation of camps is infrequent, but the location of a new camp close to an old one is a common occurrence. Therefore, these left-behind artifacts will be recovered, either (a) in the immediate future (in a few months' time), when the band again sets up camp in the area, or (b) any time before (within weeks) when a member of the band passes close by during a foraging trip.

When the band abandons the residential camp natural agents begin to act on and transform the site. There are three initial processes that manifest themselves immediately after the abandonment: (1) deterioration of the structure of the shelters; (2) disintegration of the organic remains; and (3) plant coverage of the site. The action of carnivores on deposits in abandoned camps has not been observed. Although my visits to abandoned camps were sporadic, no trace of predators was found, and the Nukak make no reference to their presence.

The first process involves a series of events that, over time, cause the collapse and degradation of the elements that make up the shelters. The sequence of deterioration is regular and consistently follows the same steps. This is, of course, a continuous process, but it can nevertheless be divided into several stages. The sequence is clearer in the rainy-season camps. Based on the observation of 93 abandoned camps, 7 principal stages have been recognized with the following, abridged characteristics:

- Stage 1: Recently abandoned camp (a few days; maximum two weeks). All or the majority of the roof leaves are still green. Crosspieces, posts, and stakes are intact and still secured. Clear and defined hearths are recognizable (Figure 5.16).
- Stage 2: Lean-to roofs are still intact, with some leaves green and others dry. Otherwise, the same characteristics as stage 1.
- Stage 3: The roof leaves are all or almost all dry. Some collapse may be in evidence. Posts and cross-members still attached. There may occasionally be incipient vegetation in the interior. Clearly visible hearths (Figure 5.17)
- Stage 4: All the roof leaves are dry, and several have fallen. Some cross-members are on the ground. Generally there is vegetation in the interior. The hearths can be identified, but at times the edges are not precise (Figure 5.18).

- Stage 5: All the leaves have fallen, as have the majority of the posts and cross-members. It is hard to recognize the shape of the camp and the location of the hearths. Young plants cover the entire occupation surface (Figure 5.19).
- Stage 6: All the posts and cross-members have fallen. Some can be identified on the ground, but not clearly. The hearths cannot be distinguished. Plant cover is denser and of low specific diversity, with plants up to 1 m tall (Figure 5.20).
- Stage 7: Poor visibility. Plant coverage is continuous and of low specific diversity, with plants taller than 1 m. Camps abandoned for more than one year are found in this last stage.

The second process brings with it the disintegration and/or the burial of the organic remains that were left on the ground. In this regard, it has been observed that the first element to degrade is the plant matter, especially the fruit shells, leaves, and pulp. The bags made from leaves—the *búrup*—also disintegrate rapidly. A few days after the abandonment there is no meat left on discarded bones; at the end of two or three weeks bones are totally clean, with perhaps only a tendon or cartilage still attached. The subsequent elements to disintegrate are the posts, cross-members, stakes, and sticks. Also included in this group are tools, such as pestles, ax handles, spears, mixing sticks, and so on. At this point in the sequence the seeds and nuts of various fruit also

Figure 5.16 Abandoned rainy-season residential camp–Stage 1

Figure 5.17 Abandoned rainy-season residential camp–Stage 3

Figure 5.18 Abandoned rainy-season residential camp–Stage 4

disintegrate. This rapid disintegration of the organic remains is in direct relationship to the intense biological activity in the tropical rainforests, since the majority of the animal biomass in this environment consists of terrestrial invertebrates that constitute a large part of the disintegrated components of the ecosystem.

Figure 5.19 Abandoned rainy-season residential camp–Stage 5

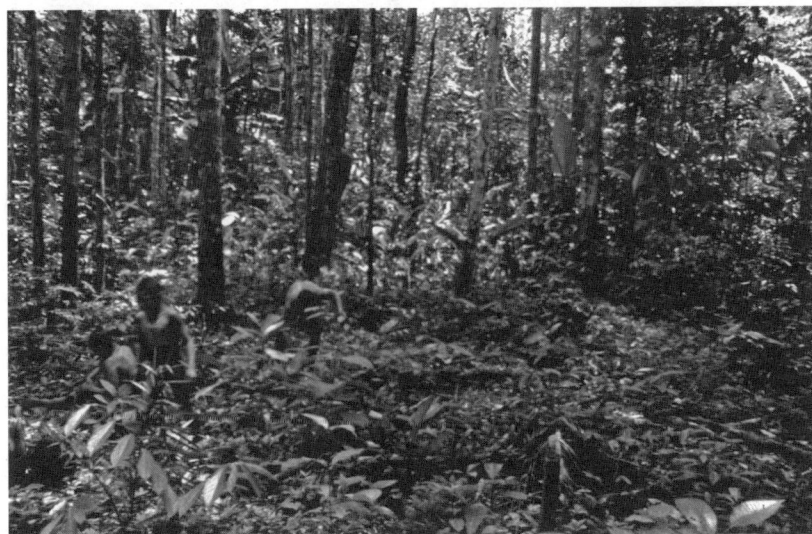

Figure 5.20 Abandoned rainy-season residential camp–Stage 6

The duration of the periods of observation have not permitted us to follow the process of disintegration of the bones or of the pottery. In general, the structure of the camp collapses, and the growth of the young plants on the previously inhabited floor begins before the degradation of these elements.

The result is that the leaf coverage and vegetation hide the bones and pottery. Therefore, even though they are not buried, they are no longer visible. In only some cases, in camps in stages 5 and 6, were large fragments of pots identified that broke *in situ*. These fragments protruded above the leaf coverage owing to their large size (in some cases half of a large vessel; Figure 5.21). Neither have the periods of observation allowed for examination of the burial processes of elements that do not disintegrate rapidly on the surface. Nonetheless, some evidence suggests that these processes are slow. For example, while cleaning the floor to have a place to sleep during a visit to a chontaduro orchard we found pottery sherds on the surface that were attributed by the Nukak to the "old ones" (making reference to ancestors).

Figure 5.21   Floor of an abandoned camp, Stage 5 or 6, with large pieces of pottery still visible

THE SYMBOLIC AND COMMUNICATIVE DIMENSION OF WASTE

Little is known as yet about this dimension of waste and discard patterns. Nonetheless, there are data that allow us to approach this subject. Discarded sherds or metal pots on abandoned camp floors are fairly informative about the people who occupied the camps and the events that occurred during their occupation. Several times during trips into the forest the Nukak stopped at abandoned camps, examining the scattered sherds and metal pots on the floor, pointing them out and mentioning specific persons and events. When

I was told that sherds in the chontaduro orchard were made by "the old ones" (see above), they also informed me that these old ones were "those who lived here and planted the chontaduro palms." A broken pot or other item is a frequent outcome of conjugal fights or arguments between kin. In a way, the sherds are the materialization of the development and the resolution of conflicts and contain codified information for the transmission not only of ideas but also, more fundamentally, of emotions. When a woman fights with her husband he will often break a pot, hurling it with force to the ground. A father, angry with his daughter, was observed breaking the only ceramic pot she had in her bag. Furthermore, there are references to the fact that when a woman dies her pots are destroyed along with all her other possessions other than her hammock, which is usually buried with her.

Cabrera, Franky, and Mahecha (1999:215) relate a case of interest concerning waste management in association with a ritual funeral. A woman who lived on the edge of the colonized zone died. Her sons cut down all the plants she had cultivated, except the chontaduro, the achiote, and the calabashes and tied the stems of yuca and sugar cane to the side of the lean-to as a type of "protection" so that the dead woman's *nemep* would not return and kill or cause other people to fall ill. A month later, when they left to live in a new lean-to, the lean-to where the woman had been buried was cleaned. They destroyed the "protective" wall and placed all the residue in the rubbish pit that was in use during occupation of the camp. This case indicates that some kind of relationship—as yet little explored—exists among waste, its location in the camp, and its protective function against *nemep* spirits.

DISCUSSION

Marked differences exist between the summer and the winter camps with respect to the quantity and the distribution of refuse. This is due to two fundamental factors: the duration of occupation and the design of the camp. In the rainy season, the periods of occupation are longer, and the shelters have precise limits. This situation generates larger and discrete formal accumulations of waste. In the dry season, occupations are shorter, and the spatial limits of the camps are relatively diffuse. Consequently, the formal concentrations of rubbish are fewer and have a random distribution pattern. This, of course, is only a general tendency, since there are winter camps that are occupied only for one night in which no secondary waste remains, and summer camps that have been occupied for longer periods of time (eight days), which generate formal secondary refuse structures.

The ethnoarchaeological information obtained from the Nukak enables the analysis of the material derivatives of some components of hunter-gatherer behavior. Bearing in mind the observations related to the occupation of the camps, the deposition of refuse, the cleaning events, and the archaeological predictions derived from this relation, one can expect that sites generated under similar conditions will present:

1. Difficulty in identifying loci associated with discrete activities. This is a consequence of the quantity of different activities that are carried out in the same space (especially around the hearth or seated in hammocks), which obliterates the traces of single tasks.
2. Concordance between the loci of multiple activities and the material remains produced by these when carried out only a few days before the abandonment of the camp.
3. Discordance between the loci of activities and the remains produced when carried out before the last cleaning event.
4. Strong positive correlation between the quantity of secondary refuse and the duration of camp occupation. The primary waste deposits, on the contrary, do not reflect the duration of occupation because they are the object of periodic displacements during the camp cleaning tasks.
5. Low correlation between the activities carried out from the hammocks and the deposits found between them and the course of leaves in the wet-season camps. This is because primary and secondary (displaced) residues are mixed in these deposits.
6. Absence of residues known as "primary residuals," in Schiffer's terms (small elements that escape the cleaning tasks), in the area of the hearth after cleaning owing to the effects of meticulous sweeping/raking of this area.
7. Presence of "primary residuals" in secondary refuse accumulations.

Observations of the Nukak also confirm the recurrence of a behavior with respect to the cleaning of the camps. When abandonment of the settlement is predicted for the near future the standards of cleanliness become more flexible, and floor cleaning occurs less frequently or does not occur at all (Fisher & Strickland 1991; Schiffer 1985; Stevenson 1982). This phenomenon has significant archaeological consequences because it implies that, under similar conditions, the remains on the camp floors represent fairly accurately the activity performed during the days prior to the abandonment (see also Fisher & Strickland 1991). It means that the camp floors are not good indicators with which to reconstruct the entire life span of the site. Nonetheless, this behavior does vary among hunter-gatherers (Binford 1983a:153–56; Murray 1980; Yellen 1977). The Aché, for example, do not sweep their camps, and therefore the displacement of waste is negligible (Jones 1993), and the Ngatatjara simply toss refuse outside the camp without creating trash heaps (Gould 1968:110–19).

Similarly, the positive correlation between the size and the extent of the secondary deposits and the duration of occupation has also frequently been identified (Hudson 1990:240; Schiffer 1985:25). This supports the hypothesis that the secondary and not the primary deposits are good indicators in the estimation of occupation time of hunter-gatherer camps. Contrarily, secondary deposits have a low degree of resolution with respect to activities carried out in the camp.

This study also confirms that the characteristics of the floor during camp occupation constitute a variable, which affects the congruency between activity and by-products and influences waste management (Fisher 1987; Gifford 1978). Although this is not technically a cultural variable, it has considerable significance for the interpretation of activity areas based on the archaeological record. On the compact, clayey surface of Nukak camps, trampling does not bury items but rather produces lateral displacement and eventually breakage. This fact reduces the congruency between a given activity and the primary waste produced, since by-products buried during camp occupation would retain a better resolution for identifying activity areas. Moreover, items that remain on the camp surface during occupation are subject to periodic cleaning events and, therefore, end up in the secondary refuse structures. In other words, the compact clayey surface makes the transit produced by human action of by-products from the activity locus to the secondary refuse structures more fluid.

Artifacts left behind with remaining use life (for example, mortars), raw material (for instance, *puiú*), and unfinished tools (for example, blowpipes) have been recorded among other hunter-gatherers, which has led to the coining of two closely related concepts: "site furniture" (Binford 1978b) and "appliances" (Gould 1980:71–2). In the Nukak case, this "site furniture" does not necessarily imply reoccupation of the camp but does indicate that the site will be revisited, whether during a residential or a logistical move, or during a foraging trip. An observation of interest, with clear and direct archaeological implications, is that the elements left behind correspond to the major steps in the technological process from unworked raw material (the *puiú*), to preforms (the unfinished blowpipes), to well-finished, highly curated artifacts such as the mortars. Therefore, in situations where some kind of "site furniture" might occur, the presence of final products alone should not be assumed. Rather, a range of artifacts in different stages of production and use should be expected.

The Nukak case also presents other aspects little explored in the ethno-archaeology of hunter-gatherers. One is the condition of the hollows that remain in the floors of the camps as a consequence of the grinding activities around the "central place." Once the mortar is removed the hole is transformed into a rubbish trap that fills up through trampling and lateral displacement. In this way, the camp floors where grinding activities take place are perforated with these traps, which become concentrations of small pieces of secondary and unintended refuse. The archaeological signature of this is quite clear and could lead to a misinterpretation, juxtaposing two unrelated components: the hole and the waste found within it.

Another interesting point is the action of children in the production and displacement of rubbish. I should clarify that other authors have drawn attention to, and superficially explored, the action of children in the archaeological record (Bonnichsen 1973; Hammond & Hammond 1981). But, they have done so, in my opinion, from a narrow perspective, considering children as "disturbing" elements of a pattern of material remains that is a product of the action of adults. Children have been considered to be like any other post-depositional, preburial biological agent, that is, modifying the spatial relationships of a supposedly "normal" record produced by adults. This is incorrect because it assumes that children do not generate an archaeological record but rather, are merely a "distorting factor" (Hammond & Hammond 1981) and are not considered as active produces of material culture. My position is very different. I consider children as active social actors in the production and the consumption of material culture and the generation and the management of discards (Politis 1999). Usually, children spend most of the day inside or around the residential camps. The maximum distance they move from the camp is dictated by the possibility of being heard by their parents. In the tropical rainforest visual contact is quickly lost, whereas auditory contact permits control over greater distances.[8]

The children are certainly among those who spend most time in the residential camps and in the immediate neighboring area, more so than any other age group. Adult women come in a close second, whereas men spend most of the day outside the camp, hunting and gathering at some distance away. Children use and produce several types of artifacts inside or around the residential camp (see Chapter 7). In this way, children are the cause of three significant processes related to refuse: (1) They produce the greatest amount of trampling inside the camp because they are there for longer periods of time and their movement is intensive. (2) While playing, they produce the most "primary refuse" in the camp's vicinity. Although this refuse is scarce and scattered, it generates a diffuse outer circle of refuse items. (3) Within the camp they modify the association between the primary residues and the activity that produced them, because they leave some and select others for their games. This last point has also been observed among other hunter-gatherers, such as the Efe (Fisher 1987:79).

It has been observed and repeatedly asserted that cleaning actions operate selectively on waste in such a way that the large pieces are displaced while the smaller sized pieces tend to remain in the primary discard locus (Binford 1978b; McKellar 1983; Nielsen 1994; Schiffer 1987, but see Tani 1995:244). This has lead to (lithic) microdebris being considered more suitable for the identification of activity areas. In the case presented in the current study, the size of the waste is not determinant in the displacement of refuse, and, in general, the cleaning episodes affect both the macro- and the microdebris. Consequently, no primary residual waste is left in the vicinity of the hearths after cleaning. However, the absence of lithic technology and the consequent lack of flakes and microflakes on the Nukak camp floors prevent an analysis that could determine which type of distribution of small waste would be generated by groups that work with stone.

Nonetheless, one of the peculiar characteristics of Nukak discard behavior is that many artifacts are abandoned when they still retain a long use life, and in spite of the great investment of energy in their manufacture. This is the case with hammocks, blowpipes, ceramic pots, and darts, all of which are broken and discarded as a result of conjugal disputes. Such behavior, which is relatively common among the Nukak, results in the introduction of elements into the archaeological record more rapidly than from the deterioration of the artifact through use. In this sense, the conjugal tensions within the band produce a specific discard pattern that cannot be understood through the principles of cost/benefit.[9]

The Nukak camp floors are covered with large quantities of food remains, material remains generated by the manufacture and maintenance of diverse tools, and elements intentionally broken owing to issues of social order. This last cause of discard has barely been explored in the study of discard patterns and their relation to the formation of the archaeological record. In a summary of discard processes, Shott (1989) mentioned six major types: breakage in production; abandonment during or after production; loss; breakage in use; recycling; and depletion. Basically, according to Shott's scheme, artifacts enter the archaeological record if there is a problem in their fabrication, when they get lost, or when their usefulness has been exhausted. In virtually none of the analyses of discard patterns among hunter-gatherers are socioideational factors taken into account. Furthermore, the Nukak case contradicts the statement that there is a directly proportional relationship between tool class use life and the effort expended in production (Schiffer 1985:33; Shott 1989:20).

Finally, this chapter also showed that the Nukak demonstrate specific behavior traits in relation to garbage and its informative power. For example, the intentional breakage of artifacts to resolve conflicts, and the consequent material correlate, has only infrequently been recorded among other hunter-gatherers. Another point to be borne in mind is the information provided by waste from abandoned camps. This is neither anecdotal nor occasional; rather, when the Nukak encounter a camp not established by their own band they systematically stop to "read" the garbage left behind to identify the people who inhabited the camp and the principle events that occurred there.

Notes

1. We only once observed the emptying of a hearth during our fieldwork.
2. In all the cases recorded during our field seasons, the colonist had given the dogs to the Nukak in recent times. In most cases the Nukak can tell which colonist gave them the dogs.
3. We have, however, noted some summer camps with roofs. One case involved the reoccupation of a winter camp, and in the other two cases the leaves had been placed for protection against occasional summer rains.
4. In one case, larger and more localized piles were observed during the summer. This occurred when a band reoccupied a camp toward the end of winter that still had its leaf roof intact. In this case, when the camp floor was swept the refuse accumulated in piles that were later burnt. Such behavior occurs only rarely.
5. In the abandoned camps close to the frontier of the colonization one also finds a variable quantity of worn-out clothing, bits of cloth, and empty containers of some industrialized foods (spaghetti, rice, and so on). These elements are no longer present at a few kilometers' distance when the camps are inside the forest.
6. We have observed on several occasions that when the blowpipe is no longer of use (generally when it splits) and it can not be mended, its owner destroys it. What remains, in the majority of cases, are many scattered fragments of cane.
7. This has been observed by other researchers who studied the Nukak (Hector Mondragón, pers. comm.)
8. Although childhood is a continuing process, one can distinguish a transition at around 7 or 8 years old. Before this age small children are always under the care of parents or older children. They remain close to the camp, and their games are usually not gender oriented. After this age they can be taking care of younger

children, explore areas to certain distances from the camp, and play more gender-oriented games. In the final part of childhood, boys may accompany their fathers on short hunting-gathering trips, and girls do the same (performing effective extractive tasks) with their mothers during gathering.

9. Neither does it seem that this regular breaking of objects through conjugal arguments has to do with an implicit social mechanism for avoiding the accumulation of items by certain individuals or families.

Chapter 6

Residential and Logistical Mobility: Daily Foraging Trips

T his chapter presents fine-grained quali-quantitative information on the several dimensions of territory and the different kinds of Nukak mobility and discusses their archaeological implications. Three types of mobility are considered: residential mobility and logistical mobility as defined by Binford (1980), and the daily foraging trips that are classified as the movements of individuals or small task parties to and from the residential camp within a single day. Finally, it discusses causes of the types of mobility and their archaeological expectations.

Hunter-gatherer mobility has been a central theme of contemporary ethnoarchaeological research. In the past twenty years this aspect of culture has been studied from a global perspective in terms of the relationship between hunter-gatherer behavior and ecological factors (Bettinger 1991; Binford 1980; Gamble & Boismier 1991; Kelly 1995). Mobility has also been seen as one of the distinctive, although by no means exclusive or constant, characteristics of hunter-gatherers (Kelly 1995; Lee & DeVore 1968:II). Nonetheless, the existing information on tropical rainforest hunter-gatherer mobility for South America is extremely limited. As such, this chapter contributes original information on Nukak mobility and puts to the test models commonly used to interpret the archaeological record of hunter-gatherers in general and of tropical rainforest groups in particular.

Mobility models of past foragers have been developed based on ethnographic cases (Binford 1980; Hayden 1981; Kelly 1983). However, most of these models fail to capture the complexity of the relationships among several types of mobility, and among these types and environmental, social, and ideological factors. This failure is fundamentally the result of the enormous difficulty in recording data—through archaeological eyes—on different types of mobility in contemporary forager society. In most cases, by the time ethno-archaeologists have arrived foragers have already changed their mobility pattern, and either they are moving toward sedentism or covaried factors, such as technology or subsistence, have been heavily impacted by contact with the West (for exceptions see Gould 1969; Lee 1979, 1984; Yellen 1977). This is especially true of South America, where good-quality ethnographic and ethnoarchaeological data on foragers were collected only after the groups studied had already become partly sedentary (for example, the Hupdu, the Kakwa, the Aché, the Pumé, and so on). In other cases, such as the Sirionó from Bolivia (Holmberg 1950), although groups maintained a "traditional" way of life during fieldwork, information on their mobility is scarce and nonquantitative. As a result, most comparisons of different types of mobility in forager societies have speculative components and usually leave aside considerations of the social and ideational factors that affect mobility.

The different types of mobility are closely related to the multidimensional nature of territory. In recent decades, territorial analyses among hunter-gatherers have taken two contrasting directions. In the first, they have been closely allied with the analysis of Cartesian space in relation to the physical reality of a territory and how these characteristics—especially the structure of food resources and raw materials—in turn shape human adaptation. Within this line of research, territoriality has been recognized as a property of all human populations (Dyson-Hudson & Smith 1978) and is defined as the behavioral system that controls and maintains the more or less specific use of a particular area (Lanata 1993:10). Conversely, there has been a reaction against this kind of spatial analysis, which has been accused of being environmentally deterministic. It has been pointed out that the first approach "reduce[s] human action to a series of numerical variables suitable for understanding the relationship between the friction of distance and economic and social behavior" (Gosden 1999, 154). In the second line of research emphasis has been placed both on the way nonindustrial societies perceive their land and on the ontology of landscape more broadly (Gosden 1994; Ingold 2000).

THE MULTIPLE DIMENSIONS OF TERRITORY

During our fieldwork the Nukak ethnic group regularly occupied a portion of the Amazonian tropical rainforest that was approximately 10,000 km^2, as was mentioned previously (Figure 1.2, p. 36). The Nukak concept of territory is fairly complex; it articulates spatial and ideational elements that go beyond the conditions of defensibility and resource use, the factors commonly employed to explain the territoriality of hunter-gatherer groups. There are five juxtaposed dimensions through which the Nukak perceive, use, and conceptualize the landscape. The first dimension of Nukak space can be denominated as the band territory. This is defined as a habitual and preferential—but not exclusive—area exploited by a band. Most residential relocations, camp erections, and the tending of horticultural plots take place within this territory. The procurement of resources from the residential camps is carried out within this space, as is the great majority of activities that make up the daily life of the Nukak, both inside and outside camp. Bands have certain usage rights over this territory, although its borders are lax. These rights are neither comparable nor similar to the concept of land ownership that Western society and other indigenous agriculturist societies hold (Ingold 2000). Similarly, this landscape is constructed by the members of the band and their ancestors. After generations of usage and management of the tropical rainforest they have succeeded in modifying it and making it more productive, as well as impregnating it with their traces and inundating it with symbolism. Consequently, each person has a profound and detailed knowledge of the band's territory, knowledge around which resource exploitation, residential relocations, logistics, and ritual activity are planned.

The size of a band's territory is difficult to define owing to the looseness of its boundaries. Taking into consideration that the bands always reach the edge of the floodplains of the Guaviare and Inírida rivers and that they are also in contact with a limited and known number of *colonos,* it is possible to speculate that the territory of each band oscillates between 200 and 500 km². This figure is extremely speculative and, of course, varies from band to band. In this sense, the northwestern bands (*Meu-munu*) are close to the lower limit as a consequence of the attraction created by the colonization of the Trocha Ganadera, which may have caused the overlapping of traditional territories. The southeastern bands (*Muhabe-munu*) have larger territories, some even greater than 500 km². Based on the recent history of the Nukak, and what it has been possible to reconstruct of demographic changes over the last two decades, one can speculate that most band territories before Western contact were in the range of 400–500 km².

The second dimension of Nukak territory is that of the regional group. These groups (*Wayari, Meu, Tákayu, Muhabe*; see Chapter 3) are also associated with a particular space, the boundaries of which are even less clear. As has been stated, there are spatial associations with reference to the location of particular bands within Nukak territory. Each of these *munu* extends from the watershed to either the Guaviare or the Inírida rivers, which delimit Nukak land to the north and south. Within the space shared by the regional group, members of the bands may travel without restriction, visit other bands (under certain conditions determined by kinship, and having carried out the appropriate rituals), and utilize the resources available in the area during these activities. Regional groups do not act as endogamous units, but there is a high proportion of unions formed by members of two different bands within the same *munu*. Thus, every couple has a detailed knowledge of the territories of at least two bands within the *munu*. The surface area of this territory is extremely difficult to calculate, given the laxity of the borders and the flexibility of the concept itself. However, it is possible to estimate it to be between 1,000 and 2,000 km².

Beyond the band or regional affiliation group territory, the Nukak travel to distinct regions occupied by bands with which, in general, they have little contact, although they of course know of their existence. This represents the third dimension of Nukak territory: a distant space that is known about but only rarely visited. The reasons for these journeys, when they occur, are diverse, ranging from the gathering of canes for blowpipes, visiting distant bands to monitor for potential spouses, or visiting *colonos* farms and villages out of curiosity. The limits of this territory are much harder to estimate. It is larger than the regional group territory and may include several thousand square kilometers, even incorporating the entire territory currently occupied by the Nukak ethnic group.

The fourth dimension of territory includes the places whose existences are known to the Nukak but are not visited by them. This external landscape is known about through the flow of information among bands or by means of oral tradition, but not through the direct experience of individuals or the band. Within this broad and diffuse territory the Nukak recognize the existence of places occupied long ago by the ancestors. The lands at the headwaters of the Unilla and the Itilla rivers can be included in this dimension. Their existence is known through oral tradition, and it was toward this location that the band that appeared in Calamar in 1988 was journeying in search of the Kakwa (Juan Manual Alegre pers. com.: 1990; Kenneth Conduff pers. com.: 1995). The southeastern lands are also found within this territorial dimension, from where, according to their oral tradition, the Nukak originated. This territory is considered by the ethnic group as Nukak territory, despite the fact that at present they do not know whether there are other Nukak occupying it, and information in this respect is scarce and relatively old.

The fifth dimension of territory is the mythic and ideational and exists within the framework of Nukak cosmology (see Chapter 3). This territory is conceived of as real and tangible in the physical world, despite its supernatural character. It is formed by three (maybe four if we consider the two sublevels of the intermediate world) overlapping strata (see Chapter 3). These stratified worlds have particular physical and environmental characteristics and are interconnected through features of the landscape, such as hollows and paths, as well as by spirit-ancestors who travel up and down between the layers (occasionally on winged animals), producing climatic phenomena. This fifth dimension articulates with the other four and gives the natural, human, and supernatural spaces a flat and stratified character.

For the Nukak there is continuity between these dimensions; the separation between the real and physical territory and the ideational and mythic is non-existent. Kenneth Conduff (pers. com. 1995) related to me an extremely revealing story in this respect. When the missionaries were boring holes for water for the Laguna Pavón 2 mission, the Nukak warned them about piercing through to the lower level of the world. After several meters some fine sand was found and the Nukak said, "See, you have already reached the beach of the river, which runs in the lower level." Later, when water began to emerge from the pipe, they said, "You see, now you have hit the river of the lower level!" This example is illustrative of how this fifth territorial dimension is conceived. Despite daily life taking place on Earth and within the first four dimensions, the existence of other inhabited planes influences the way in which space is conceived of and moved through.

The Nukak have an understanding of space outside their territory. The conceptualization of this "foreign space" has been difficult, because it is basically considered to be the "territories of others" and therefore does not articulate in the same way with the other dimensions. Within this "territory" the Nukak place cities such as Santafé de Bogotá and Villavicencio, and they can usually indicate their orientation, although not the distance (regarded as remote and associated with airplanes). They can also locate the village of Mitú (150 to 200 km southeast), because the Nukak who were relocated there in 1988 disseminated this information among the Nukak population. In contrast to the other Makú (Jackson 1983:148–63; Reichel-Dolmatoff 1968), the Nukak currently are not in regular contact with other indigenous groups, and, therefore, non-Nukak territory is basically thought of as the land of the *kaweni* (the whites).

RESIDENTIAL MOBILITY

Residential mobility is understood to be the displacement of all (or most) members of a band from one camp to another, which implies the definitive abandonment of the former camp and the construction of a new one. The concept of residential mobility is complimented by that of logistical mobility, in which only segments of the band—usually small groups of persons who travel in search of resources—are involved (Binford 1980).

One of the central characteristics of Nukak bands is high residential mobility (Figure 6.1). Residential camps are almost exclusively built in the first territorial dimension, the band's territory. In the periods observed, the occupation of camps (from here onward, unless specified to the contrary, "camps" refers to residential camps) varied between a single night and fourteen days. Some *colonos* mentioned occupations of almost a month in camps close to the frontiers of colonization (for example, in Caño Seco and Barranco Colorado and Franky, Cabrera, & Mahecha 1995:16) recorded maximum occupations of twenty-eight days. Table 6.1 gives an idea of the frequency and the dynamic of the residential movements and of their relationship to the camps. A minimum value is included because in some cases we arrived at a camp after it had already been occupied for a number of days, and when we left the last camp it would continue to be occupied.

Data obtained during fieldwork revealed seasonal patterns of residential mobility. In the rainy season, the mean distance between camps was 3.85 km ($n = 12$; min = 0.9 km; max = 7.2 km), and the mean length of occupation was 4.8 days ($n = 13$; min = 1 day; max = 14 days). During the dry season, distances between residential camps produced a pattern with a mean distance

Figure 6.1 Man and boy carrying some of their belongings in *búrup* during a residential move; note that the man is carrying a mortar in the *búrup*. The boy carries a pet monkey on his shoulders.

Table 6.1 Distance between Residential Camps and Number of Days in Each
Camp

Band	Distance between Camps (in kms)	Days of Stay
Rainy Season		
1990	1.5	–
1991a	3	14
1991a	6.4	4
1991a	4.2	1 (night)
1991a	7.2	1 (night)
1991a	5.3	1 (night)
1991a	5.2	2
1991a	1.7	more than 2
1991b	0.9	10
1991b	1	more than 2
1992	5.4	14
1992	4.2	more than 6
Dry Season		
1994	1.3	3
1994	3.1	2
1994	5.7	3
1994	9.7	3
1995a	5.4	3
1995a	7.1	2
1995a	16.7	8
1995a	12.5	1
1995a	18.1	1
1995a	8.9	2
1995 and b	7.3	2
1995 and b	7.1	2
1995 and b	13.4	6
1996a	6.5	7
1996b	1.37	2
1996b	5.2	2
1996b	3.1	1 (night)
1996b	4.6	1 (night)
1996b	8.31	more than 6

of 7.65 km ($n = 19$; min $= 1.30$ km; max $= 18.1$ km) and a mean occupation
of 3 days ($n = 20$; min $= 1$ day, max $= 8$ days). The overall pattern, therefore,
is that during the rainy season the Nukak remain longer in each residential
camp and move shorter distances between camps, whereas in the dry season
they occupy the camp for less time but move greater distances between camps.
By combining the data from both seasons we can estimate that each band

makes approximately 100 residential moves per year, although this value could be a little high given the fact that we spent more time with the more mobile bands. So, a more realistic figure would be 70 to 80 relocations per year, covering a total distance of between 400 and 500 km. These figures roughly coincide with those provided by Franky, Cabrera, and Mahecha (1995), who arrived at a figure of 68.64 moves per year, an occupation average of 5.31 days per camp and an average distance between camps of 6.9 km (min = 1 km; max = 28 km). (The last value is relatively tentative, because it was calculated based on walking time and not with a pedometer.) These figures yield a total distance traveled of 364 km per band per year.

Residential moves are usually made by the entire coresident group, following extant, well-defined paths in the band's territory (Figure 6.2). There are two basic types of relocation. Either the whole group travels together, or there is some distance between people as they advance through the forest. When they split into several subgroups there are two main variants. In the first, all members of a family walk together, generally with the adult male at the head, hunting and collecting along the way. In the second variant a group of men travel some distance in advance procuring complementary food, and the women and children walk behind. Usually, larger bands split into several subgroups to travel, a practice that is more frequent during the dry season.[1]

Residential moves follow time periods shorter than a yearly cycle, such that in one year the same zones of the territory are traveled through several times. This is also a logical consequence of the relationship between the high number of annual movements within a relatively small band territory. Obviously, there is a greater generic redundancy in the bands with the smallest territories. Taking the physiographic units described in Chapter 1 as a basis, we observe that the Nukak construct several camps per year in each such unit during the two seasons. The only notable exception is the absence of camps constructed in the current floodplain of the Guaviare River in either season, although this zone is visited during daily foraging trips in the dry season. Although there is no fixed pattern of displacements common to all the bands, and each band moves in a different fashion within its own territory, it has been possible to identify some recurring circuits. The *Wayari-munu* bands move along the watersheds (EE4, EE5, and AS3; see Figure 1.6, p. 50), following paths with a north-south orientation. When they arrive at the zone of high and medium terraces (SN2-SN3-SN4), east-west movements are made, traveling parallel to the floodplain of the Guaviare River. The *Meu-munu* bands display two patterns. The band south of Barranco Colorado has

Figure 6.2   Woman during a residential move following a well-defined path

a north-south displacement pattern, covering the area between the high terraces (SN2) and the ridged structural plains (EE3 and EE4). The other two
Meu-munu bands do not have direct access to the floodplain of the Guaviare
River owing to the existence of Sabana de la Fuga and the intense colonization
of the area. Therefore, they maintain a relocation pattern the principal paths
of which have a north-south orientation. The *Muhabe-munu* bands occupy
the area from the structural plains (EE1, EE2, EE3, EE4, and EE5) to the
current floodplain of the Inírida River, with principle paths of a southeast-
northwest orientation.

The decision to leave the camp is usually taken the day before the abandonment or early in the morning on the same day and is based on myriad factors.
Some are expressed orally, such as, "we go where there is a lot of honey" or
"we leave because it smells bad," and so forth. However, my understanding
of the complete set of factors that are taken into account when making the
decision to abandon camp was far from complete during my fieldwork and
subsequently. This is due not only to my limited knowledge of the language
but also to the fact that not all the reasons were verbalized—some were so
obvious to the Nukak that they did not need to mention them. Among the
recorded causes for residential movements are food procurement, the death
of a person, the sanitary conditions of the camp, and relocations to take part

in a *baak-wáadn*. Also, when a person is sick or has been involved in an accident the entire band may move to Laguna Pavón 2 in search of medical assistance. In recent times, the desire to camp close to individual *colonos* or villages seems to be a growing reason for such movements.[2]

LOGISTICAL MOBILITY

In contrast to their high residential mobility, the Nukak have a limited logistical mobility. I consider logistical mobility to be the occasions when most members of a band remain in camp (or move within the band territory) while a small group, usually comprising adult males, travels considerable distances beyond the regional group territory, covering large stretches each day (more than 10 km) and setting up camps that are occupied for only a few nights. One of the clearest examples of this type of trip are the journeys to the Cerro de las Cerbatanas (Blowpipe Hills, *e*) that men periodically make in order to collect high quality canes (*ú-baká*) for the subsequent manufacture of blowpipes (see Chapter 7). Tens of kilometers are covered on these trips, especially by the *Meu-munu* and *Tákayu-munu* bands. When they approach the highlands they must "blaze a trail," because there are no more paths. These trips are usually made by most of the adult men in a band, who are at times accompanied by youths and adults of neighboring bands. Once in the hills, they cut the canes (not true canes: they are actually stems of the pulse *Iriartella setigera*), and each person takes around 10 to 15 (although one informant mentioned only 5) that are then divided among relatives or stored unprocessed to be made into blowpipes at a later date (see Chapter 7). I did not participate in these trips,[3] but the distance can be estimated based on the location of the band territory. The more distant bands, in the western part of the territory, have to travel as far as 150 km, whereas the eastern bands need walk only a few kilometers (less than 10 km); at times the entire group would approach the Cerro de las Cerbatanas, making the men's trip a great deal shorter. It would appear that the logistical groups move along well-established paths, one of which seems to follow the watershed, passing close to Laguna Pavón 2. Until a few years ago, groups of men also journeyed to the hills south of the Inírida River, between Kinikiarí and Cerro Cocuy, in search of *ú-baká* (Kenneth Conduff pers. com. 1995). The trip to collect canes is framed by the social and ideological structure. Men bring back canes from each trip for relatives, and in this way reinforce and maintain the system of reciprocity. The trip is also a "male journey," where young men complete requirements to become proper Nukak adults.

On only one occasion did we participate in a logistical excursion during our fieldwork, during which time we stayed one night away from the camp, 12.03 km to the southeast. The group, comprising all the young and adult men from a coresident group (four in total), had originally planned to visit a chontaduro orchard and harvest fruit. But, at 2.30 p.m., after traveling 11.24 km, they hunted a caiman (cachirre, possibly *Paleosuchius trigonatus*) close to the chontaduro orchards (only 0.77 km ahead). They then decided to take the entire animal to the orchard to be butchered (see description in Chapter 9), grilled, and eaten. We arrived at the chontaduro orchard at 3.05 p.m., where they unhurriedly processed and cooked the caiman over the course of the next 2 hours and 20 minutes. It was consumed at 5.30 p.m., accompanied with recently harvested chontaduro fruit. Afterward we gathered and positioned platanillo leaves, on top of which we spent the night. Early the following day the remainder of the caiman was eaten. The group left the spot at 7.20 a.m., arriving back at the residential camp at 11.25 a.m.

In recent years some men have traveled more frequently beyond the borders of the regional territories to find wives as a consequence of the epidemics of the late 1980s (see Chapter 1) and of the reduction in number of potential partners. This has also become an important causal factor for movements within this territorial dimension. Also linked to the pressure caused by the colonization is the curiosity to see some of the *colono* villages, such as Tomachipán, Guanapalo, Caño Seco, and La Charrasquera, as well as the need for medical attention and the search for industrial objects, all of which have resulted in certain individuals traveling great distances. In some cases these journeys go beyond current Nukak territory, extending as far as San José del Guaviare and other population centers on the road to Calamar. Finally, Laguna Pavón 2 has been an important center of attraction. There are bands, families, and small groups who pass through the territories of other regional groups in order to seek medical attention at this settlement, or to exchange products.

DAILY FORAGING TRIPS

The Nukak make daily excursions in the vicinity of the residential camps in order to obtain food, raw material, and information on a variety of subjects (ranging from the location and the condition of resources to the state of specific persons or bands). The minimum number of people involved in these trips is one, and the maximum registered during our fieldwork was eleven (Tables 6.2 and 6.3). However, the groups frequently split up during the foraging trips for some of the time, or they meet another member, or members, of the band foraging nearby, and they might return together to the camp.

Table 6.2 Daily Foraging Trips during the Rainy Season

Date	Members	Departure Time	Arrival Time	Duration in Hours	Distance Traveled
31-8-92	2 Am	2.00 p.m.	4.27 p.m.	2:27	4.24 km
1-9-92	4 Am, 2 Ma, 3 Aw	7.10 a.m.	1.30 p.m.	6:20	7.74 km
2-9-92	1 Am	8.15 a.m.	12.39 p.m.	4:24	5.12 km
3-9-92	1 Am	7.49 a.m.	3.4 p.m.	7:56	16.20 km
4-9-92	1 Am	8.00 a.m.	1.39 p.m.	5:39	8.79 km
5-9-92	6 Am, 2 Ma, 3 Aw	8.10 a.m.	4.53 p.m.	8:43	8.96 km
6-9-92	1 Am	1.20 p.m.	5.00 p.m.	3:40	4.30 km
7-9-92	3 Aw, 2 Am, 1 Ma, 1 Fa, 1 b	9.00 a.m.	1.55 p.m.	4:55	5.70 km
9-9-92	1 Am	7.35 a.m.	11.02 a.m.	3:27	4.23 km
11-9-92	1 Am	6.50 a.m.	4.47 p.m.	9:57	15.64 km
12-9-92	1 Am, 1 Ma	7.15 a.m.	4.00 p.m.	8:45	15.30 km
15-9-92	1 Am, 1 Ma	9.43 a.m.	6.00 p.m.	8:17	8.40 km
16-9-92	3 Aw, 2 Fa, 1Am, 1 b, 1 g	8.10 a.m.	1.05 p.m.	4:55	3.50 km
17-9-92	1 Am, 1 Ma	9.18 a.m.	4.15 p.m.	6:57	8.20 km

Key: Am = adult man; Ma = male adolescent; Aw = adult woman; Fa = female adolescent; b = boy; g = girl

Table 6.3 Daily Foraging Trips during the Dry Season

Date	Members	Departure Time	Arrival Time	Duration in Hours	Distance Traveled
22-1-94	2 Am, 2 Aw, 1 Fa	7.35 a.m.	4:54 p.m.	9:19	11.09 km
25-1-94	3 Am	8.37 a.m.	1:35 p.m.	4:58	14.56 km
27-1-94	1 Am, 2 Aw	9.30 a.m.	4:36 p.m.	7:04	7.50 km
28-1-94	1 Am	1.00 p.m.	4:29 p.m.	3:29	5.31 km
30-1-94	2 Am	8.05 a.m.	2:19 p.m.	6:14	8.90 km
31-1-94	1 Am, 1 Fa, 1 b	8.20 a.m.	2:02 p.m.	5:42	5.92 km
2-2-94	1 Am	12.24 p.m.	2:04 p.m.	1:40	3.06 km
3-2-94	1 Am	8.39 a.m.	2:30 p.m.	5:51	9.53 km
4-2-94	1 Am, 1 Aw	8.11 a.m.	10:30 a.m.	2:19	2.18 km
4-2-94	1 Am, 1 Ma	12.06 p.m.	4:30 p.m.	4:24	10.70 km
29-1-96	3 Am	7.54 a.m.	3:40 p.m.	7:46	8.32 km
30-1-96	2 Am	8.40 a.m.	6:40 p.m.	10:00	13.10 km
31-1-96	2 Am	9.16 a.m.	6:50 p.m.	9:34	9.20 km

Key: Am = adult man; Ma = male adolescent; Aw = adult woman; Fa = female adolescent; b = boy

Daily foraging parties vary based on the composition of the parties and their respective objectives. I formed the impression that when a person or a group leaves the camp on a foraging trip, rather than having a single object-ive (that is, to hunt, collect honey, gather fruits, and so on) they have several options, related to the area in which they will be trekking, the season, their needs, and the social setting. The only exception is the communal hunting of peccary (see Chapter 9); in the recorded cases the peccary herd had already been located, and the group organized the party with a well-known and spe-cific purpose, although, as will be shown, not an exclusive one.

It has been difficult to estimate the minimum distance traveled on the daily foraging trips. Therefore, although there is a time-distance continuum, in the present study I have set an arbitrary radius of 1 km to separate two different kinds of off-camp daily activity. I consider the "immediate surroundings of the camp" to be the area within a 1-km radius from the residential site. Within this area, camp inhabitants frequently gather fruit, honey, and other bee-hive products, go fishing, collect leaves for the roof or for making bags, obtain bark and vines for cord, and, occasionally, if there is an orchard or a chagra nearby, they might also collect cultivated products. These activities are per-formed daily and with no specific planning or organization. Basically, the person or persons leave the camp for a short while carrying one or two re-quired tools, usually only a machete or an ax, and return soon after with something (Figure 6.3). Given the dynamic, the frequency, and the contingent nature of these short displacements they were difficult to record in detail.

Beyond the exploitation of the residential camp surroundings, daily foraging trips maintained a similar pattern in both seasons: $\bar{x} = 8.30$ km (round-trip) in the rainy season ($n = 14$; min = 3.50 km; max = 16.20 km) and $\bar{x} = 8.41$ km (round-trip) in the dry season ($n = 13$; min = 2.19 km; max = 14.56 km). The annual average is therefore 8.36 km ($n = 27$). An important observation is that the distance covered in the foraging trips does not increase in relation to the occupation time of the camp, as can be seen from Tables 6.2 and 6.3, based on a random sample of daily foraging trips. Neither is there an observ-able drop in the foraging returns as the occupation of the camp proceeds (see Tables 8.14 to 8.17, Chapter 8).

Tables 6.2 and 6.3 provide only a rough idea based on two variables (distance and time), as well as the composition of the party, of the structure of daily foraging trips. Nonetheless, a great range of variation can be distinguished in these trips. In Appendix I, detailed records are displayed of a random sample of daily foraging trips. This sample includes a variety of possible combinations in terms of member composition, equipment carried, distance covered, and

Figure 6.3 Man and boy leaving the camp for a short foraging trip in the immediate vicinity

results obtained. It gives a good idea of the complexity of each trip and the wide range of variation in this kind of daily excursion. Moreover, an imprecise "ritual time" must be included in the calculations to obtain a realistic view of the many activities carried out on each trip. By "ritual time" I mean the time dedicated to performing a ritual that generally has the objective of negotiating with the spirit-ancestors for the use of certain resources. This ritual, consisting of a series of formulas that all the adults know, usually develops around nonacoustic communication, and it is, therefore, technically impossible to measure its duration, start, and finish (Figure 6.4). By virtue of these difficulties, rituals have not been included in the list of foraging trips, although they are embedded in many of the activities recorded.

Figure 6.4 Man performing a nonacoustic ritual sitting in front of the monkey he has just hunted

Another activity which is not registered in this sample, but which appears to be common during the daily foraging trips, is sexual relations between partners. As has been noted (Chapter 4), Nukak camps lack privacy, and although sexual activity takes place as silently as possible, it is frowned on. Couples habitually take advantage of the daily foraging trips to have times of intimacy (Figure 6.5). However, there are no trips undertaken specifically for this purpose; rather, sexual relations take place in between the execution of other activities. Obviously, when couples planned to have sex during a particular excursion, they avoided our company. If we followed them regardless (obviously through ignorance), we would find ourselves abandoned in the middle of a trail, far from the camp, and with little idea of the way back.

Figure 6.5 Young couple in a moment of intimacy during a daily foraging trip; note the pet monkey on the woman's shoulders.

The set of daily foraging trips displayed in Appendix I illustrates the following issues.

1. The vast majority of daily foraging trips are multipurpose. For this reason, the equipment carried is usually appropriate for facing the various potential options (Figure 6.6). Even when the proper tool is not available, the party members may try to obtain a particular resource using an expedient tool or a tool designed for another purpose if the occasion presents itself. Examples include hunting a caiman with a sharpened stick, throwing a

Figure 6.6 Man during a daily foraging trip during the dry season; note that he is carrying a blowpipe, darts, a machete, and an ax.

machete in an attempt to kill a bird, breaking a honeycomb with a stick and collecting the honey in an expedient leaf bag, and so on.

2. The composition of the foraging trip is fluid and might change during the expedition owing to fission or annexation (Figure 6.7). Also, people who start the trip together might return together but spend most of the journey apart. Daily foraging trips include $\bar{x} = 3$ participants ($n = 27$; min = 1; max = 11).

3. On some trips time is dedicated to the education of children in the many activities involved in hunting, fishing, and collecting.

4. During the excursions, activities are carried out which do not have an immediate result. That is, there is no measurable return on arrival back at camp, but these activities nonetheless form part of a sophisticated mechanism of resource management. Examples include the cutting of palms to grow palm grubs (*mojojoy*), visiting areas with concentrations of certain trees to ascertain if their fruit is ripe, visiting abandoned camps to monitor the regeneration of plants, checking the location and condition of honeycombs in order to decide whether to relocate the camp, and so on.

5. A further activity incorporated into the trips is collecting artifacts left in protected places for future use. These may be in abandoned camps, beside a path, or hidden almost anywhere. Artifacts may also be retrieved for relatives who had left them hidden in specific locations.

Figure 6.7   Group of Nukak eating honey during a daily foraging trip

Finally, according to our data there is a tendency for agnates to accompany one another on the daily foraging trips. This broadly coincides with the observations of Cabrera, Franky, and Mahecha (1999:149), who recorded the following percentages for group composition: 51.85% agnates; 39.95% agnates and affines; and 8.79% affines.

FINAL CONSIDERATIONS

The several types of mobility, the multipurpose nature of the daily foraging trips, and the articulation of these aspects with the several dimensions of territory highlight the complexity of issues such as mobility and territoriality in hunter-gatherer societies. This fact demonstrates the difficulties of interpreting the various kinds of mobility through the archaeological record, and it constitutes a warning in regard to the apparently easy and universal correlations made between environment and type of mobility. Although the latter tendency allows some trends to be identified, this particular case study poses questions that must be examined from an alternative perspective.

In terms of territory, the dominant idea among the Nukak is not related to defensibility and ownership but to use, construction, and perception. For the Nukak, territory is much more than the physical reality of the portion of land they occupy or the place where resources to live by can be found. The territory, in any one of its five dimensions, is perceived as something tangible, real, and interconnected. It is also the result of the activity of *Mauroïjumját* and of powerful spirits-ancestors, usually referred to as having lived only a few generations ago, who transformed the texture of the Earth's surface. They brought trees, planted chontaduro palms, created animals, and made rain and storms. The action of the spirit-ancestors has not ceased, since they are still continuously modifying the landscape; this action is identifiable, for example, in the *nemep wopyii* (places recently modified by the *nemep*).

Another concept that is challenged based on this study is that of "defensibility" an idea closely associated with that of exclusivity. "Territorial defensibility" seems to be a notion more appropriate to understanding the behavior of certain animal communities (Eisenberg 1981), or the manner in which nation-states secure their boundaries, than to comprehending attitudes toward territory among foragers. As has been shown, there are basically no territorial conflicts among the Nukak, and each band freely uses an area of the rainforest with diffuse limits. Presently, there are areas that are rarely visited and many areas that are unoccupied.[4] As far as relations with neighboring indigenous groups is concerned (for example, the Puinave and the Kurripaco), territory is not a cause of conflict, because each group knows its traditional use, and consequently there have been no invasions of Nukak territory. Accordingly, neither land nor resources appears to be an issue, and, therefore, there is no need to "defend" a particular space. One would expect this type of attitude to be present among other hunter-gatherers with similar demographic profiles and resource availability. This is also the case among the Alto Parucito Hotï and neighboring groups (the Yabarana and the Piaroa), who respect the ancestral territory of this former ethnic group without the Hotï having to take a defensive stance, at least in practical or material terms. Whatever the case, the need for a territory to be defendable, both for past and present foragers, must be shown in each particular instance and not considered as a universal *sine qua non* condition for all such populations.

It could be argued that the low population density of the Nukak, whether recent or long term, prevents the appearance of territorial behavior based on "defensibility." However, this does not appear to be the case. In this instance the right to utilize a space is not based on the capacity to defend it but rather on the capacity to (a) construct it, (b) know and use it, and, finally, (c) perceive it. To "construct it" refers to the fact that the present landscape is the result of human action, of both immediate ancestors of the group in question and long-term anthropic activity from the time humans first settled the place.

This has not only modified the resource structure, that is, the physical reality of the land, but has also changed the texture of the landscape. It has been inundated with meanings, charged with symbolism, and sacralized. "Knowing it" refers to inhabiting a space and using its resources, for which one must have a detailed knowledge of its structures and how to exploit them. This is achieved only through daily occupation over a long period of time, most probably several generations. Hence, a band's territory is not merely an area that they exploit but rather it is an area that they know how to exploit. Although resembling a play on words, this has profound implications. It is relatively easy to arrive somewhere and use the resources that are available, but it is not so easy to use this same space over the long term with a high level of efficiency without negatively affecting its productivity. This is achieved only through a detailed knowledge of the resources available in time and space, which in turn is obtainable only through the prolonged, daily occupation of a particular area. The final factor is perception. This is significant because whether or not resources are exploited and visits to particular areas are rare, most non-western groups—hunter-gatherers and villagers, nonhierarchical and ranked societies—perceive their land as possessing sacred connotations and symbolic significance (Ärhem 1998; Myers 1986; Reichel-Dussan 1989). In other words, the "mental territorial map" of these societies includes areas where resources have to be used in specific ways and following ritual formulas, whereas other areas will not be exploited, occupied, or visited regularly. Such areas, which have strong mythical and cosmological significance, though they are not regularly occupied, are equally perceived as being part of their territory. A clear-cut example of this in the Amazon is the *Cerro de los Hombres Chiquitos* ("Hill of the Little Men"), a place perceived as theirs by various riverine villager groups in the Apapopris area, each one bestowing a different meaning on the land and "using" it distinctively (Van der Hammen 1992).

Therefore, I propose that territorial defense is by no means a universal condition through which hunter-gatherers maintain their territory, and nor is it the most relevant characteristic of their territorial behavior. Undoubtedly, the multiple dimensions of territory are difficult to grasp through the archaeological record, but this does not justify their reduction to one dimension—that of band territory—and the focus on one factor—defensibility or control—if we are fully to understand the complexity of territorial behavior and landscape perception of forager societies (see also discussion in Ingold 1996b).

In regard to residential mobility, the Nukak appear to be at the extreme for lowland South American hunter-gatherer groups, and for the rest of the world. Nonetheless, early indicators of other Makú also suggest high frequencies of residential movements. Several authors in the nineteenth and early twentieth centuries signaled the nomadic nature of the Makú. For example, McGovern (1927:148) wrote, "They were without any settled abode, wandering in small bands through the forest, never staying longer than a few days in any one place." However, in the early twentieth century differences began to be noted; the mobility of the Makú appears to have lessened, and at this time, the mobility of the other Makú began to become differentiated from that of the Nukak. During Reid's study of the Hupdu (1974–1976) residential mobility was limited and groups remained in the same camp for two to six years. Logistical mobility occurred when hunting areas were more than a half day's distance from the camp, in which case several or all the Hupdu families who lived in the same camp moved into the forest to hunt, fish, and gather fruit (Reid 1979). On average, the families made this trip once a month; the duration varied between 2 and 30 days. During these foraging trips the Hupdu constructed small camps of lean-to shelters (similar to the residential camps of the Nukak) that they occupied for three to five days. These relocations were fairly frequent and allowed the Hupdu to exploit distant and diverse areas. Reid calculated that each family spent around 70 days per year in the rainforest on these foraging trips, and that adult men and adolescents may have participated for as many as 100 days. The foraging trips inside the radius exploited from the camp occurred almost daily: ". . . they go out from their settlements to distances of up to three hours walk away, returning from a different route" (Reid 1979:30). In order not to exhaust the hunting areas close to the camp it was important that the Hupdu return to the same area only after two weeks had passed. During the 1960s, the Kakwa appear to have had a mobility pattern similar to that of the Hupdu, although fewer details are available. Silverwood-Cope (1990:74) estimated that the Kakwa in the area of the tributaries of the Macú-Paraná ". . . live only a few years—sometimes months—in each village." Furthermore, based on the account of a 40- to 45-year-old adult, he calculated that this individual had moved semipermanent residences approximately every five years. Obviously, the Kakwa spend an indeterminate period of the year away from their camps on foraging trips, during which time they also construct lean-to dwellings similar to the Nukak rainy-season residential camps. Silverwood-Cope did not specify the time they spend in the rainforest hunting and gathering. According to the data recorded for them, the Yuhup and Nadöb pattern would appear to be closer to that of the Kakwa and the Hupdu than the Nukak. In other words, they spend a large part of their time in residential camps, entering the forest only on logistical trips during which time they construct temporary camps that they inhabit for a few days at a time (Münzel 1969–1972; Pozzobon 1983). In this sense, the mobility pattern of these Makú is similar to the Hotï (see Politis & Jaimes Ms; Storrie 1999; Zent & Zent 2002).

Following the "forager-collector" model proposed by Binford (1980), which is extremely popular in the archaeology of hunter-gatherers, we see that the Nukak must be positioned close to the first pole. They certainly move consumers to food resources by setting up new residential camps and thus map onto an area's resource locations. Foragers have high residential mobility and very limited logistical mobility. This is the case among the Nukak for whom the adjustment to the spatial and seasonal variation in the availability of resources is made by changing residential mobility, while logistical mobility and daily foraging trips remain the same year-round in terms of frequency, distance, and periodicity. The difference in residential mobility between seasons is not characterized by the area covered by excursions but rather by the frequency of moves and the distances between camps. However, this does not explain the high mobility rate, especially taking into account that residential moves are made and a new exploitation area (or "foraging radius," after Binford 1982:7–8) is occupied before an observable decline occurs in the available resources obtainable from the surrounding area (see Chapter 8) or an increase in the distance to find them.

A possible historical causal factor that should be taken into account—although there is not much information in this respect—is the relationship between present-day Nukak mobility and the practice of "slavery" to which the Makú were submitted for hundreds of years during the recent past.[5] Such an inquiry is complex for a number of reasons. First, as has been demonstrated, the Nukak have substantially different behavioral patterns to other Makú who live in a similar environment. As a result of the absence of long-term historical information on the former group, they can not be substituted for by the latter. Nonetheless, one suspects that the Nukak were exposed to the raids carried out by certain tribes, such as the Tukano and the Desana, to secure Makú as "slaves" or wives (McGovern 1927; Spruce 1908). This may have produced greater levels of mobility as a defensive strategy. Martius, writing in the early nineteenth century in this regard, made one of the clearest references. He wrote that the Japurá River Makú were mentioned by some Indians who were specialists in taking other Indians as slaves and that these raids profoundly modified their activities (Münzel 1969–1972:141). Nonetheless, the situation as related by nineteenth-century and early twentieth-century travelers does not seem to be adequately explained by the concept of slavery[6] but rather fits within that a sort of symbiosis (Jackson 1983). Consequently, the state of knowledge on the subject does not allow a judgment to be made of whether or not these raids were conducted on the Nukak in the past, and if they were, in what way mobility was affected.

In terms of environmental exploitation, mobility can be seen as a result of placing the residential camps close to certain resources when they are available and/or abundant. This means entering places during a certain time of the year when the availability of some food resources is at its highest and using them appropriately, then moving on to another area before having a negative impact on the sustainability of these resources. A schematic circuit of resource exploitation has been identified (see Chapter 8 and Cabrera, Franky, & Mahecha 1999). However, the Nukak abandon camp when many products are still abundant—from animals to wild fruit—that are not found further away, which therefore generates a negative investment cost-benefit energy balance. Tables 8.14 to 8.17 show that relocations to new areas are made even when food remains plentiful. Taking this into account, I argue that there are no obvious resource limitations that would prevent the Nukak from staying in their residential camps for longer periods of time. The causes for their high residential mobility must be sought elsewhere.

First, there is an economic derivative of high residential mobility, because it produces abundant abandoned camps that in turn became patches of edible plants throughout the territory. The Nukak construct a residential camp that, after being abandoned, is transformed into a type of "wild orchard," augmenting the resource potential of the area. This sophisticated settlement and mobility system is connected to the various layers of the rainforest, as the Nukak displace the lowest stratum of the rainforest ecosystem but leave the forest canopy intact. This is a sort of horizontal slip that creates patches without disturbing the natural stratification of the tropical rainforest. In the long term, residential camps are not established where there is a high concentration of resources, since the establishment and subsequent abandonment of these camps foment such concentrations.

Second, the Nukak relocate for social reasons, mainly to perform meeting rituals (baak waádn). This was recorded several times as bands moved quickly through the forest to establish a residential camp on the border of their territory in order to perform rituals in conjunction with a neighboring band.

Third, the Nukak periodically abandon a camp and move to a new area as a response to poor sanitary conditions. This happens especially during the dry season when a great deal of fish is consumed and discarded around the camps, or when the camps are close to the flood plain of the Guaviare River.

Fourth, on occasion the Nukak abandon a camp when a person dies or when there is fear of powerful and malevolent spirits in the surrounding area. Certain persons having nightmares can also influence the decision to move camp. Obviously, the death of a person does not occur often, although there was a significant peak during the early contact period (see Chapter 1), and as a consequence this factor has a low influence on annual mobility averages.

Fifth, it would appear that the Nukak frequently relocate for sociopsycological motives. In other words, they simply like to shift camps, regardless of a consideration (conscious or subconscious) of the high cost/low return energy balance produced by some of these moves. For them, camp relocations are general strategies for economic, social and ideational purposes, and they feel that this is a typical Nukak custom that is deeply engaged in their worldview. They simply enjoy this sort of continuous residential motion.

It would be extremely difficult to estimate the weight of each of these five main causal factors on the general system of residential mobility. At times, the performing of the *baak waádn* is the most significant factor. At other times, the fear of malevolent spirits or, in a third case, the desire for fish or honey is the cause. None of these factors operates in isolation, and all of them have the additional and permanent benefit of creating a "virtuous circle" of edible resource patches.

Logistical mobility does not seem to be significant in terms of food resources, as would be expected in groups with a significant forager component in their mobility strategy. The primary goals are the procurement of raw materials (canes and possibly stone in the recent past), the performing of a kind of "rite of passage" to adulthood, and the maintenance of the kinship system. Hence, the Nukak appear to be fairly different from the other Makú and hunter-gatherers for whom logistical mobility is often embedded in food-procuring forays (Binford 1982). Although, of course, hunting and gathering are carried out during Nukak trips to feed the participants.

Logistical expeditions and daily foraging trips are almost invisible in terms of archaeological remains. On the contrary, residential mobility leaves abundant traces, since the highest concentration and variety of material items are discarded in the residential camp. The only clear archaeological indicators of logistical trips are the small transient camps occupied for one night. Almost nothing seems to be left behind except a hearth and a little food debris. The other off-camp activities, both daily foraging trips and logistical journeys, also result in very little discarded material. Such items, when they occur, include darts or bits of darts in places where hunts have taken place; extremely occasionally the broken tip of a spear that was damaged during the hunting of peccary; a few fallen trees; and very little else. However, there are some important effects of Nukak behavior as far as archaeological interpretation is concerned. Most fruit with juicy pulp, such as the Moraceae (that is, *patataá* [*Helicostylis tomentosa*], *yedn* [*Perebea xanthochyma*], *yé* [*Maquira guianensis*], *bijnidé* [*Naucleopsis mello-barretoi*], *echawdi* [*Perebea guianensis*], and so on) and some Euphorbiaceae (that is, *chiíri* [*Hyeronima alchorneoides*]), are eaten unprocessed in the forest close to the tree and are not therefore transported to the residential camp. This means that their seeds usually remain around the tree, or are randomly dispersed by human feces. As such, archaeological visibility is low, and the possibility of recognizing the off-site consumption of fruits and seeds, even under good preservation conditions, is extremely low. On the contrary, most palm fruit (such as moriche, seje, *juiú, yaab butu, popere,* and so forth) and tree nuts (such as *guaná,* juansoco, platanillo, *koró-paanjat,* and so on) require some kind of processing and must be transported to the residential camp to be prepared for consumption (removal of the shell, boiling, grinding, and so forth). In the latter case, the seeds have a much higher chance of being discarded inside the camp and subsequently of becoming part of the garbage piles and incorporated into the process of augmenting the wild orchards. These species will have much greater archaeological visibility. Consequently, this example draws attention to human diet reconstruction based on plant remains of any kind from archaeological deposits, in as much as certain fruits and nuts would clearly be over represented. In this context, we would expect an under representation of fleshy fruit, maintaining the illusion of low plant use diversity during the formation of the archaeological deposit (see also King 1994:189).

The multipurpose nature of the daily foraging trips is not a characteristic exclusive to the Nukak. The Nadöb, for example, during their frequent trips into the forest combine several activities, including fruit collection, tracking animals, wood procurement, eating insects, and so on. Significantly, the men may take their sacred flutes with them (Münzel 1969–1972:153), which would further indicate that these tasks are embedded within ritual practices. The Hotï also provide another good example of the variety of tasks performed on foraging trips, some of which do not produce obvious benefit (Politis & Jaimes Ms; Storrie 1999).

The scarcity, or even absence, of products obtained on daily foraging trips may mislead an analysis based on the trade-off curve between energy expended and energy obtained. As we see, there are many results of foraging trips, not all of which are of an economic character or measurable in units of energy.

Cutting palms to promote the development of grubs and checking the regeneration of palms are examples of nonimmediate economic returns. Collecting a relative's blowpipe or obtaining information on a neighboring band by visiting their abandoned camp are activities that operate in the social plane. The time dedicated to a ritual for communicating with the spirit-ancestors is also a routine that cannot be represented in an energy equation and must be understood within the ideational sphere or cosmological framework. Finally, the pleasure of walking in the rainforest with relatives, of teaching how to hunt to a young son, and the desire for intimacy and sexual relations, are other psychological and emotional causes, the benefits of which are based on personal well-being.

These observations and interpretations highlight the difficulties involved in an archaeological examination of issues such as territory, territorial behavior, and the causal factors of mobility patterns, both logistical and residential. From my perspective the case presented here suggests that the reductionism of the functional-ecological model leaves aside important features of human behavior (see also Ingold 1996a). These models, which currently dominate the archaeological literature, do not capture the wide range of causal factors that affect territory and mobility in past and present foragers and must therefore be amplified or replaced by more inclusive and less biased ways of investigating hunter-gatherers.

Notes

1. Cabrera, Franky, and Mahecha (1999:109) mention that during their fieldwork the western and eastern "local groups" (referring to eight distinct groups) "moved through the forest to the greatest extent." However, they provide figures that indicate that only 58.70% and 59.49%, respectively, of the trips were made within the rainforest. Contradictorily, they stated that 40.64% and 7.56% of journeys were made outside the forest, within colonized areas. Apart from the incongruence of these figures (since the latter two do not add up to 100%, and no explanation is given for the missing 34%), they are significantly different from the data recorded during my fieldwork. With the exceptions of the band contacted in the savannah in 1990 and the band that settled south of Barranco Colorado, all other coresident groups made their residential camps and movements within the rainforest.
2. One of the *Meu munu* bands that displayed a traditional pattern of mobility during fieldwork in 1991 and 1992 had by 1994 settled on the edge of a *colono* plantation. They had cleared their chagra and had spent months in the same spot.
3. The only non-Nukak person I know who has been on one of these trips was Kenneth Conduff.

4. It is not clear if these unoccupied areas are the product of recent demographic decline or are simply the consequence of the traditional Nukak mode of land occupation.

5. There are several antecedents concerning slavery. In earlier periods, the Tukano sold the Makú as slaves to the whites. A Franciscan Missionaries document from 1892 prohibited forever the capture and sale of Makú to the whites by the Tukano from the upper river Tiquie (Giacone 1955:3).

6. McGovern (1927), for example, was surprised that the Makú, who could survive perfectly well in the rainforest, much better than their supposed masters, did not escape. He could not understand why they remained in this state of involuntary servitude.

Chapter 7

TRADITIONAL TECHNOLOGY

Several decades ago Malinowski (1935:460) dismissed "the purely technological enthusiasm" of ethnography, continuing a trend of undermining the significance of the study of material culture and technology and affording it a peripheral status within anthropology (Pfaffenberger 1992:492). As a consequence, contemporary studies in non-Western societies on the subject are rather limited, leaving archaeologists lacking a potentially powerful source of analogical reasoning. Following on from the discussion in Chapter 2, the result has been that archaeologists have begun to record this type of information for themselves, establishing the basis for the development of the subdiscipline of ethnoarchaeology.

For the sake of clarity, in this book I use the classic definition of technology to differentiate it from material culture. Hence, technology is seen as an activity or process, whereas artifacts are the products of that process. Material culture is consequently an outcome of technology and should not be considered as equivalent (Spier 1970:2–14). In his foundational paper on the topic Binford (1962) also warned against equating technology with material culture.

In anthropology and archaeology there has been growing recognition that objects are not merely the simple and submissive mirror images of human actions, that they play a role in shaping and activating the cultural and social relations within which they are embedded (Appadurai 1986; Hodder 1986; Tilley 1999). Several recent books and papers have unpacked the concept of technology (Dobres 2000; Ingold 2000; Lemonnier 1993; Pfaffenberger 1992), shedding new light on the complexity of the processes of production, use, and discard of artifacts. Material culture has recently been analyzed as "solid metaphor," an approach in which the idea that objects "work to link different cultural domains and construct meaning relates first of all to their internal qualities, their shape, structure, color, texture, and form" (Tilley 1999:263). In essence, these new studies depart from the dominant technocentric view of material culture that had stressed its practicality, instrumentality, and rationality. Alternative views now consider the evolution of techniques as a process of objectification and externalization, rather than a process leading toward increased complexity, as was more commonly understood to be the case (Ingold 2000:321). This same point was made some time ago by Marx, who discussed the notion of objectification as a process through which material culture becomes an active component in social relations (McGuire 1992:103). Basically, the clear-cut distinction between the domains of technical and social phenomena has been challenged, and artifacts are being analyzed as polysemic and multifunctional objects that operate simultaneously in several different dimensions.

Studies of technology in the archaeology of hunter-gatherers have been, and still are, heavily dominated by what is known as the "Standard View of technology" (Pfaffenberger 1992:495–96), which argues for the preeminence and almost exclusive dominance of the utilitarian dimension of material culture. This view also highlights the fact that contemporary approaches to prehistoric technology are based on a modern, technocentric vision of the world. Thus the focus has shifted more recently to an attempt to understand nonindustrial technology in its own terms (Dobres 2000).

From a processual perspective, which is closely associated with the "Standard View," technology has been understood as comprising the assemblage of artifacts that a society produces to resolve distinct types of problems (Fitzhugh 2001; Nelson 1992; Schiffer & Skibo 1987; Shott 1989; Torrence 1983, 1989). From this position, artifacts are not considered as an end in themselves but rather are understood to be produced within the context of a broader strategy that human beings design with the object of confronting their social and physical environments. The problems that a society must resolve through the production of technology are diverse but essentially linked to survival, both in terms of food procurement and the development of protection from climatic agents. Among the problems are "obstacles to achieving maximum return on investments of time and energy [. . .] that are addressed by 'rational strategies for problem solving' (Binford 1978a:453) within a given context" (Nelson 1992:60). In relation to subsistence, technology is one of the multiple strategies used to increase access to resources in terms of their time-space distribution and to reduce the risks of accessing them (Torrence 1989:58). According to this view, technology and technological organization are seen as receptive to environmental conditions, including "resource predictability, distribution, periodicity, productivity, mobility [. . .;], size, and patchiness of resource areas [. . .] and potential hazards" (Nelson 1992:59–60). In most variants of processual archaeology technology is defined almost exclusively by artifacts and their employment in the utilitarian dimension (Bousman 1993). Analytical efforts are addressed toward measuring and discovering levels of efficiency in attaining energy from natural resources.

A step toward recognizing the multidimensional condition of material culture was taken in the early work of Binford (1962). In the classic article, "Archaeology as Anthropology" (1962), he initially established a differentiation in the primary functional context of objects, proposing the existence of three types of objects: technoeconomic, sociotechnic, and ideotechnic. At the time this undoubtedly opened up a new and stimulating field of inquiry. Nonetheless, the model brought with it certain problems that persist in the archaeology of hunter-gatherers. First, although Binford was explicit that these were primary functional contexts (that is, not exclusive ones), his model atomized functions that are essentially coexistent and difficult to understand in isolation. The category of "primary functional context" was in some ways considered by default as the only, or principal, dimension of use. Second, Binford considered the variability in the technoeconomic components of archaeological assemblages as fundamentally explicable within an ecological frame of reference. Seen in context, this has lead to a form of ecological functionalism in the interpretation of hunter-gatherer material culture.

A second dimension of technology is the social. In archaeology an early discussion of this dimension was also put forth by Binford (1962), who argued that artifacts operate on two dimensions. The first was instrumental, linked to "utilitarian" function, and the second was related to symbolism and social meaning. Subsequent studies have refined this idea and expanded the understanding of material culture as symbolic in various directions (Hodder 1982, 1986; Wiessner 1990; Wobst 1977). As such, material culture has been addressed from the matrix of social relations, as well as being seen as a means of asserting ethnic identity. According to Ingold, ". . . the 'correspondence' between technical forces and social relations is not external but internal, or in other words, the technical is one aspect of the social" (2000:318). From this perspective, material culture is fundamentally conceived of as a "language," a medium loaded with coded information embedded in a symbolic framework operating within the social domain (Pfaffenberger 1992:505) a view that has recently been developed by Schiffer (1999). Objects have become increasingly disembedded from social relations in the modern world, which has created the current separation between technology and society (Ingold 2000:322). This has lead to a strong bias in understanding nonindustrial technologies. For hunter-gatherers studies the example presented and discussed by Gould (1980) of what he calls the "righteous rocks" is revealing. He clearly demonstrates that Australian Aborigines went to extraordinary lengths to obtain good quality stones for reasons more closely linked to the socioideational realm than to more ordinary considerations such us flaking or edge-holding properties.

The third dimension is the ideational. It has been referred to also as the "ritual dimension of technical activity" (Pfaffenberger 1992:501). It is the least explored within archaeology and anthropology and is almost absent in hunter-gatherer studies (see Brumm 2004; Gould 1980; Ridington 1982; Taçon 2004 for exceptions). According to the Standard View, and to almost all definitions (Chatters 1986:352), technology is considered to be an *affective act*, as opposed to an ideational one (Pfaffenberger 1992:501). Spier (1970:2) makes a clear and explicit statement in this respect by keeping all "magico-religious means" out of his definition of "technology." This view partially originated in the desacralization and alienation of material culture by modern Western rationality. However, as ethnographic studies in nonindustrial societies show, artifacts and the techniques involved in their production and use are embedded in the ideational order (among many examples see Boivin 2004; Hodder 1982; Pineda Camacho 1974; Ridington 1982). In such societies, technology is indissoluble from "ideas of spiritual or ancestral involvement in the production process" (Tilley 1999:57). Material culture acts within this sphere in two basic and related ways. On the one hand, some artifacts are "connectors" between different cosmological levels; because of their inherent nature they are vehicles of communication with the supernatural. The case of the "righteous rock" is a clear example. Such stones have a totemic character through which they relate the members of patrilineal cult-lodges with places where important mythical and sacred events took place (Gould 1980).

Another example is the stone axes of the Andokes of the Colombian Amazon. Many of these axes were obtained by the Indians through the excavation of archaeological sites, through complex rituals that connected the ancestors with the living, and in some form they were transformed into transgenerational objects (Pineda Camacho 1974). However, artifacts may share some sort of "living essence" with human and nonhuman beings; in a sense, they can be said to have "souls" (see also Boivin 2004). I am not referring exclusively to what have been called "sacred objects," whose primary or only function is to take part in ritual or other means of interaction with the supernatural. These objects were characterized by Binford (1962:219) as "such items as figures of deities, clan symbols or symbols of natural agencies." On the contrary, I include within this category the array of everyday artifacts that have an apparent primary function in the instrumental or social level but that simultaneously and inherently act within the ideational order.

Needless to say, these three dimensions operate concurrently and are not easy to separate, even for analytical purposes. Nevertheless, the instrumental and the social are usually more evident and less problematic, whereas the ideational is more difficult to grasp and understand from the perspective of Western rationality. At the same time it is also clear that not *every* artifact in *every* society operates simultaneously in the three dimensions. What must be understood is not so much the operation and the function of specific objects, as if they were isolated entities, but the socio-ideo-technical domain of technology as a whole. In Amazonian societies some objects are only instruments for specific, mundane purposes with little social consequence attached to them; they possess neither a "soul" nor a spiritual essence. However, they do belong to a cosmologically organized system that intersects the instrumental, the social, and the ideational. If understanding the several layers of meaning of material culture is the objective of study, then objects must be approached with their status as part of this system in mind.

Based on the preceding considerations, in this chapter I focus on the analysis of traditional Nukak technology, discussing the three dimensions within which it operates. However, I approach the following description from the instrumental plane, leaving aside the other two for a separate section. As such, I concentrate on three formal axes: manufacture, morphology, and use. Subsequently, I discuss how Nukak artifacts operate within the social and the ideological spheres, examining the symbolic and sacred elements involved.

I begin by discussing how Western items have been incorporated into the Nukak material culture repertoire. Then, I analyze the technology that is primarily linked to subsistence activities. To such ends, the corpus of Nukak tools has been classified into the following categories: (1) hunting and fishing weapons; (2) elements used in the gathering of both plant products and insects; (3) artifacts used in food preparation; (4) expedient objects utilized in transportation and food storage. In addition to this group of items, there is a series of tools that are important to Nukak life but are not related to subsistence. This group includes furnishings and accessories, which will also be described in this chapter. Other relevant technology related to architecture was discussed in Chapter 4.

THE NUKAK AND THE ADOPTION OF WESTERN TECHNOLOGY

Until only a few decades ago, the Nukak were almost certainly technologically self-sufficient, insofar as they supplied themselves with all necessary objects without having to resort to foreign elements. However, in recent years they have incorporated metal tools, primarily axes, machetes, and pots. In some bands this incorporation appears to have occurred prior to contact with the New Tribes missionaries, who reported that during their first encounters with the northeastern bands they observed metal axes and machetes in very poor condition (Kenneth Conduff, pers. comm.:1994). However, Cabrera, Franky, and Mahecha (1994:172) argue that the Missionaries were responsible for introducing these items into Nukak culture. Until a few years ago, *guadua* (bamboo cane) knives and stone axes were still used in the western bands. This information came from Monicaro, who remembered that during his infancy his parents still used such tools (approximately the 1980s). There is a further series of elements that have replaced traditional tools, including lighters, scissors, mirrors, fishhooks, and clothing. The generalized introduction of these tools has resulted in the progressive replacement of their traditional equivalents.

The incorporation of foreign technology does not derive from a process in which the Nukak are replacing their artifacts with Western ones in a mechanical and automatic fashion. The new objects are reinterpreted and inserted into specific social contexts and begin to play diverse roles within Nukak culture. As is discussed further on, the new elements are frequently incorporated owing to the prestige that they bestow on their owners, rather than simply because of the technological advantages they imply when compared to traditional artifacts. The traditional and foreign technologies articulate in a complex dynamic that operates simultaneously within the three dimensions of the meaning of material culture.

A further point to highlight is that the acquisition of foreign technology is not always irreversible. There are stages at which it is still possible to return to the use of traditional artifacts without much difficulty, even if these have been left aside for a long period of time. Several examples that were recorded are fairly representative. During the first field season, I saw several individuals from the *Meu-munu* bands making fire with two sticks (Figure 7.1). They possessed few Western artifacts and lacked matches. In subsequent years, the other bands that I visited, also *Meu-munu* and *Wayari-munu*, both possessed matches (which they kept carefully in plastic bags, and I did not observe them make fire with sticks. I assumed they had abandoned this practice and were losing the ability to make fire. Nonetheless, in 1996 in one of the *Wayari-munu* bands that had been in contact with Laguna Pavón 2 for several years, one of the adult men (in his mid-thirties) made fire with two sticks during several hunting and gathering trips (we were able to film the entire process in detail). In this example, the man neither made an attempt to obtain matches later on in Laguna Pavón 2, nor did he ask us for any. Confronted by the absence of matches, he simply returned to making fire the way he knew. In another case, an ill adult man was taken to Bogotá where he stayed in the house of members of the New Tribes Association for several weeks while recuperating, where I first met him. He was fully dressed, eating food that is commonly eaten in Bogotá, and skillfully manipulating various Western objects. A few weeks later I met him again, in Nukak territory. He was following a traditional way of life and behavior, and in fact was the only adult within his band who did not wear shorts or trousers, wearing instead his traditional breech cloth (*dú*). With these two examples I hope to have shown that the incorporation of

Figure 7.1   Man making fire in the traditional way with two sticks

Western items is not necessarily a one-way process, as long as traditional knowledge is preserved and the system of production of these objects, including the social and ideational aspects involved, is still active. In these circumstances, the Nukak, and presumably other hunter-gatherers as well, are able to return to the manufacture of those objects that had been replaced by Western technology.

TRADITIONAL TECHNOLOGY

Hunting and Fishing Weapons

The Blowpipe   The blowpipe (*ú*) is the principal hunting weapon and plays a vital role in Nukak subsistence. It is made from a single piece of cane, exclusively by adult and young men. There are two types of cane used in the manufacture of blowpipes. The first is called the *ú-baká* (translated as "the truth one"), and the second, the *ú-yé*. The former is actually the trunk of a palm tree (*Iriartella setigera*), 4 to 5 m high and 1.5 to 4 cm in diameter (Cárdenas & Politis 2000:57). These canes are a pale brown color, light to carry, and, according to the Nukak, "grow one at a time." These canes are obtained from the slopes of the Cerro de las Cerbatanas. In the past they were also brought from other hills to the south of the Inírida River[1] (see Chapter 6 and Figure 1.5, p. 48). It would appear that this species grows at a certain height above sea level, and so its distribution is restricted to these rocky heights. The properties that the Nukak refer to when explaining their preference for these trees are their length and lightness. The expeditions made to secure these canes cover a great distance, given that the Cerro de las Cerbatanas is on the eastern edge of Nukak territory. The men bring back less several canes each, which they hollow out and select during the return journey. Although they are used primarily for the manufacture of the individual's own blowpipe, they are frequently brought back for relatives who did not take part in the expedition.

The second type of cane, the *ú-yé*, is darker and heavier, obtained from a species found in several places within Nukak territory and unidentified in a previous ethnobotanical study (Cárdenas & Politis 2000). Even though easier to obtain than the *ú-baká*, it is less widely used owing to its inferior quality. Cabrera, Franky, and Mahecha (1994:196) refer to it as *u* or *tewpede*, identifying it as *Bactris monticola*, a plant whose fruit is also edible.

The blowpipe is the main hunting tool, accounting for most of the arboreal fauna that is procured, among which monkeys and birds found in the highest part of the canopy (above 20 to 30 m) are conspicuous (Figure 7.2). This weapon is used daily year round[2] and in all sectors of the territory. All adult and young men own their personal blowpipe. Much time is dedicated to the care of these, because they are essential for the acquisition of food and cannot be replaced as easily as other tools. Nukak men are constantly straightening them, cleaning them, and carrying out test shots for height and precision. If it is necessary to leave blowpipes stored somewhere (generally in the roofs of the winter camps), stoppers are fitted in the ends to prevent the intrusion

Figure 7.2   Man hunting a monkey with a blowpipe during a daily foraging trip

of insects. On special occasions they are painted red with achiote (*Bixa orellana*) or *ééro* (*Arribidaea chica*). From an early age boys practice and play with smaller, toy versions or use poor quality canes as expedient blowpipes (see Politis 1999 and Figure 5.4, p. 136).

The manufacture of blowpipes is an eminently masculine and individual process. One of the most complete accounts we have was recorded in July of 1991 in Band-1991b. On this occasion, Wuaú and other members of the band made blowpipes from a *ú-yé*. The details of the fabrication of Wuaú's blowpipe are as follows:

1. The process began at 8.00 a.m. The exterior of a 3.54-meter-long cane was scraped with a knife. Subsequently, the entire length of the cane was rubbed with guamo leaves (*Inga fastuosa*).
2. A fire was started on the outskirts of the camp, and Wuaú started to heat the cane (Figure 7.3).
3. At regular intervals he straightened the cane in the angle formed by a crossbeam and a post of the dwelling contiguous to his; this process lasted approximately 50 minutes (Figure 7.4).
4. He then cut segments from the ends of the cane, leaving it 3.3 m long. Meanwhile, other younger men began making their blowpipes in the fire Wuaú had built outside the camp.
5. At 9.55 a.m. he tied the blowpipe between two posts of the dwelling opposite his (in this case, that belonging to Boóri) and began to introduce sticks of approximately 2 m length and 1 cm to 2 cm width into the cane (Figure 7.5). At intervals he forced water into the hollow being formed. As the sticks fell apart at the ends, and the transverse walls of the cane split, he replaced them with others. This process continued until 10.15 a.m., at which point Wuaú went fishing.
6. At 4.30 p.m. Wuaú returned with *juiú* fruit (*Attalea* sp.), fish, and new sticks, and immediately went back to hollowing out the cane. He began the same process from the other side with the fresh sticks. He shortened the end he had already started to a height of 75 cm from the floor.
7. By 5.20 p.m. the cane had been fully hollowed out. He began to pass sticks through from one end to the other in order to smooth out the inside surface.
8. The two ends of the blowpipe were shortened, and sticks and water continued to be introduced.
9. At 6.15 a.m. the following day, Wuaú untied the cane and brought it to the hearth at his dwelling where he shortened it a further 20 cm with a knife. He then heated it slowly. At this point several children started to burn their canes in the fire outside the camp that Wuaú had used the day before.

10. At 7.00 a.m. he made a dart and began to test the blowpipe in the central space of the camp. He fired four or five test shots with the improvised dart.

11. At 7.30 a.m. he began to form the mouthpiece in his hearth, removing a further 5-cm length of blowpipe. He then went out gathering.

12. At 4.30 p.m. he resumed work on the mouthpiece and on the farther end. He put a type of black tar (*mapa*) on both ends (Figure 7.6). He also fitted a tar plug (*mantahuát*), to be used as "sights," 36 cm from the end opposite the mouthpiece (where the dart exits). Meanwhile, the youths continued to make their blowpipes in a more expedient fashion.

13. At 8.30 a.m. Wuaú went hunting with the blowpipe. At 8.50 a.m. he cut a fresh stick and for five minutes continued hollowing out the cane. Subsequently the blowpipe was used regularly to hunt with.

The blowpipe had a final length of 3.1 m and weighed 1.7 kg. The external diameter was 2.8 cm and the internal diameter (of the orifice) between 1.7 and 1.8 cm. In general, the adults' blowpipes are between 2.5 and 3.5 m long, the adolescents' between 2 and 2.5 m, and the children's less than 2 m. The weights vary according to the type of cane and the length of the blowpipe.

The fabrication of the blowpipe was interspersed with other activities, which is also common during the manufacture of other tools. As noted, it took two days for Wuaú to make the blowpipe, during which time he performed other

Figure 7.3 Wuaú started to heat the cane in an *ad hoc* fire

Figure 7.4 Wuaú straightening the cane in the angle formed by a crossbeam and a post of the dwelling contiguous to his dwelling

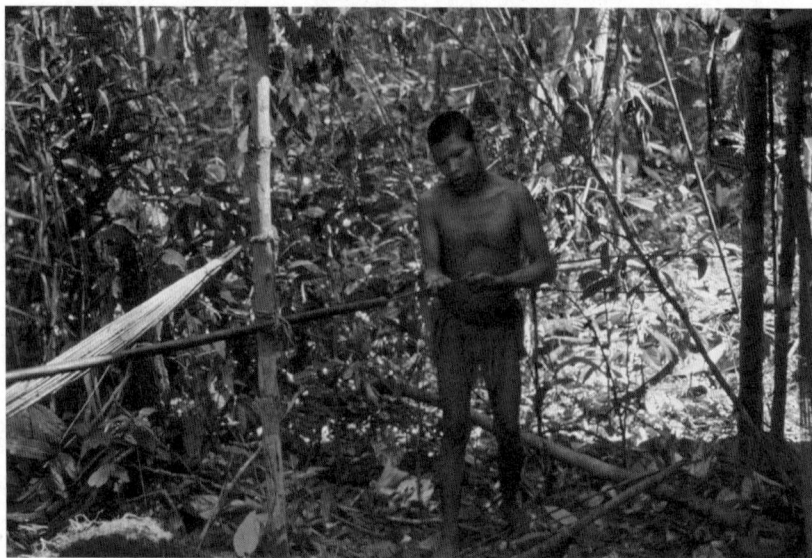

Figure 7.5 Wuaú has begun to insert sticks into the blowpipe, having tied it between two posts of the dwelling opposite his

Figure 7.6 Wuaú applying a type of black tar (*mapa*) on both ends of the blowpipe

tasks, such as gathering fruit, fishing, and preparing darts. Consequently, the net time calculated for the manufacture of this blowpipe, after the cane had been acquired, was approximately four to five hours.

Blowpipe Darts (*terú*)   Darts are made from the petiole spines of seje palm (*Oenocarpus bataua*). The points are poisoned with a substance called *manyi*, obtained from the *parupi* vine (*Curarea tecunarum*). The most brittle part of the spine is used; the point is sharpened, and any imperfections are removed. Wild cotton from the flowers of *puiú (Ceiba petranda)* or *puiú meru* (*Pachira nukakika*) is placed on the lower part of the spine by spinning the dart rapidly and subsequently fastening the cotton with thin tucum palm thread (*Astrocaryum aculeatum*) (Figure 7.7). The darts are approximately 60 cm long. Cabrera, Franky, and Mahecha (1994:198) indicate that the length of the darts depends on the status of the man and is especially related to his age. As such, an adult uses 60–75 cm darts, an adolescent 50–55 cm, and children less than 40 cm. At approximately 4 cm from the head a small cross-incision is made so that in the eventuality of the dart breaking, it will do so at this point and the poisoned spine will remain in the body of the victim.

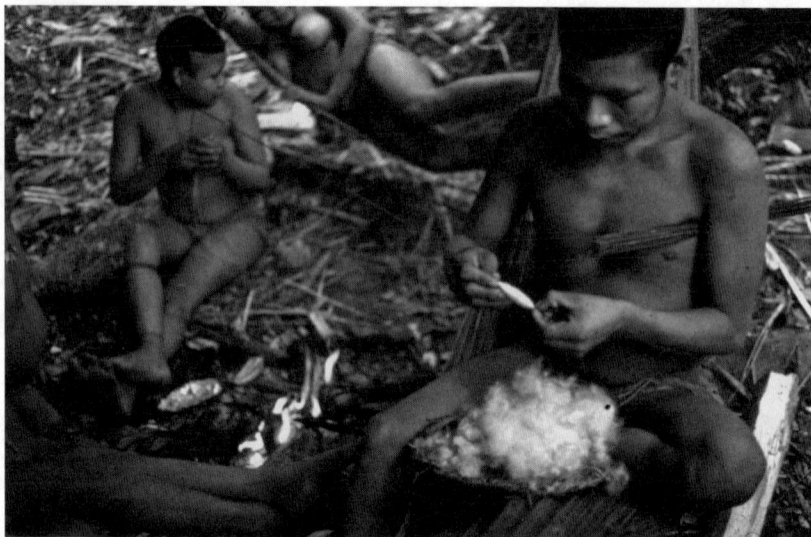

Figure 7.7   Man placing wild cotton on the lower part of the spine by spinning the dart rapidly and subsequently fastening the cotton with thin tucum palm thread

Darts are carried in a small sheaf made from a piece of dried platanillo leaf and tied with tucum palm thread so the poisoned points are kept protected. They are then stored in a leaf container to prevent them getting wet or damaged. This quiver is carried in the hand and may contain 30 or 40 darts. The darts are poisoned on a daily basis early in the day, before the men go out hunting and/or gathering.

The poison called *manyi* (regionally known as "curare") is made from the bark of the *parupi* vine, which is scraped with a knife (Figure 7.8) and cooked in plenty of water while the maker stirs the mixture and removes the impurities that rise to the surface. The liquid progressively turns a dark red color and increases in viscosity until it has the consistency of caramel. After cooking for several hours it is stored in a small pan covered by part of a leaf or a cloth. Every adult man possesses his own pot of *manyi*.

Glue Darts   The glue dart is far less common form of dart; it was not observed during our fieldwork. It consists of the hard part of the tucum palm leaf, with *puiú* cotton fastened to one end. Glue, known as *wed,* is used instead of a point, which is prepared by a cooking process (Cabrera, Franky, & Mahecha 1994:181). It must also be soaked in saliva before being attached to the dart. These darts are used to hunt certain birds: the glue sticks to their feathers, causing them to fall to the ground (Gualteros Ms).

Figure 7.8   Man scraping the bark of the *parupí* vine to make curare

Spears (*ñúmu*)   Men make these weapons from long strips of the trunk of the zancona palm (*Socratea exorrhiza*), by breaking and smoothing sections of the fibrous stem. The external fibers are removed with a machete, the body is rounded, and the ends are then sharpened, forming a conical point. The spears are approximately 2.5 m long and 2 cm in diameter. They are relatively light and extremely durable. They are frequently stained red with achiote or *éóro*, in a similar fashion to the blowpipes. These weapons are used mainly for hunting medium-sized land animals such as peccary. They may occasionally be used to spear fish. At times they are left in strategic locations, on the edge of paths or in abandoned camps. In most cases the men transport them when residential relocations are undertaken. The use of spears is far more sporadic than blowpipes, as they are associated with the hunting of animals that are infrequently available (that is, peccary).

We recorded the manufacturing process of spears several times during our fieldwork seasons. This generally begins in the outskirts of the camp. The surface of the wood is cleaned with a machete while the piece is supported on the crossbeam of a dwelling (Figure 7.9). The spear is then heated in the hearth of the domestic unit (Figure 7.10) and straightened using nearby posts and crossbeams as support. The process is repeated several times (Figure 7.11).

Figure 7.9   Man cleaning the surface of a spear with a machete while the spear is supported by the crossbeam of a dwelling

Figure 7.10 Man heating a spear in the hearth of a domestic unit

Figure 7.11 Man checking the straightness of a spear while he heats it in the hearth of the domestic unit

At intervals the surface of the spear is rubbed with leaves. When the spear is sufficiently straight, the two ends are sharpened into conical forms. Finally, the spear is occasionally rubbed with *eóro*, giving it a dark red color. The process is carried out in a discontinuous fashion, interspersed with other activities.

It has not been possible to calculate exactly the net production time; it is estimated at approximately two hours. The points of the spears are frequently retouched with a machete or a knife during hunting trips.

Bows   Bows are used by men. They are made for fishing during the dry season (Figure 7. 12). The bow is a length of wood, smoothed with a machete. The bowstring is made from tucum palm fibers. They are used to fire harpoons with metal or bone points. Smaller versions are also made and are generally employed by children when fishing after the *barbasqueo*[3] of a section of stream, or for playing. Besides being highly seasonal, these small bows are entirely expedient, generally being discarded after a day's fishing.

Figure 7.12   Young man fishing in a creek with a harpoon and a bow during the dry season

Harpoons (*dii*)   Harpoons are the complementary element of the fishing bow (Figure 7.12). The light yet durable petiole of a palm known as *pahp* (*Batris maraja var. maraja*), or the rachis of the inflorescence of *dii* (*Gynerium sagitatum*), are used as shafts. A 15–29 cm long point made from palm bark is attached to one end, having been previously cleaned and thinned. A fragment of monkey bone or even a piece of metal is fastened with tucum palm thread and some resin or dark wax (*dimni*) to the sharpest end of this point. The point is then rubbed and smoothed to improve penetration, in some cases using the rough surface of an old metal pot. The most elaborate harpoons are reused. Occasionally, smaller harpoons are made that lack bone points, often merely utilizing a piece of fiber of seje trunk (as used in the manufacture of darts) from which the bark is removed and one end is sharpened. In general, harpoons are used in conjunction with the expedient bows already mentioned. A harpoon belonging to an adult man is about 1.80 m long.

Harpoons are used when a stretch of stream or a pool has been subjected to a *barbasqueo*, when advantage can be taken of the toxic effect of the barbasco to harpoon the slow-moving fish near the surface. The weapons are generally employed on small- or medium-sized fish. Only adult men make and use them; women, and especially children, employ small, disposable projectiles. The fact that harpoons are associated with the practice of *barbasqueo* implies that these harpoons—like bows—are seasonal tools manufactured only during the dry period.

Fish Traps (*mei*[4])   These traps are made by men using a special, as yet unidentified, vine and seje leaves. They are conical in shape with one closed end (Figure 7.13). They are inserted in small dams also made with seje leaves and are checked by the men on food procurement trips. During our fieldwork we observed the use of these traps only during the rainy season. Consequently, the quantity of fish that was trapped was small, and frequently no fish were caught at all.

Figure 7.13   Man checking a conical fish trap during the rainy season

Other Elements Used in Food Procurement

This section includes a series of elements, all of an expedient nature, which are commonly used in diverse food-attainment activities.

Tree-Climbing Hoops   These are small hoops made from bound vines. They loop around both feet in such a way that a good grip is achieved on the tree trunk, enabling one to climb with less effort. Children of both sexes and men use them.

Expedient Bags, or catarijanos (*búrup*)   These bags are made from fresh plantain leaves (of several species, principally *Heliconia psittacorarum, Heliconia stricta,* and *Heliconia hirsuta*). They are folded in half, and each end is securely tied and finished in a tress that is attached to the opposite end and serves as a carrying strap. Their manufacture takes only a few minutes and is carried out by men, women, and children. Generally, plantain leaves are placed inside the *búrup* to prevent the contents, especially small fruit, from falling through the cracks. Although expedient in character, some are occasionally reused if they are still in good condition. Men always carry a small *búrup* in which they transport their *puyú* cotton. *Búrup* are also hung from the roof supports of the dwellings to keep them dry.

Torches   Torches are made from dry seje leaves whose ends are lashed together with a vine to prevent them coming apart. A stick is fastened to the lower end as a handle. They are made by men and are used to smoke out beehives from a neighboring tree or from the ground.

Pitchforks   These are used fairly frequently. A short stick is attached firmly with a strip of bark or vine to one end of a pole. They are maneuvered from a neighboring tree in order to pick racemes from spinney or irregularly barked palms such as the peach palm.

Carrying Straps   Carrying straps are used to elaborate the tresses that are attached to very large *búrup* and women's baskets, or even simply to carry small children more comfortably. They are also used frequently as lashing. These straps are made from the inner bark of several different types of tree.

Poles of Various Lengths and Widths   These poles function as expedient harpoons or spears. They are used to hunt certain animals when the appropriate tool is not at hand. They are fairly long (1–3 m) and straight sticks, one end of which is fashioned into a point with a few blows of a machete. We observed their use in a caiman hunt. The animal was removed from its den using a lure made from a pole and a bark pivot. Once the caiman was out, its head was spitted with a pole sharpened at one end. These expedient poles are also used to hunt armadillos after they have been forced out of their dens with fire and smoke, or to hunt fish intoxicated with barbasco.

Plant Product Procurement and Food Preparation Utensils

Sieves and Wicker Baskets (*werep*)   The sieve is fabricated by both men and women. Two people may be involved in their elaboration. Not everyone makes these implements; they are one of the few Nukak artifacts made by specialists, and also one of the most frequently shared items. We have not been able to establish why this is the case; the ability required to make sieves does not appear to be different from that necessitated for other objects. Nonetheless, the case remains that not all Nukak make them. This fact was also recorded in one of the New Tribes reports (IANTC 1990a), which stated that only a few people know how to make these items. An example was given in which a hammock was exchanged for a sieve. It is possible that the limitations on the manufacture of sieves are not of a practical order; possible social or ideational factors involved in their production may yet have to be understood.

Only one or two sieves are found in each band, and they are used by all the family groups. The green stems of *bórop* (*Ischnosipbon arouma*), a herb that grows abundantly in disturbed zones, are used in their production. The stems are split lengthways into several sections and then interwoven, leaving open spaces in a hexagonal pattern of open or closed weave according to their planned usage. Then, a loop of thick vine is made to which the stitched mesh is attached using thinner pieces of vine. The sieve is used to sift or strain seje, *guaná* (*Dacryodes peruviana*), and other fruits.

Some of these sieves are employed fairly frequently to prepare drinks from seje, chontaduro, and moriche. Their diameter varies from 40 to 50 cm. They are mounted on a triangular framework of sticks on a tripod approximately 60 cm above the ground. A container to collect the processed liquid—generally an aluminum pot of considerable size—is fitted to the lower part. The cooked seje is placed in the sieve and is strained with pressure from both hands (Figure 7.14). During residential moves the sieves are generally used as lids for the baskets carried by the women.

Figure 7.14 Woman straining seje with a sieve

Mortars   Mortars are used to grind various fruit and seeds and are almost always used by women and girls. These tools are made from a section of tree trunk[5] 24–30 cm in diameter and 50–70cm tall, of which the central part is burnt and the inside scraped out. The fire is stoked by blowing through a hollow cane made from the folium of the tucum palm. In this way the process can be managed and control is maintained over the shape of the hollow. Mortars are made by women, although men also participate by collecting the trunks. There are two ways of making mortars, individually or collectively. In the former case, a single woman carries out the entire process. In the latter, several women take turns blowing the embers inside the hollow. The burnt parts are then extracted with a machete, and the mortar takes shape.

Mortars are used to process seje, platanillo seeds, and any other plant found from which a flour can be made (Figure 7.15). They are also used to soak fruit in water. Cabrera, Franky, and Mahecha (1994:165) mention that they are employed to grind maize. Mortars are generally utilized when the band is located in an area that abounds in particular plant products. They are occasionally transported when a band relocates. Otherwise they are left in the abandoned camp, usually on a platform to avoid contact with the ground that

Figure 7.15 Woman sifting platanillo flour using the side of the basket; the platanillo seeds had been ground in the nearby wood mortar.

would speed up deterioration, and may be retrieved when the band returns to the area. If they are taken to the new camp they are generally transported by the men in a *búrup* made specifically for the task.

The active grinding element—the pestle—is a straight stick of medium thickness (5–10 cm) that varies from 1.2 to 1.5 m in length. The bark is removed from the stick, is smoothed, and one end is flattened. This tool is far more expedient than the mortar and is always discarded when a camp is abandoned; not once did we see pestles transported from one site to another.

The use of the pestle and the mortar to grind plant products transforms the surface of the camp. In effect, as plants are processed the mortar becomes increasingly embedded in the ground. At first this is advantageous for the woman who is grinding, since greater purchase is achieved with the partially buried mortar. Nonetheless, it eventually becomes too deeply buried and uncomfortable to use. It is then moved to a new spot, leaving behind a hole some 50 cm deep in the old location, and the process begins again (Figure 7.16). Camps occupied during an intense grinding period have circular holes in the spaces between the domestic units (see Chapter 5).

Ceramic Pots (*wámnu*)   Almost all the bands studied during our fieldwork possessed ceramic pots. We saw few among the western bands (one or two per band), whereas among the eastern bands they were more abundant. In general, these pots are used to transport or store fruit and liquids (Figure 7.17), as well as to gather honey or palm grubs. In no case did we observe the manufacturing process. Gualteros (Ms:15) states that the pots are made by women from a particular type of clay, which is formed and baked in a bonfire in a hollow dug for the purpose. He also mentions that on only one occasion did he see mud representations of animals. The degreaser used is the ash[6] of an unidentified tree that is mixed with the clay.

We observed pots of various sizes during our fieldwork, although always within the small to medium range. The largest pot recorded had a mouth diameter of 53 cm. They are generally undecorated black bowls lacking handles. Some have an inverted lip. At present the production of these pots is dying out, since they have been comprehensively replaced by metal pots obtained through exchange at Laguna Pavón 2 and the homesteads of the *colonos*. Although the pots are the property of a specific family group they may be used by any member of the band.

Bamboo Knives (*waá*)   At present we know of no band that uses these knives regularly. Their existence in the past is confirmed through oral testimonies and the exceptional cases in which they have been observed in use. They are made from a fairly durable and sharp cane from which sharp-ended fibers are extracted. They are principally used to skin game before it is cooked. Monicaro stated that his mother used knives that "she got from canes like bamboo that grew on the banks of the rivers, and used them to cut monkeys." Cabrera, Franky, and Mahecha (1999:272) recorded a case of the skinning of a monkey using 1-cm-wide strips of the sharp-edged bark of a bush called *buk*.

Figure 7.16 Garbage-filled holes left by mortars in the camp floor; note the abandoned pestle.

Figure 7.17 Girl with a ceramic pot used to collect *koró-paanját* during a daily foraging trip

Stone Axes (*nemep´chak*)   Stone axes were used prior to the introduction of metal axes. There are no known groups that still use them, although there is evidence that some western bands did until the late 1980s. Owing to the scarcity of stone in the region they must have been valuable objects used for considerable lengths of time. References to stone axes were also made when we were told of the use of the boles of *Aspidosperm excelsum* (*pewe-na*) as handles (*chak naát*). Some Nukak told us that when the metal axes arrived, "in the time that influenza arrived, we threw the *nemep'chack* into the *pipireras* [chontaduro orchards]."

The Nukak believe that the stones for the axes, found on riverbanks, were left there by thunder. A New Tribes report corroborated this association, since they have gathered testimonies from the Nukak that stone falls from the sky. The raw material for the fabrication of axes is restricted to the rocky outcrops on the Inírida River, the Blowpipe Hills to the east of Nukak territory, and the Mapiripana floodplain in the extreme east of the Department of Guaviare. It is probable that during times of exceptional drainage of the Guaviare and Inírida rivers well-rounded hard rocks appropriate for working may be found.

Today the metal axes are fundamental in food procurement activities, given that they are used to fell trees to collect fruit, to obtain firewood, and to gather honey, as well as in the construction of camps and to clear land for gardens, and so forth. Undoubtedly, the metal axes currently occupy a central role in Nukak subsistence, probably more important than that played by stone axes in the past.

Graters   The grater consists of a fragment of the spinney *zancos* (epigeous roots) of the zancona palm (*Socratea exorrhiza*). They are used to process sweet yucca, peach palm, moriche, and plantain and to produce a paste generally used in the concoction of soups and the preparation of drinks. These are expedient tools, normally manufactured by women. They are made by splitting the *zancos* into sections approximately 1 m long that are passed through the fire until the surface is thoroughly cleaned. These sections are later attached to a thick piece of wood, and the protuberances on the surface are used to grate.

Gourd Containers   These receptacles are made from the dried shells of various fruit. The smallest, known as *uúni*, are fabricated from *Lagenaria siceraria*, a creeping vine with rounded fruit common in Nukak orchards. The medium and large ones, known as *peyé* or *peyé-darúa*, are obtained from *Posadaea sphaerocarpa*, another creeping vine that grows in secondary areas. To make these containers the fruit are split lengthways when ripe and dry, the endocarp is removed, they are cleaned, and their insides are dyed with a substance called *chía*. These receptacles are used to serve food, draw water from holes, drink from, and in handling liquids in general. They are frequently damaged, whether in family quarrels, children's games, or everyday accidents. They are occasionally obtained through exchange with *colonos* who grow *Lagenaria* in their gardens.

Stirrers (*duri*; also called *kahyak* by Gualteros)   These tools consist of sticks with multiple forks used in the preparation of seje or for mixing any other food being prepared. The ends of the sticks are cut just above the fork, and the bark is removed. Given that they are used with great frequency they are often kept, although they can be replaced easily and quickly. They average 40 cm in length.

Spits or Grills   Grills made with green sticks are used to smoke certain game (monkeys, fish, peccaries, and so on). A triangular-shaped base is constructed over which several sticks are positioned in the form of a grill. The grill is kept in place by attaching it with vines to the triangular base. They are made quickly, and their size is in direct relation to size of the prey. The location of these grills is also related to the kill. When used to burn the hair of peccary, they are located close to the hunt site. However, in the majority of cases they are positioned within the camps or close by.

Besides being used to burn the hair of peccary or agouti, grills are used to preserve monkeys, fish, and any type of meat in general by smoking. The fire is located below the grill. When the fur of an animal is to be burned, dry seje leaves are used as fuel because they produce a high, active flame. In all other cases dry firewood, or, preferably, dry palm trunks are utilized. Grills are constructed frequently during the dry season, when every dwelling uses one for drying fish (Figure 7.18).

Figure 7.18   Triangular wooden grill used to smoke fish during the dry season

Furnishings and Accessories

Hammocks   Hammocks are one of the most important elements in the lives of the Nukak. Their fabrication is an exclusively female task. The first step involves making a ball of fibers from the epidermis of moriche leaves (*Mauritia flexuosa*), the threads of which are twisted with *éóro* (*Arrabidaea chica*) on the thigh into balls several meters long. On other occasions a preexisting hammock is unstitched and the recovered cord rolled into a ball. The second step consists of positioning a beam so it is supported by the posts of a dwelling at a height of approximately 0.9–1.2 m. Forked sticks are then attached to the extremities of the beam, and the ends of the hammock are wrapped over them. The ends of a thread are tied to the forks, and every 20 cm perpendicular threads are positioned that incorporate every new pass of the longitudinal thread. The transverse threads, generally of tucum palm fibers, are organized in rows hung side by side on the longitudinal thread. They are also soaked in wax (*wed*) to make them more durable. At every new pass of the longitudinal thread the transverse threads cross, moving the role from back to front. After tightening, the role is passed back again. If the ball of longitudinal thread runs out, the process is continued with a fresh ball. With every pass of the longitudinal thread a large buttonhole forms by the forks at each end, to which is attached a thick cord 30–40 cm long from which the hammock will be hung (Figure 7.19)

The hammocks are cared for by the women and transported with their baskets during camp relocations. As with the ceramic pots, the hammocks are damaged and sometimes burnt during conjugal fights. Consequently, one often finds abandoned camps with partially burnt hammock fibers around the hearth. Moreover, they are sometimes burnt when a woman dies, although it appears to be more common for them to be buried with the corpse.

Baskets   Baskets are an abundant element within Nukak material culture. They are used and fabricated by women. Every family group has at least one large basket, enabling them to carry all their belongings and leftovers during camp relocations (see Figure 6.2, p. 169). These large baskets are sometimes used to transport plants during gathering trips. Women also make smaller baskets to store small items, such as mirrors, scissors, *éoro*, knives, and so on.

To make a basket, a vine[7] is split in half after the bark has been removed. Then, a radial weave is created from segments of equal length (depending on the desired capacity of the basket) through which the vine is passed, simultaneously intercalating it and describing a circumference. In this way a cylindrical form is achieved. When the length of the weft has been covered, the

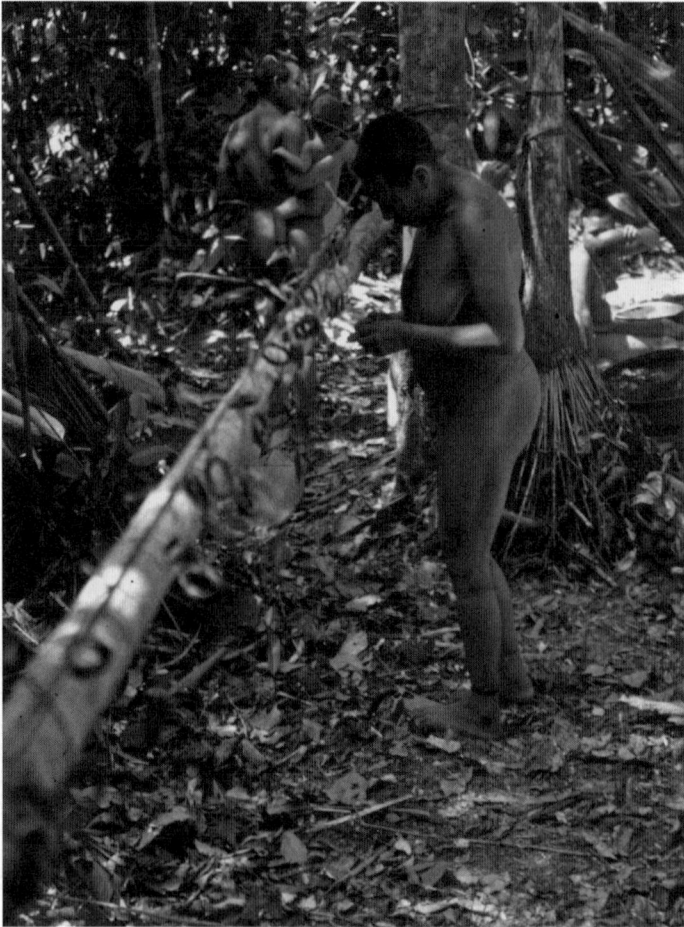

Figure 7.19 Woman making a hammock

protruding ends are trimmed and a lip is attached using the same vine without it being cut. The edge is supported by a thin fiber, sewing it in front and behind the weave of the basket wall. These baskets are tough and durable.

Guayuco or Loincloth (*du'*)   The *guayuco* or loincloth is the only traditional garment that the Nukak wear. It is worn exclusively by men, including adults, youths, and boys above a certain age (five or six years old). The women are always naked, wearing only bracelets (*kdn'yii*) on their ankles and calves. At present, both men and women are increasingly incorporating all forms of western dress.

The raw material for the manufacture of the *guayuco* is the inner bark of the *Courotari guianensis*[8] tree, stripped, cleaned, and unraveled by the men (Figure 5.2, p. 134). It has occasionally been observed that still-green fallen trees are used. A sheet of bark 20–30 cm long is stripped and taken to the camp, where the fabrication of the *guayuco* takes place. The sheets of bark are attached to a piece of tucum palm fiber in a rectangular section. They are unraveled in strips 1 or 2 cm wide and passed through two threads, creating a knot that progressively moves toward one end. When this process is finished, the strips of bark are completely unraveled. Finally, the inner part is dyed with achiote or *ééro*. The *guayuco* are made by men, although women occasionally help make them for their sons when they reach the appropriate age to wear one. An account recorded by the missionaries (IANTC 1993) suggests that the Nukak believe that when they emerged into the middle world through the hole in the earth, both men and women were naked. However, the men were embarrassed and so donned their *guayucos*.

Bracelets (*kdn'yii*)   These are bands made out of tucum palm fibers to the required size by women. Both sexes use them tightly worn around their ankles, under their knees, and (only the men) around their wrists. They are made by hand, weaving tucum palm fiber from a thin thread dyed with *ééro*. When actual bracelets are not available they are temporarily replaced with unprocessed strips of tucum palm fiber. Bracelets are also made for babies within the first few days of life.

Musical Instruments   The principal musical instruments of the Nukak are flutes and panpipes, both played by men. Flutes (*petna* or *mikuepát*) are made from a deer tibia or a jaguar humerus. Three holes are made on the flattest side of the bone, and the end is carefully smoothed to take a beeswax mouthpiece. The orifice that is blown through is profusely dyed red with *ééro* and generally adorned with rows of colored beetles.[9] Nearly all the bands we encountered during our fieldwork had these flutes, especially the youths, who would take them along when they visited other bands. As has already been observed, the flute has a high symbolic and ritual value, not only among the Nukak but also among a number of other Amazon groups.

The panpipe is made from small, hollow canes that are cut into pairs of equal length, with each pair successively shorter than the previous one. One end of the canes in both rows is blocked with wax. The tubes are tied together with tucum palm cord and occasionally decorated with rows of beetles or bird feathers. They are also dyed red.

Paint   The paint used on both the body and face, as well as many objects, is taken exclusively from two plants, achiote and *éóro*.[10] The aril of achiote seeds is an intense red and is used in two different ways. The first is to rub it directly onto the surface to be painted (the body, fibers, objects, and so on) with no prior preparation, merely dissolving it in saliva in the hand. The second method is to boil and compact it into loaves of paint. Achiote was found frequently in nearly all Nukak orchards.

Éóro is a plant the leaves of which are used to prepare a red colored dye similar to achiote. Dried leaves are boiled in water, and stems and pieces of bark of *bíri*[11] are added. Once it has thickened, after an entire day's cooking, it is left to sit, and the viscous substance is packed into pocket-shaped pieces of cloth that are suspended over a hearth to dry the colorant and allow it to compact. The resultant paste is applied directly to the body with the hand, or with the help of a small stick in the case of face painting. It is diluted with saliva in the same way as achiote. This substance may act as an insect repellent, but this has yet to be confirmed.

Small Leaf Box (*pa'chaa'*)   These are fairly rigid boxes made from palm leaves (*káénidé*, after Gualteros Ms), similar to shoe boxes but much smaller. They are made from several layers of leaves and are sometimes dyed red. They are traditionally used to store blocks of paint and other small personal objects, such as piranha jawbones or bone spatulas.

Bone Spatulas   These artifacts are made from the shaped and polished long bones of monkeys. They are 10–20 cm long, and on one end a beveled edge is created. They are commonly used to apply body or face paint. They may also be used for other circumstantial activities (seed extraction, perforation, and so on). They are made by both men and women and are stored in small baskets kept on the floors of the dwellings. These artifacts are used by individuals.

Poisons   The Nukak concoct two types of poison, curare and barbasco. Curare (*mányi*) has already been described in the section on dart preparation. Barbasco (*núun*) is an icthyotoxin that is obtained from the roots of a vine (*Lonchocarpus nicou*) that grows close to watercourses. Approximately 30-cm-long pieces of the root are macerated by beating them with sticks. They are then placed in streams that have previously been dammed. The milky substance that is released is icthyotoxic and dilutes in the water, poisoning the fish and forcing them to rise close to the surface. In this state they are caught by women standing in the water using their bare hands, a machete, or a stick.

They are also harpooned from the riverbanks by the men, although this fishing technique is inspired by motives other than mere food procurement, since prestige is gained through demonstrations of skill and good aim. The quantity of fish acquired by men using this method is insignificant compared to that obtained by women catching the fish by hand.

Barbasco is also used by men in suicide attempts, which are usually motivated by conjugal problems. These suicides are normally unsuccessful; the wife rapidly comes to her husband's aid, forcing him to drink liquids until he vomits out the poison. The ingestion of barbasco can be seen, therefore, as an extreme way to reestablish relations after serious conjugal arguments.

Fire Sticks (*iigni tuaré*)   These are sticks employed in starting fires. The active stick is 30–50 cm long, at one end of which a point is created. This is generally an extremely straight hardwood stick. The passive element has several hollows approximately 1–2 cm in diameter. The active stick is placed over an orifice of the passive stick and is rubbed energetically while pressing downward with force, producing sufficient heat to enable dry fibers to catch fire (Figure 7.1). In the cases we recorded in 1996 a piece of *tujana'* (*Pausandra trianae*) stem was always used as the active element, whereas a portion of parched stalk of the same species, 20–30 cm long, served the passive role. Furthermore, pairs of *tujana'* sticks used for the same purpose have been observed tied together in various camps.

Teeth Bead Necklaces   The Nukak frequently possess monkey-teeth bead necklaces. The fangs of larger primates are generally selected, and a hole made with a knife. The fangs of howler monkeys (*Alouatta seniculus*) are the most sought after and are hung from a string of tucum palm fibers. Children and adolescents have a large number of fangs on their necklaces (20 or 30) and sometimes wear two at the same time (Figure 7.20). Adults, however, use necklaces with fewer teeth, generally only three or four. When a boy or a girl dies he or she is buried with his or her necklace. Feline fangs are also used in necklaces, but far less frequently. Felines are killed only in exceptional circumstances (see Chapter 9), and, consequently, the fangs are usually obtained from carcasses. The most sought after are the larger jaguar teeth.

Piranha Jawbones   The sharp teeth of piranha jawbones are used by the Nukak to cut their hair. The hair is cut in a layered fashion, much the way Western hairdressers cut with razors. Piranha jawbones are also used to notch hunting darts and function as knives and carving tools more generally. They are rare today, having been replaced by scissors. In the early 1990s the *Meu munu* bands had a number of these jawbones that they used frequently.

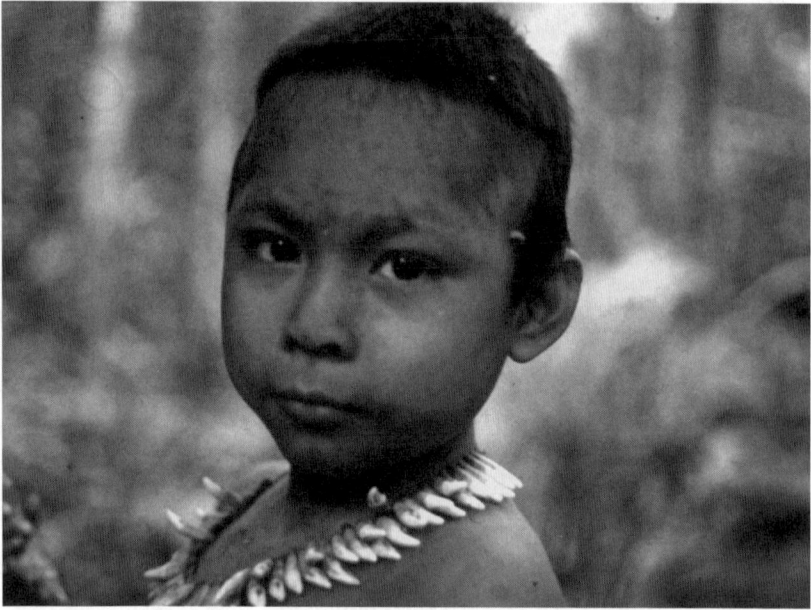

Figure 7.20 Boy with a tooth-bead necklace

They are generally stored in a small basket or in the leaf boxes together with other personal accessories.

Miscellaneous   There are artifacts that the Nukak use that we have not had the opportunity to observe during our fieldwork but have been recorded by other researchers and by the New Tribes missionaries. Included in this group are tree bark trumpets, called *pênpetiwat*, which are of ritual use and are now extremely rare (Cabrera, Franky, & Mahecha 1994:191; Gualteros Ms:14).

Toys   The Nukak fabricate a series of objects that are used for recreation and learning by their children. Children make up almost half the total current Nukak population. In a sample of 357 individuals, 135 (37.8%) were under 10 years old; this number increases to 175 (49%) if we consider all individuals below 15 years of age (Franky, Cabrera, & Mahecha, 1995:2). These children, especially those in the first age group, spend much of the day inside or around the residential camp, where they produce and use three classes of artifacts:

- Class 1. Artifacts designed specifically for play (toys). Typical toys are bark hammocks, rounded stones, fruit spinning tops, and large rings made of vines. These artifacts do not have homologues among the adults' tools.

- Class 2. Artifacts that replicate adult objects but are smaller and poorly made. They are used for the same function or for play. Examples include bows, harpoons, blowpipes, darts, baskets, pottery vessels, gourd vessels, and spears (Figure 7.21).
- Class 3. Adult artifacts, whole or broken, that are used for play. Examples include any adult artifact that has the potential to be used in play. The most frequent are metal axes, machetes, vessels and pestles.

Figure 7.21   Boys fishing with small bows and harpoons in a nearby pond

Class 1 artifacts are generally made by the children themselves (at times with the help of their parents), with minor modifications, or even with no shaping at all (such as the case of the rounded stones). Within this class it is of interest to mention the stones that Nukak children sometimes bring back from the Cerro de las Cerbatanas when the entire band approach these hills in order to gather canes for blowpipes. These rounded pebbles are carried from one place to another for weeks or months until they are finally abandoned or lost in the camps or their surroundings. They are used principally by children for play; no other function has been observed.

Class 2 contains far more artifacts and includes practically all the tools made by adults, merely reduced in scale. An important distinction must be made in this second class. On the one hand, adults make smaller versions of artifacts so they may be used by children, fulfilling a function similar to that of the full-sized objects. The only difference between adult and children's artifacts is their size, which is appropriate for the age and size of the child, but the quality of fabrication and the function are identical (for example, gourd and pottery vessels). On the other hand, there are replicas of adult tools, made by the children themselves or their parents for play or practice. Children do not use them for the same functions as adults do, although their use can be similar, and they are of a lower quality. The lower quality is due to two reasons: (1) When they are made by adults the technology has an expedient character—owing to the ludic goal of the artifacts, they are not made with the same care; (2) when children make them, the lower quality is the result of limitations in technique. The size of these artifacts is in relation to the size of the child. Virtually any size possible may be produced within a particular range. In the case of blowpipes, for example, the smallest we recorded was 0.82 m long. From there on, they gradually increase in size until the adult tools reach 3.2 m. The difference between adult and child blowpipes is determined by the relationship that exists between the length of the tool and the stature and ability of the user.

The third class is made up of unmodified adults' artifacts; only the activity of the children influences their spatial distribution. This class is the most utilized by the youngest children who pick up any object close by to use as a toy.

Children's artifacts are also differentiated from adult ones by their discard loci. Children discard the vast majority of their objects within the residential camp or its immediate vicinity, while adults tend to do so far from the camp where many activities are carried out (hunting, gathering, butchering of peccary, and so on). One of the most interesting cases is that of darts, as children play with blowpipes frequently and conduct target practice within the camps, although these darts do not include curare (poison). As a consequence, small darts—sometimes whole—are left on the floors of abandoned camps as a result of this activity.

The Social and Ideological Dimensions of Nukak Technology

These dimensions of Nukak technology are not as well known as the instrumental dimension, but the available information allows us to begin to envisage their significance. Firstly, it is quite clear that some objects circulate among bands as gifts or tokens of welcome. The elements we recorded employed in this way were pieces of *éóro* or achiote and fragments of mirrors. These are the kind of artifact that a person[12] gives to someone from a different band when he or she is visiting their camp.

Pottery has some communicative value among the Nukak, although it is not decorated in any fashion.[13] It functions, in a way, as a distinctive feature of Nukak identity. In one recorded case, a group of young Nukak were guiding a small research team out of the forest during a three-day trip from their camp to the *colono* village of Caño Seco. The only bowl they carried with them was of ceramic (Figure 7.22). It would appear that they preferred this pot to the lighter and more resistant metal pots, of which they had several in the camp, owing to the external value of pottery. Moreover, Gualteros (Ms) mentions that pots may also be buried with the body of an adult woman.

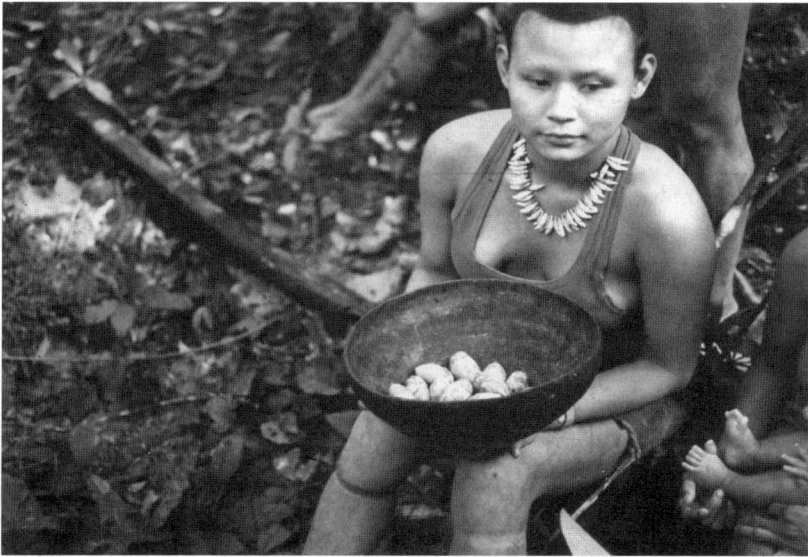

Figure 7.22   Woman carrying a ceramic pot during a visit to Caño Seco

A further indication of the multiple dimensions within which pottery functions is found in Nukak myths. We have managed to record and translate (with the help of Israel Gualteros) a woman's account of the origins of the clay used in ceramic making. She related that there are two beings called *Chák´naugú* that resemble humans but are of indeterminate sex (Chapter 3). They travel together along the banks of the rivers and streams. At times they can be seen prowling around these areas in the early morning at sunrise. The dregs of these beings—that only women may collect—are the clay used to make ceramics.

The blowpipe is an object of unmistakable and powerful social significance. The early stages of production—the men's trip to the Cerro de las Cerbatanas to collect canes—is organized around kinship. The members of the party must bring back canes for their agnates; not only for those who remain in camp who contribute to the maintenance of the family group of the male travelers but also for relatives who belong to related bands. The circulation of canes is a complex system of reciprocity, involving the canes in larger networks that incorporate men from diverse bands, although all participants usually belong to the same *munu*. The following example is illustrative of the complexity of the circulation. During a daily logistical trip in the dry season a man arrived at a creek that was low and started to search with his hand (his view was impeded by the muddy water) in the pools in the creek bed. After five or six minutes of searching, weaving his hand around the bottom of the pools, he withdrew a cane, which he took with him the remainder of the journey back to his camp. He later explained that this cane was left there weeks before by a relative who had asked him to collect it when he crossed that creek. He planned to meet with his relative sometime in the future, probably a few weeks later. This example demonstrates the complexity of the circulation of canes and information among the different bands.

The process of making a blowpipe is also loaded with social implications. The spaces in the camp involved in the different stages in the fabrication of blowpipes link the various domestic units together and in a way replicate the circulation of kills through the camp. As has been noted, the first step in blowpipe manufacture takes place outside the camp, at an *ad hoc* hearth. The subsequent manufacturing stages rotate through various dwellings until the process concludes with the fixing of the mouthpiece in the maker's shelter. He then tests the blowpipe in the central space of the camp. This series of steps mirrors the circuit traveled by game that has been hunted with the blowpipe (see Chapter 9) and is frequently left by the hunter at the camp's edge. Once inside the camp, the animal is cooked at one hearth and the parts distributed to the various domestic units. As such, the manufacturing circuit of the blowpipe reproduces the circulation of prey obtained with this weapon and also binds the technological process to the kinship networks that connect members of the residential band.

The *kd'nyii* have significant communicative value; they are made with similar yet subtle variations in weave that are indicative of the band and woman who made them. When strangers with a *kd'nyii* (we, for example) encounter a band, the women observe it closely, inferring who made it and where they live. The manufacturing of the *kd'nyii* is also related to the-world-above; their manufacture by people of that world results in good or bad wild guamo crops in the intermediate world.

Although outside the sphere of traditional technology, the procurement of metal objects is also related to the social dimension. It is obvious that metal artifacts are now widely used among the Nukak and are highly esteemed. Most bands have a significant quantity of them, which should obviate the necessity of acquiring more. However, young men still secretly visit *colono* farms to steal these artifacts, gaining prestige and demonstrating their bravery. These raids include an aspect of danger, and, although the farms are usually approached when the *colonos* are away, there are many stories, both among *colonos* and Nukak, of pursuits and hostility when the *colonos* find their ranches liberated of all metal objects. It is quite clear that on some occasions the procurement of pots is the main goal of these trips, whereas at other times the chief cause is the prestige and reputation gained.

The ideational dimension of specific items, notably blowpipes, darts, dart poison, pottery, and bone flutes, is evident. These artifacts function to unite different cosmological levels. In some sense they are also connected to people through their living essences. The ideational dimension of the blowpipe, an artifact with an undeniable utilitarian function and simultaneous symbolic value, is reflected in the way this item is treated when it is broken or the user dies. In the former case, if the blowpipe is bent and cannot or should not be straightened, or if it is cracked, it is carefully and completely destroyed. I have observed this process on two occasions, and it is evident that this act of destruction is deliberate and planned. In the same vein, when the user dies his blowpipe is completely destroyed and his *manyi* disposed of. Although we were not able to elicit a clear explanation from the Nukak as to why this occurs, a likely interpretation is that the destruction is carried out to "protect" the previous owner because part of his living essence remains in the blowpipe. If another person were to use it, the person "connected" with the blowpipe and his spirits would be adversely affected. There are clues that support this interpretation. In general, hunters may not eat ripe fruit or sweets, because this would affect the toxic power of the *manyi*. Clearly, hunter and *manyi* are interconnected, and what happens to the former affects the latter and vice versa.

Another story told to me by an adult Nukak was fairly illustrative in this respect:

> "Before, I hunted many monkeys; every time I went out I hunted at least ten. When I got back to the *wopyii* [camp] I didn't share them. I kept them all for myself. One day, without my being aware of it, Yukdaa [a Nukak from the same band, the oldest of the *Wayari munu*] blew on my *chicha*. Afterward, I couldn't

hunt as many monkeys any more. Now I hunt only two or three. From then on the darts come out bent, they don't come out straight anymore from the blowpipe."

In this case, the "blowing" on the *chicha* did not affect the man as much as the blowpipe and darts. In other words, what was ultimately affected was the efficacy of the blowpipe and the darts, whereas the *chicha* and the Nukak man were the vehicles through which the energy traveled from Yukdaa.

It appears that very sweet food can affect the *manyi* (curare), not only through the medium of men but also through women. Women who have lived for a while with the *colonos* are considered responsible for making the *manyi* ineffective through eating too much *panela* (raw sugar) (Cabrera, Franky, & Mahecha 1999:204). When a man dies, his *manyi* must be unmade, and no other man may use it. Men may borrow and lend *manyi* among themselves, but only by adhering to particular kinship rules.

In a New Tribes report, an account of the curare creation myth is given:

After many years, a woman called Nanabet, the wife of Maúrótjumjat [a male ancestor with the power of re-creation], sent her husband to climb and collect many seeds from a particular tree because she was very hungry. After eating a great deal, and being extremely full, she began to urinate over the jungle. To the east and west she urinated upwards, and her urine fell over the trees and vines. Some trees and vines became envenomed. This venom is the curare that is used today on the points of poison darts. (IANTC 1992d:1)

Bone flutes also operate heavily in the ideational dimension, since they link the people of the intermediate level with the ancestors/spirits of the upper world. Men play these flutes on specific occasions, especially at night in the camps. They also carry them on long trips, and it appears that communication with ancestor-spirits is more important during such times, probably for reasons of additional protection. On one occasion we encountered two young Nukak men traveling from their band to an area close to the *colono* frontier. The only object they were carrying was one bone flute each. Obviously, it is not mere coincidence that the flutes are made from the bones of the two animals that, together with the tapir, embody the most powerful spirits in Nukak cosmology, the jaguar and the deer. In a narrative related by Wenna of his "rite of passage" (recorded by the New Tribe missionaries in 1989), he said that at the beginning of the rite he "scraped and worked on a deer bone," and after several days he awoke carrying a flute. He recounted that he did not often play the flute during puberty, but that ". . . later they taught me to think, what did they teach him? For me to be like this, they said. Afterward, they taught me to play the flute." In this narrative, although obscure for us, there is a clear association between thinking and playing, suggesting that he was taught how to think by being taught how to play the flute.

FINAL CONSIDERATIONS

A primary, essential conclusion that underpins the significance of Nukak technology must be stated. Technology is of central concern for Western people. However, for other peoples this is not necessarily the case. The main preoccupation of Australian aborigines appears to be kinship (Ingold 2000:313), whereas for the Nukak it is the *tak´weyi*, their relatives, or the chontaduro harvest. For the Nukak, technology and technological progress do not appear to be matters of great concern, as they are for the West. Although at present it is certainly the case that the Nukak are concerned with acquiring metal axes and machetes, this need is easily and quickly fulfilled owing to the relative abundance of metal tools since the early 1990s and the tools' durability. Other than a few specific objects, all others are made, used, and discarded in an easy, routine, and relaxed fashion. The production of objects for hoarding or trade is not a preoccupation. Almost everything is for personal or family use, utilizing raw materials from the surrounding area (palms, vines, clay, bark, and so on) and the individual's own skill. Every Nukak knows how to make virtually everything he or she will need during his or her lifetime, and the basic materials for making these items can be found within the band's territory. Exceptions include canes for good-quality blowpipes and, in the past, rocks for stone axes, but probably nothing else.

A further, fundamental observation must be made. On analyzing the inventory of artifacts that constitute traditional Nukak technology, we note that a sexual division exists in the production and the use of all such items. The objects classified as "hunting and fishing weapons" are clearly male artifacts, with perhaps the exception of fishing tools, since expedient harpoons can be made and used by women. Those utensils destined for food preparation are fundamentally female, with the exception of the sieves and the mortars, in whose manufacture men may occasionally play a role. The "other elements used in food procurement" are not clearly characterized by gender, given that their expedient and temporary character mean that these artifacts can be made by anybody. There are exceptions, such as when a task is clearly associated with one sex. Torches are a case in point, as the procurement of honey is an exclusively male task. Similarly, the elements classified as "furnishings and accessories" can not be attributed as a group to one sex, although the majority can be assigned specifically to one sex or the other.

From the perspective of the first dimension of technology, that is, the utilitarian, Nukak tools can be analyzed based on Binford's (1977a, 1979) proposal concerning hunter-gatherer technological organization and planning. The majority of hunting and fishing weapons (blowpipes, harpoons, spears, and so on), as well as food preparation utensils (mortars, sieves, and so on), can be considered curated artifacts. In this sense, the weapons can be included within what Binford (1979) has called "personal gear," whereas the food preparation artifacts represent "household gear." Both groups of artifacts share the characteristics of curated elements: they are specialized in their function, their manufacture must be planned in advance and requires several steps that take a certain amount of time, and, finally, they must be maintained throughout their use life (Binford 1979:282; but see also Nelson 1992 for discussion of an alternative usage of the concept of "use life"). Conversely, the artifacts classified as "other elements used in food procurement" are of an expedient nature and can be included within the category of "situational gear" (Binford 1979). These artifacts are manufactured rapidly for specific purposes. In contrast to curated tools, their fabrication is not planned. Therefore, the raw materials available at the site of manufacture are utilized. In terms of energy, "Expediency refers to minimized technological effort under conditions where time and place of use are highly predictable" (Nelson 1992:64). Nukak artifacts that are clear examples of expedient technological behavior include pestles, tree-climbing hoops, and *búrup*.

The preceding technological categories generate variegated discard expectations and can consequently be used to interpret the archaeological record. Household gear rarely leaves the domestic area (except, obviously, during relocations), and personal gear, according to Binford (1979:278), is usually repaired and maintained within the camp. The expedient tools, however, are discarded at the locus of use, having served their purpose. The performance of Nukak artifacts with regard to discard corroborates positively with this model. Blowpipes, spears, harpoons, and other hunting and fishing tools are repaired and usually discarded, broken, in the residential camps, whereas the expedient spears, torches, tree-climbing hoops, and forks are left where they were made and used.

Some curated items are also left or occasionally hidden at a camp for future use. Such items include blowpipes (at times incomplete), mortars, and pottery. The former are usually placed on the beams beneath the platanillo leaves, the ends being covered with plant-fiber lids. Mortars are placed on top of the triangular grills if there are any in the camp. Otherwise, small *ad hoc* wooden platforms are built to house them. Pottery is usually stored close to the chontaduro orchards, to be used during the chontaduro feast for *chicha* preparation. In addition, large *búrup* containing wild cotton are sometimes stored in the roof of abandoned camps, beneath the plantain leaves. Undoubtedly, in such cases considerations of energy expenditure influences the manner in which the Nukak decide how to make, use, repair, and/or recycle their artifacts.

Nukak technology shows quite clearly how the three dimensions of meaning—utilitarian, social, and ideational—act simultaneously, affecting the way artifacts are produced, used, and discarded. I argue that the importance and the weight of each dimension is not fixed through the lifetime of an artifact but is situational, changeable, and neither unidirectional nor irreversible. Also, the supposedly clear-cut distinction between an artifact's "function" while circulating within the living, "systemic" context (in the words of Schiffer [1976]) and the postdiscard archaeological context is challenged. The entire concept of "use life" (Schiffer 1976:60) should be reviewed, although the estimation of tool use lives, in the classic sense of the concept (when artifacts are actively used by people in their primary utilitarian dimension), remains a valid and helpful way of approaching the material side of technology and artifacts (for example, see Shott 1989). In the Nukak example, broken pottery and a burned hammock left on the camp floor contain coded information for the future visitors of that place. These broken pieces tell stories to those who can interpret them, stories that are important to the Nukak, providing them with knowledge of their relatives, other people, and events that take place in their lands. In this sense, the primary instrumental dimension is diluted and the broken and discarded objects, seemingly already out of their systemic context, retain their social dimension and acquire a new, unprecedented communicative function.

To take the blowpipe as an example, the first point to be made is this: how can the time and energy expended in making a blowpipe be measured? The second point is that even if it were possible to measure both variables, what would such a measurement mean? In order to tackle the first issue, should we measure the time and the energy used to travel to the Cerro de las Cerbatanas? If so, we would have to take into account the fact that during the journey the men carried out other activities (ranging from hunting and gathering to performing rituals) and also brought canes for relatives, hence maintaining the social network. They also collected all sorts of information, including the current yield of particular trees, the state of affairs of certain bands, and the situation at the *colono* frontier. How is it possible to measure, or even to estimate, the energy expended on each of these activities? Moreover, in what units should the information gathered be measured? Once the men have returned with the canes they are given to other men on the basis of their kinship, a process not measurable in any unit of energy. Finally, the blowpipe is used, let us say, for "utilitarian" purposes (that is, hunting monkeys) but ends its use life suddenly, long before its normal usage has produced waste, when it is broken into many pieces by an angry partner during an argument. The simple, energy-oriented approach would result in a fictitious conclusion: a great deal of energy expended for little return. Is this correct? Does it reveal something about the efficiency of the blowpipe, or, instead, is it informative of the way the Nukak solve kinship conflicts?

Some would argue that what happens to a broken blowpipe is merely anecdotal and that in the long term a pattern will emerge in the relationship between the time and the energy expended on the weapon and the amount of food energy obtained with it. This is not completely true. Each blowpipe has a unique trajectory and is subject to all sorts of contingencies. Some endure until they are over-used; others survive until a wise Nukak "blows on the *chicha*" of the user. Still others remain in use for a short time, until destroyed during a conjugal argument. Cabrera, Franky, and Mahecha (1999:203) also recorded several cases of deliberate breakage of blowpipes, such as the case of a woman who broke the blowpipe of her husband when she found out he had had sexual relations with her sister when she (the sister) had recently given birth to a daughter.

Even so, admitting that energy and time is expended for nonutilitarian purposes leaves open the question of how to measure the proportion of energy used for the instrumental, the social, and the ideational dimensions. The problem is not only practical (in terms of our ability to dissect the time and energy used for different purposes) but also conceptual. How can the weight of the social and the ideational in any given artifact or technological system be estimated? In some societies it could be minimal, as it can be at certain times within a single society, but in others it could be extremely significant. Thus it is incorrect to assume that the socioideational aspects are secondary and to take for granted that instrumental aspects are determined by material needs, technological ability, or energy equilibrium alone.

Finally, the information presented in relation to children's artifacts has several important implications for archaeology. Children represent a significant percentage of human populations and spend much of their time inside residential camps. Analyzing the data gathered from the Nukak and comparing them to other South American foragers and North American Plains Indians (see Politis 1999) enables several common patterns to emerge. The following expectations can thus be postulated. First, it must be anticipated that a high proportion of archaeological remains from hunter-gatherer residential camps will be children's artifacts and their by-products. Second, it should also be possible to identify, in a given context, to which class an artifact belongs. Third, adults and children's artifacts do not separate into discrete clusters. There is a full range of variation in size and quality depending on the age of the user, his or her stature and ability, and the situation. At one end of this range are the smaller, poorly made artifacts; at the opposite end are the larger and better-quality objects, with an infinite possible range of combinations in between. Fourth, the recognition of a variety of clusters generated by children is another independent indicator that can be used to confirm the function of the site as a residential camp.

Bearing in mind the first point, one should expect the remains of children's activities to include a wide range of residues that are not the function of a *chaîne opératoire* aimed at the production of artifacts to be used in technoeconomic tasks or as items of symbolic value. These artifacts and their residues will have different trajectories that fall outside the expectations generated by the more usual models of the optimization of raw materials. Based on ethnographic information from hunter-gatherers, one can anticipate that sites generated by this type of society in the past, when residential camps are in evidence, will contain significant percentages of artifacts produced by children. These will range from those produced by practicing the reduction of nodules, training with primary and secondary flakes, to the fabrication of various generally poor-quality artifacts. The same can be expected for pottery, with training in the decoration and manufacture of vessels. Hence, one should expect quantities of clay and small recipients molded by children—who accompanied adults during the production process—to be present at ceramic production locus.

The normative perspective within archaeology relies on the reasoning that the ethnic or the cultural distance between different populations in the past can be measured in terms of the degree of similarity between archaeological assemblages (Jones 1997:25). Processual archaeology signaled differences in site function, modes of resource exploitation, and technological strategies as sources of archaeological variation within a single society (see Binford, 1977a, 1978a, 1979 among many others). However, the latter perspective has resulted in a degree of "technocentrism," since it has considered artifacts to be simple tools used for strictly practical and functional purposes without addressing other dimensions of material culture, such as its social and symbolic content. The consideration of age groups in the formation of the archaeological record generates novel perspectives, because they constitute a significant source of artifactual variation whose utilitarian dimension varies according to the age group to which the user belongs.

Technological activities are not only the consequence of planned tasks, consciously directed toward the obtainment of functionally efficient artifacts. They are also the result of learning and teaching processes. Among the old people, the production of objects in particular ways also signifies a means of maintaining status and prestige. The technological ability of older people has its particularities that should be reflected in the trends of the archaeological record. Bearing in mind such considerations opens up a new horizon in the study of hunter-gatherer material culture, since it is clear that the record produced is multidimensional and responds to a variety of causes, among which are included teaching and learning, diversions and games, and the management of objects to maintain social prestige. What percentage of residue did a linear process in the production of a set of utilitarian artifacts produce? How much of this derives from the recurrent and constant action of children playing and practicing within the camps? Aside from a few exceptions (for example, Bodú, Karlin, & Ploux 1990; Dawe 1997; Nami 1994; Park 1998), this postulate has not been advanced in past hunter-gatherer lithic technology studies. Undoubtedly, the answer is complex and different for each case study. In principle, however, the best way of approaching the analysis is from a perspective that provides space for multiple agents, not all of whom attempt to use raw material optimally. Neither may they be sufficiently trained and skilled or worried about obtaining useful and efficient artifacts in technoeconomic terms.

Old people as well as children make artifacts in a distinct fashion and with purposes beyond the strictly utilitarian. Adolescents also fabricate specific objects, generally related to rites of passage. As such, it is fairly clear that different age groups within hunter-gatherer societies generate a variety of utensils that do not function solely within the technoeconomic sphere but rather embody multiple dimensions of meaning related to learning, entertainment, status, teaching, ritual, and so on. With an appropriate methodology it will be possible to see how material culture transforms itself over the lifetime of individuals and how this generates different trends in archaeological deposits.

Notes

1. They were identified in this mountainous area, located in the Nukak Natural Reserve, by M. Córdoba and A. Etter (Cárdenas & Politis 2000).
2. As stated in Chapter 9, men do not hunt monkeys for approximately one month after their partner has given birth. At such times, they probably do not use their blowpipes.

3. The action of poisoning with barbasco (see Chapter 8).
4. The name in Nukak is taken from Cabrera, Franky, and Mahecha (1994:219).
5. Identified as juansoco (*Couma macrocarpa*) by Cabrera, Franky, and Mahecha (1994:185).
6. According to Cabrera, Franky, and Mahecha (1994:173) it is called *ki* (*Licania* sp.).
7. Cabrera, Franky, and Mahecha (1994:188) identify this vine as *we* or *bui* (*Heteropsis* sp.).
8. In previous publications, the tree from which the bark for the *guayuco* is obtained was identified as *Eschweilera* (Cabrera, Franky, & Mahecha 1994) or *Cariniana* sp. (Gutiérrez Herrera 1996). Nonetheless, it is probable that both identifications are incorrect, as was discussed in Cárdenas and Politis (2000:48).
9. Cabrera, Franky, and Mahecha (1994:190) identify this as *Euchroma gigantea*.
10. Cabrera, Franky, and Mahecha (1994:166) call it *kedā* and describe it as a plant cultivated in the Nukak gardens. Furthermore, in their Table 4 they classify it as psychotropic. Besides being a vegetable dye we have information concerning its use as a psychotropic substance for magical and religious ends (although we have never experienced this effect). See discussion in Chapter 10.
11. Cabrera, Franky, and Mahecha (1994:Table 6) identify it as *Caruocar glabrum*.
12. The cases recorded during our fieldwork largely concerned women who were visiting other women from nearby camps.
13. Gualteros (Ms:15) is alone in mentioning that he once saw two zoomorphic ceramic figurines.

Chapter 8

SUBSISTENCE

Forager subsistence has always been a central issue in anthropology, archaeology, and bioanthropology. In fact, subsistence was the original criterion used to separate hunter-gatherers from other kinds of societies. Although other criteria were later added, including mobility, social organization, and sharing, subsistence remains the key to categorizing and, according to some people, understanding any given forager society. In hunter-gatherer studies in general, and in particular of those groups inhabiting the rainforest, there exist two central ideas that have permeated research and tainted the image of these societies for the last fifty years: first, that there is a close relationship between the abundance and availability of food resources and other social and cultural traits, so that the former determine the latter (Bettinger 1991; Binford 1980; Hassan 1981; and so on). For example, Hassan (1981:7) argued that, "the population density of hunter-gatherers is a reflection of the amount of resource yield given certain resource choices and level of food consumption." The second dominant idea concerns the potentiality of the tropical rainforest for hunter-gatherer subsistence. When ecological functionalism was at the peak of its popularity it was argued that the rainforests were poor environments with a severe lack of carbohydrates, protein, and calories in general (see revision in Hames & Vickers 1983). This widely accepted representation nurtured the Bailey-Headland model, which has been developed and proposed several times since 1986 (Bailey 1990; Bailey & Headland 1991; Bailey et al. 1989, 1991; Headland 1987; Headland & Bailey 1991) and has promoted lively debate (Brosius 1991; Cavelier et al. 1995; Colinvaux & Bush 1991; Mercader 1997; Stearman 1991; Towsend 1990). In early papers, Headland proposed that carbohydrates were the limiting factor, whereas Bailey and associates also took into account fat and other sources of nutrients (see similarities and differences in Headland & Bailey 1991). In a later paper, they conclude that, "in the absence of purposeful forest clearing for the purposes of cultivation of domesticated or semidomesticated plants,

humans have never subsisted for sustained periods in tropical forest environments" (Bailey & Headland 1991:266–67). Domestication and forest clearance
were considered to be the two prerequisites for living successfully in the
rainforest, without which foragers would not survive unless they obtained
crops from neighbors. Finally, Bailey and Headland reinforced the argument
that calories, not protein, are the limiting factor for tropical rainforest foragers.

The idea about the existence of "limiting factors" to the human occupation
of the Amazonian rainforest has a long tradition in anthropological studies.
Poor soils, sparse faunal resources, the lack of efficient transportation, and
isolation from the main centers of cultural invention (the Andes) were presented as limiting factors that explained the lack of social complexity in the
region (Steward & Faron 1959). This was particularly marked in the *terra
firme*, the interriverine areas with poor soils (Meggers 1971). Only in the
várzea (the floodplains of the main white water rivers), where annual flooding
produced silt-rich soils, were the limiting factors reversed. Lathrap (1968)
continued to develop the idea of the poverty of the *terra firme* habitat but focused on the concept of devolution. While many related studies were carried
out based on this assumption (see reviews in Carneiro 1995; Hames &Vickers
1983; Neves 1999; Sponsel 1986), Gross's hypothesis (1975) deserves particular mention, since he expanded the model of animal protein as the limiting
factor for Amazonian populations. Carbohydrate deficiency has also been
put forward as a critical factor in population density (Milton 1984) and occupation of the *terra firme* generally.

The conclusions reached by these important studies have inspired a tradition
in Amazonian research that explains human adaptation in the region by em-
phasizing that the lack of resources makes it particularly difficult for foragers
to subsist in *terra firme*. Scarcity, poverty, and constraint are often used to describe the effect of the Amazonian landscape on human settlement. Since
the negative aspects of the Amazon have been emphasized, it is not surprising
that environmental factors have emerged as the major limiting factor on human
adaptation. For a number of years a significant effort was devoted to identifying
a single "ultimate limiting factor" (Milton 1984:219).

An important feature of the discussion of the viability of hunter-gatherers
in the Amazon is that there are few detailed and quantitative studies on human
diet (among the exceptions see Dufour 1994; Milton 1984; and so on). Most
of the data used in the extant models has been based on impressionistic,
anecdotal, or rough estimates of annual diet. This is especially true in regard
to the diet of foragers. Silverwood-Cope's (1972) and Reid's (1979) frequently
cited dissertations provided good quality data on subsistence, but, as noted,
by the time both projects were carried out the Kakwa and the Hupdu based
their subsistence on cultivated manioc.

In this chapter, I present original data on subsistence. To estimate diet, all the food that entered the camp over a specific period of time was weighed with a hand scale. We recorded food intake for a total of 69 days—39 days in the wet season (July, August, and September 1991 and 1992) and 30 days during the dry season (January and February 1994 and 1995). Obviously, these data cannot be translated directly into diet percentages owing to two main problems: (1) a large quantity of food is consumed outside the camp during daily foraging trips and was therefore technically impossible to weigh; and (2) the edible part of each resource varies significantly.

Furthermore, in this chapter Nukak subsistence is characterized and examined to evaluate the existing model related to tropical forest foragers. The archeological implications of Nukak behavior are also discussed. The quantitative and qualitative data obtained for the Nukak during my fieldwork are complemented by those of Cabrera, Franky, and Mahecha (1999), who provide a good record of year-round economic activities. Ruth Gutiérrez Herrera's graduate dissertation (1996) and the unpublished works of Hector Mondragón are also used.

A corollary subject tackled in this chapter is the manner in which hunter-gatherers manipulate or manage plant resources. Orthodox concepts of plant domestication have recently changed in the context of people-plant interaction (Harris 1989:18; Hecht & Posey 1989:185–86). The distinction between domesticated and undomesticated is no longer clear. Between these two categories exists a broad spectrum of plants that, although not domesticated in the classic sense of the term, are nonetheless manipulated through human intervention (Harris 1989; Posey 1984a, b; Rindos 1984). Clement (in Dufour & Wilson 1994:115) proposed the terms semidomesticated, cultivated, and managed as three main intermediate stages. Other authors include ideas such as "tolerated," "protected" (see Dufour & Wilson 1994), "tamed" (Groube 1989), "plant husbandry" (Higgs & Jarman 1972; Shipek 1989), and "incidental domestication" (Rindos 1984). Moreover, it has been agreed that "incidental domestication"—the spread (conscious or not) of wild plant species by humans and the genetic changes that resulted from this process—is probably as old as humankind and is not generally the concept of domestication used by archaeologists (Price & Gebauer 1995:17).

My aim is not to examine or offer hypothetical explanations concerning the origins of agriculture/horticulture by using the Nukak as potential living representatives of a past evolutionary stage in the development of plant domestication. I do not consider them to be "protocultivators" or "incipient farmers" who are involved in an irreversible process of plant domestication, moving toward an agricultural/horticultural stage. Instead, I want to describe and examine the processes involved in the use of plants and bring attention to their effects on contemporary and past societies. Finally, I discuss social and ideological factors, advocating that they are crucial in highlighting different aspects of the continuum of ecological change involved in the people-plant interaction. To this end, the scant but significant data related to the symbolic dimension of trees and plants are examined.

During our fieldwork, Nukak subsistence was based on the following types of resources: animal products; nondomesticated plants; domesticated plants; fish, crabs, and other aquatic products; insects and insect by-products; and food from the *colonos*, including both processed and unprocessed products. These resources contributed in different ways to the annual diet, varying significantly by season and between bands. *Colonos'* foodstuffs played a greater role for the bands that had more contact with the *colonos* and that were more westernized.

NONDOMESTICATED PLANTS

One pillar of Nukak subsistence consists of gathering wild and "manipulated" plant species. Women, men, and children make excursions from the camp daily to collect fruit, seeds, and roots (see Chapter 6). They carry the procured plant products in bunches, or they separate the fruit from their stems and transport them in expedient bags (*búrup*), baskets, and occasionally metal and pottery bowls. During these expeditions and procurement trips band members usually eat fruit and nuts close to the source tree (Figure 8.1).

Women usually depend on men for collecting plant products, especially palms, since the trees have to be felled or climbed to reach the fruit. Both tasks are generally carried out by men, or, in the latter case, by boys. The fruits gathered by women alone are, therefore, those that grow closer to the ground, such as platanillo, *koró-paanját* (a species of the Myristicaceae family), and tubers. This does not mean that women do not participate significantly in fruit gathering as they do in most hunter-gatherer societies; this case differs because most fruit grows in the canopy. Usually, men cut down the trees, leaving the women and children to gather the fruit. Women and children are more active in harvesting the chagras when the camps are located close by (less than 1 km), since most cultivated products are easily gathered without assistance or tools (Figure 8.2).

Ethnobotanical studies indicate that the Nukak exploit a variety of plant resources. Cabrera, Franky, and Mahecha (1999) counted 83 nondomesticated species used, of which 43 were identified. Gutiérrez Herrera (1996) mentioned the use of 53 species, including 43 noncultivated and 10 cultivated species found in the chagras. Among the noncultivated, 33 were used as food, while

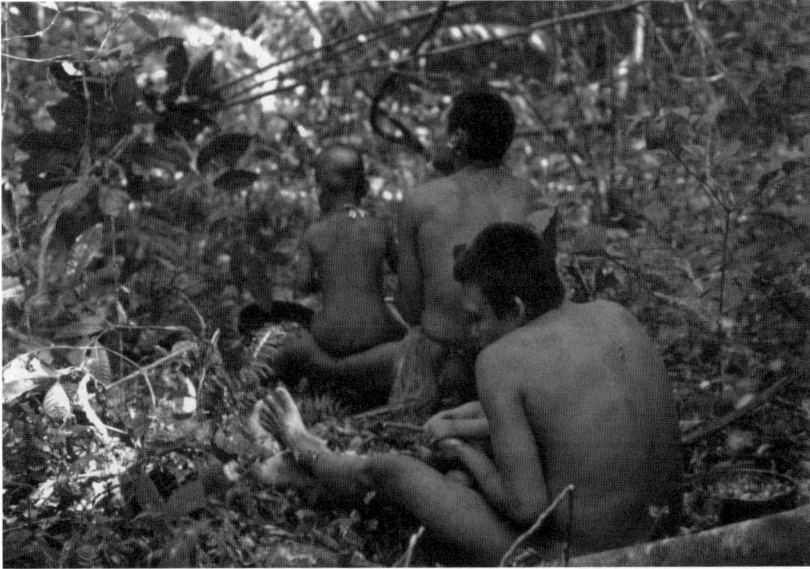

Figure 8.1   Nukak family eating *koró-paanját* close to the tree during a daily foraging trip

Figure 8.2   Group of women harvesting in a chagra; note the monkeys on the shoulders of the two women.

8 of the cultivated species were eaten. Cárdenas and Politis (2000) identified 113 utilized species, which encompass the great majority of the plants recorded in the two previous studies. Among this list of species, 90 are noncultivated

(Table 8.1) and 23 are cultivated (Table 8.2) (the majority of which were incorporated within the last decade). Seventy-six of these species are used as food. Only 7 species present in earlier studies were not recorded by Cárdenas and Politis, the addition of which would bring the total of identified plants to 120. All these figures must be considered as minimums, since more ethnobotanical research must be carried out to fully identify the whole range of plants used. However, when one compares the data obtained by the authors named above with those from other authors who mention plant utilization (Gutiérrez Herrera 1996; Mondragón Ms; Reina 1990), it appears that the major plant food resources have now been recorded.

The best-represented family is Arecaceae (Palmae) with 15 species. Its palm products are used as food but also for making artifacts, building the lean-to dwellings, and as a bed for palm grubs. The Moraceae family, the fruit of which is used exclusively as food, is ranked second with 10 species. In third place is Burseraceae with 5 species, used mostly as food. The Palmae are not only the most numerous but also yield the most kilos of product, both as foodstuff and for other uses.

With regard to wild plants, although Nukak subsistence includes the exploitation of at least 77 species (see Table 8.1) the key plants are far fewer. During the annual cycle, seje (*Oenocarpus bataua*), platanillo (*Phenakospermum guianensis*), and *juiú* (*Attalea* sp.) fruit (Figure 8.3) are regularly exploited in great quantities and with high frequency. The fruits of these trees are available most of the year round.[1]

Seje is a 15-m- to 18-m-tall solitary, naked palm, with infrafoliar infrutescence. The fruits are ovoid, black-purple, 2–4 cm in diameter, and with a thin oily mesocarp. The fruit is widely used by the Nukak and is either eaten immediately or mashed to make a type of milk (Figure 8.3). A man climbs the palm and detaches the racemes. Later, they are shelled by persons treading on them to loosen the fruit over a bed of platanillo leaves laid flat on the ground. They are subsequently deposited in a *búrup* (made from the leaves of the same seje) and transported to the camp where they are consumed. Occasionally, an entire raceme is carried to the camp without first being shelled. The cooked fruit is sometimes mashed with honey and pollen and the juice consumed. This palm is also used in the manufacture of several utensils (see Chapter 7). It is abundant in some parts of the territory and was seen germinating in almost all the abandoned camps. The other two species of *Oenocarpus, popere* (*O. mapora*) and patabá or *yuabutu* (*O. bacaba*) are eaten in a similar fashion, but far less frequently.

The platanillo (also called tarriago regionally) grows up to 18 m tall, 10–15 cm in diameter, with distich leaves 4 m long and 50 cm wide. This species is

Table 8.1 List of Noncultivated Species Used by the Nukak (modified from Cárdenas & Politis 2000)

Specie	Family	Nukak Name	Spanish or Regional Name	Use
Abuta grandifolia (C. Mart.) Sandwith	MENISPERMACEAE	*Mamutuka*		Food
Aechmea rubiginosa Mez	BROMELIACEAE	*Kamuku/o*	Piñuela	Food-Tool
Alibertia cf. edulis (L. C. Rich.) A. Rich. ex DC.	RUBIACEAE		Perita	Food
Anthurium sp.	ARACEAE	*Buu*	Tripa de Pollo	Construction
Arrabidaea chica (Humb. & Bonpl.) Verl.	BIGNONIACEAE	*Kená* or *Éóro'*		Decoration
Aspidosperma excelsum Benth.	APOCYNACEAE	*Peve-na* or *Chak naát*	Castillo	Tool
Astrocaryum aculeatum G. Mey.	ARECACEAE	*Wamni*	Cumare	Food-Tool
Astrocaryum gynacanthum Mart.	ARECACEAE	*Máam* or *Weí*		Food
Attalea maripa (Aubl.) Mart.	ARECACEAE	*Kurá*	Palma Real or Palma Amarga	Food-Construction
Attalea sp.	ARECACEAE	*Jutú*		Food
Bactris maraja Mart. var. Maraja	ARECACEAE	*Pahp*	Chontilla	Food-Tool
Batocarpus amazonicus (Ducke) Fosberg	MORACEAE		Árbol del Pan	Food
Bellucia pentamera Naudin	MELASTOMATACEAE	*Túkare*	Guayaba de Mico	Food
Brosimum guianense (Aubl.) Huber	MORACEAE	*Juutuna* or *Binire*		Food
Cariniana sp.	LECYTHIDACEAE		Abarco	Tool
Caryocar glabrum (Aubl.) Pers.	CARYOCARACEAE		Castañita	Food
Cecropia sciadophylla C. Mart.	CECROPIACEAE	*Ñun*	Yarumo	Food
Cedrelinga cateniformis (Ducke) Ducke	MIMOSACEAE	*Dídn*	Cedro Achapo	Decoration
Ceiba pentandra (L.) Gaertn.	BOMBACACEAE	*Puyí*	Ceiba	Tool
Clathrotropis macrocarpa Ducke	FABACEAE	*Tepá*	Fariñero	Medicine
Couma macrocarpa Barb. Rodr.	APOCYNACEAE	*Wee*	Juansoco	Food-Decoration
Couratari guianensis Aubl.	LECYTHIDACEAE	*Dú*		Tool

(Table 8.1 continued)

(Table 8.1 continued)

Specie	Family	Nukak Name	Spanish or Regional Name	Use
Curarea tecunarum Barneby & Krukoff	MENISPERMACEAE	*Parupi'*	Curare	Toxic
Dacryodes chimantensis Steyerm. & Maguire	BURSERACEAE	*Kupé*		Food
Dacryodes peruviana (Loes.) J.F. Macbr.	BURSERACEAE	*Guaná ó Waná*		Food
Dacryodes sp.	BURSERACEAE			Food
Dialium guianense (Aubl.) Sandwith	CAESALPINIACEAE		Pepa Agria	Food
Doliocarpus sp.	DILLENIACEAE	*Yiik tekere*		Tool
Duguetia quitarensis Benth.	ANNONACEAE	*Tiuveibdu'*		Food
Duguetia spixiana C. Mart.	ANNONACEAE	*Wipichacum*		Food-Tool
Duroia hirsuta (Poepp. & Endl.) Schum	RUBIACEAE	*Maám-ára*		Food
Duroia maguirei Steyerm.	RUBIACEAE	*Tau*		Food
Eschweilera spp.	LECYTHIDACEAE	*Diina*	Borojó Silvestre	Construction
Eugenia sp.	MYRTACEAE	*Chictucari*	Cargueros	Food
Euterpe precatoria Mart.	ARECACEAE	*Yúbudi*	Açaí	Food-Tool
Garcinia macrophylla C. Mart.	CLUSIACEAE	*Akaká*	Bakurí	Food
Geonoma cf. *deversa* (Poit.) Kunth	ARECACEAE	*Blui*		Tool
Heliconia hirsuta L.f	HELICONIACEAE		Platanillos	Tool
Heliconia psittacorum L.f	HELICONIACEAE		Platanillos	Tool
Heliconia stricta Huber	HELICONIACEAE		Platanillos	Tool
Helicostylis cf. *tomentosa* (Poepp. & Endl.) C.C. Berg	MORACEAE	*Patataá*		Food
Heteropsis tenuispadix Bunting	ARACEAE	*Buu*	Yaré	Construction
Hyeronima alchorneoides Allemao	EUPHORBIACEAE	*Chiíri*		Food
Hymenaea oblongifolia Huber	CAESALPINIACEAE	*Karápa*		Food-Tool
Ichnanthus breviscrobs Döll	POACEAE	*Pedn*		Tool-Decoration

Scientific name	Family	Indigenous name	Spanish name	Use
Inga alba (Sw.) Willd.	MIMOSACEAE	*Chitá*		Food-Decoration
Inga fastuosa (Jacc.) Willd.	MIMOSACEAE	*Wapdeja*	Guamo	Food
Iriartea deltoidea Ruiz & Pav.	ARECACEAE	*Juruda-wa*	Bombona	Food
Iriartella setigera (Mart.) H. Wendl.	ARECACEAE	*Ú-Baká*		Tool
Iryanthera ulei Warb.	MYRISTICACEAE	*Koró-paanját*	Mamita	Food
Ischnosiphon arouma (Aubl.) Körn.	MARANTACEAE	*Bórop*	Guarumo	Tool
Justicia pectoralis Jacq.	ACANTHACEAE	*Éuyi*		Decoration
Lacunaria sp.	QUIINACEAE	*Mupabuat*		Food
Lonchocarpus nicou (Aubl.) DC.	FABACEAE	*Nuún*	Barbasco	Toxic
Manilkara bidentata (A. DC.) Chev.	SAPOTACEAE	*Namaru*	Balata	Food
Maquira guianensis Aubl.	MORACEAE	*Yé*		Food
Mauritia flexuosa L.f.	ARECACEAE	*Eü or Uj*	Moriche	Food-Tool
Micrandra sprucei (Baill.) R.E. Schult.	EUPHORBIACEAE		Siringa Blanca	Food
Micropholis guyanensis (A. DC.) Pierre	SAPOTACEAE	*Bíyup*		Food
Mouriri cauliflora C. Mart. ex DC.	MELASTOMATACEAE	*In or ig*		Food
Myroxylon sp.	FABACEAE	*Ukéa´*		Decoration
Naucleopsis mello-barretoi (Standl.) C.C. Berg	MORACEAE	*Bijnidé*		Food
Naucleopsis ulei (Warb.) Ducke	MORACEAE		Lechero	Food
Niphidium crassifolium (L.) Lellinger	POLYPODIACEAE	*Maiku´ját*		Medicine
Oenocarpus bacaba Mart.	ARECACEAE	*Yáab butu*	Patabá	Food-Tool
Oenocarpus bataua Mart.	ARECACEAE	*Yáab*	Seje óMil Pesos	Food-Tool
Oenocarpus mapora H. Karst.	ARECACEAE	*Popere*		Food-Tool
Pachira nukakika Fernández Alonso (inedita)	BOMBACACEAE	*Puyá-meru*		Tool
Parinari montana Aubl.	CHRYSOBALANACEAE	*Yei*		Food
Parkia multijuga Benth.	MIMOSACEAE	*Mu*		Tool
Passiflora vitifolia Humb. & Bonpl. ex Kunth	PASSIFLORACEAE		Granadilla de Monte	Food

(Table 8.1 continued)

(*Table 8.1 continued*)

Specie	Family	Nukak Name	Spanish or Regional Name	Use
Pausandra trianae (Müll. Arg.) Baill.	EUPHORBIACEAE	*Tijana'*		Combustion
Perebea angustifolia (Poepp. & Endl.) C.C. Berg	MORACEAE	*Echauchu*		Food
Perebea guianensis Aubl.	MORACEAE	*Echaudi*		Food
Perebea xanthochyma H. Karst.	MORACEAE	*Yedn*		Food
Phenakospermum guyanense (Rich.) Endl.	STRELITZIACEAE	*Juná*	Tarriago or platanillo	Tool-Construction.-Food
Philodendron victoriae Bunting	ARACEAE	*Burikeii*		Medicine
Pourouma bicolor C. Mart.	CECROPIACEAE	*Yen*		Food
Pourouma sp.	CECROPIACEAE	*Mëu*		Food
Pouteria caimito (Ruiz & Pav.) Radlk.	SAPOTACEAE	*Juutana*	Caimo	Food
Pradosia sp.	SAPOTACEAE	*Tegebu*		Food
Protium crassipetalum Cuatrec.	BURSERACEAE	*Cheñe*		Food
Pseudolmedia laevis (Ruiz & Pav.) J.F. Macbr.	MORACEAE	*Chuu'tukéri*		Food
Salacia cf. *impressifolia* (Miers) A.C. Sm.	HIPPOCRATEACEAE	*Uamao*	Güeva de Tigre	Medicine
Siparuna decipiens (Tul.) A. DC.	MONIMIACEAE	*Juru*		Medicine
Socratea exorrhiza (Mart.) H. Wendl.	ARECACEAE	*Ígi-jere*	Zancona	Tool
Theobroma glaucum G. Karst.	STERCULIACEAE	*Ígi*		Food
Theobroma obovatum Klotzsch ex Bernoulli	STERCULIACEAE	*Igi-baká*	Cacao de Monte	Tool
Theobroma subincanum C. Mart.	STERCULIACEAE	*Eu*		Food
Trattinnickia glaziovii Swart	BURSERACEAE			Tool

Table 8.2 List of Cultivated Species Used by the Nukak (modified from Cárdenas & Politis 2000)

Specie	Family	Nukak Name	Spanish or Regional Name	USE
Anacardium occidentale L.	ANACARDIACEAE		Marañon	Food
Ananas comosus (L.) Merr.	BROMELIACEAE	*Cupuri* or *chuú*	Piña	Food
Annona muricata L.	ANNONACEAE		Guanabana	Food
Bactris gasipaes Humb. & Bonpl. ex Kunth	ARECACEAE	*Báyup* or *Juyuni*	Chontaduro	Food
Bixa orellana L.	BIXACEAE	*Mée*	Achiote	Decoration
Capsicum chinense Jacq.	SOLANACEAE	*Tubni-dé*	Ají	Food
Carica papaya L.	CARICACEAE		Papaya	Food
Colocasia esculenta (L.) Schott	ARACEAE		Mafafá	Food
Crescentia cujete L.	BIGNONIACEAE		Totumo	Tool
Dioscorea trifida L.f.	DIOCOREACEAE		Tábena	Food
Gynerium sagitatum (Aubl.) P. Beauv.	POACEAE	*Wékiri*	Caña brava	Tool
Ipomoea batatas (L.) Lam.	CONVOLVULACEAE	*Dii*	Batata	Food
Lagenaria siceraric (Molina) Standl.	CUCURBITACEAE	*Kuudn*		Tool
Macoubea guianersis Aubl.	APOCYNACEAE	*Dárua*		Tool
Manihot esculenta Crantz	EUPHORBIACEAE	*Ucuye*	Ucuye	Food
Musa paradisiaca L.	MUSACEAE	*Jeedn-iíbu*	Yuca	Food
Nicotiana tabacum L.	SOLANACEAE	*Ji-ni*	Banano	Food
Posadaea sphaeroarpa Cogn.	CUCURBITACEAE	*Júup*	Tabaco	Psicotropic
Pourouma cecropifolia C. Mart.	CECROPIACEAE	*Peye-Dárua*	Tarralí	Tool
Rollinia mucosa (Jacq.) Baill.	ANNONACEAE		Caimarona	Food
Saccharum officinarum L.	POACEAE	*Mene*	Anón amazónico	Food
Xanthosoma sp.	ARACEAE	*Turú*	Caña de azúcar	Food
Zea mays L.	POACEAE	*Wéá* or *Káná´*	Boré	Food
			Maíz	Food

Figure 8.3 Processing of seje seeds in the residential camp

widely used by the Nukak; they roof their camps with its leaves, and it produces fruit year round. Of the fruit, the red aril of the seed is chewed for its
oily liquid (Figure 8.4). Platanillo seeds are ground into flour, wrapped in green

Figure 8.4 Woman chewing the red aril of the platanillo seed; note the pet monkey
suckling her breast

leaves, and boiled; they are a good source of carbohydrates (Figure 8.5). The shells are used as fuel as they burn well. Platanillo are always eaten in camp because they require processing. Both men and women gather them and transport either the entire raceme or just the fruit in *búrup*. This species is abundant around the camps, but its germination within them is low owing

Figure 8.5 Woman wrapping platanillo flour in green leaves to be boiled.

to the intense consumption of the seeds. Sectors of high concentration of this species have been observed in different regions of the territory.

The *juiú* is a 10 m-tall palm, solitary and naked, that grows on solid ground. Its fruit is valued for its high energy content. It is generally eaten unprepared or grilled on a wooden-stick grill, either at the foot of the tree or in the camp (Figure 8.6). The nut inside the fruit is occasionally eaten.

Figure 8.6 Man eating fruits of *juiú* close to the tree during a daily foraging trip

The Nukak also consume the fruit of moriche (*Mauritia flexuosa*), koró-páanjat (*Iryanthera ulei*), patataá (*Helicostylis cf. tomentosa*), palma real (*Attalea maripa*), guaná (*Dacryodes peruviana*), kupé (*Dacryodes chimantensis*), juansoco (*Couma macrocarpa*), bijnidé (*Naucleopsis mello-barretoi*), and many others (see Table 8.1). Most of these fruits are collected in large quantities and in varying frequencies depending on when the plants bear fruit (see Tables 8.3, 8.4, 8.5, and 8.6). In the case of seje, *popere*, patabá, *juiú,* and *guaná*, the fruits are mashed to extract oils and other nutritional substances and are ingested in a milklike form or as chicha, which increases their nutritional value. It was also observed that some tubers, such as *chidna* and *hum*,[2] provide significant quantities of carbohydrates. The latter tuber seems to be "manipulated" by the Nukak, who appear to promote the growth of the wild plant through certain practices.

During the dry season the average quantity of wild fruit brought into the camp was 2.54 kg per person/per day (*n* = 30; see Table 8.7), whereas during

Table 8.3 Weight of Wild Vegetables Brought into the Camp during July 1991

| | Band A | | | | | | | | Band B | | | | | | | | | Total kg. by Species |
| | | | | | | Date | | | | | | | | | | | | |
Species	11	12	13	14	15	16	17	18	19	20	21	22	23	24	25	26	27	
Echaudi	7	–	–	–	–	–	–	–	–	–	–	–	–	–	–	–	–	7
Na'iorende	0.4	–	–	–	–	–	–	–	–	–	–	–	–	–	–	–	–	0.4
Juú	20	–	4.5	25	X	3.5	27	–	3	–	27.5	9.5	35	–	–	–	19	174
Koró-paanját	0.5	–	–	–	–	–	–	–	–	–	–	–	–	–	–	–	–	0.5
Popere	–	2.5	6.5	11	5.5	–	–	–	–	–	–	–	–	–	–	–	–	25.5
Uii	–	–	X	–	–	–	–	–	–	–	–	–	–	–	–	–	–	X
Seje	–	–	–	–	30	–	–	–	–	9	–	–	–	–	–	–	–	39
Yiubeli	–	–	–	–	–	X	–	–	–	–	–	–	–	–	–	–	–	X
Guaná	–	–	–	–	–	–	X	45	8.5	40	–	70	3	5	58	3	20	252.5
Patataá	–	–	–	–	–	–	X	1	–	–	–	–	1.2	–	X	–	–	2.2
Teruke	–	–	–	–	–	–	–	30	–	7.5	–	–	–	–	–	–	–	37.5
Moriche	–	–	–	–	–	–	–	–	2	–	–	–	–	1	X	–	–	3
Nut	–	–	–	–	–	–	–	–	4	50	–	–	–	2	–	–	–	56
Platanillo	–	–	–	–	–	–	–	–	–	–	12	–	–	–	–	12	–	24
Chidná	–	–	–	–	–	–	–	–	X	–	–	–	7	1.5	–	–	–	8.5
Caraigua	–	–	–	–	–	–	–	–	–	–	–	–	–	–	28	–	–	28
Total by day	27.9	2.5	11	36	35.5	3.5	27	76	17.5	106.5	39.5	79.5	46.2	9.5	86	15	39	**658.1**

X = means presence (no quantitative data recorded)
Underlined dates are travel days.
All amounts are expressed in kg.

Table 8.4 Weight of Nondomesticated Vegetables Brought into the Camp during August and September 1992

| | Date | | | | | | | | | | | | | | | | | | | | | Total kg. |
Species	30	31	1	2	3	4	5	6	7	8	9	10	11	12	13	14	15	16	17	18	19	by Species
Platanillo	X	20	49	39	—	58	—	—	—	1	—	31	—	2.5	—	19.5	—	95	11	30.5	X	356.5
Moriche	X	18	6	3	9	27	26	—	15	9	17	—	—	—	—	—	—	—	—	—	—	130
Moriche processed	—	20	—	—	—	7	12	—	—	—	—	—	—	—	—	—	—	—	—	—	—	39
Seje	X	40	65	—	—	47	14	53	25	—	90	13	17	30	80	28.5	15	98.5	—	46	—	662
Nanere	—	—	0.3	—	—	—	—	—	—	—	—	—	—	—	—	—	—	—	—	—	—	0.3
Yédn	—	—	—	27	—	—	—	—	—	—	—	—	—	—	—	—	—	—	—	—	—	27
Juii	—	—	—	—	—	—	—	—	—	—	38	—	—	—	6.5	—	—	—	—	—	X	44.5
Piñuelo	—	—	—	—	—	—	—	—	—	—	2	—	—	—	—	—	—	—	—	—	—	2
Hum	—	—	—	—	—	—	—	—	—	—	—	—	0.2	—	—	—	—	—	—	—	—	0.2
Total by day	X	98	120.3	69	9	139	52	53	40	10	147	44	17.2	32.5	86.5	48	15	193.5	11	76.5	X	**1261.5**

X = means presence (no quantitative data recorded)
Underlined dates are travel days.
All amounts are expressed in kg.

Table 8.5 Weight of Nondomesticated Vegetables Brought into the Camp during January and February 1994

Species	22	23	24	25	26	27	28	29	30	31	1	2	3	4	Total kg. by Species
Koró-paanját	3	0.5	2	25.8	15.5	120.4	48.8	74	29.1	16	25	102.1	34.5	129	625.7
Hum	2														2
Platanillo	19.5							8	14	47.5			6		95
Uei	2		20												22
Seje	13		15.5	14			25	26	57.5	28	61		45		285
Yubutí		1.5													1.5
Nuyó			3.5												3.5
Yaáb butu					38	11.8		26							75.8
Huyapet										0.5			2.5		3
Kurundé pununile											1	3			4
Tekeren-búnende												2.1			2.1
Juiú												16	3.5		19.5
Meeu												1.6	1		2.6
	39.5	2	41	39.8	53.5	132.2	73.8	134	100.6	92	87	124.8	92.5	129	**1141.7**

Underlined dates are travel days.
All amounts are expressed in kg.

Table 8.6 Weight of Nondomesticated Vegetables Brought into the Camp during January and February 1995

Species	20	21	23	24	25	26	27	28	29	30	31	1	2	3	4	5	Total kg. by Species
Platanillo	–	95	2.6	41	12	–	–	0.2	3	–	–	–	–	–	–	–	153.8
binire	–	54.5	0.1	–	–	–	–	–	–	–	–	–	–	–	–	–	54.6
juiú	–	–	–	–	12	–	–	–	–	–	–	–	–	–	–	–	12
Seje	–	47.5	–	92	10	10	–	–	3	25	–	–	–	13	10	–	210.5
Ñeendé	–	–	–	–	–	–	–	–	–	0.2	–	–	–	–	–	–	0.2
N'pede	–	–	–	–	–	–	–	–	–	–	–	–	2	–	–	–	2
Uei	2	–	–	–	–	–	–	–	–	–	–	–	–	–	–	–	2
Total by day	2	197	2.7	133	34	10	–	0.2	6	25.2	–	–	2	13	10	–	**435.1**

Underlined dates are travel days.
All amounts are expressed in kg.

the rainy season the average was 2.8 kg per person/per day ($n = 38$ days; see Table 8.7). These figures indicate that the quantity of wild vegetables that entered the camp varied between 2.06 and 3.3 kg per person/per day, and that there is no significant variation between the two seasons. Also, the values do not vary in relation to number of band members.

Table 8.7 Nondomesticated Vegetables Brought into the Camp

Band	n of People	n of Days	Average per Person/per Day
Rainy Season			
1991a	10 to 15	8	2.21 kg.
1991b	9 to 22	11	2.37 kg.
1992	24	12	3.33 kg.
1992	18	8	3.32 kg.
Dry Season			
1994	27	14	3.02 kg.
1995	14 to 16	16	2.06 kg.

As I stated, these values must be taken with caution, since the net weight entering camp does not equal the edible amount. In some cases, such as the fruit of the palms, the edible portion of the fruit is small, and although the seeds are mashed to extract additional nourishment, a large part is discarded. In other cases, such as the Moraceae, which are fleshy and juicy, the entire fruit is consumed. The most notable seasonal variations are that in the wet season the most frequently eaten fruit are moriche, *popere, guaná*, and the related species *kupé,* cumare, and *teruke*; in the dry season the most represented species are *koró-paanját, bijnidé*, and *patataá*.

With regard to differences related to the consumption of fruits during trips through the forest and fruits that are transported to be eaten in the camps, we make the following observations:

1. The majority of the most abundant fruits that require processing and are hard-shelled are transported to the camp where they are processed and eaten. This group includes all the palms (moriche, seje, *juiú, yáabbutu, popere*, and so on), some Burseraceae (*guaná* and *kupé*), *koró-paanját*, the platanillo, and juansoco.
2. The species that produce large quantities of fruit that do not require processing and are highly fleshy with a soft exocarp are eaten at the foot of the tree, generally by all members of the group, until that individual plant's supply of fruit has been exhausted. Small quantities are occasionally carried to the camp if it is within a short distance. Within this group are included

all the Moraceae (*patataá, bijnidé, yé, echawdi, yedn,* and so on) and some Euforbiaceae (*chiri*).

3. A third category is made up of species with small yields whose fruit can be ingested with no processing and have low alimentary values. This category includes fruits that are eaten only as an alternative or as a complement while the group is moving through the forest. They are not transported to the camp, and, owing to the limited supply of fruits, only a few members of the group eat them at the foot of the plant. This category is extremely heterogeneous and includes a wide variety of species (for example, *maám´árá, chutukeri, in,* and so forth).

ANIMAL RESOURCES

The other pillar of Nukak economy is the exploitation of vertebrates. Almost daily one or several preys are brought into the camp, monkey being the staple. During my fieldwork, 47.7% of days monkeys were hunted (usually several) in the wet season, and 40% of days during the dry season (see Tables 8.8 to 8.11). Cabrera, Franky, and Mahecha (1999:267) recorded that in a sample of 404 hunting events, 239 (59.1%) corresponded to monkeys. Among the several species of monkey living in the area, the most commonly hunted are howler (*m´habu,* araguato [*Alouatta* sp.]), brown capuchin (*wap* or maizero [*Cebus apella*]), woolly (*patchu* or churuco [*Lagothrix lagothricha*]), squirrel monkey (*ikip* [*Saimiri sciureus*], tamarins (diablillo [*Saguinus negricollis*]), and titi (*awa* or Negro [*Callicebus torquatus*]). Gutiérrez Herrera (1996:72) and Cabrera, Franky, and Mahecha (1999:268) also mention the less frequent hunting of four other species, identifying two as the nocturnal monkey (*dugup,* leoncillo [*Aotus trivigatus*], and mico de noche [*Aoutus vociferans*]), brown pale-fronted capuchin (maicero cariblanco [*Cebus alfibrons*]), and pygmy marmoset (titi pigmeo or pielroja [*Cebuella pygmeaea*]). All species are hunted using blowpipes and poisoned darts, either by individuals or small parties of up to four men (see Chapter 6). The carcasses of the monkeys are carried back to camp where women are responsible for their butchering, preparation, and cooking (see Chapter 9). Men's status becomes evident during the transportation of the monkeys: an older hunter can have another hunter carry his kill, or he may decide to transport prey he did not hunt.

Other animals hunted by the Nukak include peccaries, in particular the white-lipped peccary (*Tayassu pecari*). The presence of herds of peccary is unpredictable. When one is encountered, the band's hunters participate in a communal hunt to intensively exploit this resource. The weapon used for these hunting expeditions is a wooden spear about 2 m long, with fire-hardened conical tips at both ends (see Chapter 7). In these types of hunting episodes it is common to secure around three or four animals. They are then cooked and smoked over a large fire located on the periphery of the residential camp (see Chapter 9). The peccary is taboo to most women, and the idea of eating its meat is distasteful to them. In contrast, the men eat peccary meat in great quantities for up to three days after the hunt.

Tortoises (*Geochelone denticulata*) are consumed frequently by the Nukak. They are hunted year-round; every four or five days at least one is captured. Birds, such as panjuil (wattled curassow [*Crax globulosa*] and nocturnal curassow [*Nothocrax urumutum*]), tente (grey-winged trumpeters), pavas (Spix's Guan [*Penelope jacquacu*]) (Figure 8.7), ducks, and others, are also hunted regularly (see also Gutiérrez Herrera 1996:73–5). During our fieldwork other animals were occasionally killed, including agouti (*Dasyprocta fuliginosa.*), caiman (*Caiman sclerops*), armadillo (*Dasypus novemcinctus*), frogs, and unidentified small rodents. Eggs from birds and aquatic animals (such as tortoises) were also occasionally gathered but never in great quantities. Other researchers (Cabrera, Franky, & Mahecha 1999; Mondragón Ms) also mention that the

Figure 8.7 Young man showing two Spix's Guan he recently hunted with blowpipe

Nukak occasionally hunt other species, such as collared peccary (*Tayassu tajacu*), American opossum (*Didelphis marsupialis*), paca (*Agouti paca*), "cachirre" (*Paleosuchius trigonatus*), and coatimundis (*Nasua nasua*). I did not record the hunting of any of these animals during my fieldwork.

Although almost all the Nukak bands possess dogs, these were not observed assisting in the hunt, except on one occasion with an agouti. However, the Nukak state that they do in fact use dogs to hunt collared peccary and small rodents.

For the Nukak most of the larger animals are subject to formal taboos. Tapir (*Tapirus terrestris*), deer (*Mazama* sp.) and jaguar (*Panthera onca*) are proscribed, at least in part because they are considered sacred animals that embody spirit-ancestors. Nukak taboos surrounding smaller animals appear to be highly selective. In general, Nukak women, especially pregnant women, cannot eat all that men eat and children can eat even less than women (see discussion in Chapter 9). In this sense, the hunting and the consumption of animals are strongly mediated by the ideational domain.

During our fieldwork in the rainy season the Nukak brought into camp an average of 0.306 kg per person/per day (n = 39 days) of processed and unprocessed game meat (see Tables 8.8 and 8.9), distributed in the following way:

- Band 1991a   3.00 kg per day   0.27 kg per person/per day
- Band 1991b   2.97 kg per day   0.09 kg per person/per day
- Band 1992   12.20 kg per day   0.56 kg per person/per day

Note that the high quantity of meat in the 1992 sample is due to the two peccary hunting events that occurred during our stay. The values obtained were taken after processing (see Chapter 9); therefore, they represent the weight of consumed meat, minus the bones. However, since peccary hunts are rare, the figure given must be placed in the upper limits of the meat-consumption range.

During our fieldwork in the dry season an average of 0.237 kg per day/per person (n = 30 days) of unprocessed game meat was brought into the camp (see Tables 8.10 and 8.11). This was distributed in the following way:

- Band 1994   7.28 kg per day   0.27 kg per person/per day
- Band 1995   2.88 kg per day   0.20 kg per person/per day

In the 1995 fieldwork season a peccary hunt was recorded, which would have modified markedly the averages of meat per person per day. However, this event took place outside the period during which we were recording and

Table 8.8 Weight of Animals (Except Insects and Derivates) Brought into the Camp during July 1991

| | Band A | | | | | | | Band B | | | | | | | | | | Total kg. |
| | Date | | | | | | | | | | | | | | | | | |
Species	11	12	13	14	15	16	17	18	19	20	21	22	23	24	25	26	27	by Species
Howler monkey	6	–	–	–	–	–	–	–	–	–	–	–	–	–	–	–	–	6
Titi monkey	–	–	–	–	–	–	–	–	0.5	–	–	–	–	1.5	–	5.5	–	7.5
Squirrel monkey	–	–	–	–	–	–	–	–	1.5	–	–	–	1.25	–	–	–	–	2.8
Brown capuchin	–	–	–	–	–	–	–	–	–	–	2	–	–	4	–	–	–	6
Parrot	–	–	–	X	–	–	–	–	–	–	–	–	–	–	–	–	–	X
Bird	0.05	–	–	–	–	–	–	–	–	–	–	–	X	–	–	–	–	0.05
Pava de monte	–	–	–	–	1.5	–	–	–	–	–	–	–	–	–	–	–	–	1.5
Tortoise	–	5.5	–	–	7.5	–	–	–	–	–	–	–	2	–	–	–	–	15
Armadillo	–	–	–	–	–	–	–	–	–	–	–	–	–	–	–	–	X	X
Crab	X	–	–	–	–	–	–	–	–	–	–	–	–	–	–	–	–	X
Fish	X	–	–	–	–	–	–	X	4.8	–	X	–	0.6	X	1.5	–	–	6.9
Frog	–	–	–	–	–	–	–	X	–	–	–	–	–	–	–	–	X	X
Total by day	6.05	5.5	–	X	9	–	–	X	6.8	–	2	–	3.85	5.5	1.5	5.5	X	45.7

References: X = means presence (no quantitative data recorded)
Underlined dates are travel days.
All amounts are expressed in kg.

Table 8.9 Weight of Animals (Except Insects and Derivates) Brought into the Camp during August and September 1992

Species	Date																					Total kg. by Species
	30	31	1	2	3	4	5	6	7	8	9	_10_	11	12	_13_	14	15	16	17	18	19	
Howler monkey	6	–	–	–	–	7	–	–	–	–	–	–	9.5	–	–	–	–	–	12	–	–	34.5
Brown capuchin	4	5.5	3	7	–	–	–	–	9	–	17.5	–	5.5	–	–	3.5	4	–	–	2	–	61
Squirrel monkey	–	–	–	–	6	1.5	–	–	2	–	–	–	–	–	–	–	–	–	–	2.5	–	12
Woolly monkey	–	–	–	–	–	7.5	–	–	–	–	–	–	–	–	–	–	12.5	–	6	–	–	26
White-lipped peccary	–	–	37.2	–	–	–	60	–	–	–	–	–	–	–	–	–	–	–	–	–	–	97.2
Tortoise	–	–	9	–	–	–	8	–	–	–	–	–	–	–	–	–	–	–	–	–	–	17
Fish	–	0.7	–	0.9	–	0.5	–	–	–	–	1	–	7	–	–	2.2	–	0.2	–	–	–	12.5
Tente	–	–	–	–	2	–	–	–	–	–	–	–	–	–	–	–	–	–	–	–	–	2
Birds	–	–	–	0.3	0.3	–	–	–	–	0.25	0.5	–	0.2	–	–	–	–	–	–	–	–	1.55
Crab	–	X	–	–	–	–	–	–	–	–	–	–	–	–	–	–	–	–	–	–	–	X
Frog	–	–	–	–	–	X	–	–	–	–	–	–	–	–	–	–	–	–	–	–	–	X
Caiman eggs	–	–	–	–	–	–	–	–	0.4	–	–	–	–	–	–	–	–	–	–	–	–	0.4
Total by day	10	6.2	49.2	8.2	8.3	16.5	68	–	11.4	0.25	19	–	22.2	–	–	5.7	16.5	0.2	18	4.5	–	**264.15**

X = means presence (no quantitative data recorded)
Underlined dates are travel days.
All amounts are expressed in kg.

Table 8.10 Weight of Animals Brought into the Camp during January and February 1994

Species	22	23	24	25	26	27	28	29	30	31	1	2	3	4	Total kg. by Species
Squirrel monkey	2	–	–	–	–	–	2.5	–	–	–	–	–	–	–	4.5
Woolly monkey	–	–	6.5	5.5	–	5.3	–	10	–	–	–	–	5.5	–	32.8
Brown capuchin	–	–	–	3	–	–	–	–	5	–	–	–	6.5	–	14.5
Tortoise	–	–	7	–	–	–	–	5.5	2.5	–	3	–	8	–	26
Parrot	1.5	–	–	–	–	–	–	–	–	–	–	–	–	–	1.8
Birds	0.5	–	–	–	–	0.3	–	–	–	0.3	–	–	–	0.2	1
Small rodent	–	–	0.3	–	–	–	–	–	–	–	–	–	–	–	0.3
Pava	–	–	–	1	–	3.7	–	–	–	–	–	1	–	–	5.7
Tente	–	–	–	4	–	1.4	–	–	–	–	–	–	–	–	5.4
Duck	–	–	–	–	–	–	–	–	–	–	–	–	2.5	1.5	4
Total	4	–	13.8	13.5	–	10.7	2.5	15.5	7.5	0.3	3	1	22.5	1.7	**96 kg.**

All amounts are expressed in kg.
Underlined dates are travel dates.

Table 8.11 Weight of Animals Brought into the Camp during January and February 1995

Species	20	21	23	24	25	26	27	28	29	30	31	1	2	3	4	5	Total kg. by Species
Woolly monkey	–	–	–	–	–	–	–	–	–	–	–	–	–	–	16	–	16
Howler monkey	2	–	–	–	–	–	–	–	–	–	–	–	–	–	–	–	2
Squirrel monkey	–	–	–	2	–	–	–	–	–	–	–	–	–	–	–	–	2
Brown capuchin	–	–	–	.	–	1.6	–	–	–	–	–	–	–	–	–	–	1.6
Tortoise	–	–	–	–	–	–	–	–	–	6.5	–	–	–	–	–	6	12.5
Paujil	3.5	–	–	–	–	–	–	–	–	–	–	–	–	–	1	–	4.5
Agouti	–	–	–	–	–	–	–	–	–	4	–	–	–	–	–	–	4
Caiman	–	–	–	–	–	–	–	–	–	–	–	–	–	–	–	7	7
Small bird	–	–	0.2	–	–	–	–	–	–	–	–	–	–	–	–	–	0.2
Total by day	5.5	–	0.2	2	–	1.6	–	–	–	10.5	–	–	–	–	17	13	**49.8**

Underlined dates are travel days.
All amounts are expressed in kg.

weighing diet systematically, and therefore it was not included within the tables indicating consumption of hunted animals.

The figures presented indicate that there is no substantial seasonal variation and that the limits of meat consumption vary between 0.09 and 0.56 kg per person/per day. However, since these averages are based on a series of observations made over several days, in a few cases there were days on which meat was not eaten.

INSECT AND INSECT BY-PRODUCT RESOURCES

The two main resources in this category are honey (and other beehive products) and palm grubs. Periodically, palm grubs (weevil larvae), called *mun* generically by the Nukak and regionally known as mojojoy, are collected by all members of the band. The great majority of these palm grubs are weevil larvae (Coleoptera) from the genus *Rynchophorus*. During the rainiest months (July–September) the larvae are collected in large quantities and often brought into the camp ($n = 39$ days, 60% of days; Tables 8.12 and 8.13), whereas in the dry season this activity decreases (only a few larvae were recorded eaten at the foot of trees during daily foraging trips, but they were never taken to camp). It was not possible to weigh the quantity of palm grubs consumed since they were eaten immediately. Nevertheless, it was possible to estimate that the Nukak consume between 0.05 and 0.10 kg per person/per day during the wet months. There is no quantitative information for the transitional months.

The larvae develop in the trunks of fallen trees of four principle species— seje, chontaduro, moriche, and cumare. The first is the most abundant and is the most widely distributed in Nukak territory. It is likely that some palms are purposefully felled to create beds for the development of the larvae, as has been observed in other Amazonian groups (Balick 1986; Dufour 1987). The growth time for these larvae is approximately three months, between the moment the tree is cut down (conveniently sliced with an ax at several places along the trunk to favor colonization by the weevils) to when it is split lengthwise and the larvae extracted. Among the different larvae collected, the chontaduro larvae appear to be the largest. Other insects were occasionally also collected, but in smaller quantities. These included caterpillars (Lepidoptera) and small larvae from cumare fruit.

Collecting honey and the contents of hives such as royal jelly, propolis, and larvae contributes significantly to the Nukak diet, especially during the dry season. Honey is occasionally collected during the winter but does not provide a significant quantity of food (Tables 8.12 and 8.13). Cabrera, Franky,

Table 8.12 Weight of Insects and Derivates Brought into the Camp during July 1991

Items	Band A									Band B								Total kg. by Species
	Date																	
	11	12	13	*14*	*15*	*16*	*17*	18	19	20	21	22	23	24	25	26	27	
Palm grubs	–	–	–	X	–	X	–	–	X	–	X	–	–	0.1	4.5	–	–	4.6
Honey	–	–	–	–	–	–	–	–	–	–	1	–	–	–	–	–	–	1
Total by day	–	–	–	X	–	X	–	–	X	–	1	–	–	0.1	4.5	–	–	**5.6**

X = means presence (no quantitative data recorded)

Underlined dates are travel days.

All amounts are expressed in kg.

Table 8.13 Weight of Insects and Derivates Brought into the Camp during September and August 1992

Items	Date																					Total kg. by Species
	30	31	1	2	3	4	5	6	*7*	8	*9*	*10*	11	12	*13*	14	15	16	17	18	19	
Palm grubs	X	–	0.5	0.4	–	0.2	0.5	–	0.25	1	0.8	–	0.3	0.1	–	0.5	–	X	–	0.2	–	4.75
Honey	–	–	–	–	–	–	–	–	–	–	–	–	–	–	0.5	–	–	–	0.4	1	–	1.9
Total by day	X	–	0.5	0.4	–	0.2	0.5	–	0.25	1	0.8	–	0.3	0.1	0.5	0.5	–	X	0.4	1.2	–	**6.65**

X = means presence (no quantitative data recorded)
Underlined dates are travel days.
All amounts are expressed in kg.

and Mahecha (1994:191) found that large quantities of honey were collected in May/June and October/November. The species of bee identified include several genera, the most abundant being *Trigona* and *Melipona* (Cabrera, Franky, & Mahecha 1999; Cárdenas & Politis 2000).

During fieldwork in the dry season—January and February 1994 and 1995—the average amount of honey and beehive product recorded was 0.441 kg per person/per day ($n = 30$ days) (see Tables 8.14 and 8.15). In 1994, $\bar{x} = 0.703$ kg per person/per day, and in 1995 $x = 0.180$ kg per/person per day. The large discrepancy between the two years is due to two factors. First, in 1995 the band with which the data was collected circulated for a time near their cultivated plants and dedicated less time to gathering honey. Consequently, the amount of honey obtained in the sample days was less. Second, during this period of fieldwork the research team was composed of one person only (see Chapter 1), and therefore the weight values were only of stuff that entered the camp, since it was not possible to weigh what was obtained and consumed at the foot of the hive (which did occur in some cases in 1994).

The average 0.441 kg daily consumption of honey per person must be understood in the context of two factors. First, the material weighed was at times pure honey (100% edible) and at other times was honey in pieces of honeycomb, including a variable proportion of the wax cells that, although chewed, are not ingested. As such, not all the recorded weight always corresponded to actual honey. I estimate that between 60% and 70% was pure honey, and the rest represented the hive in which it was contained. The second factor is that the majority of the honey that was weighed arrived at the camp. It was not possible to weigh the honey and other honeycomb products consumed intensively at the foot of the source tree during daily foraging trips or during residential mobility, although this activity was observed on repeated occasions. Consequently, considering both factors, it is estimated that the values presented represent a minimum consumption of honey per person during the dry season, the actual consumption being greater, especially among adult and young men who ate honey more frequently during the daily foraging trips (see Chapter 6).

Honey is obtained by burning the hive and lowering it from the tree (occasionally the tree is cut down). A large proportion of the honey is then eaten on the spot. The rest is stored in expedient leaf bags. In the latter case, part of the honeycomb with honey in its cells is kept. During such honey-consumption events, when the entire band is close to the hive, feeding is intense (Figure 8.8). On one occasion it was observed that a ceiba (*Ceiba pentandra*) of great height (it extended beyond the forest canopy) was cut down with the only apparent immediate motive of gaining access to a large honeycomb in its trunk (Figure 8.9).

FISH AND AQUATIC ANIMALS

Fishing is a common and productive activity during the dry season (Tables 8.14 and 8.15) and occurs, but less frequently and less productively,

Figure 8.8 Couple eating honey on the spot where the honeycomb was lowered

Figure 8.9 Two young men cutting down a ceiba tree to get access to a large honeycomb

the remainder of the year (Tables 8.16 and 8.17). Regarding fishing techniques, the Nukak use conical traps made from plant fibers (see Chapter 7, Figure 7.13, p. 207), water-borne poison (barbasco [*nuún*], obtained from the root of *Lonchocarpus nicou*), bow and harpoon (with both metal and bone points), and metal fishhooks. Usually, traps and hooks are used in the wet season, when individuals or small parties fish, and the catch is generally small. The technique of poisoning the water with barbasco is practiced during the dry season, when the rivers and creeks are low. The process is carried out in the lower reaches of the waterways, close to their mouths. The recorded barbasco fishing events took place in the SN (alluvial plain of the Guaviare River, Figure 1.6, p. 50), and the whole band participated. The adult and young men construct containment dikes in the creeks to diminish the current and submerge the previously crushed root of *Lonchocarpus nicou*, disseminating the toxic substance in the water (Figure 8.10). Subsequently, the adult and young women position themselves in the creek with sticks, machetes, and baskets and strike and grab at the fish stupefied by the poison (Figure 8.11). The catch is then placed in baskets to be taken to the camp. In the case of certain species of catfish that do not surface but rather take refuge in underwater caves at the base of the creek bank, the women remove them with their hands or sticks. Meanwhile, the men wait at the side of the creek, or hunt a few fish with bow and harpoon for sport.

Table 8.14 Nukak Subsistence during the Dry Season: Band 1994

Date	Nº of Individuals	Plant Gathering	Hunting	Fishing	Horticulture	Honey and Beehive Products	Food from Colonos
22-1-94	27	39.5	4.0	8.0	–	12.5	–
23-1-94	27	2.0	–	15.0	–	22.0	–
24-1-94	27	41.0	13.8	15.0	–	6.5	–
25-1-94	27	38.8	13.5	56.2	49 (chontaduro)	25.0	–
26-1-94	27	53.5	–	–	–	40.6	–
27-1-94	27	132.2	10.7	1.8	–	23.3	–
28-1-94	27	73.8	2.5	2.0	–	87.0	–
29-1-94	27	134.0	15.5	–	4.1	2.5	–
30-1-94	27	100.6	7.5	–	2.3 (plátano)	20.7	–
31-1-94	27	92.0	0.3	8.0	–	17.7	–
1-2-94	27	87.0	3.0	57.0	–	X	–
2-2-94	27	124.8	1.0	1.5	–	–	19.5
3-2-94	27	92.5	22.5	8.5	0.6	9.0	–
4-2-94	27	129.0	1.7	–	–	–	–
Subtotal	–	1140.7	96.0	173.0	56.0	266.0	19.5

Total 1752

X = means presence (no quantitative data recorded)
All amounts are expressed in kg.
Underlined dates are travel days.

Table 8.15 Nukak Subsistence during the Dry Season: Band 1995

Date	N° of Individuals	Plant Gathering	Hunting	Fishing	Horticulture	Honey and Beehive Products	Food from Colonos
20-1-95	14	2.0	5.5	–	1.5	4.0	–
21-1-95	14	156.5	–	–	–	–	–
23-1-95	14	2.7	0.2	8.0	14.6	3.0	1.5
24-1-95	14	135.0	–	1.8	–	2.5	–
25-1-95	14	34.0	–	–	0.2	1.0	0.2
26-1-95	14	10.0	–	–	27.2	1.5	–
27-1-95	14	–	–	9.5	72.2	–	–
28-1-95	14	0.2	–	9.3	–	7.2	–
29-1-95	14	6.0	–	–	2.8	8.0	–
30-1-95	14	25.0	10.5	1.7	–	0.1	–
31-1-95	14	25.0	–	–	17.0	3.0	–
1-2-95	14	–	–	31.8	8.2	–	–
2-2-95	14	2.0	–	15.5	–	6.0	–
3-2-95	14	43.0	–	3.0	43.0	–	–
4-2-95	16	10.0	17.0	–	–	–	–
5-2-95	16	12.0	13.0	–	–	4.0	–
Subtotal	–	463.4	46.2	80.6	186.7	40.3	1.7

Total 818.9

All amounts are expressed in kg.
Underlined dates are travel days.

Table 8.16 Nukak Subsistence during the Rainy Season: Band 1991

Date	N° of Individuals	Plant Gathering	Hunting	Fishing	Horticulture	Insects and Derivates	Food from Colonos
Band 1991a							
11-7-91	10	27.4	6.05	0.5	–	–	–
12-7-91	10	2.5	5.5	–	–	–	–
13-7-91	10	11.0	–	–	–	–	–
14-7-91	10	36.0	X	–	–	X	–
15-7-91	10	35.5	9.0	–	–	–	X
16-7-91	12	3.5	–	–	19.5	X	–
22-7-91	12	22.5	3.5	?	?	–	–
24-7-91	15	50.0	?	?	?	?	–
Subtotal		188.4	24.05	0.5	19.5	–	– **Total 232.45**
Band 1991b							
17-7-91	9	27.0	–	–	X	–	X
18-7-91	26	75.0	0.3	X	–	–	–
19-7-91	25	18.5	2.0	4.8	–	X	–
20-7-91	25	106.5	–	–	–	–	–
21-7-91	25	39.5	2.0	0.8	–	X + 1 h	–
22-7-91	24	79.5	–	–	–	–	–
23-7-91	24	46.2	3.7	–	–	–	–
24-7-91	22	9.5	5.5	1.3	–	0.1	–
25-7-91	22	86.0	–	1.5	–	X	–
26-7-91	22	15.0	5.5	–	20.0	–	–
27-7-91	22	39.0	2.0	–	–	–	–
Subtotal		541.7	21.0	8.4	20.0	1.1	– **Total 592.2**

X = means presence (no quantitative data recorded)

h = honey

All amounts are expressed in kg.

Underlined dates are travel days.

Table 8.17 Nukak Subsistence during the Rainy Season: Band 1992

Date	N° of Individuals	Plant Gathering	Hunting	Fishing	Horticulture	Insects and Derivates	Food from Colonos
30-8-92	24	X	10	–	–	X	–
31-8-92	24	198.0	5.5	1.0	25.0	–	3.5
1-9-92	24	120.2	49.25	–	4.0	0.5	–
2-9-92	24	69.0	7.3	0.9	–	0.4	–
3-9-92	24	9.0	8.3	–	45.0	–	5.0
4-9-92	24	139.0	16.0	0.5	–	0.2	1.0
5-9-92	24	52.0	61.0	–	–	0.5	–
6-9-92	24	53.0	–	–	–	–	–
7-9-92	24	40.0	11.0	–	–	0.25	–
8-9-92	24	10.0	0.25	–	–	0.5	9.5
9-9-92	24	147.0	18.0	0.5	–	0.8	–
10-9-92	24	44.0	–	–	–	–	–
11-9-92	18	17.2	15.2	7.0	55.0	0.3	–
12-9-92	18	32.5	–	–	18.0	0.2	–
13-9-92	18	86.5	–	–	30.1	0.1 + h	–
14-9-92	18	48.0	3.5	2.2	21.5	0.8	–
15-9-92	18	15.0	16.5	–	15.5	–	–
16-9-92	18	193.5	–	0.2	12.7	X	–
17-9-92	18	11.0	18.0	–	14.3	0.4 h	–
18-9-92	18	76.5	4.5	–	5.0	0.2 + h	–
Subtotal	–	1361.4	244.3	12.3	246.1	5.1	19.0	**1888.2**

X = means presence (no quantitative data recorded)
h = honey
All amounts are expressed in kg.
Underlined dates are travel days.

Figure 8.10 Man crushing *Lonchocarpus nicou* root, in order to disseminate the toxic substance in the creek

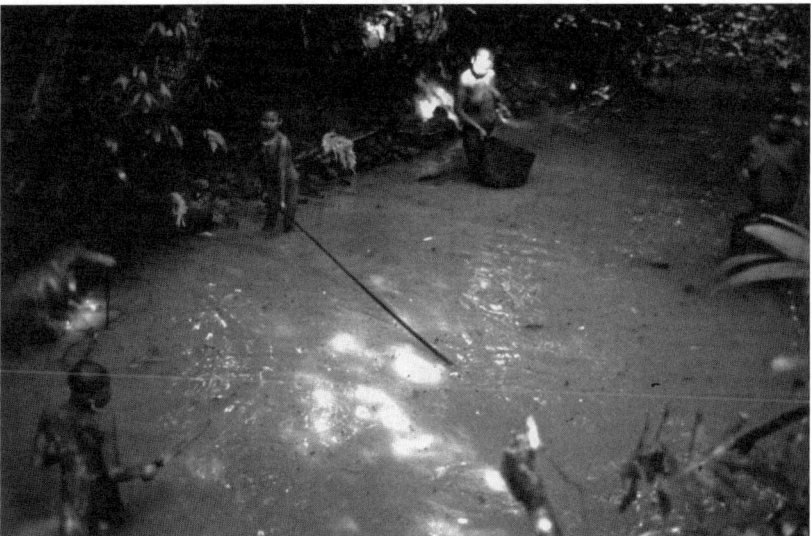

Figure 8.11 Women and girls catching fish stupefied by the poison

During the dry season, fishing using barbasco produced on average 0.457 kg per person/per day ($n = 14$) in 1994, and in 1995 0.306 kg per person/per day ($n = 16$). Therefore, $\bar{x} = 0.381$ kg per person per day during the dry season.

Fish is not eaten where it is fished; it is always brought to the camp and gutted. The figure obtained, therefore, represents fairly accurately the amount of fish consumed by people in the camp. Since productivity far exceeds daily consumption, the Nukak smoke the fish on triangular wooden-stick grills (Figure 7.18, p. 216). Through this cooking technique consumption can be deferred, since the fish keeps for several days without going off. Owing to the high residential mobility during this season, smoked fish is almost always carried from one camp to another during relocation.

During the wet season, fishing constitutes a far lower percentage of the daily diet. Generally, a few fish are caught with traps or hooks and are consumed the same day. The Nukak have devised an ingenious method of attracting fish when hook fishing. They attach a disemboweled parrot (the viscera hanging from the abdominal cavity) to a branch so that it touches the water. The Nukak cast their hooks at this spot where the fish concentrate. Fishing produces a ridiculously low average (0.0007 kg per person/per day) during the wet season, although it was not possible to weigh the fish that entered camp on some occasions (see Tables 8.16 and 8.17).

Gutiérrez Herrera (1996) provides a list of fish species consumed by the Nukak based on samples obtained in creeks that feed the Guaviare River. The list includes *Adontostemardius* sp., *Astronotus ocellatus*, *Auchenipterus* sp., *Brachyplatystoma flavicans*, *Chicla ocellaris*, *Colossoma brachypomum*, *Gymnotus carapo*, *Haplosternum* sp., *Hypophthalmus* sp., *Leiarius mamoratus*, *Mylossoma duriventre*, *Plasioscion* sp., *Potamotrygon* sp., *Pseudoplatystoma tigrium*, *Pterygoplichthys multiradiatus*, *Pterygoplichthys* sp., *Rhamphichthys rostratus*, *Serrasalmus humeralis*, *Sorubimichthys planiceps*, and *Sturisoma nigrirostrum*.

Freshwater crabs are also occasionally eaten. They are generally gathered by children on the swampy creek beaches during the dry months. One species of crab (*ñaku*) frequently collected in the vicinity of Laguna Pavón 2, within the watershed (EE4 and ES in Figure 1.6, p. 50), was identified as *Zilchopsis emarginatus*. Gutiérrez Herrera (1996, 95) also identified this species as that gathered by adults near Caño Hormiga, close to or in the alluvial plain of the Guaviare River (SN, Figure 1.6).

On the muddy beaches of the rivers and creeks, batrachian of various genera and species are also gathered by adults and children during hunting and gathering trips. Gutiérrez Herrera (1996) recorded the consumption of frogs of the genus *Leptodactylus* sp. Cabrera, Franky, and Mahecha (1999:283) state that the greatest consumption of batrachian occurs between April and May, at the beginning of the rainy season. In May, when the streams begin to swell, this activity is at its peak of productivity. One band studied gathered 15 kg in a day.

CULTIVATION

Another component of Nukak subsistence is the products cultivated in fields dispersed throughout the forest. Currently, 23 cultivated plants have been identified in various kinds of field (Cárdenas & Politis 2000, see Table 8.2 and Tables 8.14 to 8.17). Some correspond to plants recently incorporated into Nukak horticultural practices as a product of relationships with New Tribe missionaries and *colonos*. Among them the following stand out: *Anacardium occidentale* (cashew), *Carica papaya* (papaya), and *Pourouma cecropiifolia* (caimarona). Plants that originated in other continents and were incorporated in the recent or remote past into the crops of the indigenous American peoples were also found among the species cultivated by the Nukak, such as mafafa (*Colocasia esculenta*, from south Asia), plantain (*Musa paradisiaca*, from Asia), sugar cane (*Saccharum officinarum*, from New Guinea), and *Lagenaria siceraria* (from Africa) (Purseglove 1968, 1972).

There are three main types of field. The first seems to be the most traditional and is small, usually consisting of a few peach palms (locally known as chontaduro palms or pipire [*Bactris gasipaes*]), and sometimes achiote (*Bixa orellana*) and plantain (*Musa paradisiaca*). These fields generally consist of open spaces surrounded by chontaduro palms (Figure 8.12). They also contain felled chontaduro used for the breeding of palm grubs. These orchards are places that have been utilized for generations, and their importance is both economic and symbolic (see below).

The second type of cultivated field is the chagra, which is usually less than one hectare in size and contains a greater variety of species than the first field type. Chagras are generally found a few kilometers from the frontier of colonization but still within the rainforest, or close to Laguna Pavón 2. This type of cultivated field is similar to the slash-and-burn fields of the indigenous Amazonian cultivator groups (see Meggers 1996; Oliver 2002), and they include an intermixed variety of species that ripen at different times of the year (Figure 8.13). Thus the chagra is kept productive for most of the year. The commonest cultivated domesticated species are sweet manioc, sugar cane, plantains, pepper, "tavena" potato, yams, pineapple, and papaya. Several gourds of different genera are also found (*Lagenaria siceraria, Posadaea sphaerocarpa, Crescentia cujete*) and are used principally as containers (see Chapter 7).

Nukak bands usually control a few fields of each type within their circle of mobility and sometimes place their camp nearby to exploit the cultivated plants or to carry out agricultural tasks such as slash-and-burn clearing and sowing. In the area around Laguna Pavón 2 there are several chontaduro orchards and larger chagras, each of them controlled by a different band. It is

Figure 8.12 Small cultivated field with some chontaduro palms

Figure 8.13 Slash-and-burn field

highly probable that the presence of the Mission attracted Nukak bands and influenced the location of the cultivated plots, although the area was already a frontier between the territory of several bands belonging to two main *munu* (*Wayari* and *Muhabeh*). At present it has an unusually high concentration of cultivated fields.

The third field type is a recent addition and is obviously an adoption of *colono* practices. It is characterized by a large slash-and-burn area, usually greater than one hectare, and is less diverse. These slash-and-burn fields are generally located close to the *colono* settlements and sometimes adjoin them. This type of horticulture is now practiced by the bands that have become semisedentary and that in addition to spending most of their time near the *colonos* are occasionally employed by them to harvest coca leaves. I recorded two of these fields near the *colono* settlements on the western limits of Nukak territory.

Cultivated plants are also found in isolated groups at various other types of location. For example, it is relatively common to find a chontaduro palm beside a path. It is not clear whether this is due to incidental cultivation—the product of discarding the seeds when the fruit is eaten—or whether this represents the conscious planting of seeds or seedlings in specific areas of the territory.

The issue of Nukak horticultural practices prior to recent contact remains a little-explored subject. Previous work (Cabrera, Franky, & Mahecha 1994; Mondragón Ms) has promoted the idea that the Nukak possessed traditional, small-scale horticulture that was gradually replaced by introduced species. Some of the first data available on the topic were collected by the priest Tulio Alfredo Gómez, who visited the territory in 1966 after the "Charras massacre." Gómez mentioned that the "Macús" (at the time they had yet to be given their generic name) had cultivated fields: "Nevertheless, the commission discovered small gardens of cane, maize, manioc, plantain, yams, and *pupuña* [chontaduro] . . ." (*El Espectador*, 20 May 1966). Cabrera, Franky, and Mahecha (1994) suggest that the Nukak in the past cultivated other species, such as bitter manioc, but that this practice later disappeared. Information gathered by the missionaries during the 1980s also supports this hypothesis.

Our work further lends weight to the preceding idea, and it seems highly probable that during the precontact period the Nukak cultivated chontaduro, maize, sweet potato, achiote, tobacco, and bitter manioc, among other plants. Bitter manioc is no longer cultivated, although the Nukak still know how to reduce its toxicity during preparation (Israel Gualteros pers. comm.). In general terms a reasonable proposal would be that some cultigens were present prior to Western impact, and, in spite of their importance certainly varying over time, they have maintained a low-level value in the composition of the

Nukak diet. This proposal is based on the absence of technology aimed at the exploitation of cultivated species (especially manioc), which is clearly present in Amazonian horticultural groups (Meggers 1996; Oliver 2002). In the same way, the main cultural features of the Nukak are clearly oriented toward a foraging mode of life. The majority of cultivated plants that currently are found in the chagras, and that principally include sugar cane, plantain, pineapple, and papaya, are of recent introduction.

FOOD FROM THE *COLONOS*

The part played by *colono* food in the Nukak diet was always limited during our fieldwork (less than 5%; see Tables 8.14 and 8.17). Obviously, there is a gradation of importance. In the western-most bands, which have felt the impact of colonization the greatest, the percentage is higher, whereas in the eastern bands it is much lower.

Food from the *colonos* is of two types. The more significant type is the food collected when the Nukak visit *colono* friends. At such times, they generally obtain or are given as gifts by the *colonos* fruit that they do not have in their chagras. During my visits to *colono* farms with the Nukak I recorded the collection of lemons, papayas, oranges, sweet manioc, plantains, and others. The quantities are not generally large. The other type is processed foods, among which pasta, rice, sugar, salt, and even some canned goods are notable. This type of consumption is more common in the northwestern bands. Usually, the Nukak eat the food while in the camps closer to the colonization. In such camps one finds tins and plastic bags from pasta and rice, which remain after abandonment. Consumption of such food decreases rapidly the further the Nukak travel from the frontier of the colonization.

THE IDEATIONAL ASPECT OF FOOD

In this section I examine the ideational aspects of plants only; the ritual aspects of the hunting and the consumption of animals and how they appear in the archeological record are presented and discussed in the next chapter (Chapter 9). Animals and plants play a central role in Nukak cosmological conceptualization, in the temporal connections between past and present, and in the different levels of the universe (see Chapter 3). Food procurement, distribution, and consumption are a ritual practice loaded with symbolism and meaning. These activities are anchored in Nukak cosmology, and, like other aspects of daily life, the processing and the consumption of food are ways of connecting to and communicating with the spirit-ancestors, as well as being a means of negotiating social and kin relationships. Fundamentally, plants are also perceived within the Nukak logic so that "the image that one sees is the shadow of what one does not see." This idea is applicable to many things, but only in some cases could we identify it in specific phenomena. Supernatural beings are active in the food chain and participate in daily food procurement: "All the spirits in the sky help us when we are ill, and the *takwe´yi* help us to search for food" (IANTC 1992a).

Several keys to the Nukak ideational world enable the symbolism of trees to be decoded. To begin with, many of the trees of the middle world have an ancestral tree in the-world-above, including *kupé, yáabbutu, waana'* (*guaná*), *num', chíri, yúbudi, uj, yáab, ne'endé, ed* (*pununidé*) *eétchaá'chuu'dui*, and *ché'ne* (IANTC 1992d). The ripening and the abundance of fruit on the earth's trees depend on the ancestral tree-spirits and the spirit-ancestors who live in the-world-above. If the spirit-ancestors do not eat fruit from the ancestral trees, the corresponding trees from the middle world will not bear fruit. If they eat only a little the trees will bear small amounts of fruit. In the case of the *koró-paanját*, as I have stated, the abundance of fruit is in direct relation to the sexual activity of the spirit-ancestors of the-world-above. Another interesting case is that of the *chiwá* (guama silvestre), as the fruit and their husks are actually the *kdn´yii* (bracelets) of the spirit-ancestors of girls from the-world-above. If these spirit-ancestors make a great many *kdn´yii* then this tree will bear an abundance of fruit; if they make them long then the guama will be long. If, on the contrary, the spirit-ancestors of girls from the-world-above make poor-quality *kdn´yii* while playing and practicing, then the earthly crop of guama will be bad (IANTC 1992d).

One of the principal foods of the *nemep* is the fruit of a tree called *tkéri*. Certain plots within the forest with undeveloped herbaceous cover are considered to be *nemep wopyii*,[3] places used and managed by the *nemep*. These localities are dangerous at night and to be avoided; camping nearby is not advisable. Particular trees are considered *nemep* layers, and the spirits supposedly dwell there.

Seje is also mentioned as the food of the *takwe´yi* (IANTC 1992a). In the middle of the-world-above there is a *kupé* tree, which occupies a central position in this world. It is of supreme importance, as it appears to have been the first tree in existence. Furthermore, it is the "brother" of the *guaná*, a species of the same genus that is prominent in the Nukak diet and highly "managed." Some wild tubers, such as *cud*, contain venom that is said to come from the inhabitants of the-world-below and that can cause people of the middle world to fall ill. It is possible only to "inhale" this venom through certain shamanic formulas, songs, or "cleanings" that particular men and women are able to perform (Cabrera, Franky, & Mahecha 1999:170).

Curare (*Curarea tecunarum*) is another plant with mythical connotations. It was created by *Nanabet*, the wife of Mauróijumjat (the ancestral hero), who urinated over the forest in ancient times, impregnating some large creeping plants and trees with the substance from which the Nukak extract the poison (see Chapter 3).

Beyond the chontaduro orchards' economic importance they have considerable symbolic and social significance, as previously mentioned. In or around these orchards certain people are buried, significant events are said to occur (that is, "we discarded the stone axes in the *pipireras* [the regional name for the chontaduro palm orchards] when we got the metal axes," or "our great grandparents are buried in the pipireras"), and they are frequently used as sites for the *baak wáadn* meetings. The ritual meetings take place in February and March, the months in which the fruit ripen. The *baak wáadn* also have the character of recurring funeral wakes for the dead, especially those who have died most recently (see Chapter 3).

In one of the chontaduro fields I found pottery shards scattered on the surface. I was told by the Nukak that they belonged to their "grandparents." Generally, chontaduro orchards are found deep in the rainforest, far from colonized areas. They were established by "the elders" and can be traced back at least three generations. They also say, "now we no longer plant chontaduro, all that there is was planted by our grandfathers; now we harvest the fruit. . . ." However, with the rapid advance of colonization (which is producing dramatic deforestation) these fields are increasingly close to the edge of the rainforest.

The chontaduro also appears in Nukak origin myths. When the first Nukak emerged in the middle world from the-world-below, they brought chontaduro with them in bags. It is interesting to note that the mythical antiquity of chontaduro coincides with botanical studies that indicate that chontaduro was domesticated in the northwest Amazon, where larger and more evolved varieties of the plant exist (Clement 1989).

The areas of high *guaná* concentration are also the sites of *baak wáadn*. These concentrations of *guaná* have been promoted by human action (see below) and are highly sacralized. The ritual fiestas take place at night. A chicha of *guaná* is drunk, prepared on the days prior to the meeting in the camp where the ritual takes place. During the gathering of the fruit and the preparation of the chicha the women repeatedly sing songs alluding to the place and their desire to be there during the harvesting of the fruit.

Finally, the case of the *éóro baká* is interesting and demonstrative, both of how plants act in the intermediate world and of Nukak ontology. There exists a vine called *éóro* or *kená* (*Arrobidea chica*), the leaves of which are boiled and processed to obtain a red-colored substance. The body and many objects are painted with this colorant (see Chapter 7). This substance is considered the "image" ("that which one sees") of the *éóro-baká* (in other words, "the truth drug"). The *éóro-baká* is a substance that *takwe´yi* bring from the Cerro de los Cerbatanas and give to the spirit-ancestors. This substance can be "seen" only by the old and powerful ones (shamans), who perceive it as a red halo, for example, around the head of certain animals (see Chapter 9). Apparently, in the intermediate world (the real world, according to Western ontology), there exists only one *éóro*, the botanical species *Arrobidea chica*; the other *éóro* (the *baká,* the true one) has only a metaphysical existence. Still, both *éóro* operate together in Nukak cosmovision; one (the colorant) is the "shadow" of the other (the one that truly exists for the Nukak). The latter supplies the drug that enables states of shamanic trance and allows one to see things that ordinary beings do not. This case is a good example of the contrast between Nukak and Western ontology. For the Nukak, true existence, "the real," is what the *éóro baká* contains (hence the use of the *baká* suffix, which means "the real," "the proper"), which is the substance that is not seen yet exists in the world of supernatural beings. On the contrary, according to Western ontology reality resides in the world of botanical species, the other remaining a purely metaphysical plane.

THE ANNUAL CIRCLE AND THE CREATION OF WILD ORCHARDS

The Nukak's high mobility appears to have several causes, one of which is the production of resource patches. Residential relocations occur long before depletion in resources can be observed (at least in quantitative terms). In this sense, mobility can be seen as a result of establishing residential camps close to certain resources when they are abundant. This implies being in a specific area at a certain time of year, when the availability of particular food resources is at its greatest. These resources are used appropriately, and the band moves to another area before a negative impact is made on resource productivity. During the dry season economic decisions are associated with access to waterways and streams where fish can be obtained in abundance, and with areas with concentrations of beehives. In January and February, during the harvest, chontaduro orchards and chagras are the focus. In winter, access to patches of certain palms and hunting strategies play major roles in organizing mobility.

Nukak mobility is also partially a consequence of a sophisticated strategy for management and use of forest resources. This implies that while the phenotypes or genotypes of a particular species are not being modified their natural distribution is affected and they become concentrated in certain forest sectors. Included in the spectrum of species affected in this way are palms (such as seje), platanillo, and the *popere* and *guaná* trees that occur in unusual concentrations throughout the rainforest. The high density of some of these species in Nukak territory has also been noted by other authors (Cabrera, Franky, & Mahecha 1999; Gutiérrez Herrera 1996) and by the New Tribes missionaries (Andres Jiménez pers. comm.). The manipulation of these and perhaps other species seems to be associated with activities related to Nukak mobility. One such activity is the cutting down of trees and plants during residential camp movements and during hunting and gathering excursions. This is forest management through selective clearing, subtle and perhaps insignificant in the short run but much more significant in the long term. The second and more important activity that favors the concentration of certain species is residential relocation. When the Nukak abandon their camps the ground is covered with large quantities of seeds of the fruit consumed during occupation. In some cases, the number of discarded fruit seeds could reach several thousand (Figures 5.14 and 5.15, pp. 146–47). Although many of these seeds have been processed in various ways (for example, mashed), others are intact and maintain a high germinative potential. In some cases, for example seje, human processing favors the growth and propagation of the species, since the maceration of the seeds (through which the epicarp and mesocarp are removed) increases their germinative potential (Balick 1986).

In this sense, the species with the greatest opportunity to germinate in the abandoned camps are those that belong to the fruit group with hard exocarps that must be processed, including the palms (that is, seje, *juiú, yáab butu, popere*), some Burseraceae (*guaná* and *kupé*), *koró-paanját*, platanillo, and juansoco (see above). Even so, there is always the possibility that they develop as isolated seedlings in the same way as the other groups, the fruit of which are not brought to the camps in abundance. For this reason, the presence in abandoned camps of numerous seedlings of palms, Burseraceae, and even some Moraceae is noteworthy. They are transported to the camps where the transformative processes do not compromise the viability of the seed. In other cases such as the platanillo, the fruit of which is taken to the camps but the processing destroys the seeds, the recorded germination is low.

This high concentration of seeds places some species in an advantageous position in a tropical rainforest environment, which is typically highly competitive for sunlight and nutrients. These favored species are precisely those that the Nukak consume intensively. The Nukak also modify the natural distribution of every plant they consume, in varying degrees. The frequent relocation of residential camps, consequently, produces different derived food sources in the form of "wild orchards," which the Nukak frequent in their mobility cycles. In other words, the Nukak leave a resource patch behind when they abandon and relocate a camp. They are creating *domuses* (in the sense of Chase 1989) to which they can return in times of high productivity. The conceptualization of environment exploitation is framed by Nukak cosmology, resulting in a "map" of the territory where places are favored or forbidden.

Residential camp construction encourages the generation of these wild orchards. The surface area of these camps oscillates between 32 m^2 and 178 m^2, depending on the number of domestic units (see Table 4.1, p. 106). There are no significant variations between seasons. In the process of camp construction, the herbaceous layer, shrubs, small-, and sometimes medium-sized trees are felled and removed. The majority of the medium-sized trees and all the large trees are left, so that the camp area is covered by the forest canopy, which creates a filtered shade typical of tropical rainforests. As a result, when camps are abandoned no clearing is left nor is the plot invaded by vines and shrubs, which grow quickly and aggressively in areas exposed to direct sunlight (Kricher 1989:81) and would therefore compete successfully with seje, platanillo, and other plants frequently consumed by the Nukak within the camps. Thus the abandoned camps avoid becoming "jungles" of tangled vegetation. Furthermore, edible wild species are not destroyed by subsequent human activity owing to the fact that abandoned camps are usually not reoccupied (Figure 8.14). During the summer the dry roof leaves that remain on the shelters are sometimes burned, as are the garbage piles, creating a fine layer of ash that increases the fertility of the compacted soil.

This pattern of behavior creates patches of edible plants throughout the territory. The Nukak construct a residential camp that, after being abandoned, is transformed into a type of wild orchard, which augments the resource potential of the area. This sophisticated settlement and mobility system is also connected to the rainforest layers, as the Nukak displace the lowest stratum of the rainforest ecosystem and leave the forest canopy intact. This is a type of horizontal displacement that creates patches without disturbing the natural stratification of the rainforest. From a long-term perspective, one can conclude that residential camps are not established where there is a high concentration of resources since this concentration is promoted by the establishment and subsequent abandonment of residential camps. This pattern alters the density and distribution of edible plants through means other than domestication (see also Brosius 1991:131–32; Rival 1998b; Zent & Zent Ms:17).

The impact of this transformation is difficult to estimate, but one can get an approximate idea of the magnitude of the area affected on the basis of the

Figure 8.14 Plants of edible species growing in an abandoned camp

surface area occupied by the residential camps (see Chapter 4). Bearing in mind that a band constructs between 70 and 80 camps a year, the area altered through this process can be estimated at as much as 6,400 m² per band. The area peripheral to the camp where seeds are also discarded, and the multiple modifications that are produced by movement through the forest (which are extremely difficult to measure or even estimate), must also be taken into consideration.

Even so, not every concentration of trees should be interpreted automatically as having been created through human agency, since there are several palms (for example, moriche and platanillo) that naturally form large dense stands, which makes them an attractive resource (Cárdenas & Politis 2000; Dufour & Wilmson 1994:119). There are species that form dense populations through intrinsic reproductive strategies—*Caryodendron orinocensis* (inchi) is a case in point. Also, platanillo develops in areas with unstable soil and has been observed in large concentrations on the tops of the low ridges that characterize a good part of the physiography of Nukak territory (especially in EE5, EE4 and ES—Figure 1.6, p. 50). Moriche (*Mauritia flexuosa*) is another species that forms stands and is naturally abundant in poorly drained soils. Furthermore, in studies carried out in several Amazonian regions with no recent human intervention areas of high concentration of species of Myristicaceae, such as *Iryanthera ulei* (*koró paanját*), have been observed (Cárdenas, Giraldo-Cañas, & Arias 1997). Moreover, some species, such as *Tachigali paniculata*, were found highly concentrated in areas close to new gardens and are not utilized by the Nukak. Also, patches of *Duroia hirsuta* are detectable in other areas within Nukak territory. In the nearby Middle Caquetá, high concentrations of species utilized by the Nukak have also been identified, such as *Iryanthera ulei* (*koró paanját*), *Dacryodes chimantensis* (*kupé*), *Oenocarpus bataua* (seje), and *Mauritia flexuosa* (moriche) (Duivenvoorden & Lips 1993:85–86). Other authors have noted stands of *Euterpe* spp. and *Orbignya phalerat* (Henderson, Galeano, & Bernal 1995). The former grows naturally in flood river areas, whereas the latter develops well in disturbed or unstable areas (Dufour & Wilson 1994:119).

The preceding information indicates that the concentration of some species in the tropical rainforest is not a phenomenon exclusive to the Nukak territory and cannot be attributed solely to direct or indirect human intervention. Consequently, it should not be assumed that all identified areas of high density in Nukak territory are the product of anthropic activity.

DISCUSSION

The first point to stress is that the potential resources of the tropical rainforest are sufficient to maintain sustained populations of hunter-gatherers at far higher densities than those of the present-day Nukak. The wide variety of plant and animal species and their high annual productivity ensure a balanced diet throughout the year. With regard to the animal component of their diet, the Nukak support themselves by hunting mammals and birds and fishing, but the consumption of insects and their by-products also occupies a prominent place. While for the other Makú groups the drier season was by far the best for hunting (Milton 1984; Reid 1979; Silverwood-Cope 1972), there does not seem to be significant variation throughout the year in relation to game availability for the Nukak. Actually, the few peccary hunting events recorded in the rainy season increased significantly the average meat intake in my sample.

Concerning the plant aspect, it is clear that the diversity of wild species exploited and the high productivity of those that are the pillars of Nukak subsistence guarantee the year-round procurement of essential nutritional components. Several bromatological and phytochemical studies of tropical forest palm and tree fruit note the high nutritional content of many species (Balick & Gershopp 1981:267; Borgtoft & Baslev 1993; Collazos & Mejía 1987; Gutiérrez Herrera 1996:105; Morcote-Ríos et al. 1998; Sotomayor et al. 1998). The high fat and carbohydrate content of several palm genera (*Oenocarpus, Attalea, Mauritia, Bactris*, and so on) and fruit trees (*Couma, Phenakospermum*, and so forth) are especially notable, as well as the quality of the oil they produce (especially *Oenocarpus*). The high productivity of the species involved must also be highlighted, which in some cases (such as the species of the genera *Oenocarpus* and *Attalea*) produce fruit for almost the entire year. Despite it being impossible to carry out a detailing of the nutritional components of each one of these species here, a comparison between the results of the phytochemical analyses of the principle species consumed and the recorded gross daily values of the samples obtained that entered the camps (see Tables 8.14 to 8.17) clearly signals the abundance and nutritive quality of the tropical rainforest in Nukak territory. Similar studies also stress the abundance and quality of nondomesticated resources based on which the Nukak maintain their annual diet with high nutritive levels (Morcote-Ríos et al. 1998; Sotomayor et al. 1998). These data do not support the existence of alimentary limits of any type that could impede the viability of medium density populations of hunter-gatherers in these interfluvial tropical forest environments.

Furthermore, there are a number of fairly abundant plants with edible fruit or roots available in the territory that are ignored by the Nukak. To the extent that we were able to record them (although there are doubts in this regard) there are no particular ideological reasons for why these plants are not consumed; rather, there is simply no tradition of their consumption. A notable case is that of açaí (*Euterpe precatoria*), a relatively abundant palm in Nukak territory and highly productive (Dairon Cárdenas pers. comm. 1996). This palm is known to the Nukak who use the trunk as a bed for palm grubs and the rachises of the infrutescence as a broom. However, they do not eat the flesh of the fruit, which has a high nutritive value and which indeed is eaten by many Amazonian groups. This example draws attention to the fact that there is a subexploitation not only in terms of the quantity of available products but also in terms of the variety of potential resources.

Data recorded from other Makú before their diet became based on the cultivation of bitter manioc also support the viability of forager populations in the tropical rainforest. For example, in reference to the Makú, McGovern (1927:148) stated, "they were acquainted with no form of agriculture, eating only the wild fruit of the forest." Further, during a visit to a camp—probably not the band's residential camp but a transient men's camp (only four men were seen there)—he wrote, "the only food I could see in the Posgas [Makú] settlement was a large number of fruit-seeds from a certain kind of wild palm, which the other Indians use only for obtaining a dark purple dye" (McGovern 1927:180–81). Giacone (1955:5) also stated that the Makú, in contrast to other neighboring Indians, "live off the forest, which produces varied fruit, insects, reptiles and abundant game. All the men are great consumers of *ipadú*, which is well prepared in great quantities." An important observation is that the contemporary manioc-based Makú can broaden their diet significantly if they are under food constraints. In the sedentary settlement of Nova Fundaçao, where all food resources except manioc were scarce, daily diet included nocturnal wood rats, freshwater crabs, small armored catfish, pipefish, and other small aquatic animals (Milton 1984:14).

The Nukak case, and that of other Makú (Dufour 1987; Giacone 1955; Milton 1984; Terribilini & Terribilini 1961:4), supports the recognition that one resource that has not been identified as significant in hunter-gatherers' diet is insect consumption (see review in Sutton 1995). This intake is important for the other Makú groups; it is a good complement to their diet when other resources are not so abundant. They are also significant sources of fat (especially palm grubs), an element that was thought to be scarce in the Amazonian rainforest. For example, the Kakwa consume four types of insect: two species of palm grubs, one species of caterpillar, and termite soldiers (Milton 1984:14). This food is of greatest value between July and September when game is hardest to hunt and is theoretically most lean. Palms grubs of the genus *Rhynchophorus* stand out. Their composition indicates that for every 100 g of edible portion (in this case virtually the entire larva) there is 24.3 g of protein and 55 g of fat, which represents 661 Cal (Dufour 1987:89).

Caterpillars also have a high nutritional value (100 g = 455 Cal; 52.6 g of protein and 15.4 g of fat).

Finally, as we have seen, during the dry season fishing produces high average per-person daily intake in an interriverine environment, where fishing is usually assumed not to be significant. Fishing with barbasco and the use of stick grills to dry the fish, and so defer consumption, provides the Nukak with an excellent complement of animal protein during the dry season (see Tables 8.14 and 8.15) and therefore enables them to maintain high nutritional levels. During the dry season other Makú, such as the Yuhup and the Nadöb, also consume significant quantities of fish, which become the principle source of animal protein (Schultz 1959:122; Pozzobon 1983:79).

Conclusion

The Nukak are a hunter-gatherer group that collects, manipulates, and cultivates plants to varying degrees, and hunts primates, birds, tortoises, peccaries, and some rodents. The intensive consumption of palm grubs, honey, and fish during certain periods of the year enables them to maintain a balanced diet. This dietary breadth, combined with the high productivity of the components, allows the Nukak to sustain high nutritional levels year round. Their multiple exploitation strategies allow them to manage the rainforest and increase its productivity. Improvement of productivity is not only related to the adoption of new crops and to the development of better agricultural techniques but also directly linked to the manipulation of nondomesticated plants. Game meat is relatively reliable and abundant year round.

In spite of the use of domesticated species it is clear that the Nukak economy revolves around the exploitation of nondomesticated plants and animals. In fact, the collection of produce such as seje, platanillo, *juiú, koró-paanját*, moriche, *guaná*, and others greatly exceeds the quantity and variety of resources obtained from cultivation. During the rainy season, the "seje-platanillo" duplex plays an important role. These plants not only provide food but also are a source of other products important to Nukak life: leaves for lean-to roofs and expedient basket construction, fibers for dart manufacture, and beds for palm-grub breeding.

Traditional Nukak horticulture also played an important role in both subsistence and the social and ideational spheres. The chontaduro-achiote combination has a strong symbolic significance. Thus, when a person dies the plants he or she planted are cut down, except the achiote and chontaduro. The places with the most intense significance are the chontaduro and achiote orchards. These places are related to the ancestors, since the palms connect past and contemporary generations. The elders planted them or used these plots for cultivation, and now their descendants consume the chontaduro fruit. Some of the major representations of the symbolic aspect of the chontaduro orchards are the performance of *baak-wáadn* in or near these spots and the inhumation of the deceased. These palms, therefore, materialize the connection through time between generations; this connection can be represented in the ordinate axis ("Y") (Figure 8.15). Complementarily, achiote is also cultivated in these orchards and is essential for all kinds of rituals. Red paint obtained from the achiote seeds is used on a regular basis for body decoration and to color many objects (hammocks, spears, guayucos, and so on). Red paint is constantly present in Nukak daily life, and the colors and the designs have a variety of meanings that encode social information. In this sense, achiote is a vehicle for social communication and interaction in the present; thus, this connection can be represented in the abscissa axis ("X"). Chontaduro[4] and achiote are solid metaphors that link the two axes, the past and the present, connecting the cross-time relations with the spirit-ancestors and the synchronicity of contemporary social relations.

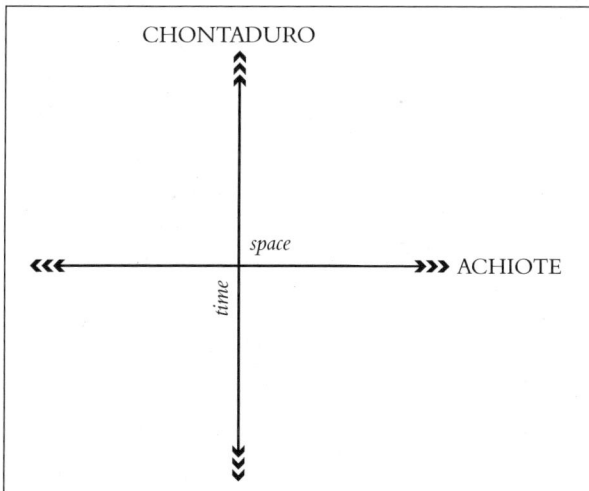

Figure 8.15 Schematic representation of the symbolic associations of achiote and chontaduro use

It has been widely accepted for some time that after a prolonged period human feeding behavior alters local flora (Rindos 1984, 1989). In this way certain plant species are placed at a competitive advantage (Rindos 1989:2) or are in some sense "protected." The Nukak provide a good example of this practice. They make residential movements and occupy a new exploitation area (or *foraging radius*, after Binford 1982:7–8) before an observable decline occurs in the available resources obtained from the surrounding area. Their well-balanced and varied diet indicates that no clear limitation in food resources exists that would prevent a longer residential camp stay or a higher population density. I argue that high mobility is related to a strategy aimed at concentrating and managing forest resources, as well as being the result of social and ideological factors. The symbolic significance of plants and animals undoubtedly conditions the way forest resources are exploited and determines which species will be used and which will not. Symbolic factors will also condition who eats the food obtained. The composition and annual structure of Nukak subsistence at the present time is the result of the intersection of the alimentary properties of the plants and their productivity, the available technology to obtain and process the products, and the ideational and cosmo-logical aspects that, independently of energy equations, regulate the use of the tropical rainforest resources.

Notes

1. All taxonomic determinations were done by botanist Dairon Cárdenas from the Instituto Amazónico de Investigaciones Científicas SINCHI.
2. This tuber is probably the one mentioned by Cabrera, Franky, and Mahecha (1999:290) as *cud*, *hud*, or diuji.
3. The term *wopyii* is generic and appears to be used by the Nukak to refer to any place transformed by human or spirit agency. In this sense, the Nukak call a residential camp a *wopyii*, as well as a chagra or a place used or modified by a *nemep*.
4. Chontaduro is also important for other Makú. For example, the Nadöb Kabori (Schultz 1959:119) also conduct a ritual associated with this fruit. They have also planted chontaduro, which are found in stands of palm in the forest.

Chapter 9

ANIMAL EXPLOITATION, PROCESSING, AND DISCARD

Theoretical and methodological advances in recent years have contributed significantly to improving our understanding of the zoo-archaeological record (for example, Behrensmeyer & Hill 1980; Binford 1988; Blumenschine 1986, 1989; Haynes 1985, 1987; O'Connor 1996, 2000; Mengoni Goñalons 1999, Miotti 1998; Miracle & Milner 2002; Reitz & Wing 1999). The ethnoarchaeology of hunter-gatherers has played a major role in these developments, providing models for the interpretation of the spatial arrangement of bone remains and their correlation with past human activities, especially in relation to economy and subsistence (Bartram 1993; Binford 1978a, 1981, 1984; Gould 1969; Lupo 1994, 1995; O'Connell, Hawkes, & Blurton Jones 1988a, 1988b, 1990; Yellen 1977). In contemporary research, special attention is given to bone assemblages to assess two principle factors that contribute to the formation of the archaeological record of past foragers. One is the cultural information that the spatial arrangement and context of bone features contain with regard to faunal exploitation, including patterns of hunting, transportation, butchering, processing, consumption, and discard (Binford 1981; Brooks & Yellen 1987; Kent 1987; O'Connell, Hawkes, and Blurton Jones 1988a, 1990, 1992). The second factor is the taphonomy of bone assemblages and the ways in which nonhuman factors contribute to site formation (see Behrensmeyer & Hill 1980; Borrero 1990a, 2001; Guiterrez 2004; Haynes 1987, 1988a, b, 1991; Kerbis Peterhans et al. 1993; Lyman 1994).

Most ethnoarchaeological studies that have investigated vertebrate faunal exploitation have been carried out among hunter-gatherers inhabiting open environments, such as the Arctic (for example, the Nunamiut), the African and the Australian deserts (for example, the !Kung San and Alyawara), or mixed savannah woodlands (for example, the Hadza). In the majority of these cases, the focus has been on large mammal exploitation and its archaeological consequences in order to provide an analogical framework to be used in explaining the zooarchaeological record (Binford 1978a; Bunn & Kroll 1986; O'Connell, Hawkes, & Blurton-Jones 1988a, b; Shipman 1983; see review in David & Kramer 2001). Less attention has been given to the exploitation of small and medium-sized mammals and their contribution to archaeological site formation (for exceptions see Bartram, Kroll, & Bunn 1991; Jones 1984; O'Connell & Marshall 1989; Yellen 1991a, b). Even less attention still has been paid to tropical rainforest foragers who remain somewhat elusive in the existing models of hunter-gatherer faunal exploitation and carcass management.

Carcass transport patterns among contemporary hunter-gatherers are highly variable and have been the subject of lively debate (see review in Mengoni Goñalons 1999:9–39). The key issue addressed has been isolating which factors affect contemporary hunter-gatherer decisions in relation to carcass transportation. In other words, what kinds of criteria are used by hunter-gatherers in the decision to transport certain body parts and leave others? The issue was originally discussed years ago by White (1952, 1953, 1954), who argued on the basis of only two ethnographic examples (O'Connell, Hawkes, & Blurton-Jones 1988a) that the representation of bone elements in camp sites is usually inversely proportional to body size (large animals were represented by fewer elements and vice versa) and that these differences are the result of transport patterns. White's initial model gave rise to a long list of studies of the intervening factors in the formation of faunal assemblages (for example, Binford 1978a; Borrero 1990b; Gifford-González 1993; Klein 1976; Landals 1990; Lyman 1994; Metcalfe & Jones 1988; O'Connell, Hawkes, & Blurton Jones 1988a, 1990; Speth 1983; Thomas & Mayer 1983).

The various ethnographic examples that fueled the debate on carcass transportation and related decision-making strategies have shown that over and beyond the general patterns each hunter-gatherer group has its own way of transporting body parts. They also demonstrate that each prey can be treated differently owing to many factors, including body size, hunting party composition, nutritional value, processing cost, distance to residential base, availability of other resources, logistical planning, condition of the carcass at the time of encounter, gear at hand to effect field processing, time and date, and other circumstances (see for example the reviews by Gifford-González 1993 and David & Kramer 2001:123–25). A central idea in the debate is that processing and transport behavior is basically understandable in terms of cost and benefit and that hunter-gatherers tend to maximize net nutritional returns relative to the cost of field processing and transport to the residential camps.

Beyond cost-benefit relationships and materialist causes, few other factors have been explored in previous studies that address the issues of why foragers hunt some animals and not others and how they move carcasses or body parts from one place to another. The social dimension is one such factor, especially when one considers the issue of the division of game among members of the group and the way in which this is influenced by social relationships (Barnard & Woodburn 1991; Speth 1990; Woodburn 1991). Ideational factors and their potential archeological implications have been only scantly covered in previous studies (for exceptions see Jones 1978; Zimmermann Holt 1996a, b). For example, food taboos have rarely been taken into consideration despite the long-standing recognition in the ethnographic and anthropological literature that animal taboos have both complex symbolic and utilitarian motivates and that such taboos articulate the subsistence and ideational spheres (for example, Douglas 1957, 1966; Garine 1994:246–50; Tambiah 1969; Valeri 2000:43–113). Food taboos among many Amazonian indigenous groups have been the subject of an intense debate centered on their frequency and significance (Balée 1989; Beckerman 1980; DeBoer 1987; Descola 1994; Kiltie 1980; Reichel-Dolmatoff 1985; Ross 1978, 1980). However, the influence of cosmology, religion and beliefs—so prevalent in ethnographic accounts—have been virtually ignored in the analysis faunal exploitation patterns in the archaeology of past hunter-gatherers, thereby perpetuating the rift between anthropological and archeological approaches and narrowing interpretative horizons (Politis & Saunders 2002).

Although I do present new ethnographic data on food taboos it is not my intention here to review the extensive anthropological literature on this subject or to rehearse the arguments concerning their origins, function, or universality. Many papers and books have reviewed and discussed these issues in detail from very different perspectives (Douglas 1957, 1966, 1990; Harris 1990; Valeri 2000, to mention just a few). To simplify presentation of the data, and because the concept of taboo is notable for the distinct uses that different authors have made of it, I will use the term "taboo" interchangeably with prohibition, avoidance, or sign of danger (see also Valeri 2000:45).

Some materialist ecological models have explained food taboos in the Amazonian rainforest as an adaptive mechanism to preserve scarce prey such as deer and tapir (Ross 1978); or they have argued that such taboos have their origin in a long-term information chain related to the low return of rarely encountered prey (Kaplan & Hill 1992); or that they have adaptive functions, minimizing overexploitation, diversifying exploitation, and maximizing consumption of fat (Meggers 1996:192). However, the adaptive advantage of such taboos has not been tested against long-term data, nor have there supposed nutritional benefits during anomalous conditions of scarcity been proven. Other authors have seen Amazonian food taboos as cultural practices within a pure ideological domain in relation to a body of beliefs in which animal myths are central elements (for example, Descola 1994; Hugh-Jones 1979; Lévi Strauss 1969). In this sense, the anthropomorphization of animals is understood as a manifestation of mythical thinking used as a code to translate forms of popular knowledge (Descola 1994:98; but see Ingold 1994 for a different view). A third perspective is that taboos function in the social plane and are frequently the means for in-group, out-group distinctions (DeBoer 1987:45). Critical of the former approaches, DeBoer (1987:45) has stated that, "between the natural and mind the whole world of human social activity [. . .] is left fiddling." A fourth position is taken by Reichel-Dolmatoff (1976, 1985), who conceived of taboos as a form of ecological accommodation but from the ideational sphere. This model is related to Ross's (1978), but with greater development of the mythic components of the belief system.

Ethnoarcheological research derived from the Nukak provides an excellent opportunity to examine the cultural aspects of faunal remains assemblage formation and to discuss how cultural inferences can be made from bone assemblages. In this chapter I summarize the data on the Nukak exploitation of land vertebrates and their bone refuse patterns. The archeological implications of both sets of practices are also examined and discussed. I further address the different ways in which small and medium-sized mammals are incorporated into the material remains produced by tropical rainforest foragers. Finally, I explore the effects of the ideational order—especially animal food taboos—on the formation of bone assemblages. In investigating the latter issue I examine a range of evidence concerning species avoidance from both the Nukak and other Amazonian groups.

HUNTED AND TABOO ANIMALS

Although a variety of potential prey is available to the Nukak, few animals are actually hunted. As stated in the previous chapter, a number of species are hunted with different degrees of intensity, including monkeys, birds, tortoise, peccaries, armadillos, and agouti. Following earlier work (Jones 1978; Politis & Martínez 1996), I have classified vertebrates found in the area into three main size categories: small (below 10 kg); medium (between 10 and 50 kg); and large (above 50 kg). As such, the major vertebrates that inhabit the region can be grouped as follows:

- *Small*: All species of monkey, tortoise, armadillos, agouti, paca, coatimundi, smaller rodents, and birds.

- *Medium*: White-lipped peccary, collared peccary, deer, capybara, anteater, and caiman.
- *Large*: Tapir and jaguar.

The Nukak recognize four classes of animal. First, there are those that embody spirit-ancestors, the majority of which live in the "house of the tapir." Second are those animals that Mauroijumját created from an elemental material. Third are those animals that in the past were Nukak but were transformed owing to a generally catastrophic event, such as falling into the water during the great flood. Finally, there exist animals the origin of which is unclear—they are said to be those that "always have been."

The animals that embody spirit-ancestors (most of the larger local animals) are taboo for all band members. These include tapir (*Tapirus terrestris*), deer (*Mazama* sp.), anteater (*Myrmecophaga tridactyla*), freshwater otter (perro de agua, *Lutra longicaudis*), jaguar (*Panthera onca*), and related smaller felines such as the little spotted cat (tigrillo, *Felis tigrina*). For a variety of conceptual, symbolic, and mythological reasons large animals are considered to be "like people," and it is completely forbidden to kill and/or eat any of them. These animals are members of the "house of the tapir" and are actually the *yorehat* spirits of the ancestors who "dress in the shirt of" or "get inside" the animals to travel the intermediate world, using the salt licks as gateways (see Chapter 3). These spirit-ancestors have three "shirts." If the three shirts of one of these spirits were to be killed "people would be finished, everything would end."

Attitudes about the consumption of tapir are particularly revealing of the diverse ways in which lowland Amazonian societies articulate total or partial taboos with everyday life. The tapir is probably the most powerful animal, and hunting and eating it are totally prohibited. The tapir does not appear to be comparable to the jaguar with its double status (some jaguar are considered powerful spirit-ancestors, whereas others are not, see below), since it is always the embodiment of a spirit-ancestor. I have never observed the consumption of tapir meat or the use of any of its body parts (that is, teeth, bones, skin, and so on). It is also the master of the house, and special constructions are built for it in the intermediate world (see Chapter 4). The Nukak take every possible precaution to avoid tapir and will ignore the animal's tracks if they come across them. When tracks are encountered (a not infrequent occurrence), Nukak identify them, indicate the direction taken by the animal, discuss it, but never follow. According to Nukak mythology killing a tapir angers thunder, the spirit-ancestor of a powerful enemy. The power of this animal also manifests itself in its remains. For example, a woman (probably an epileptic) attributed her fits and health problems to the fact that her mother had bathed her as a child in a place contaminated by tapir excrement (Cabrera, Franky, & Mahecha 1999:209).

Jaguars and related small felines like the little spotted cat are also considered powerful spirit-ancestors. However, not all jaguars are seen as fierce spirit-animals that attack people, especially when they do not act like them (see below); some are simply dangerous predators. Although the Nukak do not hunt jaguar they will kill one if it threatens people, as was the case when an old jaguar was killed by three hunters at the Cerro de las Cerbatanas after it had attacked a young Nukak (Andres Jimenez, pers. comm.:1995). On this occasion the men removed the large canine teeth and made them into a necklace but did not use the animal's skin or consume its meat. When jaguars approach camps at night the Nukak prepare their spears and shout loudly and aggressively. The possibility that the jaguar is in fact a zoomorphized spirit-ancestor is implied by the Nukak habit of constructing a wall of seje leaves around the camp: a physical and symbolic barrier against malevolent spirits represented by the nocturnal prowling feline.

The other conspicuous member of the "house of the tapir" is the deer. This animal is apparently like the tapir, because it always embodies a spirit-ancestor and is never hunted or eaten. Only deer bones taken from carcasses found in the forest are used to make the *mikuepat* flutes (see discussion in Chapter 7). Although only one name has been recorded for deer, during an interview a Nukak woman referred to various classes of deer, implying that more than one species is known.

The paca, a member of the "house of the tapir," is also taboo. We did not see this animal hunted or eaten during our fieldwork, even though paca are relatively abundant along the banks of rivers and streams. Gualteros (Ms) also mentions that paca are a taboo food for all members of the group, information corroborated by informants in several different interviews. However, Cabrera, Franky, and Mahecha (1999) record the occasional consumption of paca, and Gutiérrez Herrera (1996:74) mentions that "they are eaten frequently." This last statement must be taken with caution owing to the short period of observation undertaken by the author, as well as her lack of knowledge of the Nukak language. The discrepancies between different authors may be due to the paca having been taboo until recently. In the past several years, especially in the northwestern bands most exposed to the effects of colonization, this prohibition has gradually relaxed as social practices are transformed.

The freshwater otter and the anteater have an ambiguous status, since they belong to the "house of the tapir" and can be considered people, but they are rarely mentioned. Furthermore, these animals are not currently found in Nukak territory, nor are their remains. I did not record the consumption of these animals during any part of my fieldwork; nor do they appear in the lists of consumed animals published by other authors.

The animals created by Mauroijumját are generally small, and the majority may be eaten. They are members of no "house." In some form they are thought of as created to be "given" to the Nukak, although in the past some of them were the objects of greater restrictions. Within this group are included monkeys, pavas (Spix's Guan), paujiles (curassows), other birds, and many fish. These animals were created from things in the past. For example, the night monkey (*dugup*) was made from small bark bags made by the Nukak. An unidentified large fish (*ñamú*) was created from a sieve. Although none of these animals is entirely taboo, there are restrictions tied to them for specific people or genders. For example, locally the Nukak recognize two species of Spix's Guan: the white, which inhabit the floodplain, and the red, which live in the hinterland. Women may not eat the white Spix's Guan or the curassows because they will become thin.

The animals that resulted from Nukak transformed in the past are, in general, medium sized, and most are taboo for one or other gender or a particular category of people (the sick, newborns, parents, a specific clan, and so on), exemplifying what are called "specific taboos" (Basso 1973:16; Ross 1978). This type of taboo includes the two species of peccary, caiman, capybara (*kék´chut, Hydrochaeris hidrochaeris*), and tortoises. When they are considered prey, these animals are hunted with spears but no venom. The most interesting case is the white-lipped peccary, the processing and consumption of which are forbidden for women and children.[1] During our fieldwork on only one occasion did two women eat peccary viscera. In fact, most women show great discomfort even at the idea of eating peccary or smelling smoked peccary meat. In Nukak mythology peccaries were originally people who ate seje fruit from the ancestral palms and were transformed into the animal. The caiman is another case—like the capybara and tortoises, caiman were Nukak who fell into the water during the great flood and were transformed. Some informants indicated that they would not eat caiman, whereas others said that women do not eat caiman. In an interview with two women, one stated that she would eat caiman and the other said she would not. Clearly, the prohibition on eating caiman affects women, but not all women, so it is possibly linked to clan affiliation as well as gender. Neither any other researcher nor I have ever witnessed the hunting or consumption of capybara.

A few smaller animals, such as sloth (*Bradypus sp.*) and some birds, including several types of duck, are also considered inedible, but for more mundane reasons that do not appear to have mythological connotations. They may be included within the category of animals that "always have been." In a single interview I heard mention of river dolphin, but with no allusion to its status. They were never caught during my fieldwork, nor have they been recorded in the work of other researchers. Other edible animals such as the agouti are also included in this list. The agouti does not belong to a particular "house," and its origin is mundane: "they come from hollows in the ground."

In the past the list of taboo animals was longer. Presently, the Nukak say that the "old ones" did not eat the two largest monkeys in the area: howler and woolly monkeys. Neither did they eat caiman, capybara, or any species of piranha, "because they were afraid"; and the women had even more restrictions. Present-day Nukak, who in fact still find the smell of howler monkey distasteful, still remember the old taboos. One must remember that the ancestral memory of the Nukak is short; the "old ones," or the "grandparents," are comparable to the "ancestors." Consequently, when the grandparents or "old ones" are referred to it is difficult to know if this means only two generations back or if they are referring to ancestral time. During this imprecise time, some mentioned that "their food" (referring to the ancestors) was eaten, perhaps suggesting that some of the animals created by Mauroijumját did not yet exist and that these are important in their present diet (such as the larger monkeys and fish).

Pregnant women have an important series of restrictions. They may not eat howler monkey, caiman, or armadillo, because they are harmful—the women will become thin and turn yellow. They may eat Spix's Guan, tinamou, fish, and abundant fruit, especially *patataá* when it is available. Also, a pregnant women's husband can bring her only certain kinds of food, such as toucan (*Ramphastidae* sp.) and certain unspecified types of tortoise. Parents of a newborn baby are forbidden to eat certain kinds of animal food, such as howler monkey and various kinds of birds and fish, for a period ranging from two to four weeks. During this period the family diet is based on wild and domesticated vegetables and honey.

Women also must abide by similar restrictions when they are menstruating, although with slight differences. Note that women with babies apparently do not have sexual relations until weaning has taken place when the infant is between two and three years old (Cabrera, Franky, & Mahecha 1999:200). Furthermore, when adults or children are sick they are forbidden to eat certain kinds of animal food that at other times are allowed. In general, Nukak women cannot eat everything that men eat, particularly when pregnant, and children can eat even fewer things than women can. Children may not eat caiman, as well as the general taboos and the white-lipped peccary taboo.

Some species of fish, duck, and Spix's Guan appear to have the status of "antifood," insofar as they may cause wasting, a situation that closely parallels the Barasana notion of *wisiose* (Hugh-Jones 1979:92). This category can be broadened to include many more animals in specific situations and in some ways alludes to the relations between people and animals rather than one specific situation. As such, in accordance with clan, the state and situation of a person, some species are transformed into antifood—a complex phenomenon that I have yet to understand in its full depth. However, although the Nukak do not purposefully hunt coatimundi (*Nasua nasua*), opportunistic kills do occur. In one case, a coatimundi was hunted and killed but not eaten; one of the hunters stated that he could not eat the animal because it would make him "thin," but another hunter commented that eventually he would eat it. Several genera of duck, the "pato agujeto," the "pato negro," and the "pato real" are also forbidden to all members of the group, not for any obvious mythic reason but because their meat is believed to cause wasting. The same principle works for other fowl such as the red Spix's Guan. The only parts of these animals used are the breast feathers for adornments, especially those of the "pato agujeto." The agouti is also on this list. In an interview a woman stated that she ate this mammal once in a while, while another woman from the same band commented that she did not because it made her extremely thin. The same applies to white Spix's Guan and curassows, which make women thin (see above).

Aquatic animals have an important place in Nukak cosmology. This status is due to the existence in the rivers of a "house" for the floodplain, which is located beneath the ground and harbors animals that are perceived as "crowded" and abundant. Consumption of aquatic animals is also subject to prohibitions. The Nukak recognize a wide variety of fish subject to total, partial, or no taboo. The details of how these taboos operate remain obscure. Piranhas provide an interesting case: some species are taboo for everyone, some for women only, and others are edible to all. In all cases the jaw of the piranha has two uses, to cut hair and to notch hunting darts.

Beyond this complex series of food taboos and restrictions there are also restrictions on how certain prey are consumed. The most obvious, which has already been mentioned, is that certain animal parts cannot be eaten by the hunter, although there is a degree of flexibility that operates within Nukak ontology. In the case of monkey heads, the explanation for the taboo is that the hunter's "aim would fail" in future hunts. Eating the head of a peccary would "sting" the hunter, later causing him severe pain, and he would not be able to hunt peccary again in the future. Even so, some "old ones" (who are considered to be powerful people) do occasionally eat the heads of peccary piglets. This conduct around heads is related to the belief that the "truth drug" (*éóro-baká*, see Chapter 8) is found in the heads of animals and above all in the heads of animals from the "house of the tapir" and the "floodplain house." This red substance is found in the heads of many animals, including the peccary, but only the wisest old people can "see" it. This concentration of *éóro baká* substance explains the avoidance of the consumption of the head of various animals. Other animals, such as the agouti, do not contain this substance, and so may be eaten by anyone.

In summary, Nukak animal consumption taboos are complex and, in some cases, situational. In general, animals that embody spirit-ancestors and are members of a "house" are totally taboo (primarily large and some medium-sized animals). Small animals created by *Mauroijumját* are generally edible, and some are eaten regularly. They are, however, subject to a series of specific taboos related to a person's state (pregnant women, fathers of a newborn, menstruating women, and so on). Animals that were Nukak transformed by some special event in the past are generally medium-sized and are subject to more marked specific taboos that affect a gender or age group. Animals that "always have been" are generally small and have a double status: they are either not eaten because they are considered indelible or anyone may eat them.

Hunting and Processing Strategies

Hunting and processing strategies were recorded for both small and medium-sized vertebrates. During fieldwork the hunting and processing of the most frequently hunted vertebrates were observed and recorded several times each, including white-lipped peccary ($n = 6$); monkey ($n = 37$); tortoises ($n = 6$); birds ($n = 8$); and caiman ($n = 1$).

White-Lipped Peccary

The hunting of white-lipped peccary was observed on three occasions—twice in the rainy season and once in the dry season. The rainy-season hunting trips were recorded in detail. They covered distances (round trip) of 7.74 km and 8.96 km. The first left base camp at 7.10 am and returned at 1.30 pm. By 9:10 a.m. two peccaries had been killed. The second hunt started at 8:10 a.m. At 11:05 a.m. the peccaries were killed, and the meat was taken to the main camp at 4:14 p.m. All the hunters in the band participated in the hunts, as well as three or four women. The women accompanied the hunting parties but did not participate in the killing or the processing activities. The hunting parties consisted of five adult men and two adolescents, plus three visiting adolescent men from another band. Two different scenarios were observed. The first involved a chance encounter whereby a woman trekking through a swampy area discovered signs of peccary. The second situation involved an organized hunt when expectations of success were high, as suggested by the maintenance of spears and butchering equipment as well as matches being brought for the initial burning of the carcass.

In both situations the hunting parties traveled directly along previously used paths to swampy areas traversed by peccaries. In these areas the hunters followed the peccary tracks in single file, the men ahead of the women (Figure 9.1), until they were close to the animals, at which point they stopped and sharpened their spear points a final time. The hunters then moved closer to the peccaries until they could hear them. They stopped again, conversed and made signals confirming the location of the animals. They then dispersed and partially surrounded their prey in a semicircle. At this stage they were within a few meters of the animals and threw their spears. The peccaries, some wounded with spears (generally in the hind limbs), at times attacked the hunters but generally would flee the area at random with the hunters in pursuit. Both men and women assisted in relocating the wounded peccaries, which were typically 10 to 30 minutes from the hunt site. The wounded animals were finally killed with a spear through the neck or chest region (Figure 9.2). The other end of the spear was used, as the weapon may have broken in two during the animal's flight. On one occasion an animal that did not die from

Figure 9.1 File of men and women on a peccary hunting trip

Figure 9.2 Wounded peccary killed with a spear

the spear strike was struck between the eyes with a club. In the first hunting event an adult and a juvenile peccary were killed, whereas in the second four peccaries were killed, one adult, two subadults, and a juvenile.

The peccary carcasses were hoisted onto the back of a hunter, fore and hind limbs of one side of the animal on either side of the hunter's neck. Heavy animals often required two hunters to carry them (Figure 9.3). The carcasses were then transported to a dry area inside the swamp where the hunters had regrouped, and the carcasses were prepared for further transportation. The legs of the peccary were roped together using strips of bark.

The carcasses were then transported to a treeless open area outside the swamp close to a water source. Here, a wooden grill was constructed on top of which the peccaries were placed and a fire was lit underneath using large dry leaves (usually of seje), which produce tall flames (Figure 9.4). The hair of the peccaries was soon singed off. The carcasses were removed from the grill before the skin became charred. They were placed on leaves to keep them clean, and they were then butchered (Figure 9.5). By this stage the adolescent men had carried leaves containing water to the butchering location. This water was slowly and continuously poured over the area being cut. This keeps the hands of the butcher and the area surrounding the cut clean of dirt and

Figure 9.3   One hunter helps another carry his kill out of a swamp

Figure 9.4   Young man burning the hair off a peccary

charred skin and allows greater control of the cutting process. This is also done because of a belief in the impurity of blood and the necessity of avoiding contact with it, or of quickly washing away any trace that remains on the hands.

Figure 9.5 Man butchering a peccary

The dismembering sequence is as follows (a machete is used):

1. Each forelimb is removed by a cut that begins at the middle of the neck and extends around the shoulder blade.
2. The head is chopped off at the neck (midcervical) and discarded a few meters away from the butchering area.
3. A cut is made halfway down the abdomen and across to the hind limbs, which are then splayed open, exposing the lower intestines.
4. The testicles and tail are removed.
5. A cut through the skin and muscles is then made from the throat down the chest as far as the previous posterior cut, releasing the stomach and the intestines.
6. The skin and muscles (belly sheet) surrounding the stomach are cut away in two pieces.
7. The viscera are removed and placed to one side.
8. The hind limbs and pelvic girdle are removed from the rib cage as a single unit with a careful cut through the lumbar region.
9. The hind limbs (femur, tibia, fibula, tarsals, metatarsals, and phalanges) are then removed from the pelvic girdle that, with the sacral vertebrae, remains intact.
10. The viscera—by this stage covered with flies—are then sorted. Lungs, heart, liver, and kidneys, all of which are very carefully cleaned, are placed

in an expedient basket (*búrup*). The intestines, stomach, glands, and other remaining organs are discarded at the same location as the head.
11. All the butchered portions are then placed into expedient baskets for transportation to the camp.

In the first hunting event the adult and the juvenile peccary were butchered almost simultaneously, which took approximately 35 minutes. On the second occasion the four peccaries were butchered in a process (in pairs in two main episodes) that took 1 hour and 10 minutes. This would suggest that individual peccaries take approximately 25 minutes each to butcher.

A total of 13 body parts from the first hunt were returned to the main camp. All were weighed to the nearest 10th of a kilo with a pocket spring balance: hind limb (3.5 kg), pelvis (2.5 kg), pelvis (2 kg), rib cage (2.5 kg), belly sheet (2.5 kg), hind limb (2.5 kg), belly sheet (2 kg), ribcage (5.5 kg), forelimb (3 kg), forelimb (3 kg), hind limb (2.5 kg), forelimb (2.75 kg), and viscera (3 kg). The remaining six parts were taken to the small camp belonging to the young hunters, a dwelling located close to the band's residential camp that was occupied for several days. A total of 27 parts from the second hunt were brought back to the main camp. Their weights were as follows: forelimb (3 kg), forelimb (1.5 kg), ribcage (4 kg), forelimb (2.5 kg), ribcage (2.5 kg), ribcage (5 kg), ribcage (0.5 kg), forelimb (4 kg), hind limb (0.5 kg), pelvis (1.5 kg), hind limb (2 kg), belly sheet (2.5 kg), belly sheet (1.5 kg), belly sheet (1 kg), heart, liver and kidneys (0.5 kg), liver and other viscera (4 kg), hind limb (2.5 kg), hind limb (2 kg), hind limb (0.5 kg), pelvis (0.5 kg), belly sheet (0.5 kg), hind limb (2 kg), hind limb (1.5 kg), hind limb (1.5 kg), pelvis (2 kg), pelvis (2.5 kg), and hind limb (0.5 kg). Three or four limbs and some pieces of belly sheet went to the young hunters' camp.

A triangular grill was then constructed from sticks on the periphery of the main camp area (Figure 9.6). The meat was placed on top and a small fire lit underneath. A roof of leaves was positioned over the grill to prevent the meat from getting wet. Only the hunters, men, and juvenile boys consume peccary meat and marrow. The viscera were boiled in a small bowl placed on the fire beneath the grill and were consumed first. Some meat was also boiled at this stage. The remainder was smoked for about two and a half days, during which period particular portions were consumed in roughly the following order: ribcage, pelvis, and then flesh cut from the upper parts of the limbs. During the second and third days the belly sheets and the meat on the bone were eaten. On the third day the grill was no longer used, and the remaining portions (parts of the belly sheet, which at this stage were very dry, and the bones and remaining attached flesh from the fore and hind limbs) were brought inside the camp and hung over the domestic hearth. By the fourth day the peccary was completely consumed.

Figure 9.6   Men eating peccary off the grill outside the camp

The bones of several portions (ribs, vertebrae, and pelvis) were discarded near the grill. Long bones such as the femora (sometimes broken), tibia, and fibula were discarded inside and around the camp. Phalanges were likely discarded inside the camp. Only the largest long bones such as the femora were broken; the others remained complete. Long bones were cut open with a machete and the marrow removed with a stick.

Monkey

The hunting of monkeys occurs on a daily basis. Hunting parties vary in number from one to four adults, usually male (see Chapter 8). The Nukak appear to follow an encounter hunting strategy, hunters traveling to various places within the camp catchment area. Hunters generally proceed through the rainforest on known paths that may pass by abandoned camps. They will stop and listen for monkeys, imitate their calls, and then listen again. They are also guided by signs, such as fruit eaten by monkeys found at the foot of trees. On sighting monkeys the hunters run through the rainforest, leaving the paths and attempting to get as close as possible to their prey (Figure 9.7). At this stage, when it is practicable to do so, the blowpipe is loaded and fired.

Figure 9.7 Man approaching his prey just before shooting a dart

The hunters attempt to position the blowpipe as near vertical as possible directly beneath the monkeys. Each time the hunter hits his prey with the first dart he invariably repeats a series of gestures. He lets out a shout from the bottom of his chest, a sound like "ough!!" and begins to chase the monkey, heedless of the noise he may be making. This initial shout always takes place at the same moment and would be considered a ritual gesture.

After the first dart hits the monkey, the animal reduces its speed as the poison takes effect. It is then hit by more darts and dies within 20 to 30 minutes, larger animals taking longer. The monkey will either fall to the ground (the most frequent event) or remain in a fork or branch of a tree in agony until a hunter retrieves it. The hunters return with intact carcasses to the camp where the monkeys are butchered and cooked exclusively by women, who generally use a metal knife to disarticulate the carcasses and cut away the tissue. Before the use of metal knives this task was carried out with a sharpened bamboo cane fiber (see Chapter 7). The monkey carcass is rotated over a fire, and the hair is carefully burnt from the skin, although this sometimes exposes the joints, at which stage burning ceases (Figure 9.8). It is then washed in water to remove the ash, burnt skin, and hair. The complete dismembering sequence has been recorded in detail. The sequence varied little over the observed period, and the carcass is turned into primary butchering units. Viscera are removed and most of them discarded, especially the stomach and the intestines.

Figure 9.8 Woman burning the hair off a monkey in the domestic hearth

The sequence is as follows:

1. The head is cut off at the first cervical vertebra.
2. The hindquarters (the femur, tibia, fibula, and the tarsals, metatarsals, and phalanges) are cut from the carcass.

3. The forelimbs (scapula, humerus, ulna, radius, carpals, metacarpals, and phalanges) are then removed (Figure 9.9).
4. The muscles surrounding the trunk and belly are fleshed from the carcass, exposing the viscera. These are removed and most of them discarded, especially the stomach, the intestines, and the gall bladder.
5. The carcass is cut transversely into two portions, the first consisting of the thorax (ribs, thoracic vertebrae, and the breastbones) and some lumbar vertebrae. The second consists of the remaining lumbar, vertebrae, and the pelvis.
6. The tail is separated from the sacrum.

Figure 9.9 Woman butchering a monkey; she is removing the forelimbs

During this process the butchered portions are carefully washed and may be piled on a leaf or placed directly in a bowl. Before being placed in the bowl, primary butchering units are partially cut at the elbow and the knee, which are twisted without fully disarticulating the unit. The portions are then boiled and subsequently fully disarticulated into smaller, secondary units.

The cooking location and the distribution of the cooked portions vary with the quantity and the size of the monkeys. When the catch consists of only one or two animals these are cooked in the successful hunter's hearth, and the secondary butchering units are distributed roughly equally among the other members of the band. This results in the distribution of portions of the same monkey among different households with separate hearths. When the catch consists of several small monkeys (for example, tamarins and titis) they are distributed whole among the families in the band, to be butchered and consumed. In these cases both preparation and consumption of single animals occur at the same household, in contrast to the first type of distribution.

Long bones are occasionally cut open for their marrow (Figure 9.10). The bones of large monkeys (that is, howler monkeys) are cut with the machete along the diaphyses (see Appendix II). The bones of small monkeys are generally broken with the teeth, leaving distinctive marks. The marrow is sucked from the bone or removed with a stick. The head is usually cracked in the occipital region with a machete or against a tree or post and the brains sucked from the skull or removed with the fingers and subsequently eaten (Figure 9.11).

The head is commonly the last portion to be consumed. It is usually kept in the hunter's household and may also be carried between camps. A hunter cannot eat the head of the monkey for ideational reasons, so his wife and children consequently eat it (see above).

Tortoise

Tortoises are usually encountered by chance during hunting or gathering trips or when the band is moving to a new camp. Tortoise bones are left at both the kill/processing site and at the camp. When this prey is encountered and the hunters have the proper gear with them they usually butcher the animal *in situ*, leaving behind the ventral carapace, the dorsal shell, and some viscera. However, if the tortoise was encountered and no machete or ax was at hand, the hunters bring the prey to the camp unprocessed. Once in the camp the tortoise is butchered, consumed, and discarded. Both men and women participate owing to the hardness of the shell, the strength of two people being required to butcher it.

The dismembering sequence is as follows:

1. The ventral carapace is broken and torn away where it joins the dorsal shell using an ax or machete.

Figure 9.10 Man cutting the epiphysis of a long bone to access the marrow

2. The hind limbs and pelvis are cut from the dorsal carapace. They are pulled away from the shell together, and a cut is made between the pelvis and the attached fat and the shell. The fat is saved.

3. The tail is also pulled out and cut from the main body.

Figure 9.11 Girl eating the brain of a monkey

4. The liver is removed and cut open. The gall bladder, which contains a bitter substance, is carefully removed. On one occasion a female tortoise was killed and eggs removed.
5. The head and neck are cut and removed.

The dorsal and ventral carapace and most of the viscera are discarded, either in the camp or at the kill site.

Birds

During our fieldwork we observed birds being hunted exclusively with blowpipes during daily foraging trips and brought back to the camp whole. Women butcher medium-sized birds and fowl such as tente, Spix's Guan, curassows, ducks, and tinamou (see Chapter 8). Butchering is done with a knife and is slightly different for each species of bird. In the case of the tente the sequence observed ($n = 3$) is as follows:

1. The feathers are plucked.
2. The carcass is placed over the domestic hearth and burnt superficially until the skin is more or less black.
3. A pot is filled with water, and the skin is carefully washed.
4. The carcass is cut longitudinally from the thorax to the tail with a knife.
5. The tail and tripe (intestines) are removed with a knife and discarded (these are eaten immediately by any dogs in the camp).
6. The distal parts of the feet are twisted, and then the feet are sliced but not deeply enough to separate them from the body.
7. The abdomen is opened with a transversal cut. The viscera are removed and discarded.
8. The body cavity is washed with water.
9. The gutted body is boiled, along with the head and partially cut feet.

The sequence recorded for pavas is as follows ($n = 5$):

1-3. See the tente sequence.
4. A low transversal cut is made close to the tail, which may touch the head of the femur, and the viscera are removed (including the intestines).
5. The body is split by hand into two parts according to the cut. The feet and pelvis are put to one side and the wings, breast, nape of the neck, and head to the other.
6. The viscera are put back inside the abdominal cavity, which is tied with a vine so they are held fast inside the body.
7. The feet are boiled, having been partially cut.

If several birds were hunted they are either processed and cooked in the domestic hearth of the hunter and afterward shared, or the whole carcasses are distributed among other families who finish the preparation.

Caiman

The hunting and butchering of caiman was recorded only once, in the dry season, during the only logistical trip on which I accompanied the Nukak (see Chapter 6). On one other occasion we recorded a caiman being brought into the camp, but we were unable to observe it being butchered and consumed in detail. In the former case caiman signs were found by chance in a small, almost dry creek, and the hunters followed the tracks to a den in the banks of the creek, the entrance of which was partially submerged. Once the hideout was located a very simple but effective device was prepared to pull the caiman out of its layer. This tool consisted of a long stick with a "ball" of inner bark (phloem) wrapped around one end. The end of the stick was shoved aggressively several times into the den, irritating the caiman, who bit the bark-ball fiercely and with great strength. The hunters then pulled on the stick, dragging the caiman out of its burrow. An expedient spear (a stick with a sharpened end) was made and used to kill the caiman once it was in the open.

The butchering of the caiman was performed with a machete according to the following sequence:

1. The caiman was skinned by making a cut below the head and pulling the skin down to the back legs, removing it whole.
2. The nape of the neck was sliced with a deep cut through the muscle. A similar cut was made in the abdomen.
3. The esophagus and trachea were cut. The viscera were removed.
4. The head was cut off and discarded.
5. The front left leg was cut on the inner side but not deep enough to separate it entirely.
6. The front right leg was cut on the inner side.
7. The body was divided into two parts with blows from the machete. The first part included the thoracic box and the front of the body; the second consisted of the hips, back legs and tail.

The caiman, divided into these butchering units, was placed on a wooden grill located near the butchering site. All members of the hunting party consumed it during the evening and the following morning. Nothing was taken to the women and children in the residential camp.

Bone-Discard Pattern

The Nukak have three kinds of bone-discard patterns in regard to hunted animals. One type is associated with monkeys, birds, and small mammals (armadillos, agouti, and smaller rodents); the second pattern is associated with the white-lipped peccary; and the third case consists of tortoise.

Since monkeys are brought whole to the base camps to be butchered there is no refuse left at any other site. Monkey bones are generally discarded in a random fashion around the consumption site. This usually takes place during the evening, which makes the discard of bone refuse difficult to observe. Some household areas, such as the hearth and surrounding area, show higher bone concentrations because the Nukak often eat in their hammocks. Monkey bones are also tossed in the zone between the hammock and the leafy walls of the winter dwelling. They usually follow the trajectory of other discarded items, eventually ending up in the trash heaps (see Chapter 5). The only exception is the head, which is sometimes taken by the Nukak when they move to a new camp. In these cases the head is abandoned between camps or in the new camp. Since the head is usually the last part to be consumed it is occasionally dropped in the domestic hearth during the camp occupation or just before its abandonment. Birds, armadillos, and small rodents follow the same discard pattern—the whole carcass is taken into camp, where it is butchered, consumed, and discarded.

White-lipped peccary bones are disposed of in a rather different sequence. Their bones are discarded in three main locations (Figure 9.12): (1) The head and some viscera are discarded at the hair-burning and butchering spot close to the swamp. (2) The ribs, vertebrae, pelvis, and scapulae are discarded in the area around the grill established on the outskirts of the base camp. Some long bones, such as humeri and femurs, may also be discarded around the grill. These bones are sometimes broken for marrow extraction. (3) Other long bones, such as tibias, fibulas, ulnas, metacarpals, and metatarsals, as well as the carpals, tarsals, and phalanges, are discarded inside and around the residential camp.

The third type of bone discard is associated with tortoise. Tortoise bones may be left at both the kill/processing site and at the camp. If hunters with the proper gear encounter the prey they usually butcher the animal *in situ*, leaving behind the ventral carapace, the dorsal shell, and parts of the viscera. However, if the tortoise is brought to the camp unprocessed it is butchered, consumed, and discarded in that one location. In the latter case the dorsal shell often freely circulates within the camp during the occupation and usually ends up in the "central place" of the wet season camps (see Chapters 4 and 5).

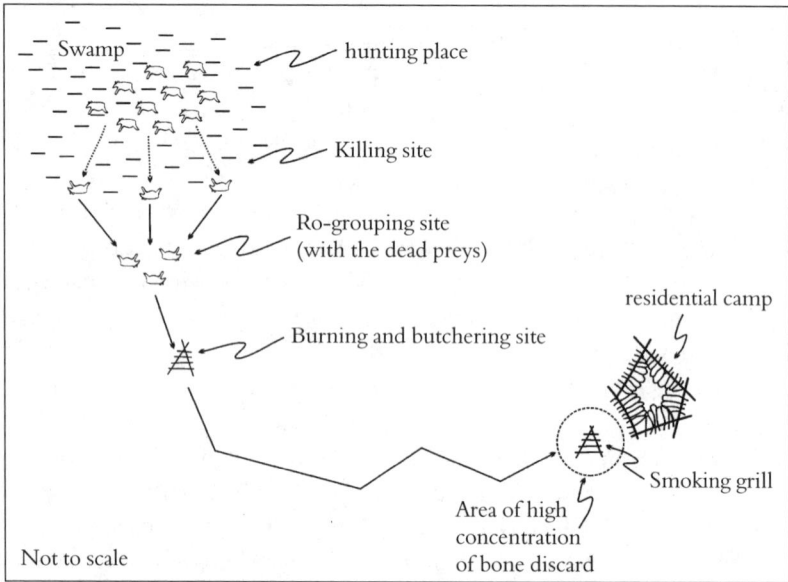

Figure 9.12 Schematic sequence of the hunting, processing, and discard of a peccary

Bones of any of these three types discarded inside the camp may be displaced owing to the action of secondary consumers (for example, dogs), the cleaning of certain areas of the camps, and children's games. Although the vast majority of vertebrate bones are discarded, a small percentage is used as raw materials for both curated and expedient tools (see Chapter 7). Monkey bones are occasionally used as expedient tools for processing the prey carcass (for example, for prizing the mandible from the skull).

ARCHEOLOGICAL VISIBILITY OF BUTCHERING PATTERNS AND BONE DISCARD

The first issue to be addressed is the sequence from skinning to consumption. The typical—though not universal—sequence for large animals includes the following steps: skinning, dismemberment, filleting, and consumption, including marrow extraction (see Binford 1981). In contrast, Nukak butchering techniques do not include the skinning of either small or medium-sized mammalian prey, except for the caiman. For example, with white-lipped peccary the hair is burnt and then the carcass is dismembered. It appears to be easier to burn, grill, and eat the skin than to remove it with a metal knife or traditional instrument such as a cane-fiber knife. It should also be noted that the absence of skinning is not a direct consequence of the size of the animal, since the only prey that is skinned—the caiman—is intermediate in size compared to those that are not skinned. Other hunter-gatherer groups, such as the !Kung San, do skin small and medium-sized prey (Yellen 1991a:9–12), and the Hotï occasionally skin howler monkeys and small felines to make bags from their skin (Politis & Jaimes Ms). The fact that only the caiman was skinned is also related to the Nukak concept that things with hair are impure and dirty. As such, the caiman is skinned because it is hairless and does not require "purification," whereas peccaries and monkeys are burnt as part of the cooking-purification process.

Dismembering into primary butchering units prior to cooking was observed in all cases involving white-lipped peccary, monkey, tortoise, caiman, and agouti,[2] but the hair was burnt from the carcasses of all hairy animals over a naked flame. The same process occurred with birds after the feathers were removed. The Nukak do not fillet in most vertebrate dismemberment processes. Only in the case of white-lipped peccary is filleting used to strip meat from the upper limb bones after they have already been roasted/smoked.

The last stage of the sequence is consumption, which produces the most bone damage (see Appendix II). Monkey, peccary, and bird bones are broken to access the marrow, the consumption of which has been observed consistently in large mammal exploitation (Silberbauer 1981), as well as in medium-sized and small mammals (Politis & Jaimes Ms; Silberbauer 1981; Yellen 1991a). Taking into account the processing sequence as a whole it is clear that most bone damage is produced in the last stage. This observation supports Yellen's (1991a) statements recording a similar pattern of small mammal processing among the !Kung. He also pointed out that most previous studies focused on the marks produced during the early stages of processing, placing emphasis on the practices associated with the initial dismemberment.

The Nukak carry the whole carcass of small animals with no preliminary butchering from kill to camp sites. The same pattern has been recorded among many groups, such as the I Ioti (Politis & Jaimes Ms; Storrie 1999), the !Kung San, the Aka pygmy hunters (Yellen 1991a), the Dobe (Brooks & Yellen 1987), the G/Wi (Silberbauer 1981), the Awa-Guajá (personal observation), and the Aché (Jones 1993). In the Nukak case, the first obvious implication for archaeology is that there are no visible signs of the kill site. The only remains, if any, that might be found after the killing of monkeys or birds are a few pieces of broken darts scattered in the vicinity. In the case of armadillos and agouti nothing at all remains at the hunting place. Medium-sized mammals such as white-lipped peccary are initially butchered close to the kill site at a specific location—the burning and butchering site (Figure 9.7)—where the head, some viscera, and a hearth are the only distinguishable features. This assemblage would have some archaeological visibility, but again, it will be extremely low when compared with large mammal primary processing sites from other environments (for example, savannah, grasslands, tundra, and so on). Thus the Nukak case suggests that under comparable cultural contexts in the Amazonian tropical rainforest one would expect to find higher frequencies of bone, including all or most of the skeleton, in the residential camps and their immediacies. In this sense, the pattern of bone distribution throughout the landscape shows a high concentration of monkey bones (although skulls may be found in other sectors) and a few agouti, armadillo, and bird bones in circumscribed locations (less than 200 m², approximately). In the case of the white-lipped peccary, the area covered by discarded bones is larger and shows spatial segregation. Some bones are disposed inside the camps, whereas others are thrown near the roasting/smoking grill located on the edge of the camp. Furthermore, heads are left in the initial butchering location, producing a wider distribution of peccary bones throughout the landscape, although these are scattered and of low archeological visibility.

The action and consequences of secondary consumers on faunal assemblage composition and site structure has been a topic of some concern (for example, Binford 1981; Bunn & Kroll 1986; O'Connell, Hawkes, & Blurton-Jones 1992; Kent 1993). The effect of such consumers is significant in relation to both large and small mammals (Yellen 1991b:166–72), and they are thought to contribute to the formation of archeological sites in varying degrees of importance. In the case of the Amazonian rainforest the situation is quite different. There are no wild scavengers that significantly affect the bone deposit after abandonment. The fact that the Nukak take the entire carcass into the camp in most cases reduces the possibility of animal scavenging at both kill and processing sites. Small animal bones are usually discarded with no meat attached since the Nukak clean them thoroughly. So, with the exception of marks left by domestic dogs (see Appendix II) the bone assemblages exhibit greater integrity because they have not been modified by secondary consumers. This again is a marked difference when compared to large mammals from open environments where predatory scavenging would frequently mask the traces of human exploitation.

The discard and archaeological visibility of bones is strongly mediated by the ideational realm, especially food taboos. The clearest case involves the tapir—its sacred status means that none of its bones are ever found in deposits created by the Nukak. Other animals from the "house of the tapir," including the anteater, the freshwater otter, and the paca (see discussion above), are also in this group, although they have less symbolic power. In the case of deer, jaguar, and little spotted cats, the only bones present are those elements from which artifacts of important symbolic content are made, such as bone flutes and teeth-bead necklaces. Such elements are the metonymic manifestation of the spirit-ancestors embodied by these animals. The piranha taboo is both partial and unlike those applied to other animals, since they are not a common food resource. This may partly be due to their sharp predator's teeth and local taxonomic associations with other animals possessing similar dentition (for example, Crocker 1985:285–86). But, as previously stated, piranha jaws have two uses. First, they are hair-cutting implements, "purifying" instruments with ideational-aesthetic significance because they make the Nukak clean and attractive. Second, they are used to notch hunting darts, which are in turn used to hunt other animals. Thus, the strong predatory capacities of the piranha are transferred to hunting equipment by their mandibles. Archaeologically, in residential camp contexts one would find all parts of piranha except the highly curated jaw. Almost complete skeletal remains could be interpreted as indicating that piranha were primarily a food resource rather than a provider of jaw-tools possessing two use categories.

TRANSPORT

When we test the previous models against the Nukak data some general cost-benefit principles underlying the Nukak's decisions concerning carcass treatment and consumption can be found. It is clear that the Nukak treat small and medium-sized prey differently, which is partly related to the cost of processing and transportation. On the one hand, small animals that are not subject to taboo, such as monkeys, some birds, and agouti, are consumed intensively, and it therefore seems more efficient to carry the entire carcass to the residential camp to be processed. On the other hand, medium-sized prey may be too heavy to carry whole (although we recorded Nukak men carrying *búrup* with more than 40 kilos of wild fruit for several kilometers) and are less intensively exploited (a larger proportion of viscera and the head are not consumed). Consequently, the carcasses are butchered at the processing site, and parts that will not be eaten are discarded. This behavior reduces transport costs and makes it easier to carry the edible portions in smaller units.

As expected, the Nukak treat the carcasses of their prey differently than do large mammal hunters. They do not take into account the relationship between the edible tissue and the body part to which it is attached. Except for white-lipped peccary heads and some viscera everything is transported to the residential camp regardless of the relationship between bone and associated edible tissue. Moreover, no stripping as a means of reducing transport costs was recorded at the processing sites. Therefore, utility indices for monkey or white-lipped peccary cannot be used to predict or explain Nukak transport patterns. The distance between the kill site and the residential base does not seem to be a critical factor in deciding how the carcasses will be transported. Carcasses have been transported to the camp sites from various distances, ranging from a few meters (on the few occasions when the animal was hunted near the camp) to approximately 9 km. The composition of the hunting party does not affect the transport decision in any way. Hunting parties ranging from a single man to seven men treated the carcasses in exactly the same manner. The availability of other resources does not seem to have any impact either: prey hunted as the sole product during a foraging trip and prey hunted alongside other resources obtained in the same trip are transported and butchered in the same way. Finally, logistical planning and the time of day have no impact on decisions related to the transport and butchering of prey.

Tortoise are treated differently from other prey, demonstrating that the serendipitous availability of hunting gear carried by the Nukak when prey is captured is a critical factor. If they have the proper tools the tortoise is butchered at the site of capture, but if adequate tools are not at hand the tortoise is transported whole to the residential camp to be processed. Therefore, for tortoise, gear at hand does affect decisions related to transport and butchering.

Above and beyond energy-related factors my research has shown that certain food taboos are critical to the Nukak when making decisions about processing, transportation, consumption, and discard. If we compare the pattern of white-lipped peccary processing, transportation, and consumption with the same sequence in monkeys, we see major differences that can partially be explained by taboos. All members of the band consume monkeys at the residential camp. They are hunted and transported by men and butchered and cooked by women, who, along with teenagers and children, are in charge of their distribution among coresidents. Monkeys are butchered and cooked in the household sphere and shared by everybody. In contrast, white-lipped peccaries are hunted and butchered far from the residential camp and then cooked and eaten in the area surrounding the camp. These activities are the exclusive domain of adult and young men; women and children do not participate.

What factors are taken into account when decisions related to transport and dismemberment are made? Size is one such factor—only small mammals are brought to the camp unbutchered. Even so, there are other factors to take into account. It seems that those prey that are consumed by everybody are taken whole into the camp so that women can participate in tasks related to processing, cooking, and distribution. Monkeys pass from men to women's hands through a continuous process of acquisition, preparation, and consumption. In the case of the white-lipped peccary, only men—the hunters—participate in the entire process, which occurs almost completely outside the household sphere. The women and children are not involved in any of the tasks. There is no need, in which case, to bring the prey whole to the camp and introduce it into the household sphere. Note that some immature peccaries (6.5 kg) were processed in the same way and at the same place, even though they weighed less than some monkeys (a howler monkey can weight up to 9 kg). Furthermore, peccary carcasses are transported whole from the kill site to the butchering site. On occasion, a single hunter carries a peccary, whereas at other times its legs are tied to a pole and two hunters carry it supported on their shoulders. This implies that no physical impediment exists to the transportation of entire carcasses from the kill site to camp site or anywhere else.

The fact that the heads of peccaries are neither eaten nor transported, even though they are considered edible by many Amazonian groups, does not appear to be based on an energy equation. Leaving the peccary head at the butchering site is related to the belief that a type of "essence," the *éóro baká*, is found inside the head of certain prey, which a hunter must not consume. Nor may the head be consumed in the camp by the rest of the band (as happens, for example, with monkeys) owing to the food restrictions placed on women and children with respect to peccary. Thus, if no member of the group may eat the head of the peccary for reasons that have nothing to do with nutritional content, to carry this body part to the camp makes no sense to the Nukak. In this case, then, body size is not the determining factor in the butchering and transportation process, which is determined, rather, by a complex ideational framework.

CONCLUSIONS

The Nukak case has two main implications for archeological studies. First, most hunted prey are small mammals that are carried whole to the camp. Therefore, specific models must be developed to understand such patterns of mammal utilization, since those produced for large or medium-sized mammals are not applicable. It seems that the proportion of edible tissue of a given body part, the distance between the kill site and the camp site, the composition of the hunting party, the time of day, and the success of the hunting event are not critical factors in determining where and how a carcass will be dismembered. From an archeological point of view the small mammal exploitation processes demonstrated by the Nukak and other groups result in the deposition of almost all bones at the camp site and nothing at the kill site. In time this pattern produces a high concentration of bone refuse in certain places, whereas other parts of the landscape (for example, the hunting territories) remain virtually bare of archeological bone deposits.

The second implication is that food taboos have important consequences for the formation of the archaeological record. For the Nukak a variety of factors—body size, food avoidance, social relations, and available gear at the kill site, among other contingencies—result in a specific distribution of bones across the landscape. In turn, food taboos for particular species mean that these species are invisible in bone assemblages created by humans. The consequences of such factors have been underestimated—non-energy-related reasons in general have not been systematically considered when analyzing hunter-gatherer decisions concerning the exploitation of certain animals (for example, see discussion in Yellen 1991a: 23–4; O'Connor 1996:12). Hence, expectations based purely on cost-benefit relationships or on the maximization of human effort do not fit the archaeological contexts generated by Amazonian hunter-gatherers. In these contexts we should expect "anomalies" or "cultural behavior that seems irrelevant or unreasonable under normal conditions" (Meggers 1996:191). These "anomalies" are, at least in part, the result of food taboos, which reflect a different conception of the interaction between people and their natural environment. For the Nukak most large animals are subject to formal taboo despite their high meat-to-bone ratio (and thus calorific attractiveness). Tapir, deer, and jaguar are proscribed partially because, as already noted, they are considered sacred and appear in anthropomorphized form in the mythical framework that supports Nukak spiritual life. As such, food taboos must have played a central role in subsistence strategies in the past and undoubtedly have significantly influenced the structure of bone assemblages.

Other Amazonian hunter-gatherers also show how bone trajectories are subject to ideational factors in disregard to their nutritional value. Rydén (1941:44–5) reported that the Siriono tied the skulls of monkeys and coatimundi to branches on the edge of pools. Skulls of caiman and other monkeys were also set up in the surrounding area. Wegner (1931:61) reported a similar phenomenon. These branches have strong symbolic meaning and are believed to prevent the pool from drying up, and they occupy an important place within Siriono cosmology.[3] Califano (1999:106) also noted that the Siriono kept the skull of prey spiked to trunks located close to hunting paths to bring luck in the hunt year round and to keep the animals from leaving. The Hotï have a similar practice, the skulls of prey being hung from the branches of trees in front of the camp or above their hearth within the shelters (Politis & Jaimes Ms). The Nadöb case contrasts to the Nukak with respect to the consumption of the head, exemplifying culturally specific factors that affect the distribution of bones in the archaeological landscape. For the Nadöb the head of hunted prey always goes to the hunter after he has distributed the body parts among his family and the other men in the group (Münzel 1969–1972:153).

The widespread association of the jaguar with shamans and spirits of the dead is found among other Amazonian groups (for example, Karsten 1968: 268–69; Reichel-Dolmatoff 1975). In these instances the animal is regarded as "fierce" and is thought to have attacked group members in the past. Even though the jaguar has the necessary characteristics to be considered a sacred, powerful animal, it does not possess intrinsic traits that prevent it being hunted and consumed. The Siriono routinely kill jaguar with a specially designed bamboo point (Rydén 1941:60). They consider it an important food resource and believe that its supernatural characteristics bestow extraordinary physical potency on whoever eats it. Jaguar meat is also extremely attractive to the Tehuelches (Musters 1871), the Ache (Clastres 1998), and many other South Americans Indians. This means that sacred animals used as living metaphors for, or solid representations of, spirit-ancestors do not have specific, universal, and intrinsic features; in other words, they are culturally and temporally specific.

Others propose that a determining factor in the exploitation of faunal resources are particular socioecological characteristics of prey (Foley 1983; Metcalfe & Barlow 1992; Steele & Baker 1993, in Mengoni 1999:13). While it can be argued that in some areas tapir are seen infrequently, the idea that "scarcity" elicits a taboo appears increasingly untenable. The Bara-Makú, Hupdu Makú, Hotï, Siona-Secoya, and other Amazonian groups, exhibit an opportunistic hunting attitude toward tapir that appears to be oblivious to Western notions of conserving "rare" species. While the Nukak proscribe tapir, the Kakwa, Yukuna, Hotï, and many other Amazonian groups actively hunt and kill this animal at night in the *salados* (salt licks). Contrary to materialist explanations, Descola (1994:338) shows convincingly that the Achuar not only hunt and kill large and supposedly scarce animals but also prohibit the hunting of more numerous smaller ones. Among the Siona and Secoya of northeastern Ecuador the scarce tapir is nevertheless hunted and consumed at every opportunity, while more abundant deer (red deer, *Mazama americana*, and "deer of the yuca," *Mazama* sp.) are hunted only rarely because they are considered evil spirits or "devils" (Vickers 1989:302).

In the Nukak case, it is notable how the mythic origin of animals plays a central role in the way in which they are hunted and how their bones appear in the archaeological record. Animals that embody spirit-ancestor and are members of a "house" are generally completely taboo and thus either they leave no archaeological trace or what trace they do leave functions primarily in the ideational sphere (that is, bone flutes, jaguar teeth). Animals created by Mauroijumjat are generally edible although subject to specific taboos related to a person's state (pregnant women, fathers of newborn babies, menstruating women, and so on). They leave an archaeological record in the residential camps from which can be inferred their regular and relatively generalized consumption by all band members. Animals who were Nukak transformed by a special event in the past are subject to more definite specific taboos that affect an entire gender or age group, especially women and children. The best example in this case is the peccary: these animals leave a different bone assemblage than do the other two animals in this class, and they provide enough traces to enable them to be identified as manifesting food restrictions.

To conclude, I maintain that although materialist factors retain their potential to affect human predation of animals, cosmology plays an equally significant and, on occasion, more important role (Politis & Saunders 2002). In the Nukak case, the management of carcasses and the spatial distribution of bones across the landscape are results not only of economic decisions but also of social and ideational factors embedded in indigenous Amazonian cosmologies, including food-related taboos. Even though such factors are not usually taken into consideration I believe they are of great importance to the formation of the zooarchaeological record.

Notes

1. This, at least, is what happened in the bands with which I did fieldwork. Apparently some women from other bands do eat white-lipped peccary. Cabrera, Franky, and Mahecha mention only one case of a collared peccary hunt, when the carcass was carried to the camp and cooked on a communal hearth. On this occasion, the women ate very little.
2. We were unable to observe the only two cases of armadillo processing that took place during our fieldwork.
3. Based on Nordenskiold's account (1922:122), the caiman is a sacred animal. He reports how his friendly relationship with the Siriono disappeared when one of his helpers shot a one on sight.

Chapter 10

FINAL CONSIDERATIONS

The research I have developed and discussed in the previous chapters demonstrates the complexity of Amazonian forager behavior and enables particularities of the hunter-gatherers of the region to be distinguished. Even though throughout my research I focused on recording and analyzing certain ecological aspects of Nukak behavior, I believe that this ethnoarcheological research could be included in what has been called the "New Synthesis" in Amazonian studies (Viveiros de Castro 1996), or the "Revised Paradigm" (Stahl 2002). This is a new perspective on Amazonian cultural development that emphasizes historical circumstances and takes into account the socioideational dimension of these societies. Within this framework I have summarized and discussed several issues of major interest for archaeologists, although it is my belief that some of the subjects tackled in this book are also of interest for social anthropologists and human ecologists. This last chapter distinguishes the main subject areas covered in this book to highlight what I think are the principle contributions of this study.

THE NUKAK AS HUNTER-GATHERERS

There are several present-day groups in the Lowlands of South America who maintain, or until recently maintained, a hunter-gatherer way of life; however, this fact need not imply that they do not practice—or have not practiced—some type of small-scale horticulture (Wilbert & Simoneau 1992). Examples are the Amahuaca (Lathrap 1968), Waorani (Yost 1981; Rival 1996), Xokleng (Henry 1941), Cuiva (Arcand 1972, 1976; Hurtado & Hill 1986), Pumé (Gragson 1989, Greaves 1997), and many others. Some are from the Tupi-Guaraní family, such as the Héta (Kozák et al. 1979), Awa-Guajá (Balée 1994, Cormier 2003), Aché (Hill & Hurtado 1995; Clastres 1998), and the Siriono[1] (Califano 1999; Holmberg 1950; Rydén 1941). It has been proposed that many of these hunter-gatherers, especially the Tupí-Guaraní groups, are the product of a process of "regression," having had in the past an economy with a greater reliance on horticulture that they subsequently abandoned owing to the impact of Western colonization (Lathrap 1968; Lévi-Strauss 1963:109–10). Other authors include in this stage most of the tropical South American foragers, which are considered to perhaps represent a "secondary readaptation" (Lee 1999:825), or "new adaptations, not primeval ones" (Roosevelt 1998:206). Whether this hypothesis can be tested with the available data or not the horticultural past of most of these groups does not diminish their potential for understanding the hunter-gatherer way of life. Most of them live—or lived until recently—as foragers, with minimal or no horticulture, a lack of marked hierarchies, and a pattern of high residential mobility. They have maintained this dynamic for generations and are distinctively different in subsistence terms from their more settled, horticulturist and fisher neighbors. Moreover, the historical changes in their mode of life have a simple yet profound implication: among South American foragers the adoption of horticultural practices is reversible, and the incorporation of cultivated plants into their diet is not a linear process that once embarked on cannot be abandoned. These examples demonstrate that under specific conditions that make it difficult to subsist with a large horticultural subsistence component in the Amazon, indigenous groups can return to a forager way of life, or significantly increase hunting and gathering to ensure their survival.

This "horticultural regression" also has other significant implications. Such changes are not evolutionary events but rather are fundamentally political actions determined by the history of the colonization of the continent. Horticultural regression shows that these people made decisions throughout their history in which they privileged certain values, such as political autonomy and cultural integrity, at the expense of others, such as access to commodities or the supposed alimentary security that crops may provide (see also Viveiros de Castro 1996:194).

A further interesting point concerning the Nukak is that they demonstrate the laxity of the differences among Amazonian groups and the difficulty of encapsulating such groups within categories based solely on subsistence or mobility. Although the Nukak can be characterized as mobile hunter-gatherers, they also share many aspects in common with riverine horticulturists in terms of kinship system and ideology. This can be demonstrated by the similarities that exist between the Nukak and the Cubeo or the Puinave. These groups have a comparable cosmology, and activities such as hunting, fishing, and the gathering of forest products occupy an important position not only in their economy but also in their symbolic construction of reality. In the same way, the supposed difference between Amazonian hunter-gatherers and those from the savannah is not as marked or categorical (see for example Wilbert and Simoneau 1992). In the case of the Nukak, their strong similarities with the Cuiva—the hunter-gatherer bands studied during the 1970s by Arcand (1972)—should be addressed.

A further important point is that beyond the variations through time in the wild and domestic components of diet there is another aspect that makes the differences between hunter-gatherers and horticulturists even more blurred: the strategy that enables the concentration of resources and the management of nondomesticated plants. In this sense, the Nukak cannot be considered ecologically passive, subsisting within a supposedly pristine rainforest. They modify the floral structure of the landscape, not only by the clearing of chagras but more importantly by behavioral patterns outside the category of horti-culture/agriculture. Rainforest floral structure may be modified by long-term hunter-gatherer occupations. The impact of these populations could be the result of "accidental" or "unconscious" actions (in the sense of Chase 1989), also labeled "incidental domestication" by Rindos (1984), or they could be the effect of a carefully planned strategy to improve the food productivity of the forest. In either case, it seems clear that residential mobility among the Nukak cannot be seen exclusively as a consequence of avoiding the over-exploitation of an easily depleted environment. On the contrary, the Nukak are environmental managers, generating "wild orchards," promoting some species over others, and thereby increasing the productivity of the forest.

The same process can be recognized among foragers in neighboring areas. Zent and Zent (2002 and in press) recorded 254 folk botanical species eaten by the Hotï of Venezuelan Guayana and collected valuable information in this regard. They proposed that the Hotï modify the structure of the rainforest through three main types of activity: harvest and dispersal of edible fruit trees, exploitation and manipulation of palms, and gap cultivation. The first two of these activities are closely related to the way the Nukak manage the rainforest. Among the Hotï of the High Parucito River a process of selective and intensive gathering of great quantities of a very limited variety of wild palm fruits has been recorded (Politis & Jaimes Ms). Also, the consistent discard in specific locations in the residential camps of palms products (such as uneaten seeds, shells, peels, endocarps, and so on) was observed, especially of coroba palms (*Attalea macrolepis*, Zent & Zent in press) and cucurito palm (*Attalea maripa*). Abnormal concentrations of these two species have been observed in the Hotï territory rainforest and in the form of small "forest islands" in the surrounding savannahs of the piedmont (Politis & Jaimes Ms). Similarly to the Nukak case, many seeds of these and other palms and trees remain in the residential camps in very specific places close to the Hotï dwellings. Therefore, the potential for germination is much higher compared to when ripe fruit naturally falls in the forest and must compete with a wide variety of other palms and trees. Each of these camps is a potential source for concentrated edible palms, as has been seen with the Nukak.

A telling story that was recorded by Zent and Zent (in press:17) exemplified this process. They found numerous cucurito-dominant patches during a trek toward the headwaters of the Cuchivero River. Their Hotï informant explained that some of these patches were clearly the living remains of past garden or settlement sites, and in some cases he was able to recall who had lived there. In other cases, these patches were found on ridge tops, where gardens are not normally located. In these cases it is possible that some of the cucurito patches were the result of human-set fires.

Other indigenous groups have specific ways of concentrating edible plants without being involved in classic horticultural practices. Reid (1979:28) states, with regard to the Hupdu, that when they trek through their territories, "they often passed through patches of secondary forest, in various stages of regrowth from old settlement and garden sites." Furthermore, Reid claimed he could identify these patches of secondary forest up to 40 years after their creation. For the Kakwa, who consider more than 54 species edible (although they consume far fewer), the easiest way of reaching fruit is to fell the tree. They explain that "there are so many young trees that will later bear fruit that the natural resources will never be exhausted" (Silverwood-Cope 1990:50). According to this information on Hupdu and Kakwa fruit gathering and (especially logistical) mobility, these groups are probably creating resource patches and modifying the natural density of plant species in ways similar to those described here for the Nukak. Laden (1992) observed that the Efe's forest use pattern concentrates edible plants along the paths and around ancient camps. Among the Huaorani from the Ecuadorian Amazon the distribution of several species seems to be influenced by human activities (Rival 1998b). The case of seje is notable (mentioned by Rival under the synonym *Jessenia bataua*). This palm grows along ridge tops where people collect the fruit during gathering expeditions and bring them back to camp, encouraging germination and facilitating propagation (Rival 1998b:238). It has been observed that among Amazonian native people "managed plants would also include plants that grow in cultivated areas or around living sites from seeds discarded after snack" (Dufour & Wilson 1994:116). Hutterer (1983:175) also recognized the constant influence of human population with minimal or no horticultural practices and concluded that, "certain aspects in the patchy distribution of plants in tropical forest may be an effect of long-range and continuous human presence."

The interaction between plants and humans is as old as humankind and undoubtedly resulted in changes in the distribution of gathered species from the very beginning of such interaction (see discussion in Hayden 1995). Hence, hunter-gatherers in one way or another will have always affected the natural distribution of some species, although this effect may have been of low intensity. Nonetheless, in this case, and in others such as the Efe and Hotï, the processes identified result in complex actions—conscious or not—that intersect several behavioral spheres (mobility, settlement, gathering and discard patterns, and so on) and generate a concentration of resources that significantly favors human beings.

TERRITORY AND MOBILITY

The multiple dimensionality of Nukak territory highlights the practical problems that archaeologists face when reconstructing the territory of past hunter-gatherers. Most approaches to the subject involve an explicit and implicit reductionism: territory is equated with band territory, and the principle way of defining and analyzing it is understood to be through the study of the resource structure. In other words, knowing how and when resources are available and whether or not bands exploit them allows conjectures to be made about myriad cultural aspects, from mobility to postmarital residence (Bettinger 1991; Cashdan 1983; Dyson Hudson & Dyson Hudson 1980:29–30; Ember 1975; Hassan 1981:56; Hayden 1981:377; Stein Mandryk 1993:41). A few have gone further and have explored the social dimension of territory (Barnard 1992; Pickering 1994; Silberbauer 1994).

The Nukak case demonstrates the shortcomings of these assumptions; for the Nukak their territory is much more than resources, it is considered to comprise the four physical and one metaphysical juxtaposed dimensions of territory, all of which are perceived as real. From the immediate surroundings of the camp, to distant places occupied by ancestors generations ago but that can be visited by the Nukak at anytime, everything is considered to be in some way or other "their territory": one closer and better known, the other more distant and less frequented. None is exclusive, yet none is alien. In this sense, the territoriality of the Nukak intersects the economic, the social, and the ideational. After recognizing this, a problem emerges, as usual. How can these interrelated dimensions be differentiated in the archaeological record?

If this cannot be done, is it then correct to assume that only one, usually the first (the band territory), represents "the" territory? What happens to the others and their significance in economic, social, and ideational terms?

Territoriality is without a doubt a varied behavior among hunter-gatherers. It varies with time, in space, and from one cultural group to another. While the Alaskan Eskimos have social and clearly defined spatial boundaries (presumably among bands), and territories were defended by force if required (Burch & Ellana 1994), the Nukak are lax in their band territory and fluid in the right of access to resources. They certainly will not fight among one another for land or resources. Boundaries are diffuse and dynamic, and territories are separated by buffer areas and permeable frontiers. Defense and control are practically nonexistent and are in some ways autoregulated by the members of the different bands. The Hotï provide an interesting case in point, as they too have lax territories and vague exclusivity. The sense of belonging to each territory is expressed by the relationship between hunters and supernatural beings called *čoaimo,* the invisible guardian spirits that accompany them on their foraging trips (Storrie 1999). Each territory has a specific community of *čoaimo* that protects only the Hotï hunters from this territory. To hunt beyond this area, without the protection of the *čoaimo,* is dangerous and can cause illness, death, or jaguar attacks (jaguar are the pets of *čoaimo*) (Storrie 1999:86–7). I too have traveled several times with the Hotï on hunting trips with men visiting from other territories. Even though they were fully armed with blowpipes and spears, and in spite of several opportunities, these hunters did not even attempt to hunt prey. Another interesting example is presented by Morphy (1995) of the Yolngu of Arnhem Land, Australia. On one occasion he witnessed a discussion among hunters who decided not to shoot a crocodile because it had moved from one water moiety to another, and this affected the health of the leader of one of the moieties in question. These examples illustrate ways of autoregulating the exploitation of resources of the band territories through mechanisms other than defense or repulse. They also exemplify how cosmologies are decisive in the way in which tropical forest resources are used. In short, these examples support the idea outlined by Guenther (1981) that territoriality is a cultural construct that should be approached ethnographically (to which I add historically and archaeologically) and comparatively, paying attention to the specificity of the cultural groups and without economic and materialist biased preconceived notions.

Although there have been several attempts to capture these different dimensions of territory (Andrew 1994; Binford 1980, 1983b; Casimir 1992; Ingold 2000; Lanata 1993) most such attempts fail to realize that the various levels—including the ideational—operate simultaneously and, along with other factors (that is, social and economic), shape the territorial behavior and the mobility of hunter-gatherers. Most approaches to territory explored from archaeology have desacralized space and taken the physical components as the only ones necessary for an understanding of the concept of territory. Nonetheless, the way of conceiving space, and of generating territorial behavior, is part of a general strategy of the construction of reality and identity (see discussion in Hernando Gonzalo 1999) through which ideological and social factors have a central role (see, for example, Ärhem 1998; Silberbauer 1994). If one agrees that territoriality "exists in the context of a wider set of relations between man and the environment and between individuals" (Barnard 1992:138), the link with the supernatural sphere cannot be excluded from this set of relationships, since, in fact, this sphere strongly affects how hunter-gatherers conceive, perceive, and use the physical territory (Ingold 1996b). The Nukak example of the hole that extends to the subsurface level is similar to others that reveal how the cosmological dimension (for them not a metaphysical one) intersects the different dimensions of the physical territory. The case of the Nadöb, as related by Münzel (1969–1972:178), reflects a similar perception. When Münzel explained to the Nadöb that he lived far away, farther than the Manaus, a Nadöb man, whose songs Münzel had recorded, asked him to play the recording extremely loud when he returned home. From there the Nadöb man's dead son would hear the song, because "the country of the dead" was also found beyond Manaus. Storrie (1999:99) relates a story in which a noted shaman Hotï had a dream foretelling the immanent end of the world. He announced his dream to his people, provoking widespread panic and a migration by him and several followers toward the east in search of the edge of the world and the path to the "House of Dead." He and his followers traveled some 100 km eastward, to the middle of Yekuana territory, where they stayed for a while until the death of the shaman. These examples reinforce the idea that the supernatural dimension of territory, strongly rooted in indigenous Amazonian ontology and present among other indigenous groups throughout the world, has a direct influence on the territorial conduct of hunter-gatherers, and this is revealed in the material record and its properties (that is, distribution, density, and so on).

Compared to other foragers the Nukak have some of the highest mobility rates in the world in terms of number of moves per year (see, for example, Kelly 1995:112–15, Table 4.1), but the average distance between camps is low. Other groups that come closest to demonstrating a similar pattern are the high-latitude groups, the Selknam of Tierra del Fuego and the Baffinland Inuit, both with a residential mobility estimated at around 60 relocations per year. Other groups who live at a variety of latitudes and inhabit various different environments also show high (greater than 50) residential moves. Such is the case, for example, with the Cuiva bands, which inhabit a mixture of savannah and scrub woodland penetrated by fingers of broadleaf evergreen gallery (Arcand 1972; Morey & Metzger 1974), or the Aché, who inhabit the Paraguayan tropical forest of the Eastern Brazilian Highlands (Hill & Hurtado 1995). In spite of the existence of exceptions, in broad terms the residential mobility value for the Nukak falls within the definition based on effective temperatures (ET) proposed by Binford (1980), who recognized that the higher residential mobility occurs among tropical forest and arctic hunter-gatherers. However, the fact that the number of Nukak residential relocations concurs with expectations based on the correlation between foragers and major environmental zones does not mean that environment determines mobility rates, although it does suggest that some environmental parameters affect mobility patterns. As has been shown, similar rates are demonstrated by groups that inhabit an array of major environmental zones presenting different ETs and primary biomasses. In the same way, the mobility of several hunter-gatherer groups from similar environments to the Nukak, such as the African equatorial rainforest, shows radically different patterns. In effect, the Mbuti and the Efe move residential camps five to seven times a year (Bahuchet 1992), each of which is on average a 5-km to 8-km displacement, a distance comparable to Nukak camps. The Aka relocate residentially on average six times yearly, with a distance of 6 km between camps (Bahuchet 1992).

The exploration of the causes of the high Nukak residential mobility rate must be approached from various angles. To begin with, the depletion of the foraging radius of the camp as the prime causal factor for explaining the high residential rate must be dismissed. The Nukak's well-balanced and varied diet indicates that no clear limitation on food resources exists that would prevent the existence of a longer-term residential camp or a higher population density (see discussion in Chapter 8). Of course, resource location and abundance is one of the leading—although not the only—causal factor affecting the decision about the location of new camps, but it does nothing to explain the high frequency of such moves. At least in the Nukak case residential camp moves are not made merely to avoid forest depletion, as has been postulated for the mobility of many hunter-gatherers (Bettinger 1991; Hayden 1981; Stein Mandryk 1993). Leaving aside this reason as a prime causal factor, I argue that the high residential mobility of the Nukak is related to a strategy aimed at managing and concentrating (through the creation of "wild orchards") forest resources, as well as being the result of social and ideational factors. Factors that contribute to the Nukak moving residence with such frequency include the abandonment of a camp because of a death, moving to a particular place to participate in a *baak wáadn*, the necessity of establishing contact with a distant relative, and the existence of *takwe'yi* enemies in the area.

The Nukak case has interesting implications for archaeology. In terms of archaeological visibility, the creation of "wild orchards," meaning the generic reoccupation of the same area (so-called *tethered nomadism*), would also produce patches of resources that in turn would increase the attraction of certain geographical locations. Therefore, the process is the inverse of that which has been proposed. The settlements are not located in areas of high concentration of edible resources; the concentration of resources is the result of a virtuous circle in which the settlement pattern generates these "wild orchards." If this, or similar processes, has occurred since the Late Pleistocene as the archaeological record suggests (see below) the implications for the distribution of certain palms and trees in the supposedly primary forest are tremendous.

THE USE OF PLANTS

As we have seen, gathering and management of wild plants is central to the Nukak as well as to all Amazonian indigenous peoples, the importance of which has been recorded in both the present and the past. If we turn to the archaeological record of the South American Tropical Lowlands, we can see that the use of palms and trees from the tropical rainforest has a long tradition, which allows us to explore the temporal depth of these processes.

A recent review of palms remains recorded at archaeological sites in the New World carried out by Morcote-Ríos and Bernal (2001) provides a starting point. Their review of 130 archaeological sites indicates that 29 genera and at least 50 species of palms have been identified. The best represented genera include *Acrocomia, Attalea, Bactris, Syagrus, Elaeis, Astrocaryum*, and *Oenocarpus*. Four of these genera are commonly used today by the Nukak. Some of the earliest evidence of plant use in Amazonia was recorded at the Monte Alegre site, in the north band region of the lower Amazon. Roosevelt and colleagues (1996) argue that the arrival of humans at the cave is marked by a group of four dates ranging from 11,145 to 10,875 years BP. In the lowest level of the cave abundant plant remains have been recovered, indicating the intensive use of rainforest species as early as the Late Pleistocene. Some genera from earliest levels, such as *Astrocaryum, Attalea,* and *Hymenea*, are used by the Nukak, other Makú, the Hoti, and many tropical lowland foragers. In addition, strong evidence comes from the Peña Roja site on the banks of the Caquetá River in the Amazon (Cavalier et al. 1995; Gnecco & Mora 1997). A forager occupational level has been identified and dated to around 9000 BP. The macrobotanical remains found in this level include several plant species, with palms representing 68% of the total. Many of these palm species are the same as those the Nukak, other Makú, and the Hotï currently exploit, including *Oenocarpus bacaba*, *O. bataua* and *O. mapora*, *Mauritia flexuosa*, *Attalea maripa*, and *Atrocaryum*.

These examples, as well as others from the South America lowlands (see review in Morcote-Ríos & Bernal 2001) indicate the use and early subtle manipulation of rainforest plants, especially palms, as early as the Late Pleistocene. Although the archaeological evidence is meager with reference to how this early manipulation might have happened, some abnormal concentrations of plants have been noted in tropical rainforests and attributed to past human activity. For example, sites assigned to the Mabaruma and Koriabo phases in Coastal Guayana are associated with dense patches of large bamboo (Evans & Meggers 1960:72–73). Concentrations of babaçu (*Orbygna phalerata*), chontaduro (*Bactris gasipaes*), and cumare (*Astrocaryum acueleatum*) occur at archaeological sites along the Jamarí River and the adjacent Upper Madeira. The seeds of these species have been found among habitation refuse, which indicates that they were exploited since the beginning of the site's occupation, c. 2500 years BP (Miller 1992).

However, beyond the economic dimension of plant exploitation, which is undeniable for Amazonian people, we also need to understand the crucial role of plants in the ideational and social spheres (Bloch 1998; Ellen 1998; Rival 1998a). Ethnographic accounts widely show how significant the spirits/ancestors/owners/masters that inhabit or control animate and inanimate components of the universe are for non-Western peoples. Nukak landscape is saturated with symbolic connotations. Trees are part of the way that Nukak build reality and connect the different levels of the universe. For the Nukak, chontaduro and achiote are solid metaphors that articulate two axes, between the past and the present, between cross-time relations with spirit-ancestors and the synchronicity of contemporary social relations (see Chapter 8). Chontaduro is also symbolically important for other Makú, such as the Nadöb (Schultz 1959:119), who also elaborate a ritual associated with this fruit. The Kakwa have a striking phrase that illuminates the ideational side of plants for the Makú, here explained in the words of Silverwood-Cope after having been with the Kakwa for about two years. In a vivid speech in front of a film camera he expressed his perspective on how they conceive of the forest: "it is like a warehouse. They find food in it, medicine in it . . . and they find a meaning" (Moser 1971).

Plant exploitation patterns are a consequence of both ecological and ideational factors, which must both be examined with equal intensity when we approach the study of present and past societies. Examples from other area of the world demonstrate how ideational factors have significantly mitigated the transition to rice domestication in South East Asia (Higham 1995) and northern Australia (Jones & Meehan 1989). Such examples indicate the benefits of a complementary approach to the interpretation of the archeological record.

TECHNOLOGY

Technology has been, and remains, a major concern for archaeologists and has recently become central to a growing line of research labeled as "material culture studies" (for example, Lemonnier 1992). In Chapter 7 I summarized the characteristics of Nukak material culture and technology and discussed the three dimensions of its meaning. The lesson to be learned from the Nukak, as well from other Amazonian societies, is that to understand better the behavior of foragers—in the present and the past—we should consider all these several layers of meaning in our analyses. It is patently obvious that Price's (1982, 720) piercing statement that, "whatever else a material object may represent, it is directly the energy expended on it," cannot lead to a proper understanding of how material culture and technology operate in a given society. It is not possible to maintain the separation between something supposedly objective and measurable, such as the "energy" expended on an artifact, and the social and ideational realms in which this artifact is also embedded, because this multidimensional integrity affects the production, the use, and the discard of artifacts. In other words, knowing the energy expended on an artifact and speculating how much energy could be captured during its use life tells us very little about how this artifact operated in a given society. If we split the practical and economical from the cultural and ideational, and prioritize the physical over the social or seemingly intangible symbolic dimensions, the range of factors taken into account in explaining past and present technologies from nonindustrial societies is dramatically reduced, simplified, and ultimately eliminated (see also Dobres 2000:38). Such a move is also methodologically incorrect because, as the ethnography and ethnoarchaeology of many nonindustrial societies show, artifacts operate simultaneously in different dimensions (Boivin 2004, Taçon 2004). To consider one only (the utilitarian) as if it were unique or determinant is a false starting point for any analysis. As has been suggested by Pfaffenberger (1992) and Lemonnier (1993), the economic, social, political, and ideational dimensions of the technological process cannot be meaningfully separated and put into discrete boxes (Tilley 1999:59). Of course, having been trained as an archaeologist, I am not challenging the feasibility of a starting point related to the physical properties of objects, or that the instrumental side of artifacts is probably the most evident to us (to our form of rationality). But, at the same time, the fact that this can mislead and obscure a more complete understanding of the function and the meaning of material culture in any past or present society should be noted.

It could be argued, of course, that the ontology into which the "things with souls" are embedded, although not unique is specifically Nukak, or at most pertains to the indigenous peoples of the region and affords no grounds for generalization beyond the Amazon. However, in order to stress the genuine similarities in the ways foragers and nonindustrial people in general think about their artifacts, I will introduce some examples from other regions of the world that demonstrate similar phenomena worldwide. The Ayoreo of the Boreal Chaco of Paraguay and Bolivia use long wooden artifacts with a beveled end, called *porotadí*, daily to scrape the flesh of an edible root. These artifacts, which include clanic signs engraved on them, are continually worn down through use until they reach a point at which the Ayoreo say they have "grown old." From this point forward only old men may use them, and the younger people must take extreme care when transporting them in their bags (Bórmida 1973:50–60). In 1994 I recorded that, until a few years earlier, the indigenous fishers of Tahiti had still used specific rocks to attract specific fish. These rocks, usually rounded porous volcanic rocks were, and still are, kept in the gardens of their houses. During certain times of the year, depending on the season for a particular fish, they were submerged in the water to attract and catch that fish. While in the garden they were regularly watered, "because they become thirsty and that should not happen. If that happens, they will never help us to fish again." In this case it is clear that the rocks have a "living essence" that must be cared for as if it were a living organism. The way these rocks are used, treated, and kept in the gardens is determined by the attitude toward them and the belief that they are in some sense alive. Another interesting example is the iron manufacturing process in the Cameroon Grassfields of west Africa, discussed by Rowlands and Warnier (1993). The authors argue that rituals involved in iron production are not "inessential," things that can be removed from more "rational" processes. Rather, they entail an alternative means of metaphorical thought in which alteration of both persons and things are elements of a single continuum, both equally animate and inanimate and reliant on circumstances and context. Final examples are the cases of the stone axes among the Lagdan of the New Guinea Highlands, which are considered to possess "souls," a factor that strongly affects their discard location (see Toth, Clark, & Ligabue 1992), and the "namur" rock of the Shuar, stones that care for and protect hunters and are linked to their prey (Bianchi 1981).

In short, I believe there are important implications from this ethnoarchaeological study for archaeological interpretation, above all the impossibility—both practical and conceptual—of separating the various dimensions and different layers of significance of material culture. From a methodological point of view one can concur that the starting point for analysis should be the instrumental aspects and the formal characteristics of artifacts and their raw materials, but one cannot ignore that this implies an instrumental and ecological reductionism. Of course, there are material and ecological constraints that limit the technological options of nonindustrial societies, but these are strongly mediated by social and ideational factors. As such, ethnoarchaeology can contribute greatly to a more fruitful approach that endeavors to capture these multiple dimensions and meanings of material culture. To attempt a more holistic approach to the material culture of past societies is undoubtedly an extremely difficult task (but see, for example, Flegenheimer & Bayón 1999; Sinclair 1995; Taçon 1991, 2004) but is nevertheless a worthwhile challenge.

HUNTING AND FOOD TABOOS

What emerges from the data presented in Chapter 9 is a picture of taboo far more complex than hitherto recognized. Nukak attitudes and practices highlight the potential for misinterpreting the archaeological record by ignoring the ideological nature of taboo and its embeddedness within wider cosmological structures. In the case of Amazonian aboriginal people, food taboos are widespread (Cormier 2004; Descola 1994; Kensinger & Kracke 1981; Meggers 1996:190; Milton 1997) and are significant in the way these people represent their cosmological beliefs and the various dimensions of identity, suggesting a long tradition of such taboos. In his work on Amazonian taboos DeBoer (1987) arrived at the opposite conclusion. Having analyzed a sample composed of different Amazonian groups, he identified the existence of taboos among most. Although this abundance of taboos supports their importance, the apparently low percentages (between 31% and 8%, with the exception of the sloth that was recorded in 61% of cases) lead DeBoer to propose that, ". . . anthropologists should remember that in the case of general taboos in Amazonia, they are dealing with a minority phenomenon" (DeBoer 1987:48). However, it is reductionist to analyze taboos as percentages of one or several prohibited species in a given society. General taboos are only one part of a complex system of prohibitions and restrictions around animal consumption. Owing to the size and the quantity of proscribed animals (both total and partial) and their alimentary and symbolic and sacred value, animal taboos in these societies cannot be understood as a "minor phenomenon" because they structure the exploitation of faunal resources and have a significant influence on diet. Acceptance of this argument has an important archaeological implication: it implies that we should expect, and look for, archaeological assemblages that reflect faunal exploitation performed within specific ideological frameworks in which food taboos played a key role.

Some would argue that food taboos are pragmatic and functional (Harris 1990: Ross 1978) or are part of a broader risk-reduction strategy for periods of infrequent but disastrous events (Meggers 1996:190–91). Or perhaps they exist only when societies are not influenced by strong food constrains. Several cases demonstrate that this is not true. The Nukak do not consume a significant portion of the available animal biomass (resources of high nutritional quality, such as tapirs and peccaries) for purely ideational reasons, not in order to preserve a resource for a supposed period of scarcity. In response to the same taboo among other Amazonian groups, Milton (1997:48) wrote: "if no one ever eats it, what's the point? Who benefits except tapirs?" Neither does taboo appear to overlay a risk-reduction energy equation, or an economic or health reason, by depriving women and children of abundant animal protein, such as the peccary; especially bearing in mind that when one of these animals is hunted tens of kilos of meat are made available in a single event, a part of which rots because the men do not manage to eat it before it is ruined and because smoking is an imperfect preservation method. The Hotï example reinforces the weakness of the functional and materialist argument. The Hotï, who live in a nearby region, are comparable demographically and have a similar animal availability (in terms of both diversity and density) yet have an entirely opposite conception. They consider the terrestrial animals (agouti, peccary, tapir, and capybara) to be the best food, which should be eaten by everyone (Storrie 1999:168). This indicates that relatively similar societies that live in similar environments developed totally opposite food prohibitions and restrictions. These differences do not appear to be the result of distinct adaptive strategies developed through time. On the contrary the different taboo complexes, both total and specific, seem to be the result of cultural differences (especially in terms of symbolic referents used to conceptualize the world) in the way in which identity differences are exhibited and materialized (see also Milton 1997) and of particular historical trajectories. I am not denying the possibility that some taboos benefit the long-term subsistence of a given society. However, this does not seem to be the tendency, and, besides, the possible adaptive benefits of taboos ought not to be generalized to all—and not even the majority—of Amazonian groups.

Numerous examples from other parts of Amazonia and the world lead to the conclusion that food taboos have an existence independent of energy reasons and cannot be understood within ecologico-functional conceptual frameworks (Cormier 2003; Kensinger 1981; Milton 1997; Valeri 2000). The best and most clear-cut example I know is that of the Mapuche Indians of Ruca Choroy (Southern Argentina), who are confined to the Alumine National Park. Owing to strong restrictions from park authorities and the disintegration of their traditional economy, this group suffered long periods of starvation, especially during the winter. One of their members, Roberto Pellao, while complaining of food shortages, stated in his not fluent Spanish, in front of a film camera:

> Of course, there are many fish in the lake [Alumine] and the *huincas* [white people], come and they eat them with all those spines they have. But we the Mapuche only eat animals with fur. No fish! (Preloran 1996)

Another interesting archaeological example was presented by Jones (1977:196), who showed that at a specific point in time (between ca. 3800 and 3500 BP) prehistoric Tasmanian hunter-gatherers made a conscious decision not to eat fish, despite its ready availability. Moreover, it had been a major food resource for four thousand years, and the decision to discontinue its consumption constituted a net loss of food (Jones 1978:45). This event appears to have had nothing to do with environmental change. As Jones (1978:44) pointed out, it was an intellectual event that caused a contraction in the resource availability and reduced significantly the food options (Politis & Saunders 2002).

These cases clearly illustrate the power of food taboos in everyday life and the persistence of such beliefs in spite of resource abundance or availability. Of course, many Amazonian groups have abandoned their traditional food restrictions and nowadays customarily consume animals that were sacred a few generations ago. However, this is not a consequence of the variation in food resources but of the result of the disintegration of traditional cultural patterns due to the massive impact of the West. I have seen many cases in the Amazon and in the Orinoquia that show how food taboos have been dismissed by the new generation while still being maintained by the older generations. For example, among the Piaroa and the Yabarana of the High Parucito River (Amazonas State, Venezuela) young people may kill and eventually eat formerly totally tabooed animals, such as river dolphins and freshwater otter, whereas their parents reject them emphatically. The same pattern can be seen in many Amazonian groups nowadays (Milton 1997).

Although the origin of taboos is multicausal, in the Nukak case the hypotheses I prefer explain these taboos as a result of specific ideological and mythical beliefs that have a long tradition among Amazonian indigenous peoples (see also Kensinger 1981). This body of belief has been conceptualized in various ways, from animism (see discussion in Bird-David 1999), totemism (Lévi-Strauss 1962), and ecosophy (Ärhem 1990) to cosmological perspectivism (Viveiros de Castro 1992), which all defend the existence of this type of taboo as part of an articulated body of beliefs. Leaving aside the differences in focus of these authors, within Amazonian ontology animals have a status similar to humans, and therefore their consumption is restricted and mediated by ritual complexes. Animals are considered to be related to one another and to humans in much the same way that humans are related to one another (Ärhem 1996; Rival 1996; Storrie 1999). That which animals and humans share is precisely their "humanity." Within this ideational framework one can explain the existence of alimentary taboos, especially concerning animals, independently of adaptive reasons for their origin or maintenance. In consequence, I am more inclined toward an explanation in which these phenomena are understood as the result of historical and developmental trajectories. I have the sense that the food taboos and other restrictions around consumption developed together with the economic strategies that over time formed the diet of the different hunter-gatherer groups. Throughout this process multiple elements intersected—economic, social (especially those referring to the several dimensions of identity), and ideational—and resulted in particular compositions of diet in time and space. Such diets were not based exclusively on materialist considerations, although in many cases these were surely influential, and in specific cases they took apparently maladaptive courses.

All types of taboo have often been neglected by archaeologists on the basis that they can not be found "empirically." Taboos can not be "seen" in the archaeological record. This neglect has not usually been explicit but rather basically implicit. It can be recognized in debate by a distinctive characteristic: its complete absence. With very few noteworthy exceptions (Jones 1984) food taboos have been ignored in the vast archaeological literature on the subsistence of hunter-gatherers. This is unfortunate given the widespread presence of food taboos among aboriginal (non-Western) societies around the world. I have confidence that the case presented in this book is a step toward acknowledging that ideological generative principles can be identified in a context-specific archaeological record. I hope that this case study promotes new ethnoarchaeological studies that will help to identify ideational and social casual factors in past societies.

The Western View of Amazonian Hunter-Gatherers

Several conclusions can be drawn based on the data presented. First, this research on the Nukak demonstrates, once again, how deeply influenced is the study of both past and present hunter-gatherers by Western views. Many examples in the literature clearly show that interpretations of hunter-gatherer behavioral patterns are basically a projection of the fears and concerns of Western society. A clear example is how the rainforest resources have been evaluated in economic terms, and how this has been considered to affect mobility. It has repeatedly been argued (for example Kelly 1995:121; Sponsel 1986; Whitelaw 1991:171) that tropical rainforest resources may be abundant but that they are difficult to reach (in the treetops or at the ends of branches), which reduces their potential for human exploitation. For the Nukak, who learn to climb before they can walk (they virtually hang from their mothers as babies) and who possess blowpipes, darts, and powerful poison, this statement could not be further from the truth. It is easier for them to procure canopy resources than any other. A further misconception is that, "fruit is widely scattered in space and time and seldom concentrates in any abundance" (in Sponsel 1986:74, cited in Beckerman 1979). As I have shown, the Nukak have available several nondomesticated species, especially palms such as seje, *popere, juiú*, and others, that provide abundant fruit with high nutritional value and low procurement costs, which are also highly productive and concentrated. Another trait that has been evaluated in a negative light is that in spite of having a high biomass approximately 98% of the rainforest is trunks and branches, which human digestive tracts cannot process. This is true, but the existence of palm grubs that grow in trunks has not been taken into account. The archeological data summarized above enable similar forms of life to be inferred from the end of the Pleistocene to the present. These are not just more cautionary tales; they are examples that warn against tainting our understanding of present and past nonindustrial societies with our Western worldview. We should pay more attention to the different means developed by indigenous American groups of utilizing the environment. A great effort must also to be made to understand other cultures on their own terms.

Another area in which the projection of Western thought has had a crucial impact is in understanding the adaptation of hunter-gatherers to the tropical rainforest. The anthropogenic nature of some ecosystems in the contemporary Amazonian rainforest has been a subject of intense debate in recent years (see Balée 1994; Meggers 1996, 2003; Morán 1993; Posey 1994; Roosevelt 1998; see review in Stahl 2002). In the same vein, the viability of hunter-gatherers in these environments in the total absence of domesticated plants has also been a central issue in the last two decades (see summary in Chapter 8). The idea that there are "limiting" factors to the human occupation of the Amazonian rainforest has had a long tradition. Following *The Handbook of South American Indians* (Steward 1946–1950), the Amazonian environment has been "cited by cultural ecologists as a prime example of how the environment determines and limits sociocultural evolution" (Hames & Vickers 1983:7). As we have seen, the Nukak demonstrate that the situation is quite different and that the so-called limiting factors are more a Western thought projection than a reality (see also Morán 1993; Roosevelt 1998). Certainly, the environment in which the Nukak live out their lives can support densities of hunter-gatherer populations far greater than those that they support at present or have done in the recent past. Although until recently domesticated plants were consumed only in small quantities, they are still not a critical or "keystone" resource (in the sense of Stearman 1991). Nukak keystone resources are the patches of wild edible plants that are created throughout the foraging circuit. These patches supply not only food but also raw materials essential for tools and shelter construction. Other key resources are fish, honey, palm grubs, and a small group of hunted animals, among which monkeys, birds, and tortoises stand out. I do not deny the importance of cultivated gardens, especially in more recent times, but they are important only in terms of food yield and not for raw materials (with the exception of achiote for painting). In addition, they provide no exclusive nutritional elements, either quantitatively or qualitatively. In this context, I believe that the incorporation of horticulture by the Nukak, and possibly other Amazon hunter-gatherers, should be understood as the consequence of an historic process more than as a necessity for maintaining viable populations, or the result of the evolution of subsistence strategies toward an optimum adaptation. Finally, the characterization of distinct ecological environments in Nukak territory (see Chapter 1), as well as the exploitation of these different environments by the Nukak (Chapter 8), indicates once again that supposed resources scarcity and the nonviability of hunter-gatherer populations in the Amazon are not supported by the data.

Some indirect evidence from the region also contradicts the nonviability of tropical rainforests for hunter-gatherer habitation. The Cuiva of the Llanos Orientales are an interesting case. They are typically considered a savannah group, with correspondingly greater resource availability than the forest groups. However, Arcand (1972:5) notes that, "roughly 85% of the meat consumed is obtained from the immediate vicinity of the rivers [there is a "gallery" forest that fringes the river banks, as previously explained]. In contrast, the savannahs, which are by far the largest ecological zone of the area, offer very little food and are only rarely visited by the Cuiva." This reference calls attention to the fact that given the choice of two distinct ecological environments the Cuiva prefer the rainforest.

I agree with the conclusions reached by Viveiros de Castro who argued that, "adaptationist theories take for granted the marginalist postulates of resource scarcity and optimization of yield-to-effort ratios and assume an immanent rationality of an evolutionary kind, governed by thermodynamic parameters" (Viveiros de Castro 1996:184). Viveiros de Castro's critique is oriented toward a type of ecological approach known as "evolutionary ecology" (Winterhalder & Smith 1992). Although it is true that many practitioners of this approach within archaeology conceive of it not as dogma but as a structured form of inquiry (Winterhalder 1987:313), it is equally true that some of the assumptions made in pursuing this research program are largely untested or simply wrong, and the application of the proposed models does not leave room for alternative, nonecological explanations. I hope that this book has provided examples that demonstrate the inadequacy of some of the assumptions in question as well as the limitations of the models employed.

FINAL WORDS

The Nukak present us with a fascinating case of hunter-gatherers managing their environment, conceptualizing their territory, and daily negotiating their existence with the various supernatural beings and spirit-ancestors of the distinct planes of the universe. The absolute belief that, "what is seen is the shadow of what is not seen," of what is considered real, reflects an ontology that permeates all aspects of life in this society and that without doubt conditions their daily conduct. This is not an epiphenomenon; it is the core that governs their behavior. The Nukak also demonstrate an interesting characteristic—an attitude of solidarity that reveals a level of social resistance to political centralization. This is a clear-cut example of a society all the behavioral patterns of which are oriented toward preventing the development of rank and social complexity: from Yukdaa "blowing the *chicha*" at a successful hunter because he did not appropriately share his game to the striking lack of accumulation of food and objects.

The observations and ideas presented in this book are neither designed to add a further "cautionary tale" to the long list of unexpected behaviors of hunter-gatherers nor to produce an anecdotal-type statement. On the contrary, they aim to broaden the range of variability of the forms of production of material culture and displacement of residue by hunter-gatherers and how these are reflected in the archaeological record. This range of variation brings to light the different ways that any (ethnographically and historically recorded) human activity can be accomplished. The archaeological record should be compared against this variation in order to argue, through analogy, which model corresponds to the case under study, bearing in mind the properties and characteristics of the sample in question.

As I expressed at the beginning of the book, my goal has been to contribute both data concerning the socioideational dimension (and explore methodological means of interpreting them) and information directly related to ecological and technoutilitarian aspects of material culture. Data on the former were the least obvious, the most difficult to record, and probably the least represented in this book. Nonetheless, I believe that the data and information that I was able to gather on the socioideational realm opens a small window on the wealth and variety of causal factors that contribute to the formation of the archaeological record. Finally, subordinating the symbolic and ideological aspects to economic/energy-related factors assumes that non-Western people share our logic and motivations, our pattern of rationality, our ontology. The Nukak, and many other indigenous peoples around the world, demonstrate that this is not the case.

Note

1. Although for the Siriono alternative explanations have been proposed. They could be nomadic hunter-gatherers who were "guaranized" through relatively recent contact with Guaraní tribes (Rydén 1941:125–27).

Appendix I

SAMPLE OF DAILY FORAGING TRIPS

I participated in all the daily foraging trips summarized in this Appendix. I maintained a low profile, and I never asked anyone to perform a specific task recorded for research purposes. However, I assume my presence still affected the Nukak's activities in some way. I hope my presence did not significantly alter their behavior.

Trip: September 3, 1992

Participants and gear: Kanilo (adult man) with blowpipe and darts

Time	Distance	Activity
7.49	0.00 km	Departure.
8.05	0.62 km	Stopped to eat moriche (*Mauritia flexuosa*) fruit in a low zone.
8.38	2.06 km	Short stop in an abandoned camp.
9.00	2.45 km	Stopped to defecate off the path.
9.36	4.64 km	Crossed a creek with high water level.
9.41	4.87 km	Stopped in abandoned camp. Checked young papaya and achiote plants that were growing on the floor.
10.10	5.62 km	Passed through an abandoned camp with *puyú* and seje plants.
10.59	7.35 km	Hunted two pavas (birds) with blowpipe.
11.15	7.45 km	Started the return journey.
11.20	7.51 km	Hunted three birds. One *juaine* (which he threw away) and two *iooro*.
11.50	8.53 km	Stopped at an abandoned camp (the same at which he had stopped at 10.10 hs); collected *puyú* and seje plants.

| 12.41 | 12.30 km | Hunted three small squirrel monkeys (*ikip*) during heavy rain. |
| 15.45 | 16.20 km | Arrived back at camp. |

Total products brought into the camp: two birds (*iooro*); two pavas; three squirrel monkeys (*ikip*); and some small *puyú* and seje plants.

Trip: September 4, 1992

Participants and gear: Wákaka (young male) with spear and fishing cane, and Y (male adult) with spear, fishing cane, and blowpipe.

Time	Distance	Activity
8.10	0.00 km	Departure.
8.15	0.13 km	Found Maria burning a beehive.
8.57	0.85 km	Uté and Kodiban (with an ax) joined the party. Started to split the trunk of a seje palm with the ax, looking for palm grubs.
9.10	1.80 km	Passed throughout an abandoned camp containing gourd and platanillo saplings. Stopped to trim darts.
9.45	1.80 km	The trip continued.
9.50	1.95 km	A main path was reached. The group—Wákaka, Maria, and Y—stayed together. Someone killed a bat.
10.03	2.03 km	Palm grubs eaten from the trunk of a *juiú*.
10.29	2.04 km	A *yáab butu* tree was cut down; the trunk was split with an ax to get at some palm grubs that were eaten on the spot.
12.05	2.47 km	After walking for a while the party reached a large creek.
1.05	–	The group walked along the shore of the large creek.
15.30	–	Wákaka and Maria returned to the camp. Y remained nearby cutting a tree.

Trip: September 7, 1992

Participants and gear: Enanaucoptn (adult woman) with a metal ax; Chowowo (adult woman); J'huili (adult woman); Kei (adult man) with fishing cane and machete; Y (adult man) with fishing cane and machete; Wanake (young woman); Tatree (young man); and N'dikiri (boy).

Time	Distance	Activity
9.00	0.00 km	Departure.
9.22	0.67 km	The party began to collect and eat palm grubs from a fallen seje trunk.

9.53	0.67 km	Collecting of palm grub is completed. A trunk was split to "breed" palm grubs.
9.58	0.92 km	The three adult men joined the group.
10.22	1.77 km	The group arrived at a creek and started to fish with hooks and canes.
10.30	1.77 km	While some people fished four adults collected bunches of seje fruit and made expedient bags (*búrup*).
11.32	2.34 km	The party left the path carrying the empty *búrup*, moving into a swamp area.
11.40	3.21 km	Everyone collected moriche fruit that were floating in the water.
13.55	5.70 km	Arrived at the camp.

Trip: September 11, 1992

Participants and gear: Uté (adult male) with blowpipe, darts, and a fishing cane.

Time	*Distance*	*Activity*
6.50	0.00 km	Departure.
7.17	1.05 km	Passed by an abandoned camp.
7.20	1.52 km	Passed by an abandoned camp.
8.12	4.40 km	Passed by an abandoned camp.
8.27	4.53 km	Passed by an abandoned camp.
8.37	4.68 km	Visited a cultivated spot with a rectangular house (a "house of the tapir"; see Chapter 4).
9.43	5.55 km	Started to fish.
10.13	7.09 km	Passed by an abandoned camp.
10.30	8.09 km	Stopped at a creek and caught a small fish.
11.12	8.09 km	Hunted two small birds to use as bait.
11.20	8.09 km	Caught another small fish (*tepara'aken*).
12.01	8.09 km	Stopped fishing and began the return journey to the camp.
12.10	8.15 km	Stopped at a creek and caught a medium-sized fish.
12.30	8.30 km	Attempted to hunt some birds but failed.
14.49	–	Hunted a howler monkey.
15.00	10.82 km	Stopped at the cultivated spot with the rectangular house.
16.47	15.64 km	Arrived back at camp.

Total products brought into the camp: 3 fish and 1 howler monkey.

Trip: September 16, 1992

Participants and gear: Y (adult man) with machete and ax; Maria (adult woman); Enanaucoptn (adult woman) with her daughter; Kodiban (adult woman) with her son; Dugúp (young woman); and Wánaku (young woman).

Time	Distance	Activity
8.10	0.00 km	Departure
8.30	0.64 km	In a swamp area they cut some fallen trunks longitudinally with an ax to get palm grubs that were immediately eaten.
8.46	0.91 km	A bunch of platanillo fruit was cut down but was still green. Another bunch of platanillo fruit was procured and eaten by the children. Y and Maria left the group, which remained at the spot eating platanillo fruit.
10.00	0.91 km	The children remained in the same place while the adults and the adolescents brought platanillo fruit collected nearby.
11.09	1.3 km	The adults returned to the camp with three *búrup* full of platanillo fruit.
12.30	–	More platanillo fruit collected in five *búrup*.
13.20	3.45 km	Near the camp a young woman laden with platanillo fruit fell, and the end of a stick struck her in the vagina.
13.45	3.50 km	The group arrived back at the camp.

Total products brought into the camp: many of platanillo fruit.

Trip: January 22, 1994

Participants and gear: Uté (adult man) with machete; Kanilo (adult man) with machete and ax; Krit'ti (adult woman) with basket and bowl; Kódiban (adult woman) with basket and bowl; and Ditta (young woman) with basket.

Time	Distance	Activity
7.35	0.00 km	Departure.
8.05	0.97 km	Kanilo attempted to hunt a bird by throwing his machete, but failed.
8.22	1.22 km	*Parupi'* vine was cut.
8.47	2.16 km	Palms were cut.
9.24	2.89 km	A tuber (*hím'dum*) was dug up.
9.54	3.79 km	A beehive was found, burned, brought down, and opened. All group members ate honey (*houte*) and subsequently made hidromiel ("mead").

11.03	–	Continued.
11.27	5.15 km	*Parupi'* vine was cut. A dead sloth at the foot of a tree is glanced over.
11.52	6.06 km	*Weei* palms were cut and their fruit gathered.
12.45	–	The party stopped to eat *weei* fruits.
1.05	7.15 km	Another beehive was burned and the honey collected. Everyone ate honey.
3.03	–	Continued.
3.39	8.72 km	Kánilo hunted a land turtle and transported it alive.
4.20	9.20 km	Collection of platanillo fruit.
4.54	11.09 km	The group arrived back at camp.

Total products brought into the camp: 2 kg of platanillo in a basket by Dit'ta; 1 kg of honey in a basket by Dit'ta; 6 kg of *parupi'* in a basket by Dit'ta; 10 kg of *parupi'* in basket by Krit'ti; 1.5 kg of honey in a basket by Krit'ti; 10 kg of honey in a sling by Kanilo; 10 kg of land turtle by Kanilo; 8 kg of *parupi'* in a basket by Uté; 3 kg of honey wrapped in leaves by Uté.

Trip: January 25, 1994

Participants and gear: Ú (adult man) with blowpipe, darts, and machete; Kei (adult man) with blowpipe, darts, and machete; and P'nabu (adult man) with nothing. A dog accompanied the party.

Time	Distance	Activity
8.37	0.00 km	Departure.
9.04	1.58 km	The blowpipes are left; P'nabu climbed a tree and obtained *bijnidé*.
9.47	4.00 km	The dog barked and chased an animal, possibly a tapir.
10.09	5.22 km	Ú met up with the party (he had separated from it some time earlier), bringing 3 killed tente (a kind of bird). The tente and a blowpipe are left hidden beside the path.
10.19	5.70 km	Crossed a main creek.
11.07	7.86 km	Arrived at a ceiba tree; there was a lot of wild cotton flowers (*puyú*) on the floor. They did not collect any.
11.17	8.36 km	Arrived at a chontaduro palm. They cut some racemes and put them in *búrup*.
11.28	–	They completed collecting chontaduro fruit and began the return journey.

12.09	10.95 km	They crossed the main creek. They drank water and washed themselves.
12.19	11.54 km	The blowpipe is retrieved. They cut seje fruit and carried them in a *búrup*.
12.49	14.16 km	*Koró-paanját* is gathered and placed in a *búrup*.
1.35	14.56 km	Arrived back at camp.

Total products brought into the camp: 6 kg of seje in a basket by Ú; 18 kg of chontaduro in a basket by Ú; 14 kg of chontaduro in a *búrup* by P'nabu; 2 kg of *koró-paanját* in a *búrup* by P'nabu; 4 kg of *tentes* (three birds) in a *búrup* by P'nabu; 8 kg of seje in a *búrup* by Kei; 17 kg of chontaduro in a *búrup* by Kei.

Trip: January 27, 1994

Participants and gear: Kei (adult man) with blowpipe darts and ax. His two wives later joined the party: Krit'ti (adult woman) with a basket and Chowowo (adult woman) with a metal bowl.

Time	Distance	Activity
9.30	0.00 km	Departure.
9.47	0.9 km	Kei fired a dart at a duck, but missed.
10.00	1.73 km	He gathered some seje racemes and called for his two wives, who arrived with their children.
10.38	2.25 km	He cut down a seje palm to get at a beehive. He ate the honey and put the seje fruit in a *búrup*.
11.20	4.75 km	A hollow was uncovered and a beehive removed. They consumed all the honey on the spot.
13.03	4.90 km	A halt. Kei left the group alone, without any equipment, and returned a short while later. (He was probably defecating)
13.44	6.24 km	He shot a dart at a small bird but missed.
13.48	6.45 km	Kei started to cut a tree containing *koró-paanját*, then continued with a second tree with a beehive. The women collected the *koró-paanját* and honey. All ate honey on the spot.
14.55	–	Uté appeared with an ax and his son Eibi. They were carrying a pot full of honey. Uté opened another hollow in the tree and obtained more honey.
13.56	6.69 km	They found another tree containing a beehive and burned it. They removed nothing. The women remained with the ax.
16.15	7.50 km	Kei and the children arrived at the camp.

16.36	7.50 km	Chowowo and Krit'ti arrived with honey and *koró-paanját*.

Trip: January 28, 1994

Participants and gear: Kei (adult man) with blowpipe and darts.

Time	Distance	Activity
13.00	0.00 km	Departure.
13.29	1.29 km	He encountered Enanauncopt and Chowowo who were transporting honey.
13.45	1.75 km	Tried unsuccessfully to hunt a monkey.
14.07	2.40 km	Collected gallineta (*ñok'n'debe*) eggs.
15.28	4.21 km	Hunted a bird but did not take the carcass.
16.29	5.31 km	Arrived at the camp.

Total products brought into the camp: 2 gallineta eggs.

Trip: January 30, 1994

Participants and gear: Kei (adult man) with ax; and P'nabu (adult man) with ax.

Time	Distance	Activity
8.05	–	Departure.
8.40	2.8	Stopped at a huge tree with honey. Saw a monkey.
9.04	4.02	Found and caught a land turtle.
9.40	5.07	Returned to the huge tree.
10.09	–	Started to cut the tree down.
11.45	–	Lighted a torch to burn the beehive.
12.00	–	The tree fell. Everyone ate a large quantity of honey.
12.30	–	The land turtle was butchered, and portions were placed in a *búrup*. Carapace, head, and some entrails were discarded.
12.48	–	Continued the trip with the honey and the land turtle in *búrup*.
13.50	8.12	Stopped to gather fruit (seje).
14.19	8.99	Arrived at the camp.

Trip: January 31, 1994

Participants and gear: Uté (adult man) with ax and machete; Eibi (boy) with blowpipe and darts; and Dugup (adolescent girl) with bowl.

Time	Distance	Activity
8.20	–	Departure.
8.58	0.9 km	Left path and visited an orchard. They did not collect anything.
9.03	1.58 km	A tree (*mei*) containing a beehive is felled. Dugup ate some partially burnt plantains (she had carried them from camp). Everyone ate honey. Eibi practiced with the blowpipe on small birds, but fails. His father started to teach him.
9.45	–	Continued the trip.
10.10	2.21 km	Stopped to eat honey from a beehive in the trunk of a fallen tree.
10.37	2.85 km	Walk through highlands (rolling hills). Uté carefully looked at and inspected some palms.
10.45	2.97 km	Stopped to cut down a tree with a beehive.
11.15	–	The tree falls, and everyone ate an abundance of honey.
11.31	–	The cut down a *wei* tree. Everyone ate the fruit and drank the water they contained (they are similar to coquitos). Many fruit were left behind—neither eaten nor collected. A notch was made in the trunk of a very green platanillo, which produced water. They drank copiously.
11.54	3.48 km	Stopped to cut down a tree containing a beehive. They ate and collected honey.
12.30	–	Continued.
12.45	–	They came across the skull of peccary eaten by a jaguar. They inspected it carefully and discussed it.
1.43	5.53 km	Returned to a main path. Eibi hunted a small bird and attempted to hunt others. Dugup gathered *koró paanját* and some caterpillars (*wiri*), which she stored in leaves.
2.02	5.92 km	Arrived at the camp.

Total products brought into the camp: 2 kg of *koró paanját* (unpeeled) in a *búrup* by Dugup; 1.7 kg of honey in a leaf bag; 1 small bird by Eibi; some caterpillars (less than 100 gm) by Dugup.

Trip: February 2, 1994

Participants and gear: P'nabu (adult man) with machete.

Time	Distance	Activity
12.24	0.00 km	Departure.
12.43	1.16 km	Stopped at a *juiú* palm. Cut and shaped a forked stick to collect the racemes from a neighboring tree.
13.00	–	Continued to wander around the area searching.
13.10	2.42 km	Returned to the *juiú* palm. Made a *búrup* to carry the fruit.
14.04	3.06 km	Returned to the camp.

Total products brought into the camp: 16 kg of *juiú* in a *búrup*

Trip: February 3, 1994

Participants and gear: Uté (adult man) with machete, blowpipe, and darts.

Time	Distance	Activity
8.39	00 km	Departure.
8.59	1.20 km	On the borders of a creek, attempted to hunt two big birds (*kieet*), but failed.
9.34	2.38 km	Stopped to collect fruits.
11.18	5.29 km	Stopped to cut down a tree.
12.00	5.79 km	Hunted a duck and start to pursue a woolly monkey.
12.30	–	Caught the monkey. He made a *búrup* to carry it.
12.37	6.05 km	A troop of brown capuchin monkeys showed up, and he chased them. He killed the larger two.
1.00	6.90 km	He scraped a *parupi'* vine (with which they make curare), checking its condition, and then cut several pieces.
2.30	9.53 km	Arrived at the camp.

Total products brought into the camp: 12 kg of monkey (2 brown capuchins and 1 woolly monkey); 2.5 of kg duck; and 3 kg (approximately) of *parupi'*.

Trip: January 29, 1996

Participants and gear: Tigriri (adult man) with blowpipe and darts; Edubé (adult male) with blowpipe and darts; and Popopó (adult man) with blowpipe and darts [we were asked to carry two axes].

Time	Distance	Activity
7.54	0.00 km	Departure.
8.13	0.91 km	Stop. They pointed out two trees called *axa* and *chuibún*.
8.42	1.32 km	Stopped in a *nemep wopyii*. Gathered *yaabutu* and *yee*.

| 12.10 | 4.78 km | Stopped to collect honey. Made a fire with two sticks. Popopó separated from the group. Edubé collected and ate honey for about an hour. |
| 15.40 | 8.32 km | Arrived at the camp. Popopó had arrived before bringing seje fruit. Tigriri arrived late empty handed. |

Total products brought into the camp: honey; seje fruit; *yááb butú,* and *yee*.

Trip: January 30, 1996

Participants: Tigiri (adult man) with blowpipe, darts, and two sticks for making fire; and Edubé (adult man) with blowpipe, darts, and a metal ax.

Time	Distance	Activity
8.40	0.00 km	Departure.
10.30	3.20 km	Attempted to hunt a pava but failed.
10.45	3.50 km	Successfully hunted a monkey (*yeyewa*).
11.30	4.70 km	Tried to hunt another pava. The bird was hurt but escaped.
12.10	5.78 km	Stopped in an old winter residential camp. Ate some fruit while sitting inside the camp.
14.10	8.31 km	Stopped to eat palm grubs from a seje trunk. A large quantity was eaten (several hundred larvae).
16.30	10.05 km	A tree was cut down and a beehive burned. They ate a lot of honey *in situ* and collected some 4 kg of honey to take to the camp.
18.40	13.10 km	Arrived at the camp with honey and a monkey.

Total products brought into the camp: 1 monkey; and 4 kg of honey.

Trip: January 31, 1996

Participants and gear: Tigiri (adult male) with blowpipe and darts; and Edubé (adult male) with blowpipe and darts. Two dogs.

Time	Distance	Activity
9.16	0.00 km	Departure.
10.30	3.03 km	Stopped in a *nemep wopyii*. The dogs hunted a coatimundi (*yiuai*). Tigiri killed it with a poisoned dart but left the carcass intact nearby.
11.20	3.92 km	Stopped to cut down two *bijnidé* tree. They ate a large quantity of fruit on the spot.

12.30	4.89 km	Stopped to rest. After a while Edubé collected some fibers to make darts.
13.07	5.02 km	Both men cut down a tree called *copo*, which contained a panel of wasps (*auchemdá*). They ate honey on the spot.
15.07	6.50 km	Edubé and Tigiri separated. We followed Edubé.
16.00	7.10 km	Tigiri, who brought two *búrup* full of vines for barbasco (*parupi'*), joined up again with Edube.
16.15	7.25 km	They climbed a tree that contained a beehive and ate honey in abundance.
17.00	8.10 km	Stopped to burn a beehive. Ate and collected honey in abundance.
18.50	9.20 km	Returned to the camp.

Total products brought into the camp: vines for barbasco (*parupi'*), honey, and fibers to make darts.

PATTERNS OF BONE REPRESENTATION AND SURFACE BONE MODIFICATION CAUSED BY NUKAK PREY ACQUISITION

By Gustavo A. Martínez

The Nukak case provides a good opportunity for discussing issues related to management of faunal resources by tropical forest hunter-gatherers. The focus of this analysis comprises the description and the explanation of processes related to the production of a set of material correlates produced on bone surfaces derived from Nukak activities. These modifications were produced by a set of behaviors related to hunting strategies such as prey acquisition, processing, consumption, and discarding of carcasses. Post-depositional processes also affected the assemblages. Information related to the representation of species and surface bone modifications of skeletal parts caused by humans, such as cut marks, fractures, burning, and chewing, and also nonhumans (for example, carnivores), are analyzed and discussed. These kinds of studies have been performed by many other authors in different sociocultural and environmental contexts (O'Connell 1987; O'Connell, Hawkes, & Blurton-Jones 1988a, b, 1990, 1992; O' Connell & Marshall 1989; Kent 1993; Lupo 1994, 1995). Finally, the expectations derived from the observation of hunting and processing activities is compared with the recorded patterns of bone modifications to detect a set of patterns that can be used to identify material correlates of Nukak behavior.

Detailed analyses, seen through the eyes of an archaeologist, of the bone assemblages produced by tropical rain forest hunter-gatherers are almost non-existent. Most of the cases reported belong to archetypical hunter-gatherers (see, for example, Binford 1978a; Lupo 1995). Part of the sample included in this chapter has been previously analyzed (see Politis, Martínez, & Marshall 1995). New bones deriving from further fieldwork (carried out in 1994 and 1996) and final results from the total assemblage are presented here.

Material and Methods

During fieldwork, hunting tactics, primary and secondary butchering techniques, and transport and discard patterns were recorded (see Chapter 9), and a bone collection from the camps where these activities were observed was built up. The work carried out in the lab consisted of activities such as anatomic classification of bone specimens, quantification, presence/absence, location, frequency, and features of surface bone modification such as marks, fractures, chewing, and burning. The faunal sample analyzed is presented in Table II.1.

Table II.1 Number and Frequencies of Bone Specimens Identified per Taxa and Camp; Analysis of a Faunal Sample

	Camp								
Specie	AC1-91	C5-91	C6-91	C1-92	C1/C2-92	C3-92	C1-96	Total	%
Monkey	14	40	80		29	21	23	207	66.99
Peccary				43				43	13.91
Tortoise				3			1	4	1.29
Bird							18	18	5.82
Unidentified	25						12	37	11.97
Total	39	40	80	46	29	21	54	309	100
%	12.62	12.9	25.88	14.88	9.38	6.79	17.47	100	

The bones studied were collected from both active and recently abandoned Nukak camps. The sample is composed of specimens collected in 1991 from abandoned camp 1 (AC1) and from active camps 5 and 6 (C5-91 and C6-91); in the 1992 field season from active camps 1, 2, and 3 (C1-92, C1/C2-92, and C3-1992); and, finally, from active camp 1 of the 1996 season (C1-96). The conditions under which the bones were collected were variable as regard to factors such as ground visibility, which in turn depended on the duration of the occupation, the production of garbage, and, of course, the intensity of hunting activities carried out in the camp. Also, the dynamics of Nukak mobility (see Chapter 6) do not allow enough time for collecting bones when a move from one camp to another is suddenly decided on. Therefore, the totality of the discarded bones was not collected. Although these factors can introduce bias in the representation of animal species and bones, the sample considered here is still representative of the major trends concerning bone surface modifications.

Although the sequence of carcass dismemberment and the elements used for this task have been mentioned in Chapter 9, some contextual information is crucial for the understanding of the analysis performed here. Note that marks related to butchery were made either with metal knives or machetes, which in turn affects the type of bone surface modification recorded (for example, marks, fractures, and so on). As will be discussed later, the case of chewing is a more complex process due to the fact that two agents—humans and carnivores—can be involved. These contextual properties lead to the consideration of a set of situational criteria to establish the origin of bone surface modifications. Although it is not the goal of this appendix to deal with methodological aspects linked to the complexity of the depositional formation processes generated by humans and other agents, it is important to mention some of the criteria used in this study to avoid problems in assigning specific traits to agents of production when trying to solve problems linked with equifinality (see Lupo 1994, 1995; Lyman 1994; O'Connell 1995).

Many authors (Binford 1981; Johnson 1985; Lyman 1987; Shipman 1981) have defined butchering marks. Based on some of the attributes described and used by these authors an analytical distinction is made between cut marks and blow marks in the Nukak assemblages. The morphological analysis of the cut marks was performed with the naked eye using a hand lens and in some cases a 40 × light microscope. Cut marks are straight, short (up to 7 mm), and thin lines that show a very shallow V-shaped section. This section does not always describe a symmetrical "V" but may be an oblique trait regarding bone surface. The ends of the marks are thinner and shallow when compared with their middle portion. They usually occur isolated or in closely aligned groups (maximum 7) located around the distal and the proximal epiphyses of long bones (Figure II.1) and also associated with articulation cavities of the axial skeleton (for example, acetabulums). These marks may be closely associated with other attributes such as flake scars, slices, and notches that imply tissue removal. Some of the marks present a discontinuous line owing to bone surface topography or intensity of the cut (Figure II.2, left).

Although blow marks share some attributes with cut marks, differences exist that should be stressed (Figure II.3). Blow marks are also straight and fine, but they are longer (up to 12 mm) and much deeper (up to 6 mm). In many cases they present a "U" instead of a "V" shape in section that is not always symmetrical to the bone surface but rather oblique to it. The ends and the middle sections of the marks are usually the same size, being broader and deeper than the cut marks. They commonly occur in groups (maximum 6, although the normal pattern is between 2 and 4), are not closely aligned, and although they are also spatially related they are at times located far from the long bones' distal and proximal epiphyses. These marks present a strong association with other attributes such as flake scars, slices, and notches (Figure II.3), and they do not occur as discontinuous lines.

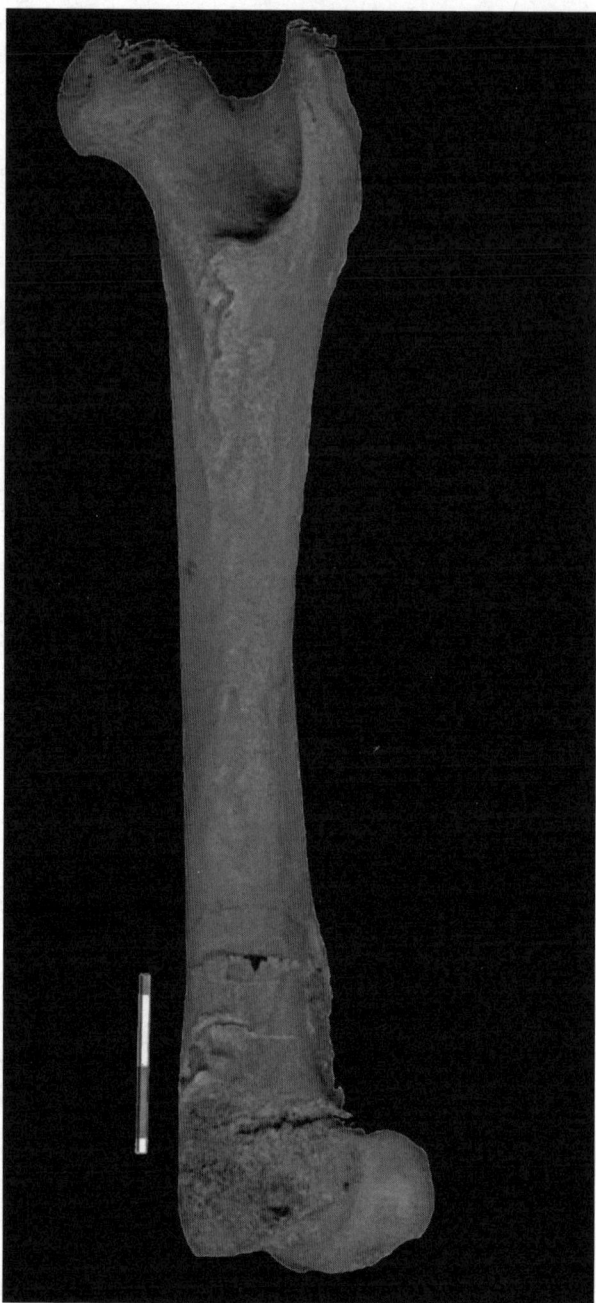

Figure II.1 Cut marks on a peccary femur head, probably produced during the dismembering process

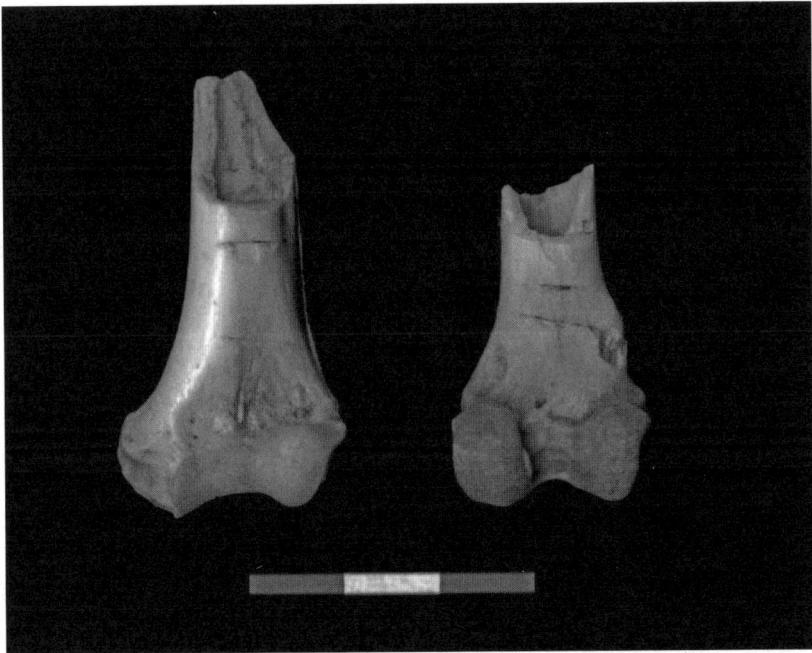

Figure II.2 (*Left*) The bone belongs to a left distal humerus of a monkey. A fracture produced by a dynamic impact (blow) can be observed. The upper blow marks are the result of previous failed attempts to break the bone. These blow marks have associated attributes such as slices. The marks located at the bottom–a very fine, short line and a discontinuous one–are probably cut marks related to the dismembering stage. (*Right)* This bone presents a similar fracture pattern to the photo on the left. In this case small flakes are still attached to the borders of the blow marks.

Modification by chewing was recorded following the criteria of various authors (see Behrensmeyer 1990,1993; Binford 1981; Blumenschine & Marean 1993; Elkin & Mondini 2001; Hudson 1993; Lupo 1995; Lyman 1994;). Traits such as punctures, pittings, scorings, pits, bone flakes, denticulate and crenulated borders, lack of spongy tissue in articular ends, and fractures were taken into account in recording gnawing damage. Fractures were divided into three main categories: helical, transverse, and oblique. Attributes associated with the borders and surfaces of the fractures such as plain-smooth, crenulated, jagged and uneven with irregular borders, and finally smashed-splintered were recorded (Binford 1981; Haynes 1988a, b, 1991; Johnson 1985; Lyman 1987, 1994). Alteration by fire demonstrates a pattern that ranges from scorching to calcinated, but here it will simply be referred to as burnt.

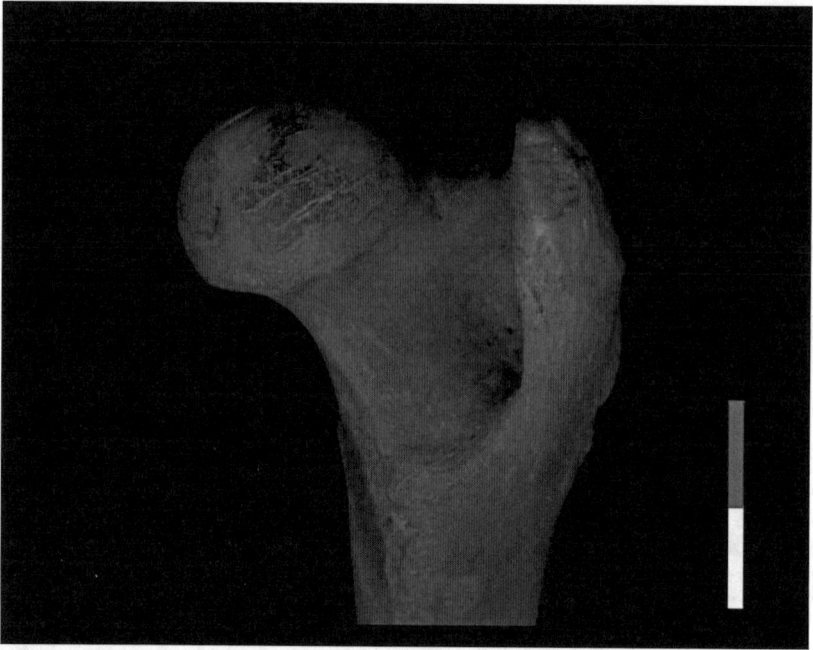

Figure II.3 Femur of peccary showing several traits produced by the dynamic impact of a machete (blow marks represented by deep cuts, flake scars, sliced notches, removal of tissue, and so on)

SAMPLE ANALYSIS

As has been stated elsewhere (Politis & Martínez 1996; see also Chapter 9), vertebrates living in Nukak territory were classified into three main size categories: small (for example, monkeys), medium (for example, peccaries), and large (for example, jaguars, tapirs, and deer). Given the different behaviors and hunting tactics employed in the acquisition and processing of prey of different size, bone surface modifications of monkey and peccary will be examined separately. Monkeys will be considered as a whole and not separated by species, since the carcass treatment of all was the same. The only peccary specie represented in the sample is the white-lipped peccary, which was the object of two separate hunting events in 1992 (Chapter 9).

The total number of specimens recovered from the camps (see Table II.1) was 309 items. The best-represented camps in terms of bone frequency were C6-91 (ca. 26%), C1-96 (ca. 17.5%), and C1-92 (ca. 15%). Considering the animal bone representation as measured in NISP, monkey is in first place (ca. 70%) followed by peccary (ca. 14%). Monkey teeth that had come loose from the maxillae or mandibles were merely counted (ca. 60). The low frequency of bone birds (ca. 6%, which were not taken into account in this analysis) is caused by the high fragmentation of such small, low density and fragile bones and is also due to the difficulties of detecting them on the ground. Needless to say, these frequencies do not represent the contribution to diet of each prey (Chapter 8) but only the bone frequencies collected per camp.

Modifications such as cut and blow marks, fractures, chewing, and burning were recorded for the two main species represented, monkey and peccary. The intensity of monkey and peccary bone surface modification can be seen in Figures II.4 and II.5, respectively. Monkey axial elements are located on the left side of the X axis of Figure II.4; the appendicular are on the right side. There is a clear pattern with regard to burning, the most affected specimen being the skull. Fracture patterns were recorded for both axial and appendicular elements. The skull is again the most fragmented item, followed by the humerus, the ulna, and the femur. Cut marks are quite evenly represented both in the axial and the appendicular skeleton, although some elements, such as mandible, scapula, pelvis, humerus, and femur present higher frequencies. Blow marks are more common on skull, humerus, ulna, femur, and tibia. Chewing was predominantly recorded on elements of the appendicular skeleton, such as humerus, radio, ulna, femur, tibia. and fibula (see Figure II.4).

Examination of the bone surface of peccary ($n = 43$) revealed that 36% show no evidence of modification (Table II.2). Some axial elements, such as vertebrae, scapulae, and ribs, as well as appendicular ones (for example, humerus and femur) show cut marks. When one compares the frequency of bone modification of monkey and peccary (see Table II.2) differences and similarities can be noted: cut marks are equally recorded in peccary and monkey bone specimens (ca. 20% and ca. 22%, respectively), whereas the main differences can be observed in dynamic marks (ca. 27% and ca. 11%), fractures (ca. 7% and ca. 34%), and chewing (0% and ca. 7%).

Table II.3 shows the different proportions of fractures, taking into account the three main categories of helical, transverse, and oblique. Figure II.6 adds information about the features of the borders and the surface fractures, divided into the following main categories: plain-smooth, crenulated, jagged-irregular, and smashed-splintered. Figure II.7 shows the number of surface modifications or traits capable of being produced by chewing, such as scoring, pitting, and punctures, represented per camp.

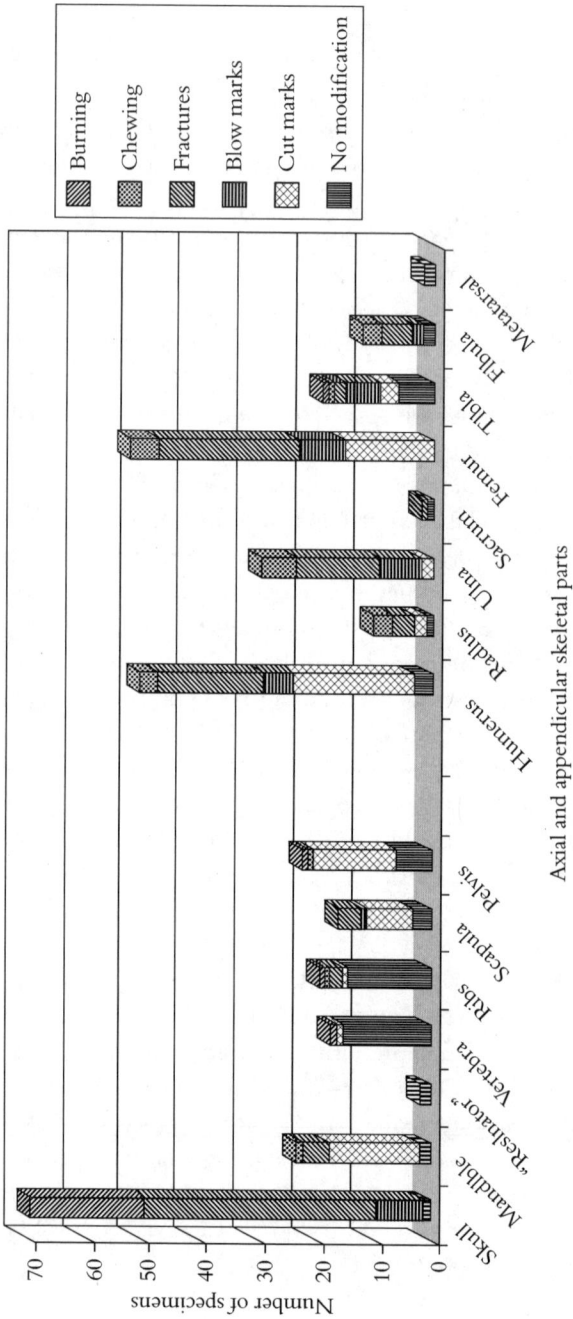

Figure II.4 Modification on the surface of a monkey bone

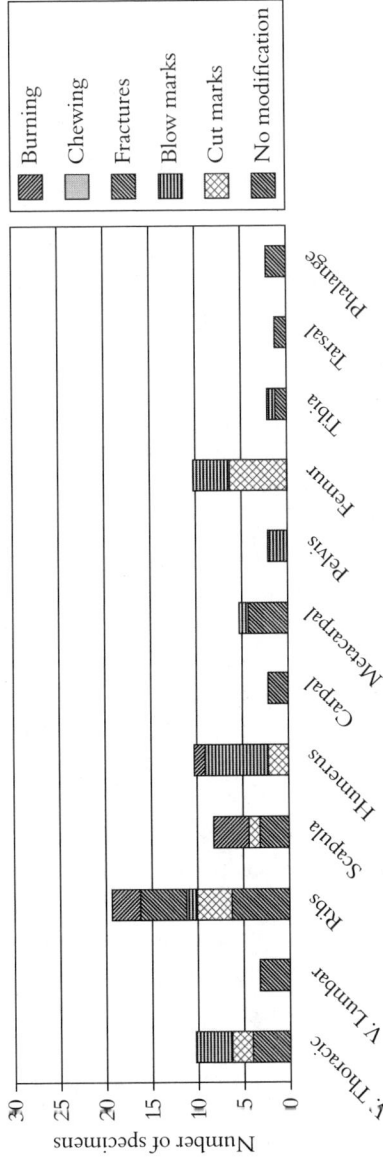

Figure II.5 Modification on the surface of a peccary bone

Table II.2 Frequency of Bone Surface Modifications on Peccary and Monkey
Bones

Specie	No Modification	Cut Marks	Blow Marks	Fractures	Chewing	Burning
Peccary	35.14 %	20.27 %	27.03 %	6.75 %	0 %	10.81 %
Monkey	16.17 %	22.1 %	11.32 %	34.23 %	7.01 %	9.16 %

Table II.3 Types of Fractures and Their Total Frequency per Camp

Specie	AC1-91	C5-91	C6-91	C1-92	C1/C2-92	C3-92	C1-96	Total	%
Helical			1				1	2	1.99
Transverse	3	19	12	4	1	1	4	44	43.56
Oblique	4	25	14	5		6	1	55	54.45
Total	7	44	27	9	1	7	6	101	100
%	6.93	43.56	26.73	8.91	0.99	6.93	5.94	100	

Discussion

The analysis performed on the seven assemblages collected indicates that, with the exception of C1-92 where peccary is overrepresented, monkeys dominate the assemblages with small, subordinated numbers of tortoises and birds (Table II.1). Therefore, the detailed analysis concentrates on monkey bones, since these constitute the greater part of the assemblages, and includes most body parts except the lower extremities.

Binford's work (1981) is used as a frame of reference for analyzing the butchering sequence that constituted skinning, dismemberment, filleting, and consumption, including marrow extraction. This discussion will concentrate on the treatment of carcasses in the base camps, divided into small (monkey) and medium (peccary) size prey.

In the case of monkey the dismembering process is carried out using a metal knife or occasionally a machete. When compared with Binford's model (1981), the Nukak technique does not include the skinning of prey. Instead, they burn the hair, and, therefore, no marks on the bones related to this stage remain. The recorded cut marks belong to different stages of dismemberment. The first stage is related to the dismembering of the complete carcass in order to obtain primary processing units (for example, rear limbs, forelimbs, and so on). The second stage involves a secondary processing step. Here, additional marks are produced when these units are subsequently semidisarticulated with partial cuts through the joints. However, the proximal and distal ends of contiguous bones are not completely separated and remain semiarticulated. This process enables "bending" of the primary processing units in order to fit them in the pot ready for cooking. In other words, this

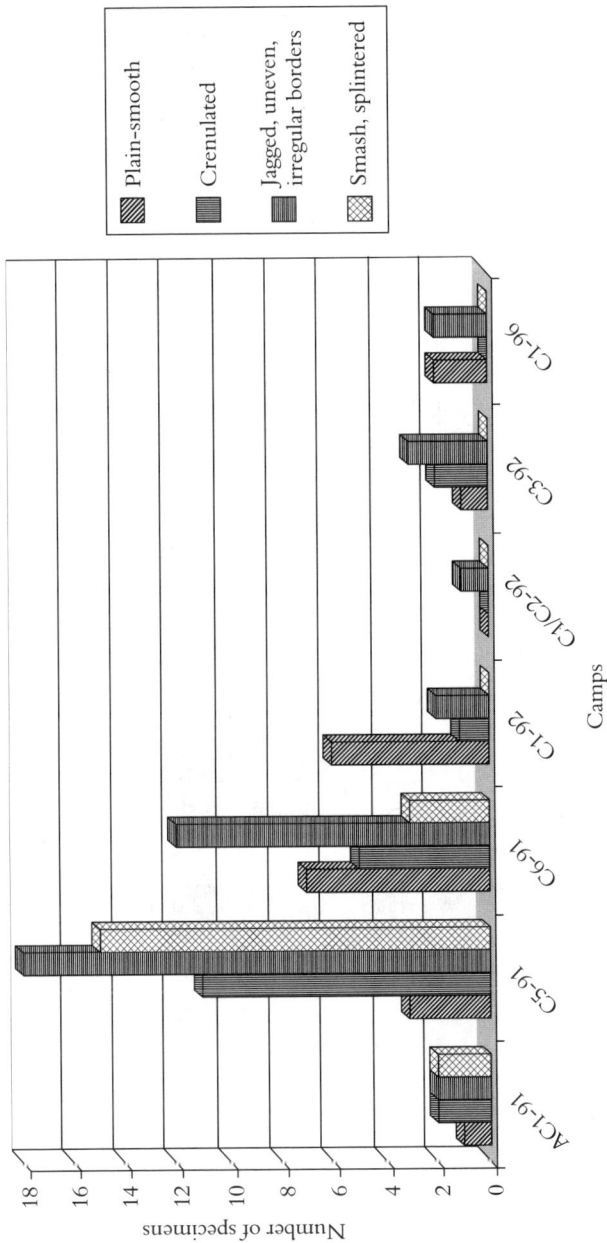

Figure II.6 Comparative chart showing number of specimens and characteristics of fractures by camp

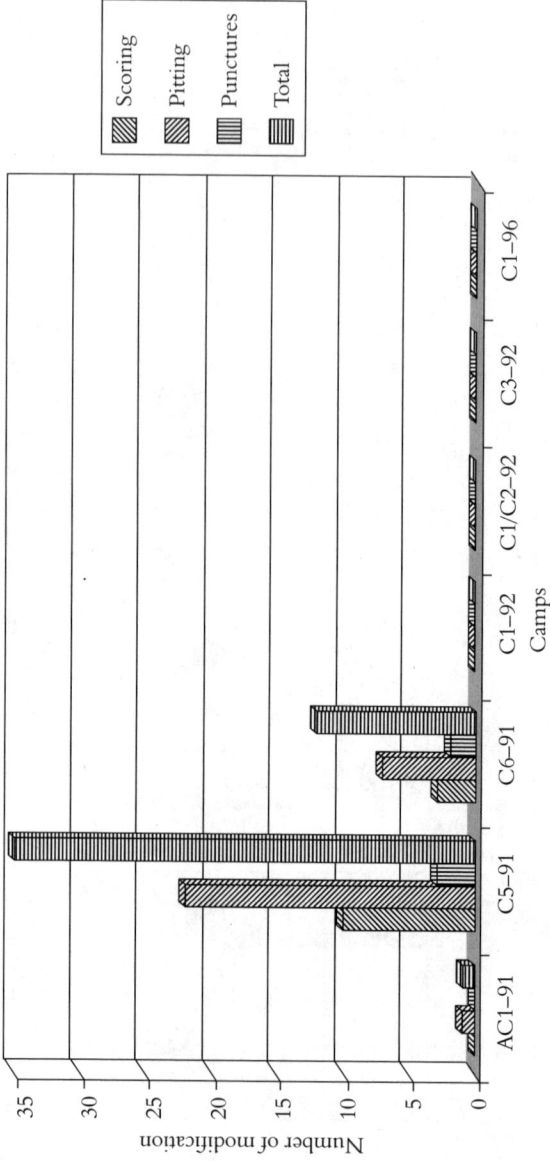

Figure II.7 Modification by chewing

second dismemberment step decreases the size of the unit without fully disarticulating the bones of the primary units, adapting them to the dimensions of the pot. Thus, at least some of the determinants of processing patterns are the sizes of both the prey and the available container, as well as the cooking technique. Filleting was not observed, and marks are not expected because tissue is removed from bone after cooking by chewing, probably because of the small size of the anatomical units. Taking into account these observations it can be concluded that the recorded cut marks were produced during the two-step dismembering process just described, with the only exception of those marks recorded on mandibles. A common practice was the disarticulation of the mandible from the skull by a cut through the masseter muscle, which produced a higher frequency of cut marks (ca. 18%) on the mandible ramus. The removal of the jaws with a knife occurs after cooking and is linked to consumption rather than processing. Therefore, cut marks on these elements are not related to the primary processing tasks, and consequently these marks are one of the last to be produced in the entire butchery-consumption process. This statement can be reinforced using the information regarding the location and the frequency of marks. Cuts in scapulae (ca. 10%) and pelvises (ca. 17%) are mainly the result of the first step of the dismembering process, involving segmentation into primary processing units. Regarding the appendicular skeleton, the major frequency of marks is on the humerus-radius-ulna (ca. 30%) and femur-tibia (ca. 22%). These marks were produced during the second step of the dismembering process.

Consumption always occurs after cooking, which means that marrow extraction—an activity that it is generally associated with the early steps of the processing of other prey (for example, ungulates)—is in this case one of the last activities in the sequence, just prior to bone discard. Consumption produces a large part of the damage represented by fractures, chewing, and, indirectly, burning (ca. 27% in total). Blow marks are represented in ca. 11% of cases and, with the exception of the skull (ca. 19%), they are located on bones belonging to the appendicular skeleton. Similar patterns can be observed for fractures and chewing, although mandibles and ribs are also affected.

Two different techniques were observed regarding consumption of marrow that primarily produce fractures. Long-bone epiphyses are removed with a knife or machete, whereas the ends of small bones are removed with the teeth. The former technique produces a low frequency of helical fractures (ca. 2%, see Table II.3), presenting plain and smooth borders (ca. 4%). This is clearly related to marrow acquisition through dynamic impacts (blows) produced with a sharp acute-edged tool (for example, knife), which works by inflicting severe damage at a specific point on the bone surface rather than over a larger area. As a consequence, the production of fractures is mainly represented by deep and long cuts, leaving little chance for the production of a spiral/helicoidal pattern along the epiphyses. Much more common are transverse (ca. 44%) and oblique (ca. 54%) fractures (see Table II.3). Although a pattern of crenulated, jagged-irregular, and smashed-splintered border damage can be observed with varying frequency between camps, C5-91 and C6-91 show the highest degree of fragmentation (Figure II.6).

Modification of bones by chewing is not well known, and preliminary studies show that similar patterns can be produced either by carnivores or humans (see discussion in Elkin & Mondini 2001). The trends in presence and the frequency of traits commonly related to chewing modification appear to be insufficient to elucidate who were the responsible agent (humans or carnivores). An experiment conducted by Elkin and Mondini (2001) carried out on captive small carnivores (foxes) that inflicted tooth damage on mid-size prey (sheep) demonstrated that traits (for example, scoring, pitting, punctures, and so on) produced by them are morphologically the same or very close to those produced by human chewing, and also that these traits share the same location on specific portions of bones. The methodological problem of equifinality focuses our view on the specificity of the context of damage production. Identification of signatures and properties of the Nukak social and ecological context regarding chewing-related agents can be taken into account in elucidating the origin of these traits. Four adult medium to small dogs were recorded at C5-91 and C6-91; a single female dog was present at C1-92, C1/C2-92, and C3-92. It was not possible to record if dogs were present at AC1-91, and they were absent at C1-96. Thus, the identification of the appropriate agent is even more difficult owing to the fact that in the camps that produced the greatest frequency of chewing (C5-91 and C6-91) several dogs were present. Although potential dog damage is expected on bone surfaces, it is notable that in these camps human chewing as a consumption technique was also observed, especially in C5-91.

The data shows that ca. 15% of the elements that present damage by chewing are related almost exclusively to C5-91 and C6-91 (see Figure II.7). Pittings are the best-represented trait (ca. 62.5%), followed by scorings (ca. 27%) and punctures (ca. 10%). Furthermore, a pattern of crenulated, jagged-irregular, and smashed-splintered border damage can be observed with varying frequency in the camps, C5-91 and C6-91 again being those that present the highest degree of fragmentation (Figure II.6).

Although some traits that were recorded in Nukak camps (for example, pittings, scoring, and so on) could be inflicted by either carnivores or humans, the absence of damage (for example, removal of bone tissue) much more commonly left by carnivores is noted. Given the scarcity of wild carnivores during the occupation of the camps, the potential producers of chewing damage are the Nukaks' dogs. They appear to be the best candidates because they would have immediate access to the freshly discarded bones. Moreover, given the short period of time between the time of bone discard and when the bones were recovered for this study (20 days maximum) the possibility of carnivores other than dogs chewing the bones can also be reduced.

As mentioned before, typical chewing features (for example, scoring, pitting, punctures, cylinders, and so forth) are not enough for deducing human or carnivore action. Nevertheless, the information summarized above, combined with fracture patterns and the size of the consumed bones, is additional evidence providing a more accurate view of the agent that caused the damage. Figure II.8 shows fractures with jagged-irregular and smashed-splintered borders ($n = 60$); they have a frequency of ca. 59% and are fundamentally associated with oblique and transverse fractures (ca. 47.5%). Most of the fractures on long bones from C5-91 and C6-91 were produced on bones of very small monkeys, such as titi and tamarins (NISP = 78). Carnivores not only inflict damage on bone surfaces but also eat bone. If carnivores had strongly affected C5-91 and C6-91 bone assemblages (consisting mainly of small monkey bones) the chances of survival and further recovery of the elements would be low. Consequently, it is suggested that the most probable agent responsible for damage caused by chewing and also for fractures inflicted on small monkey bones are humans. A further implication of this proposition is that in some assemblages the pattern of fragmentation was primarily related to consumption rather than processing.

The process of butchering of peccary carcasses is performed with metal knives and, given the size of the bones, frequently machetes. The processing-consumption process shares some common features with the monkey butchering sequence. For instance, there is no skin removal, but charring does occur, and, therefore, no cut marks can be expected regarding the first step of the sequence, or skinning. The peccary dismembering process is different to monkey. It is initiated in a special-purpose place, after which the primary processing units obtained are moved to the base camps (Chapter 9). In the small peccary sample (only C1-92; $n = 43$, see Table II.1) the frequency of cut marks (ca. 20%, Table II.2) is quite similar to those of monkeys, but the distribution of marks is restricted to only 5 elements as opposed to the 10 units affected by cut marks for monkeys (see Figures II.4 and II.5). Given the scarcity of cut marks on peccary bones it is difficult to assign them to a specific

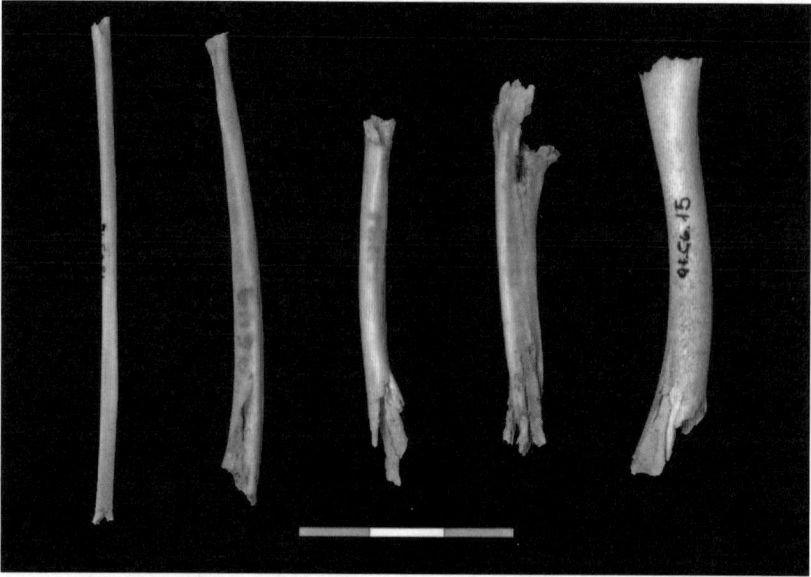

Figure II.8 Small monkey bones showing jagged-irregular and smashed-splintered borders, as well as evidence of chewing. The combination of size of bone, fractures, and chewing marks associated with the observed pattern of human chewing at the camp indicates that humans were the agents of damage.

step in the dismemberment sequence in the same way as was done for monkey. The fact that partial dismemberment is carried out in a special-purpose location, plus the scarcity of recorded marks, makes it difficult to recognize the locus of mark production, either in the processing tasks at the hunting site or consumption at base camp. Filleting for extraction of meat was observed during consumption, but the expected pattern of multiple scrape marks located on middle shafts was not recorded on bone surfaces. Instead, the position (at the ends) and the nature of the recorded marks (mainly associated with dynamic impacts) show a pattern linked with consumption related to marrow extraction (Figure II.3). Thus, filleting left no evidence on bone surfaces.

Again in a similar fashion to the case of monkeys, consumption is basically carried out in the base camp. An additional step is the process of smoking the primary processing units on a grill located beside the base camp (Chapter 9). Here, the process of bone breakage acquires relevance in relation to meat consumption and marrow extraction. The presence of dynamic marks for marrow consumption is significant in peccary bones, representing ca. 27%.

This pattern contrasts with the few fractures that were recorded (see Table II. 2). The explanation lies in failed attempts to break the bones—for each successful bone breakage and subsequent fracture several dynamic marks are produced.

The surfaces and the borders of the fractures produced in peccary bones present a different frequency of categories. Figure II.7 shows that when one compares these statistics with assemblages dominated by monkey (for example, C5-91) the plain and smooth borders are more frequent, whereas types such as crenulated, jagged-uneven-irregular, and smashed-splintered borders are less common. This pattern may also be associated with the predominance of use of machetes and their effect through dynamic impacts that produce severe linear cuts when processing larger bones for marrow extraction. For instance, proximal ends of peccary ribs usually have oblique or transverse fractures with clear plain cuts, occasionally associated with slices where part of the surface tissue has been removed. Given the skeletal part (rib) and the lack of attributes associated with chewing (such as crenulated or uneven irregular borders, pittings, scorings, and so on) it is most likely that these fractures belong to an initial stage of dismemberment produced with machetes rather than being the result of consumption processes such as marrow extraction. The decrease in crenulated, jagged-uneven-irregular, and smashed-splintered borders seems to be related to the lack of other modifications, such as chewing, which did not occur with peccary bones at all. Taking into account that four dogs were with this band, the lack of chewing and the low frequency of crenulated and jagged borders support the idea of low carnivore damage.

The frequency of burning associated with peccary bones is the same as that recorded for monkey bones (Table II.2), despite the fact that peccaries are subject to smoking, a process that is visible on bone surfaces as a bright brown coating.

CONCLUSIONS

Of principle concern is whether the evidence of hunting/processing tasks for monkey and peccary is represented by the same kinds of bone-surface modification. First, the information mentioned above referred to different size prey—small (monkey) and medium (peccary)—which has obvious consequences for transportation and ulterior treatment of carcasses. Regarding processing and consumption the technology used for both types of prey was the same, with a more intensive use of machetes in the processing of peccary, which is related to the sizes of both the prey and the bones. In this vein, the greater frequency of knife use for processing monkeys means that shallow, linear, and in some cases multiple cut marks are almost exclusively represented, while the peccary bones show other marks (for example, notches, slices, and deep cuts) associated with dynamic impacts made by the machetes. Generally, fragmentation is significant, and with regard to the elements most affected by dynamic impacts it is clear that fragments of monkey skull appear over-represented, which is a product of the high degree of processing required to obtain the brain. Fragmentation is also due to the high rates of breakage on the long-bone epiphyses of both monkeys and peccaries from marrow extraction. The distal and the proximal ends of long bones are the most affected parts due to fractures and because they are the major place of cut and dynamic-impact marks. The majority of butchering marks recorded both for monkey and peccary are produced by dynamic impacts; the rest are related to the dismembering process and belong to the two-step sequence of dismemberment recorded for monkeys. As previously stated, this process of dismemberment is difficult to recognize in peccaries owing to the fact that only a few elements show cut marks.

The identification of chewing and its origin (human or dog) is difficult to establish and highly contextual. Nevertheless, additional traits and attributes in the assemblages, generally characterized by smashed-splintered, jagged-uneven-irregular, and crenulated borders on fractures of very small monkey bones, are more likely related to human chewing. This is particularly clear in camp C5-91 where most of the monkeys consumed were very small, highlighting the idea that the size of the prey has something to do with the technique of consumption and the use or nonuse of tools. It is also noteworthy that few cut marks were recognized in this context, which implies a low investment in processing activities when dealing with very small prey.

Despite the presence of dogs at some Nukak camps the activity of carnivores and the consequent modifications of bone surfaces does not appear to be significant in bone assemblages left behind by the Nukak. This idea deserves further exploration, although there are also reasons for keeping it in mind at this stage. First, the "primary consumers" of hunted animals are the Nukak. Therefore, dogs do not have access to the prey "first hand" because these latter enter immediately into the sphere of processing and consumption, carried out intensively for both meat and marrow. Second, the processes of boiling (in the case of monkeys) and smoking (in the case of peccaries) result in fairly unattractive bone remains for carnivores. A representative case is camp C1-92, where bones of mid-sized prey (peccary) were present but dogs did not damage them. It is possible that the several steps involved in the management of the peccary carcasses (acquisition, primary butchering, and smoking in processing loci, transport of carcasses, secondary processing, butchering, and smoking in the base camp; see Chapter 9) make the bones less available for immediate consumption and less desirable for dogs as a consequence of the smoking that produces changes in bone surface (for example, the bright brown coating). Third, after consumption of the meat by humans some few bones are thrown into the hearths where they burn, and access to them is consequently reduced.

Despite the differences in the sample, similar low frequencies of burnt bones were recorded for both peccary and monkey. In the case of monkey the boiling method of cooking is implicated, burnt bones being the result of the postconsumption stage related to their disposal in the hearths. The method of smoking peccary primary processing units produced, at the most, scorching and charred patterns on bone surfaces but never reached the burnt-calcinated stage.

The Nukak case is also important for observing the way in which human behavior not directly linked with subsistence and prey treatment could have a partial material correlate in bones. In this regard, the pattern of bone surface modification of peccary bones with regard to chewing deserves special comment. Although the probability that humans did not produce this damage may be due to the size of bones, other reasons can be adduced for explaining the pattern. Factors that could determine the intensity of modifications in general, and chewing in particular, within the sphere of consumption could be partially related to social practice and ideologies, such as taboos (see Chapter 9). In this sense, because peccary is taboo for women and children, the bones are subject to a particular treatment when compared with monkey. Consequently, they undergo a strategy of management that involves fewer people, all of whom are men of a specific age. In theory, this fact could partially reduce the frequency of modifications on peccary bone surfaces. Besides, the bones are not immediately processed, consumed, and discarded. Rather, some of them remain "managed" on the grill situated beside the camp for some time (up to four days). This process delays the full consumption of units because they are eaten slowly and partially (units that have begun to be eaten are momentarily left and fully consumed later) until the flesh is completely consumed. In the meantime, some bones are permanently subjected to the smoking process, which produces the coating already mentioned. In other words, owing to the process of consumption and its particularities the elements have no meat attached when discarded, and the smoking has produced a coating and/or burning that probably makes the bones unattractive for carnivores (see also Lupo 1995). Thus, it is possible that the integrity of bone surfaces—for example, gnawing (either by carnivores or humans)—is closely related to particular human behavior linked to social and ideational components rather than with subsistence strategies or ecological conditions.

Acknowledgments

I thank Dolores Elkin and Luis Borrero for reading a draft version of this appendix and for their valuable comments and suggestions.

BIBLIOGRAPHY

Abrams, E. 1989. Architecture and energy: An evolutionary perspective. In *Archaeo-logical methods and theory*. Vol. 1. M. Schiffer, ed. Tucson: University of Arizona Press, pp. 47–87.

Acosta, L. 1993. *Guaviare, puente a la Amazonia*. Bogotá: Corporación Colombiana para la Amazonia-Araracuara.

Andrews, E. F. 1994. Territoriality and land use among the *Akulmiut* of western Alaska. In *Key issues in hunter-gatherer research*. E. Burch, Jr. and J. Ellanna, eds. Oxford: Berg Publishers, pp. 65–94.

Allen, W. 1998. *Deconstructing Harry*. Sweetland Films.

Appadurai, A., ed. 1986. *The social life of things: Commodities in cultural perspective*. Cambridge: Cambridge University Press.

Arcand, B. 1972. *The urgent situation of the Cuiva Indians of Colombia*. Copenhagen: IWGIA Document.

——— 1976. Cuiva food production, *Canadian Review of Sociology and Anthropology* 13:387–96.

——— 1981. The Negritos and the Penan will never be Cuiva, *Folk* 23:37–43.

Ardila, G. 1992a. Un grupo Nukak en el verano. Paper presented at the 6to. Congreso Nacional de Antropología de Colombia, Symposium Pasado y Presente de los Cazadores Recolectores en América del Sur. Universidad de Los Andes, Santafé de Bogotá, Colombia.

——— 1992b. Los Nukak-Makú del Guaviare: Mi primer encuentro con la gente de las palmas (etnografía para la arqueología del poblamiento de América), *América Negra* 3:171–89.

Ardila, G., and G. Politis. 1992. La situación actual de los Nukak de la Amazonía Colombiana: Problemas y perspectivas, *Revista de la Universidad Nacional de Colombia* 26:2–6.

Århem, K. 1990. Ecosofia Makuna. In *La selva humanizada: Ecología alternativa en el trópico húmedo Colombiano*. F. Correa, ed. Bogotá: Instituto Colombiano de Antro-pología, Fondo Editorial CEREC, pp. 105–22.

——— 1996. The cosmic food web: Human nature relatedness in the Northwest Amazon. In *Nature and society: Anthropological perspectives*. P. Descola and G. Pálsson, eds. European Association of Social Anthropologists. London: Routledge.

——— 1998. Power of place: Landscape, territory and local belonging in Northwest Amazonia. In *Locality and belonging*. N. Lovell, ed. London: Routledge, pp. 78–102.

Ascher, R. 1961. Analogy in archaeological interpretation, *Journal of Anthropology* 17:317–25.

Assis, V. S. 1995–1996. Um estudo da Casa Mbya pela perspectiva etnoarqueológica, *Coleçao Arqueología* 1(2):519–26.

Athias, R. 1995. Hupdë-Maku et Tukano: Les Rélations Inégales entre deux societés du Uaupés Amazonien (Brésil). Ph.D. dissertation. Université de Paris X, Nanterre, France.

Athias, R. 2003. Territoriality and space among the Hupd'äh and Tukano of the River Uaupés Basin, *Estudios Latinoamericanos* 23:1–26.

Azcárate, L. Ms. *Informe de Comisión a Laguna Pavón (Guaviare) y Mitú (Vaupes)*. Bogotá: División de Asuntos Indígenas, 1989. Ministerio de Gobierno.

Bailey, R. 1990. Exciting opportunities in tropical rain forest: A reply to Townsend, *American Anthropologist* 92 (3):747–48.

Bailey, R., G. Head, M. Janike, B. Owen, R. Rechtman, and E. Zechenter. 1989. Hunting and gathering in tropical rain forest: Is it possible? *American Anthropologist* 91:261–85.

Bailey, R., and T. Headland. 1991. The tropical rain forest: Is it a productive environment for human foragers? *Human Ecology* 19 (2):261–85.

Bailey, R., M. Janike, and R. Rechtman. 1991. Reply to Colinvaux and Bush, *American Anthropologist* 93:160–62.

Balée, W. 1989. The culture of Amazonian forest. In *Resource management in Amazonia: Advances in economic botany*. Vol. 7. D. Posey and W. Balée, eds. New York: New York Botanical Garden, pp. 1–21.

——— 1994. *Footprints of the forest: Ka´apor Ethnobotany—The historical ecology of plant utilization by an Amazonian people*. New York: Columbia University Press.

——— 1998a. Introduction to *Advances in historical ecology*. W. Balée, ed. New York: Columbia University Press, pp. 1–10.

——— 1998b. Historical ecology: Premises and postulates. In *Advances in historical ecology*. W. Balée, ed. New York: Columbia University Press, pp. 14–29.

Balick, M. 1986. Systematic and economic botany of the *Oenocarpus Jessenia* (Palmae) Complex, *Advances in Economic Botany* 3:1–140.

Balick, M., and S. Gershopp. 1981. Nutritional evaluation of the *Jessenia bataua palm*: Source of high quality protein and oil from tropical America, *Economic Botany* 35 (3):262–71.

Barnard, A. 1992. Social and spatial boundary maintenance among southern African hunter-gatherers. In *Mobility and territoriality: Social and spatial boundaries among foragers, fishers, pastoralists and peripatetics*. M. J. Casimir and A. Rao, eds. New York: Berg Publishers, pp. 137–51.

Barnard, A., and J. Woodburn. 1991. Property, power and ideology in hunting and gathering societies: An introduction. In *Hunters and gatherers 1: History, evolution and social change*. T. Ingold, D. Riches, and J. Woodburn, eds. Oxford: Berg Publishers, pp. 4–30.

Bartram, L. E., Jr. 1993. Perspectives on skeletal part profiles and utility curves from Eastern Kalahari ethnoarchaeology. In *From bones to behavior: Ethnoarchaeological and experimental contributions to the interpretation of faunal remains*. J. Hudson, ed. Carbondale, IL: Center for Archaeological Investigations. Southern Illinois University at Carbondale. Occasional Paper Nr. 31, pp. 115–37.

Bartram, L. E., M. Kroll, and H. T. Bunn. 1991. Variability in camp structure and bone food refuse patterning at Kua San Camps. In *The interpretation of archaeological spatial patterning*. E. M. Kroll and T. Price, eds. New York: Plenum Press, pp. 77–148.

Bahuchet, S. 1992. Spatial mobility and access to resources among the African pygmies. In *Mobility and territoriality: Social and spatial boundaries among foragers, fishers, pastoralists and peripatetics*. M. J. Casimir and A. Rao, eds. Oxford: Berg Publishers, pp. 205–37.

Basso, E. 1973. *The Kalapalo Indians of Central Brazil*. New York: Holt, Rinehart and Winston.

Beckerman, S. 1979. The abundance of protein in Amazonia: A reply to Gross, *American Anthropologist* 81 (3):533–60.

——— 1980. Fishing and hunting by the Bari of Colombia, *Working Papers on South American Indians* 2:67–111.

Behrensmeyer, A. K. 1990. *Experimental taphonomy workshop: Workshop outline and notes. ICAZ*:1–17. Washington, DC: Smithsonian Institution, Natural Museum of Natural History.

——— 1993. Discussion: Noncultural processes. In *From bones to behavior: Ethnoarchaeological and experimental contributions to the interpretation of faunal remains*. J. Hudson, ed. Carbondale: IL: Center for Archaeological Investigations. Southern Illinois University at Carbondale. Occasional Paper Nr. 31, pp. 342–48.

Behrensmeyer, A. K., and A. Hills, eds. 1980. *Fossil in the making*. Chicago: Chicago University Press.

Bettinger, R. 1991. *Hunter-Gatherers: Archaeological and evolutionary theory*. New York: Plenum Press.

Bianchi, C. 1981. *El shuar y el ambiente: Conocimiento del medio y cacería no destructiva*. Bogotá: Mundo.

Binford, L. R. 1962. Archaeology as anthropology, *American Antiquity* 28:217–25.

——— 1967. Smudge pits and hide smoking: The use of analogy in archaeological reasoning, *American Antiquity* 32:1–12.

——— 1977a. Forty-seven trips. In *Stone tools as cultural markers*. R. V. S. Wright, ed. Canberra: Australian Institute of Aboriginal Studies. pp. 24–36.

——— 1977b. General introduction. In *For theory building in archaeology*. L. Binford, ed. New York: Academic Press, pp. 1–10.

——— 1978a. *Nunamiut ethnoarchaeology*. New York: Academic Press.

——— 1978b. Dimensional analysis of behaviour and site structure: Learning from an Eskimo hunting stand, *American Antiquity* 43:330–61.

——— 1979. Organization and formation processes: Looking at curated technologies, *Journal Anthropological Research* 35 (3):255–73.

——— 1980. Willows smoke and dogs' tails: Hunter-gatherer settlement systems and archaeological site formation, *American Antiquity* 45:4–20.

——— 1981. *Bones: Ancient men and modern myths*. New York: Academic Press.

——— 1982. The archaeology of place, *Journal of Anthropological Archaeology* 1 (1): 31–51.

——— 1983a. *In pursuit of the past*. London: Thames and Hudson.

——— 1983b. Long-term land-use patterning: Some implications for archaeology. In *Working at archaeology*. L. R. Binford, ed. New York: Academic Press, pp. 379–86.

——— 1984. Butchering, sharing, and the archaeological record, *Journal of Anthropological Archaeology* 3:235–57.

——— 1987. Researching ambiguity: Frames of reference and site structure. In *Method and theory for activity area research: An ethnoarchaeological approach*. S. Kent, ed. New York: Columbia University Press, pp. 449–512.

——— 1988. Fact and fiction about the *Zinjanthropus* Floor: Data, arguments and interpretations, *Current Anthropology* 29:123–35.

Biocca, E.1965. *Viaggi tra gli Indi. Alto Rio Negro—Alto Orinoco. Appunti di un biologo.* Roma: Consiglio Nazionale Delle Ricerche.

Bird-David, N. 1990. The giving environment: Another perspective on the economic system of gatherer-hunters, *Current Anthropology* 31:189–96.

——— 1992. Beyond "the original affluent society": A culturalist reformulation, *Current Anthropology* 33:25–48.

——— 1999. "Animism" revisited: Personhood, environment and relational epistemology, *Current Anthropology* 40:67–91.

Bloch, M. 1998. Why trees, too, are good to think: Toward an anthropology of the meaning of life. In *The social life of trees: Anthropological perspectives on tree symbolism.* L. Rival, ed. Oxford: Berg Publishers, pp. 39–55.

Blumenschine, R. 1986. Carcass consumption sequences and the archaeological distinction of scavenging and hunting, *Journal of Human Evolution* 15:639–59.

——— 1989. A landscape taphonomic model of the scale of prehistoric scavenging opportunities, *Journal of Human Evolution* 18:345–71.

Blumenschine, R., and C. Marean. 1993. A carnivore's view of archaeological bone assemblages. In *From bones to behavior: Ethnoarchaeological and experimental contributions to the interpretation of faunal remains.* J. Hudson, ed. Carbondale, IL: Center for Archaeological Investigations. Southern Illinois University at Carbondale. Occasional Paper Nr. 31, pp. 273–300.

Bodú, P., C. Karlin, and S. Ploux. 1990. Who is who? The Magdalenian flintkanppers of Pincevent. In *The big puzzle.* C. Cziesla, S. Eichoff, N. Arts, and D. Winter, eds. Bonn: Holos, pp. 143–63.

Boivin, N. 2004. From veneration to exploitation: Human engagement with the mineral world. In *Soils, stones and symbols: Cultural perceptions of the mineral world.* N. Boivin and M. A. Owoc, eds. London: UCL Press, pp. 1–30.

Bonnichsen, R. 1973. Millie's Camp: An experiment in archaeology, *World Archaeology* 4:277–91.

Borgtoft Pedersen, H., and H. Balslev. 1993. *Palmas útiles. Especies ecuatorianas para agroforestería y extractivismo.* Quito: Abya-Yala.

Bórmida, M. 1973. Ergon y Mito: Una hermenéutica de la cultura material de los Ayoreo del Chaco Boreal *Scripta Ethnologica* 1 (1):9–68.

Borrero, L. 1990a. Fuego-Patagonian bone assemblages and the problem of communal guanaco hunting. In *Hunters of the recent past.* L. B. Davis and B. O. K. Reeves, eds. London: Unwin Hyman, pp. 373–95.

——— 1990b. Taphonomy of guanaco bones in Tierra del Fuego, *Quaternary Research* 34:361–71.

——— 1994. The extermination of the Selk'nam. In *Key issues in hunter-gatherer research.* E. Burch and L. Ellanna, eds. Oxford: Berg Publishers, pp. 247–62.

——— 2001. Regional taphonomy: The scales of application to the archaeological record. In *Animals and man in the past: Essays in honour of Dr. A. T. Clason.* H. Buitenhuis and W. Prummel, eds. ARC- Publicatie 41, Groningen, The Netherlands, pp. 17–20.

Borrero, L., and H. Yacobaccio. 1989. Etnoarqueología de Asentamientos Aché, *Journal de la Societé des Américanistes* 75:7–33.

Botero, P. 1997. *Guía para el análisis fisiográfico. Notas de clase.* Bogotá: CIAF-IGAC.

Bousman, C. Britt.1993. Hunter-gatherer adaptations, economic risk and tool design. *Lithic Technology* 18 (1–2):59–86.

Brochado, J. 1984. An ecological model of the spread of pottery and agriculture into Eastern South America. Unpublished Ph.D. dissertation. Department of Anthropology. University of Illinois, Urbana-Champaign.

Brooks, A., and J. Yellen. 1987. The preservation of activity areas in the archaeological record: Ethnoarchaeological work in the Northwest Ngamiland, Botswana. In *Method and theory for activity area research*. S. Kent, ed. New York: Columbia University Press, pp. 354–403.

Brosius, J. P. 1991. Foraging in tropical rain forest: The case of the Penan of Sarawak, East Malaysia (Borneo), *Human Ecology* 19 (2):123–50.

Brumm, A. 2004. An axe to grind: Symbolic considerations of stone axe use in ancient Australia. In *Soils, stones and symbols: Cultural perceptions of the mineral world*. N. Boivin and M. A. Owoc, eds. London: UCL Press, pp. 143–64.

Bunn, H., and E. Kroll. 1986. Systematic butchering by Plio/Pleistocene hominids at Olduvai Gorge, Tanzania, *Current Anthropology* 27 (5):431–52.

Burch, E., Jr. 1994. The future in hunter-gatherer research. In *Key issues in hunter-gatherer research*. E. Burch and L. Ellanna, eds. Oxford: Berg Publishers, pp. 441–56.

Burch, E., Jr., and Ellanna, L. 1994. Introduction. In *Key issues in hunter-gatherer research*. E. Burch and L. Ellanna, eds. Oxford: Berg Publishers, pp. 1–10.

Cabrera, G., C. Franky, and D. Mahecha. 1994. Aportes a la etnografía de los Nukak y su lengua: Aspectos sobre fonología segmental. Tesis de Grado. Universidad Nacional de Colombia, Facultad de Ciencias Humanas, Santafé de Bogotá.

——— 1999. *Los Nukak: Nómadas de la Amazonía Colombiana*. Santafé de Bogotá: Editorial Universidad Nacional.

Califano, M., ed. 1999. *Los indios Sirionó de Bolivia Oriental*. Buenos Aires: Ciudad Argentina.

Caracotche, M. S. 2001. The invisibility of time: An ethnoarchaeological study of the temporary sites of herders of the Southern Puna. In *Ethnoarchaeology of Andean South America: Contributions to archaeological method and theory*. L. Kuznar, ed. Ann Arbor, MI: International Monographs in Prehistory, Ethnoarchaeological. Series 4, pp. 87–115.

Cárdenas, D., D. Giraldo-Cañas, and C. Arias. 1997. Capítulo de vegetación. In *Zonificación ambiental para el plan modelo Colombo-Brasilero* (eje Apaporis-Tabatinga, PAT). Bogotá: IGAC-SINCHI, pp. 183–228.

Cárdenas, D., and G. Politis. 2000. Territorio, movilidad, etnobotánica y manejo del bosque de los Nukak Orientales: Amazonía Colombiana, *Informes Antropológicos* 3. Santafé de Bogotá: Universidad de los Andes-Instituto Amazónico de Investigaciones Científicas SINCHI.

Carneiro, R. 1979. Tree felling with the stone ax: An experiment carried out among the Yanomamö Indians of Venezuela. In *Ethnoarchaeology: Implications of ethnography for archaeology*. C. Kramer, ed. New York: Columbia University Press, pp. 21–58.

——— 1995. The History of ecological interpretations of Amazonia: Does Roosevelt have it right? In *Indigenous peoples and the future of Amazonia: An ecological anthropology of an endangered world*. L. E. Sponsel, ed. Tucson: University of Arizona Press, pp. 45–65.

Carsten, J., and S. Hugh-Jones, eds. 1995. *About the house: Lévi-Strauss and beyond*. Cambridge: Cambridge University Press.

Cashdan, E. A. 1983. Territoriality among human foragers: Ecological models and an application to four Bushman groups, *Current Anthropology* 24 (1):47–66.

Casimir, M. J. 1992. The dimensions of territoriality: An introduction. In *Mobility and territoriality: Social and spatial boundaries among foragers, fishers, pastoralists and peripatetics*. C. Michael and A. Rao, eds. Oxford: Berg Publishers, pp. 1–26.

Cavalier, I., C. Rodriguez, S. Mora, L. F. Herrera, and G. Morcote. 1995. No sólo de caza vive el hombre: Ocupación del bosque Amazónico, Holoceno temprano. In *Ambito y ocupaciones tempranas de la América tropical*. I. Cavalier and S. Mora, eds. Bogotá: Instituto Colombiano de Antropología-Fundación Erigaie, pp. 27–44.

Caycedo Turriago, J. 1993. Los Nukak: Transformaciones socioculturales y articulación étnica en una situación regional. In *Encrucijadas de Colombia Amerindia*. F. Correa, ed. Bogotá: Instituto Colombiano de Antropología, pp. 141–57.

Chase, A. K. 1989. Domestication and domiculture in Northern Australia: A social perspective. In *Foraging and farming: The evolution of plant exploitation*. D. Harris and G. Hillman, eds. London: Unwin Hyman, pp. 42–54.

Chatters, J. C. 1986. Hunther-gatherer adaptations and assemblage structure, *Journal of Anthropological Archaeology* 6:336–75.

Chaves, M., and L. Wirpsa. 1988. Aparecen los Nukak, *Noticias Antropológicas* 89:1–5. Bogotá: Instituto Colombiano de Antropología.

Clastres, P. 1998. *Chronicle of the Guayaki Indians*. New York: Zone Books.

Clement, C. R. 1989. *Origin, domestication and genetic conservation of Amazonian fruit tree species*. Manaus: INPA.

Colinvaux, P., and M. Bush. 1991. The rain-forest ecosystem as a resource for hunting and gathering, *American Anthropologist* 91 (1):153–90.

Collazos, M. E., and M. Mejía. 1987. Fenología y postcosecha de milpesos, *Jessenia bataua* (Mart.) Palmira. Ph. D. dissertation. Universidad Nacional de Colombia, Facultad de Ciencias Agropecuarias, Palmira.

Cormier, L. A. 2003. *Kinship with monkeys: The Guajá foragers of Eastern Amazonia*. New York: Columbia University Press.

Coppens, W. 1975. *Los Cuiva de San Esteban de Capanaparo*. Caracas: Fundación La Salle de Ciencias Naturales.

——— 1983. Los Hoti. In *Los Aborígenes de Venezuela*. Vol. 2. W. Coppens, ed. Caracas: Fundación La Salle, pp. 243–301.

Córdova, L. 1988. Misterio antropológico, *Semana* 315:36–37.

Correa, F. 1987. Makú. In *Introducción a la Colombia Amerindia*. F. Correa, ed. Bogotá: Instituto Colombiano de Antropología, pp. 123–24.

Cremonte, B. 1988–1989. Técnicas alfareras tradicionales en la Puna: Inti-Cancha, *Arqueología Contemporánea* 2 (2):5–29.

Crocker, J. C. 1985. *Vital souls: Bororo cosmology, natural symbolism and shamanism*. Tucson: University of Arizona Press.

Crumley, C. L., ed. 1994. *Historical ecology: Cultural knowledge and changing landscapes*. Santa Fe, NM: School of American Research Press.

David, N., and C. Kramer. 2001. *Ethnoarchaeology in action*. Cambridge: Cambridge University Press.

David, N., and J. A. Sterner. 1999. Wonderful society: The Burgess Shale creatures, Mandara chiefdoms and the nature of prehistory. In *Beyond chiefdoms: Pathways to complexity in Africa*. S. K. McIntosh, ed. Cambridge: Cambridge University Press, pp. 97–109.

David, N., J. A. Sterner, and K. B. Gauva. 1988. Why pots are decorated, *Current Anthropology* 29:365–89.

Dawe, B. 1997. Tiny arrowheads: Toys in the toolkit, *Plains Anthropologist* 42 (161): 303–18.

DeBoer, W. 1987. You are what you don't eat: Yet another look at food taboos in Amazonia. In *Ethnicity and culture*. R. Auger, M. Glass, S. Mac Eachern, and P. McCartney, eds. Calgary: The University of Calgary Archaeological Association, pp. 45–54.

DeBoer, W., and D. Lathrap. 1979. The making and breaking of Shipibo-Conibo Ceramics. In *Ethnoarchaeology: Implications of ethnography for archaeology*. C. Kramer, ed. New York: Columbia University Press, pp. 102–38.

Delfino, D. D. 2001. Of Pircas and the limits of society: Ethnoarchaeology in the Puna, Laguna Blanca, Catamarca, Argentina. In *Ethnoarchaeology of Andean South America: Contributions to archaeological method and theory*. L. Kuznar, ed. Ann Arbor, MI: International Monographs in Prehistory, Ethnoarchaeological Series 4, pp. 116–37.

Descola, P. 1994. *In the society of nature: A native ecology of Amazonia*. Cambridge: Cambridge University Press.

Diehl, W. 1993. Informe sobre la temporada de campo: Atención en salud. Nukak-Makú. Laguna Pavón II-Guaviare. Unpublished report. Santafé de Bogotá: Dirección General de Asuntos Indígenas.

——— 1994. Informe final: Investigación y atención en salud a la comunidad Nukak-Makú. Laguna Pavón II-Guaviare. Unpublished report. Santafé de Bogotá: Dirección General de Asuntos Indígenas.

Dillehay, T. 1998. Felines, patronyms, and history of the Araucanians in the southern Andes. In *Icons of power: Feline symbolism in the Americas*. N. Saunders, ed. London: Routledge, pp. 203–28.

Dobres, M. A. 2000. *Technology and social agency*. Oxford: Blackwell Publishers.

Domínguez, C. 1985. *Amazonia Colombiana*. Bogotá: Editorial del Banco Popular.

Douglas, M. 1957. Animals in Lele religious symbolism, *Africa* 27:46–58.

——— 1966. *Purity and danger*. London: Routledge.

——— 1990. The pangolin revisited: A new approach to animal symbolism. In *Signifying animals: Human meaning in the natural world*. R. G. Willis, ed. London: Unwin Hyman, pp. 25–36.

Dufour, D. L. 1987. Insects as food: A case study from the Northwest Amazon, *American Anthropologists* 89 (2):383–97.

——— 1994. Diet and nutritional status of Amazonian peoples. In *Amazonian Indians: From prehistory to the present. Anthropological perspectives* A. Roosevelt, ed. Tucson: The University of Arizona Press, pp. 151–75.

Dufour, D. L., and W. Wilson. 1994. Characteristics of "wild" plant foods used by indigenous populations in Amazonia. In *Eating on the wild side*. N. Etkin, ed. Tucson: The University of Arizona Press, pp. 114–42.

Duivenvoorden, J., and J. Lips. 1993. *Ecología del paisaje del Medio Caquetá (Memoria explicativa)*. Serie de estudios en la Amazonia colombiana. Vol. IIIA. Santafé de Bogotá: Tropenbos.

Dunnell, R. C. 1980. Evolutionary theory and archaeology. In *Advances in archaeological method and theory*. Vol. 3. M. B. Schiffer, ed. New York: Academic Press, pp. 35–99.

Dyson-Hudson, R., and N. Dyson-Hudson. 1980. Nomadic pastoralism, *Annual Review of Anthropology* 9:15–61.

Dyson-Hudson, R., and E. A. Smith. 1978. Human territoriality: An ecological re-assessment, *American Anthropologist* 80:21–41.

Eisenberg, J. 1981. *The mammalian radiations: An analysis of trends in evolution, adaptation and behavior*. Chicago: University of Chicago Press.

El Espectador. 1966. Nuevos descubrimientos sobre los "Macús": Conocen la agricultura y viven de frutas. Bogotá (Mayo 20), p. 4 A.

Elkin, D., and M. Mondini. 2001. Human and small carnivore gnawing damage on bones: An exploratory study and its archaeological implications. In *Ethnoarchaeology of Andean South America: Contributions to archaeological method and theory*. L. A. Kuznar, ed. Ann Arbor, MI: International Monographs in Prehistory, Ethnoarchaeological Series 4, pp. 255–56.

Ellen, R. 1998. Palms and the prototipicality of trees: Some questions concerning assumptions in the comparative study of categories and labels. In *The social life of trees: Anthropological perspectives on tree symbolism*. L. Rival, ed. Oxford: Berg Publishers, pp. 57–78.

Ember, C. 1975. Residential variation among hunter-gatherers, *Behavior Science Research* 3:199–227.

——— 1978. Myths about hunter-gatherers, *Ethnology* 17:439–48.

Eremites de Oliveira, J. 2001. A história indígena em Mato Grosso do Sul, Brasil: Dilemas e perspectivas, *Revista Territorios e Fronteiras-Prog. De Pós-Grad. Em História-UFMT*. 2 (2):115–24.

Evans, C., and B. Meggers. 1960. Archaeological investigations in British Guiana, *Bulletin of the Bureau of American Ethnology 177*. Washington, DC: Smithsonian Institution.

Fernández Martínez, V. M. 1994. Etnoarqueología una guía de métodos y aplicaciones, *Revista de Dialectología y Tradiciones Populares* 39:137–69.

Fisher, J. W., Jr. 1987. Shadows in the forest: Ethnoarchaeology among the Efe pygmies. Ph.D. dissertation. University of California, Berkeley.

——— 1993. Foragers and farmers: Material expressions of interaction at elephant processing sites in the Ituri Forest, Zaire. In *From bones to behavior: Ethnoarchaeological and experimental contributions to the interpretation of faunal remains*. J. Hudson, ed. Carbondale, IL: Center for Archaeological Investigations. Southern Illinois University at Carbondale. Occasional Paper Nr. 31, pp. 247–62.

Fisher, J. W., Jr., and H. C. Strickland. 1989. Ethnoarchaeology among Efe pygmies, Zaire: Spatial organization of campsites, *American Journal of Physical Anthropology* 78:473–84.

——— 1991. Dwellings and fireplaces: Keys to Efe Pygmy campsite structure. In *Ethnoarchaeological approaches to mobile campsites*. C. Gamble and W. Boismier, eds. Ann Arbor, MI: International Monographs in Prehistory, Ethnoarchaeological Series 1, pp. 215–36.

Fitzhugh, B. 2001. Risk and invention in human technological evolution, *Journal of Anthropological Archaeology* 20:125–67.

Foley, R. 1983. Modelling hunting strategies and inferring predator behaviour from prey attributes. In *Animals and archaeology: 1. Hunters and their prey*. J. Clutton-Brock and C. Grigson, eds. Oxford: BAR International Series 163, pp. 63–76.

Flegenheimer, N., and C. Bayón. 1999. Abastecimiento de rocas en sitios pampeanos tempranos: Recolectando colores. In *Los tres reinos: Prácticas de recolección en el Cono Sur de América*. C. Aschero, A. Korstanje, and P. Vuoto, eds. Tucumán: Ediciones Magna Publicaciones, pp. 95–107.

Franky, C., G. Cabrera, and D. Mahecha. 1995. *Demografía y movilidad socio-espacial de los Nukak*. Santafé de Bogotá: Fundación GAIA.

Freeman, L. G., Jr. 1968. A theoretical framework for interpreting archaeological materials. In *Man the hunter*. R. Lee and I. DeVore, eds. Chicago: Aldine Publishing Company, pp. 262–67.

Frias, I. 1993. Ajuar cerámico de los Piapoco: Un caso de estilo como transmisor de información. In *Contribuciones a la arqueología regional de Venezuela*. F. Fernández and R. Gasson, eds. Colinas de Bello Monte: Fondo Editorial Acta Científica Venezolana, pp. 107–38.

Friedemann, N., and J. Arocha. 1982. *Herederos del jaguar y la anaconda*. Bogotá: Carlos Valencia Editores.

Furst, P. 1973–1974. The roots and continuities of shamanism, *Arts Canada* 184/7: 33–50.

Gamble, C. 1986. *The Palaeolithic settlement of Europe*. Cambridge: Cambridge University Press.

Gamble, C., and W. A. Boismier, eds. 1991. *Ethnoarchaeological approaches to mobile campsites: Hunter-gatherer and the pastoralist case studies*. Ann Arbor, MI: International Monographs in Prehistory, Ethnoarchaeological Series 1.

Gándara, M. 1990. La analogía etnográfica como heurística: Lógica muestreal, dominios ontológicos e historicidad. In *Etnoarqueología: Coloquio Bosch-Gimpera*. Y. Sugiura and M. C. Serra, eds. México: Universidad Autónoma de México. pp. 43–82.

García, L. C. 1988. Etnoarqueología: Manufactura de cerámica en Alto Sapagua. In *Arqueología contemporánea Argentina*. H. Yacobaccio, ed. Buenos Aires: Editorial Búsqueda, pp. 33–58.

———— 1993. Qué nos cuentan las cocinas: Etnoarqueología en Inca Cueva, *Palimpsesto* 3:133–8.

———— 2001. Women at work: A present archaeological view of Azul Pampa herding culture (North West Argentina). In *Ethnoarchaeology of Andean South America: Contributions to archaeological method and theory*. L. Kuznar, ed. Ann Arbor, MI: International Monographs in Prehistory, Ethnoarchaeological Series 4, pp. 202–20.

Garine, I. 1994. The diet and nutrition of human populations. In *Companion encyclopaedia of anthropology*. T. Ingold, ed. London: Routledge, pp. 265–96.

Giacone, A. P. E. 1955. *Pequena gramática e dicionário Português, Ubde-Neheren ou Macú*. Recife: Escola Saleciana de Artes Gráficas.

Gifford, D. 1978. Ethnoarchaeological observations of natural processes affecting cultural material. In *Explorations in ethnoarchaeology*. R. Gould, ed. Albuquerque: University of New Mexico Press, pp. 77–102.

Gifford-González, D. 1993. Gaps in the zooarchaeological analyses of butchery: Is gender an issue? In *From bones to behavior: Ethnoarchaeological and experimental contributions to the interpretation of faunal remains*. J. Hudson, ed. Carbondale, IL: Center for Archaeological Investigations. Southern Illinois University at Carbondale. Occasional Paper Nr. 31, pp. 101–40.

Gilij, P. F. S. 1965. *Ensayo de historia Americana: Fuentes para la historia colonial de Venezuela*. Vols 71–73. Caracas: Academia de Historia. Originally published 1780–1784.

Gnecco, C., and S. Mora. 1997. Late Pleistocene\early Holocene tropical forest occupations at San Isidro and Peña Roja, Colombia, *Antiquity* 71 (273):683–90.

Goldman, I. 1966. *The Cubeo: Indians of the Northwest Amazon*. Illinois Studies in Anthropology Nr. 2. Urbana: The University of Illinois Press.

González, A. R. 1977. *Arte Precolombino de la Argentina: Introducción a su historia cultural*. Buenos Aires: Filmediciones Valero.

——— 1992. *Las placas metálicas de los Andes del Sur: Contribución al estudio de las religiones precolombinas*. Mainz: Verlag Phillipp von Zabern.

González Ruibal, A. 2003. *La experiencia del otro: Una introducción a la etnoarqueología*. Madrid: Editorial Akal.

Gosden, C. 1994. *Social being and time*. Oxford: Blackwell.

——— 1999. *Anthropology and archaeology: A changing relationship*. London: Routledge.

Gould, R. 1968. Living archaeology: The Ngatatjara of western Australia, *Southwestern Journal of Anthropology* 24 (2):101–22.

——— 1969. *Yiwara: Foragers of the Australian desert*. New York: Scribners.

——— 1978a. The anthropology of human residues, *American Anthropologist* 80: 815–35.

——— 1978b. From Tasmania to Tucson: New directions in ethnoarchaeology. In *Explorations in ethnoarchaeology*. R. Gould, ed. Albuquerque: University of New Mexico Press, pp. 1–10.

——— 1980. *Living archaeology*. Cambridge: Cambridge University Press.

Gould, R., and P. Watson. 1982. A dialogue on the meaning and use of analogy in ethnoarchaeological reasoning, *Journal of Anthropological Archaeology* 1: 355–81.

Gould, R., and J. Yellen. 1987. Man the hunted: Determinants of household spacing in desert and tropical foraging societies, *Journal of Anthropological Archaeology* 6:77–103.

Gragson, T. L. 1989. Allocation of time to subsistence and settlement in a Ciri Khonome Pumé village of the Llanos of Apure, Venezuela. Ph.D. dissertation. Department of Anthropology, The Pennsylvania State University.

Greaves, R. 1996. Ethnoarchaeology of wild root collection among savanna foragers of Venezuela. Paper presented at the 54th Annual Plains Anthropological Conference, October 31, Iowa City, Iowa.

——— 1997. Hunting and multifunctional use of bows and arrows: Ethnoarchaeology of technological organization among the Pumé hunters of Venezuela. In *Projectile Technology*. H. Knecht, ed. New York: Plenum Press, pp. 287–320.

Gronnow, B. 1993. Comments on analogy in Danish prehistoric studies. *Norwegian Archaeological Review* 26 (2):79 *Norwegian Archaeological Review* 90.

Gross, D. R. 1975. Protein capture and cultural developments in the Amazon Basin, *American Anthropologist* 77:526–49.

Groube, L. 1989. The taming of the rain forests: A model for Late Pleistocene forest exploitation in New Guinea. In *Foraging and farming: The evolution of plant exploitation*. D. Harris and G. Hillman, eds. London: Unwin Hyman, pp. 292–304.

Gualteros, I. Ms. *Estudio breve sobre la cultura material de los Nukak*. Misión Nuevas Tribus de Colombia.

Guarisma, V. 1974. Los Hoti: Introducción etnolingüística. Graduate degree thesis, Universidad Central de Venezuela.

Guenther, M. 1981. Bushman and hunter-gatherer territoriality, *Zeitschrift für Ethnologie* 106:109–20.

———— 1999. From totemism to shamanism: Hunter-gatherer contributions to world mythology and spirituality. In *The Cambridge encyclopedia of hunter and gatherers.* R. Lee and R. Daly, eds. Cambridge: Cambridge University Press, pp. 426–33.

Gutiérrez, M. A. 2004. Tafonomía del Area Interserrana Bonaerense. Unpublished Ph.D. dissertation. La Plata.

Gutiérrez Herrera, R. 1996. Manejo de los recursos naturales (flora y fauna) por los Nukak. Graduate degree thesis, Universidad Nacional de Colombia.

Haber, A. F. 2001. Observations, definitions and pre-understandings in the ethnoarcheology of pastoralism. In *Ethnoarchaeology of Andean South America: Contributions to archaeological method and theory.* L. Kuznar, ed. Ann Arbor, MI: International Monographs in Prehistory, Ethnoarchaeological Series 4, pp. 31–37.

Hames, R. B., and W. T. Vickers, eds. 1983. *Adaptive responses of Native Amazonians.* New York: Academic Press.

Hammond, G., and N. Hammond. 1981. Child's play: A distorting factor in archaeological distribution, *American Antiquity* 64:634–36.

Harris, D. 1989. An evolutionary continuum of people-plant interaction. In *Foraging and farming: The evolution of plant exploitation.* D. Harris and G. Hillman, eds. London: Unwin Hyman, pp. 11–24.

Harris, M. 1985. *El materialismo cultural.* Madrid: Alianza Editorial.

———— 1990. *Bueno para comer.* Madrid: Alianza Editorial.

Hassan, F. A. 1981. *Demographic archaeology.* New York: Academic Press.

Hawkes, K., K. Hill, and J. O'Connell. 1982. Why hunter gather: Optimal foraging and the Ache of eastern Paraguay, *American Ethnology* 9:379–98.

Hayden, B. 1981. Subsistence and ecological adaptation of modern hunter/gatherers. In *Omnivorous primates: Gathering and hunting in human evolution.* R. S. O. Harding and G. Teleki, eds. New York: Columbia University Press, pp. 344–421.

———— 1995. A new overview of domestication. In *Last hunters, first farmers: New perspectives on the prehistoric transition to agriculture.* T. D. Price and A. B. Gebauer, eds. Santa Fe, NM: School of American Research Press, pp. 273–99.

Haynes, G. 1985. Age profiles in elephant and mammoth bone assemblages, *Quaternary Research* 24:333–45.

———— 1987. Proboscidean die-offs and die-outs: Age profiles in fossil collections, *Journal of Archaeological Science* 14:659–68.

———— 1988a. Longitudinal studies of African elephant death and bone deposits, *Journal of Archaeological Science* 15:131–57.

———— 1988b. Mass death sites and serial predation: Comparative taphonomic studies of modern large mammal death sites, *Journal of Archaeological Science* 15:219–35.

———— 1991. *Mammoths, mastodons, and elephants: Biology, behavior, and the fossil record.* Cambridge: Cambridge University Press.

Headland, T. 1987. The wild yam question: How well could independent hunter-gatherer live in a tropical rainforest environment? *Human Ecology* 15 (4):463–91.

Headland, T., and R. Bailey. 1991. Introduction: Have hunter-gatherers lived in tropical rain forest independently of agriculture? *Human Ecology* 19 (2):115–22.

Hecht, S. B., and D. A. Posey. 1989. Preliminary results on soil management techniques of the Kayapó Indians, *Advances in Economic Botany* 7:174–88.

Heckenberger, M. 1996. War and peace in the shadow of empire: Sociopolitical change in the Upper Xingu of Southeastern Amazonia, ca. A.D. 1400–2000. Ph.D. dissertation. University of Pittsburgh. University Microfilms, Ann Arbor.

Heckenberger, M., E. G. Neves, and J. B. Petersen. 1998. De onde surgem os modelos? As origem e expansões Tupi na Amazônia Central, *Revista de Antropología* 41 (1): 69–96. São Paulo, USP.

Heckenberger, M., J. Petersen, and E. G. Neves. 1999. Village size and permanence in Amazonia: Two archaeological examples from Brazil, *American Antiquity* 10 (4): 353–76.

Henderson, A., G. Galeano, and R. Bernal. 1995. *Field guide to the palms of the Americas.* Princeton, NJ: Princeton University Press.

Henley, P., M.-C. Mattei-Müller, and H. Reid. 1994–1996. Cultural and linguistic affinities of the foraging people of Northern Amazonia: A new perspective, *Antropológica* 83:3–38.

Henry, J. 1941. *Jungle people: A Kaingáng tribe of the highlands of Brazil.* New York: Vintage Books.

Hernando Gonzalo, A. 1995. La etnoarqueología hoy: Una vía eficaz de aproximación al pasado, *Trabajos de Prehistoria* 52 (2):15–30.

——— 1999. El Espacio no es necesariamente un lugar: en torno al concepto de espacio y a sus implicaciones en el estudio de la Prehistoria, *Arqueología Espacial* 21:7–27.

Herndon, W. L. 1851. *Exploration of the Valley of the Amazon.* Made under Direction of the Navy Department by Wm. Lewis and Lardner Gibbon, part I. Washington, DC.

Hewlett, B. 1995. Cultural diversity among African pygmies. In *Cultural diversity among twentieth-century foragers: An African perspective.* S. Kent, ed. Cambridge: Cambridge University Press, p. 215–44.

Higgs, E. S, and M. R. Jarman. 1972. The origin of animal and plant husbandry. In *Papers in economic prehistory.* E. S. Higgs, ed. Cambridge: Cambridge University Press, pp. 3–13.

Higham, C. 1995. The transition to rice cultivation in Southeast Asia. In *Last hunters, first farmers: New perspectives on the prehistoric transition to agriculture.* T. D. Price and A. B. Gebauer, eds. Santa Fe, NM: School of American Research Press, pp. 127–56.

Hill, K., and A. M. Hurtado. 1995. *Ache life history: The ecology and demography of a foraging people.* New York: Aldine de Gruyter.

Hodder, I., ed. 1982. *Symbols in actions: Ethnoarchaeological studies of material culture.* Cambridge: Cambridge University Press.

Hodder, I. 1986. *Reading the past: Current approaches to interpretation in archaeology.* Cambridge: Cambridge University Press.

——— 1987. The Meaning of discard: Ash and domestic space in Baringo. In *Method and theory for activity area research.* S. Kent, ed. New York: Columbia University Press, pp. 424–49.

——— 1990. *The domestication of Europe.* Oxford: Blackwell.

Holmberg, A. 1950. *Nomads of the Long Bow: The Siriono of Eastern Bolivia.* Washington, DC: Smithsonian Institution, Institute of Social Anthropology, Publication Nr. 10.

Hosler, D. 1996. Technical choices, social categories and meaning among the Andean potter of Las Animas, *Journal of Material Culture* 1 (1):63–92.

Hudson, J. 1990. Spatial analysis of faunal remains in hunter-gatherer camps. In *Etnoarqueología: Coloquio Bosch-Gimpera*. Y. Sugiura and M. C. Serra, eds. México: Universidad Autónoma de México, pp. 219–40.

Hudson, J., ed. 1993, *From bones to behavior: Ethnoarchaeological and experimental contributions to the interpretation of faunal remains*. Carbondale, IL: Center for Archaeological Investigations. Southern Illinois University at Carbondale. Occasional Paper Nr. 31.

Hugh-Jones, S. 1979. *The palm and the Pleiades: Initiation and cosmology in Northwest Amazonia*. Cambridge: Cambridge University Press.

Hurtado, M. A., and K. R. Hill. 1986. The Cuiva: Hunter-gatherers of Western Venezuela, *AnthroQuest* 36:14–23.

Hutterer, K. 1983. The natural and cultural history of Southeast Asian agriculture: Ecological and evolutionary considerations, *Anthropos* 78:169–212.

IANTC (Informe Asociación Nuevas Tribus de Colombia). 1990a. Informe de actividades julio-agosto-septiembre. Bogotá: División de Asuntos Indígenas (unpublished).

———— 1990b. Informe de actividades octubre-noviembre-diciembre. Bogotá: División de Asuntos Indígenas (unpublished).

———— 1992a. Informe de actividades enero-febrero-marzo. Bogotá: Dirección General de Asuntos Indígenas (unpublished).

———— 1992b. Informe de actividades abril-mayo-junio. Bogotá: Dirección General de Asuntos Indígenas (unpublished).

———— 1992c. Informe de actividades julio-agosto-septiembre. Bogotá: Dirección General de Asuntos Indígenas (unpublished).

———— 1992d. Informe de actividades octubre-noviembre-diciembre. Bogotá: Dirección General de Asuntos Indígenas (unpublished).

———— 1993. Informe de actividades octubre-noviembre-diciembre. Bogotá: Dirección General de Asuntos Indígenas (unpublished).

Ingerson, A. 1994. Tracking and testing the nature/culture dichotomy in practice. In *Historical ecology: Cultural knowledge and changing landscapes*. C. Crumley, ed. Santa Fe, NM: School of American Research Press, pp. 43–66.

Ingold, T. 1994. Animals and society: Changing perspectives. In *Animals and human society: Changing perspectives*. A. Manning and J. Serpell, eds. London: Routledge, pp. 1–10.

———— 1996a. The optimal forager and economic man. In *Nature and society: Anthropological perspectives*. P. Descola and G. Palsson, eds. London: Routledge, pp. 25–44.

———— 1996b. Hunting and Gathering as ways of perceiving the environment. In *Redefining nature: Ecology, culture and domestication*. R. Ellen and K. Fukui, eds. Oxford: Berg Publishers, pp. 117–55.

———— 2000. *The perception of the environment: Essays in livelihood, dwelling and skill*. London: Routledge.

Jackson, J. 1983. *The fish people*. New York: Cambridge University Press.

———— 1991. Hostile encounter between Nukak and Tukanoans: Changing ethnic identity in the Vaupés, *The Journal of Ethnic Studies* XIX (2):17–39.

Jangoux, J. 1971. Observations on the Hotï Indians of Venezuela. Unpublished.

Johnson, E. 1985. Current developments in bone technology, *Advances in Archaeological Method and Theory* 8:157–235.

Johnson, M. 1999. *Archaeological theory: An introduction*. Oxford: Blackwell Publishers.

Jones, K. 1984. Hunting and scavenging by early hominids: A study in archaeological method and theory. Unpublished Ph.D. dissertation. Department of Anthropology, University of Utah, Salt Lake City.

——— 1993. The archaeological structure of a short-term camp. In *From bones to behaviour: Ethnoarchaeological and experimental contributions to the interpretation of faunal remains*. J. Hudson, ed. Carbondale, IL: Center for Archaeological Investigations. Southern Illinois University at Carbondale. Occasional Paper Nr. 31, pp. 101–40.

Jones, R. 1977. The Tasmanian paradox. In *Stone tools as cultural markers: Change, evolution and complexity*. R. V. S. Wright, ed. Atlantic Highlands, NJ: Humanities Press, pp. 189–204.

——— 1978. Why did the Tasmanians stop eating fish? In *Explorations in ethnoarchaeology*. R. A. Gould, ed. Albuquerque: University of New Mexico Press, pp. 11–48.

Jones, R., and B. Meehan. 1989. Plant foods of the Gidjingali: Ethnographic and archaeological perspectives from northern Australia on tuber and seed exploitation. In *Foraging and farming: The evolution of plants exploitation*. D. R. Harris and G. C. Hillman, eds. London: Unwin Hyman, pp. 120–35.

Jones, S. 1997. *The archaeology of ethnicity: Constructing identities in the past and present*. London: Routledge.

Joyce, R. A., and S. D. Gillespie, eds. 2000. *Beyond kinship: Social and material reproduction in house societies*. Philadelphia: University of Pennsylvania Press.

Kaplan, H., and K. Hill. 1992. The evolutionary ecology of food acquisition. In *Evolutionary ecology and human behaviour*. E. Smith and B. Winterhalder, eds. New York: Aldine de Gruyter, pp. 167–202.

Karsten, R. 1968. *The civilization of the South American Indians: With special reference to magic and religion*. London: Dawsons of Pall Mall.

Kelly, R. 1983. Hunter-gatherer mobility strategies, *Journal of Anthropological Research* 39 (3):277–306.

——— 1995. *The foraging spectrum*. Washington, DC: Smithsonian Institution Press.

Kensinger, K. 1981. Food taboos as markers of age categories in Cashinahua: Food taboos in Lowlands South America. In *Working papers of South American Indians, No. 3*. K. Kensinger and W. H. Kracke, eds. Bennington, VT: Bennington College, pp. 157–71.

Kensinger, K., and W. H. Kracke, eds. 1981. Food taboos in Lowlands South America. In *Working papers of South American Indians*. Bennington, VT: Bennington College.

Kent, S. 1984. *Analyzing activity areas: An ethnoarchaeological study of the use of the space*. Albuquerque: University of New Mexico Press.

——— 1987. *Method and theory for activity area research: An ethnoarchaeological approach*. New York: Columbia University Press.

——— 1990. A cross-cultural study of segmentation architecture, and the use of space. In *Domestic architecture and the use of space: An interdisciplinary cross-cultural study*. S. Kent, ed. Cambridge: Cambridge University Press, pp. 172–252.

——— 1993. Variability in faunal assemblages: The influence of hunting skill, sharing, dogs, and mode of cooking on faunal remains at a sedentary Kalahari community, *Journal of Anthropological Archaeology* 12:323–85.

Kent, S., and H. Vierich. 1989. The myth of ecological determinism: Anticipated mobility and site spatial organization. In *From hunters to farmers: The causes and consequences of food production in Africa*. J. Clark and S. Brandt, eds. Berkeley and Los Angeles: University of California Press, pp. 96–130.

Kerbis, P., J. R. Wrangham, M. Carter, and M. Hauser. 1993. A contribution to tropical rain forest taphonomy: Retrieval and documentation of chimpanzee remains from Kibale Forest, Uganda, *Journal of Human Evolution* 25:485–514.

Kiltie, R. A.1980. Comments to Ross, *Current Anthropology* 21 (4):541–44.

King, F. 1994. Interpreting wild plant food in the archaeological record. In *Eating on the wild side*. N. L. Etkin, ed. Tucson: The University of Arizona Press, pp. 185–209.

Klein, R. G. 1976. The mammalian fauna of the Klasies River mouth sites, southern Cape Province, South Africa, *South African Archaeological Bulletin* 31:75–98.

Koch-Grünberg, T. 1906. Die Makú, *Anthropos* 1:877–906.

———— 1995 [1909]. *Dos años entre los indios*. Bogotá: Universidad Nacional. Colombia.

Kozák, V., D. Baxter, L. Williamson, and R. L. Carneiro. 1979. *The Héta Indians: Fish in a dry pond*. Anthropological Papers of the American Museum of Natural History 55 (6). New York: American Museum of Natural History.

Kricher, J. 1989. *The neotropical companion*. Princeton, NJ: Princeton University Press.

Kroll, E., and T. D. Price, eds. 1991. *The interpretation of archaeological spatial patterning*. New York: Plenum Press.

Kuznar, L. A. 1995. *Awatimarka: The ethnoarchaeology of an Andean herding community*. Forth Worth, TX: Harcourt Brace College Publishers.

———— 2001a. Introduction to Andean ethnoarchaeology. In *Ethnoarchaeology of Andean South America: Contributions to archaeological method and theory*. L. Kuznar, ed. Ann Arbor, MI: International Monographs in Prehistory, Ethnoarchaeological Series 4, pp. 1–18.

———— 2001b. An introduction to Andean religious ethnoarchaeology: Preliminary results and future directions. In *Ethnoarchaeology of Andean South America: Contributions to archaeological method and theory*. L. Kuznar, ed. Ann Arbor, MI: International Monographs in Prehistory, Ethnoarchaeological Series 4, 38–66.

Laden, G. 1992. Ethnoarchaeology and the land use ecology of the Efe (pygmies) of the Ituri rainforest, Zaire. Ph.D. dissertation. Harvard University, Anthropology Department.

Laming-Emperaire, A., M. J. Menezes, A. D. Margarida. 1978. O trabalho da pedra entre os Xetá da Serra dos Dourados, Estado do Paraná. In *Coletânea de estudos em Homenagem a Anette Laming-Emperaire*. Coleção Museu Paulista, Série Ensaios, Vol. 2, 19–82.

Lanata, J. L. 1993. Evolución, espacio y adaptación en grupos cazadores-recolectores, *Revista do Museu de Arqueologia e Etnologia* 3:3–15.

Landals, A. 1990. The Maple Leaf Site: Implications of the analysis of small scale bison kills. In *Hunters of the recent past*. L. B. Davis and B. O. K. Reeves, eds. London: Unwin Hyman, pp. 122–51.

Lathrap, D. 1968. The "hunting" economies of the tropical forest zone of South America: An attempt at historical perspective. In *Man the hunter*. R. Lee and I. DeVore, eds. Chicago: Aldine Publishing Company, pp. 23–48.

Lathrap, D. 1970. *The Upper Amazon, ancient people and places*. Series Nr. 70. London: Thames and Hudson.

Layton, R. 1992. Ethnographic analogy and the two archaeological paradigms. In *Ancient images, ancient thought: The archaeology of identity*. S. Goldsmith et al., eds. Proceedings of the 23rd Annual Chacmool Conference. Calgary: Archaeological Association, University of Calgary, pp. 211–21.

Leach, E. 1973. Concluding address. In *The Exploration of culture change: Models in prehistory*. C. Renfrew, ed. London: Duckworth, pp. 761–71.

―――― 1977. A view from the bridge. In *Archaeology and anthropology*. M. Sriggs, ed. Oxford: BAR Supplementary Series, pp. 161–76.

Lee, R. 1979. *The !Kung San*. Cambridge: Cambridge University Press.

―――― 1984. *The Dobe !Kung*. New York: Holt, Rinehart and Winston.

―――― 1992. Art, science or politics? The crisis in hunter gatherer studies, *American Anthropologist* 94:31–54.

―――― 1999. Hunter-gatherer studies and the millennium: A look forward (and back). Eighth International Conference on Hunting and Gathering Societies: Foraging and Post-Foraging Societies. Japan: National Museum of Ethnology.

Lee, R., and R. Daly. 1999. Introduction: Foragers and others. In *Cambridge encyclopedia of hunters and gatherers*. R. Lee and R. Daly, eds. Cambridge: Cambridge University Press, pp. 1–433.

Lee, R., and I. DeVore, eds. 1968. *Man the hunter*. Chicago: Aldine Publishing Company.

Lemonnier, P. 1992. *Elements for anthropology of technology*. Anthropological Papers, Museum of Anthropology No. 88. Ann Arbor, MI.

Lemonnier, P., ed. 1993. *Technological choices: Transformation in material cultures since the Neolithic*. London: Routledge.

Lévi-Strauss, C. 1962. *Totemism*. Boston: Beacon Press.

―――― 1963. *Structural anthropology*. New York: Basic Books.

―――― 1969. *The raw and the cooked*. New York: Harper and Row.

Longacre, W. A. 1981. Kalinga pottery: An ethnoarchaeological study. In *Pattern of the past: Studies in honour of David Clarke*. I. Hodder, G. Isaac, and N. Hammond, eds. Cambridge: Cambridge University Press, pp. 49–66.

Lupo, K. 1994. Butchering marks and carcass acquisition strategies: Distinguishing hunting from scavenging in archaeological context, *Journal of Archaeological Science* 21:827–37.

―――― 1995. Hadza bone assemblages and hyena attrition: An ethnographic example of the influence of cooking and mode of discard on the intensity of scavenger ravaging, *Journal of Anthropological Archaeology* 14:288–314.

Lyman, R. 1987. Archaeofaunas and butchery studies: A taphonomic perspective, *Advances in archaeological method and theory* 10:249–337.

―――― 1994. *Vertebrate taphonomy: Cambridge manuals in archaeology*. Cambridge: Cambridge University Press.

Lyon, P. 1970. Differential bone destruction: An ethnographic example, *American Antiquity* 35:213–15.

Malinowski, B. 1935. *Coral gardens and their magic*. London: Routledge.

Marcus, G., and M. Fisher. 1986. *Anthropology as cultural critique: An experimental moment in the human sciences*. Chicago: University of Chicago Press.

von Martius, K. P. 1867. *Belträge zur Ethnographie und Sprachenkunde Amerikas zumal Brasiliens*. Vol. I. Leipzig, p. 547.

McEwan, C., C. Barreto, and E. Neves. 2001. *Unknown Amazon*. London: The British Museum Press.

McGovern, W. M. 1927. *Jungle paths and Inca ruins*. New York: The Century Co.

McGuire, R. 1992. *A Marxist archaeology*. San Diego, CA: Academic Press.

McGuire, R. and M. Schiffer. 1983. A theory of architectural design, *Journal of Anthropological Archaeology* 2:277–303.

McKellar, J. A.1983. *Correlates and the explanation of distributions*. Tucson: University of Arizona Anthropology Club, Atlalt. Occasional Paper Nr. 4.

Meggers, B. 1971. *Amazonia: Man and culture in a counterfeit paradise*. Chicago: Aldine Publishing Company.

———— 1996. *Amazonia: Man and culture in a counterfeit paradise*. Washington, DC: Smithsonian Institution Press.

———— 2003. Natural versus anthropogenic sources of Amazonian biodiversity: The continuing quest for El Dorado. In *How landscapes change*. G. A. Bradshaw and P. A. Marquet, eds. Berlin: Springer-Verlag, pp. 89–107.

Meggers, B., and C. Evans.1957. Archaeological investigation at the mouth of the Amazon. *Bureau of American Ethnology*. Bulletin 167. Washington, DC: Smithsonian Institution.

Mengoni Goñalons, G. 1999. *Cazadores de Guanaco de la Estepa Patagónica*. Buenos Aires: Sociedad Argentina de Antropología.

Mercader, J. 1997. Bajo el techo forestal: La evolución del poblamiento en el bosque ecuatorial del Ituri. Zaire. Ph.D. dissertation. Universidad Complutense. Departamento de Prehistoria. Madrid.

Metcalfe, D., and K. R. Barlow. 1992. A model for exploring the optimal trade-off between field processing and transport, *American Anthropologist* 94:340–56.

Metcalfe, D., and K. T. Jones. 1988. A reconsideration of animal body-part utility indices, *American Antiquity* 53 (3):486–504.

Métraux, A. 1948. The hunting and gathering people of the Rio Negro Basin. In *Handbook of South American Indians*. Vol. 3. *The tropical forest tribes* J. H. Steward, ed. Washington, DC: Smithsonian Institution, pp. 861–68.

Miller, E. 1992. *Arqueología, ambiente, desenvolvimiento*. Brasilia: Electronorte/PNUD.

Miller, G. 1977. An introduction to the ethnoarchaeology of Andean camelids. Unpublished Ph.D. dissertation. University of California, Berkeley.

Miller, Jr., T. 1975. Tecnología lítica arqueológica (Arqueología Experimental no Brasil), *Anais do Museu de Antropología* 7:5–135. Florianópolis.

———— 1979. Stonework of the Xetá Indians of Brazil. In *Lithic use—Wear analysis*. B. Hayden, ed. New York: Academic Press, pp. 401–09.

———— 1981–1982. Etnoarqueologia: Implicações para o Brasil, *Archivo do Museu de História Natural* VI–VII: 293–310.

Milton, K.1984. Protein and carbohydrate resources of the Makú Indians of northwestern Amazonia, *American Anthropologist* 86:7–25.

———— 1997. Real men don't eat deer, *Discovery* June: 46–53.

Miotti, L. 1998. *Zooarqueología de la Meseta Central y Costa de Santa Cruz. Un enfoque de las estrategias adaptativas aborígenes y los paleoambientes*. San Rafael, Mendoza: Museo Municipal de Historia Natural.

Miracle, P., and N. Milner, eds. 2002. *Consuming passions and patterns of consumption*. Cambridge: McDonald Institute Monographs.

Molano, A. 1987. *Selva adentro. Una historia oral de la colonización del Guaviare*. Bogotá: El Ancora Editores.

Mondragón, H. Ms. *Estudio para el establecimiento de un programa de defensa de la comunidad indígena Nukak*. Informe final presentado al programa de Rehabilitación Nacional (PNR) de la Presidencia de la República de Colombia. Santafé de Bogotá, Colombia. Unpublished Report. 1991.

——— 2000. La familia Tukano-Makú. www7.gratisweb.com/nukakwa/Fmaku.htm.

Morán, E.1993. *Through Amazonian eyes: The human ecology of Amazonian populations*. Iowa City: University of Iowa Press.

Morcote-Ríos, G., and R. Bernal. 2001. Remains of palm (Palmae) at archaeological sites in the New World: A review, *The Botanical Review* 67 (3):309–50.

Morcote-Ríos, G., G. Cabrera, D. Mahecha, C. E. Franky, and I. Cavelier. 1998. Las Palmas entre los Grupos Cazadores-Recolectores de la Amazónia Colombiana, *Caldasia* 20 (1):57–74.

Morcote-Ríos, G., I. Cavelier, D. Mahecha, C. E. Franky, and G. Cabrera. 1996. El manejo milenario de las palmas amazónicas: de los recolectores precerámicos a los Nukak, *CESPEDESIA* 21 (67):89–117.

Morey, R., and D. Metzger. 1974. *The Guahibo: People of the Savanna*. Acta Ethnologica et Linguistica Nr. 31. Series Americana 7. Wien.

Morphy, H. 1995. Landscape and the reproduction of the ancestral past. In *The anthropology of landscape: Perspectives on place and space*. E. Hirsch and M. O'Hanlon, eds. Oxford: Clarendon Press, pp. 184–209.

Moser, B. 1971. *The wars of the goods*. Granada Television International. Film Incorporated Video, 1991, Illinois: Chicago.

Münzel, M. 1969–1972. Notas preliminares sobre os Kaborí (Makú entre o Rio Negro e o Japurá, *Revista de Antropología* 17–20 (1):137–82.

Murray, P. 1980. Discard location: The ethnographic data, *American Antiquity* 45: 490–502.

Musters, G. 1871. *At home with the Patagonians: A year wandering over untrodden ground from the strait of Magellan to the Rio Negro*. London: Murray.

Myers, F. R. 1986. *Pintupi country, Pintupi self*. Washington, DC: Smithsonian Institution Press.

——— 1988. Critical trends in the study of hunter gatherers, *Annual Review of Anthropology* 17:261–68.

Nami, H. 1994. A young flintknapper from Misiones, Argentina, *Journal of Lithic Studies* 1:21–25.

Nasti, A. 1993. Etnoarqueología de los residuos humanos: Análisis de estructuras de sitios de asentamientos de pastores de la Puna Meridional Argentina, *Arqueología* 3:9–39.

Nelson, M. 1992. The study of technological organization. In *Archaeological method and theory*. Vol. 3. M. Schiffer, ed. Tucson: The University of Arizona Press, pp. 57–100.

Neves, E. G. 1999. Changing perspectives in Amazonian archaeology. In *Archaeology in Latin America*. G. Politis and B. Alberti, eds. London: Routledge, pp. 216–43.

Nielsen, A. 1994. Como es arriba es abajo: Evaluación crítica de las posibilidades del análisis de microartefactos para la inferencia arqueológica, *Arqueología* 4:9–41.

—— 1998. Tráfico de caravanas en el sur de Bolivia: observaciones etnográficas e implicancias arqueológicas, *Relaciones de la Sociedad Argentina de Antropología* XXII–XXIII:139–78.

—— 2001. Ethnoarchaeological perspectives on caravan trade in the south-central Andes. In *Ethnoarchaeology of Andean South America: Contributions to archaeological method and theory*. L. Kuznar, ed. Ann Arbor, MI: International Monographs in Prehistory, Ethnoarchaeological Series 4, pp. 163–201.

Nordenskiöld, E. 1922. *Indianer und Weisse in Nordostbolivien*. Stuttgart: Strecker und Schröder Verlag.

O'Brien, M. J., ed. 1996. *Evolutionary archaeology: Theory and application*. Salt Lake City: University of Utah Press.

O'Brien, M. J., and T. D. Holland. 1995. Behavioural archaeology and the extended phenotype. In *Expanding archaeology*. J. Skibo, W. H. Walker, and A. E. Nielsen, eds. Salt Lake City: University of Utah Press, pp. 143–61.

O'Connell, J. F. 1987. Alyawara site structure and its archaeological implications, *American Antiquity* 52 (1):74–108.

—— 1995. Ethnoarchaeology needs a general theory of behaviour, *Journal of Archaeological Research* 3 (3):205–55.

O'Connell, J. F., K. Hawkes, and N. Blurton-Jones. 1988a. Hadza hunting, butchering and bone transport and their archaeological implications, *Journal of Anthropological Research* 44 (2):113–61.

—— 1988b. Hadza scavenging implications for Plio/Pleistocene hominid subsistence, *Current Anthropology* 29 (2):356–63.

—— 1990. Reanalysis of large mammal body part transport among the Hadza, *Journal of Archaeological Science* 17:301–16.

—— 1991. Distribution of refuse-producing activities at Hadza residential base camps: Implications for analyses of archaeological site structure. In *The interpretation of archaeological spatial patterning*. E. Kroll and T. D. Price, eds. New York: Plenum Press, pp. 61–76.

—— 1992. Patterns in the distribution, site structure and assemblage composition of Hadza kill-butchering sites, *Journal of Archaeological Science* 19:319–45.

O'Connell, J. F., and B. Marshall. 1989. Analysis of kangaroo body part transport among the Alyawara of Central Australia, *Journal of Archaeological Science* 16:393–405.

O'Connor, T. 1996. A critical overview of archaeological animal bone studies, *World Archaeology* 28 (1):5–19.

—— 2000. *The archaeology of animal bones*. Gloucestershire.: Sutton.

Oliver, J. 2002. The archaeology of forest foraging and agricultural production in Amazonia. In *Unknown Amazon*. C. McEwan, C. Barreto, and E. G. Neves, eds. London: The British Museum Press, pp. 50–85.

Oswalt, W. H. 1974. Ethnoarchaeology. In *Ethnoarchaeology* C. W. Clewlow, ed. Berkeley and Los Angeles: University of California, pp. 3–26.

Owens, D., and B. Hayden. 1997. Prehistoric rites of passage: A comparative study of transegalitarian hunter-gatherers, *Journal of Anthropological Archaeology* 16:121–61.

Parckington, J., and G. Mills. 1991. From space to space: The architecture and social organisation of Southern African mobile communities. In *Ethnoarchaeological approaches to mobile campsites: Hunter-gatherer and pastoralist case studies*. C. S. Gamble and W. A. Boismier, eds. Ann Arbor, MI: International Monographs in Prehistory. Ethnoarchaeological Series 1, pp. 355–70.

Park, R. 1998. Size counts: The miniature archaeology of childhood in Inuit societies, *Antiquity* 72 (276):269–81.

Parker-Pearson, M., and C. Richardson. 1992. *Architecture and order*. London: Routledge.

Pfaffenberger, B. 1992. Social anthropology of technology, *Annual Review of Anthropology* 21:491–16.

Pickering, M. 1994. The physical landscape as a social landscape: A Garawa example, *Archaeology Oceania* 29:149–61.

Pineda Camacho, R. 1974. La gente del hacha: Breve historia de la tecnología según una tribu Amazónica, *Revista Colombiana de Antropología* XVIII: 437–77.

Politis, G. 1992. La Arquitectura del Nomadismo en la Amazonía Colombiana, *Proa* 412:11–20.

———— 1996a. Moving to produce: Nukak mobility and settlement patterns in Amazonia, *World Archaeology* 27 (3):492–11.

———— 1996b. *Nukak*. Santafé de Bogotá: Instituto Amazónico de Investigaciones Científicas SINCHI.

———— 1998. Arqueología de la infancia: Una perspectiva etnoarqueológica, *Trabajos de Prehistoria* 52 (2):5–20.

———— 1999a. Plant exploitation among the Nukak hunter gatherers of Amazonia: Between ecology and ideology. In *The prehistory of food: Appetites for change*. C. Gosden and J. Hather, eds. London: Routledge, pp. 99–125.

———— 1999b. La actividad infantil en la producción del registro arqueológico de cazadores recolectores, *Revista do Museu de Arqueología e Etnología* Suplemento 3: 263–84.

Politis, G., and A. Jaimes. Ms. Informe de las investigaciones etnoarqueológicas realizadas entre los Hotï (Dpto. de Amazonas, Venezuela) en enero-febrero de 2002. Unpublished report. 2002.

Politis, G., and G. Martínez. 1992. La subsistencia invernal de un grupo Nukak de la Amazonía Colombiana. Paper presented at the VI Congreso Nacional de Antropología Colombiana, Santafé de Bogotá, July 1992.

———— 1996. La cacería, el procesamiento de las presas y los tabúes alimenticios. In *Nukak*. G. Politis, ed. Santafé de Bogotá: Instituto Amazónico de Investigaciones Científicas SINCHI, pp. 213–79.

Politis, G., G. Martínez, and B. Marshall. 1995. Preliminary bone analyses from 1991–1992 field seasons among the Nukak (Colombian Amazon). Unpublished report submitted to the British Council-Fundación Antorchas. Bs. As.

Politis, G., and N. Saunders. 2002. Archaeological correlates of ideological activity: Food taboos and the spirit-animals in an Amazonian hunter-gatherer society. In *Consuming passions and patterns of consumption*. P. Miracle and N. Milner, eds. Cambridge: McDonald Institute for Archaeological Research, pp. 113–30.

Posey, D. A. 1984a. A preliminary report on diversified management of tropical forest by Kayapó Indians, *Advances in Economic Botany* 1:112–27.

———— 1984b. Keepers of the campo, *Garden* 8:8–12.

Posey, D. A. 1994. Environmental and social implications of pre- and postcontact situations on Brazilian Indians. In *Amazonian Indians: From prehistory to the present.* A. Roosevelt. Tucson: University of Arizona Press, 271–86.

Pozzobon, J. 1983. Isolamento e endogamia: Observações sobre a organização social dos indios Maku. M.A. dissertation. Universidade Federal do Rio Grande do Sul, Porto Alegre, Brazil.

——— 1992. Parenté et démographie chez les indies Maku. Ph.D. dissertation. Universite Paris VII, Paris, France.

Preloran, J. 1996. *Damasio Caitruz.* Film. Fondo Nacional de la Artes- Universidad de Tucumán.

Price, B. 1982. Cultural materialism: A theoretical review, *American Antiquity* 47 (4):709–41.

Price, T., and J. Brown. 1985. Aspects of hunter-gatherer complexity. In *Prehistoric hunter-gatherers: The emergence of cultural complexity.* T. Price and J. Brown, eds. New York: Academic Press, pp. 3–20.

Price, T. Douglas, and A. B. Gebauer. 1995. New perspectives on the transition to agriculture. In *Last hunters first farmers: New perspectives on the prehistoric transition to agriculture.* T. D. Price and A. B. Gebauer, eds. Santa Fe, NM: School of American Research Press, pp. 3–19.

Purseglove, J. 1968. *Tropical crops: Dicotyledons 2.* New York: John Wiley and Sons, Inc.

——— 1972. *Tropical crops: Monocotyledons 2.* London: Logmangroup Limited.

Ravn, M. 1993. Discussions: Analogy in Danish prehistoric studies, *Norwegian Archaeological Review* 26 (2):59–60.

Reichel-Dolmatoff, G. 1967. A brief report on urgent ethnological research in the Vaupes area, Colombia, South America, *Bulletin of International Committee on Urgent Anthropological Research* 9:53–62.

——— 1968. *Desana: Simbolismo de los Indios Tukano del Vaupes.* Bogotá: Departamento de Antropología de la Universidad de Los Andes.

——— 1971. *Amazonian cosmos.* Chicago: Chicago University Press.

——— 1972. The feline motif in prehistoric San Agustín sculpture. In *The cult of the feline.* E. Benson, ed. Washington, DC: Dumbarton Oaks, pp. 51–68.

——— 1975. *The shaman and the jaguar: A study of narcotic drugs among the Indians of Colombia.* Philadelphia: Temple University Press.

——— 1976. Cosmology as ecological analysis: A view from the rainforest, *Man* 11:307–18.

——— 1978. Desana animal categories, food restrictions, and the concept of color energies, *Journal of Latin American Lore* 4 (2):243–91.

——— 1985. Tapir avoidance in the Colombian Northwest Amazon. In *Animal myths and metaphors in South America.* G. Urton, ed. Salt Lake City: University of Utah Press, pp. 107–43.

——— 1991. *Indios de Colombia: Mundos vividos—mundos concebidos.* Santafé de Bogotá: Villegas Editores.

——— 1996. *The forest within: A world-view of the Tukano Amazonian Indians.* Devon: Themos Books.

Reichel-Dussan, E. 1989. La danta y el delfín: Manejo ambiental e intercambio entre duendes de maloca y chamanes. El caso Yukuna-Matapí (Amazonas). *Revista de Antropología* 5 (1–2):1–45. Bogotá: Universidad de Los Andes.

Reichel-Dussan, E. 1995. Comments to the historical anthropology of text, Neil Whitehead (author), *Current Anthropology* 36 (1):66–67.

Reid, H. 1979. Some aspects of movement, growth, and change among the Hupdu Makú Indians of Brazil. Ph.D. dissertation. Cambridge University Press. Cambridge.

Reigadas, M. del C. 2001. Herding today, lassoing the past, herding yesterday: Toward the ancients (livestock specialization and variability in pastoral contexts). In *Ethnoarchaeology of Andean South America: Contributions to archaeological method and theory*. L. Kuznar, ed. Ann Arbor, MI: International Monographs in Prehistory, Ethnoarchaeological Series 4, pp. 221–42.

Reina, L. Ms. *Informe de comisión entre la comunidad indígena Nukak, Corregimiento de Calamar, Guaviare*. Santafé de Bogotá: Instituto Colombiano de Antropología.

——— 1986. Análisis fonológico, lengua Juhupde-Makú, Amazonas. Unpublished M.A. dissertation. Bogotá. Universidad de Los Andes.

——— 1990. Actividades relacionadas con los Nukak, *Mopa-Mopa* 5:17–25.

——— 1992. Los Nukak: Cacería, recolección y nomadismo en la Amazonia. In *Diversidad es riqueza*. Santafé de Bogotá: ICAN, pp. 62–64.

Reitz, E., and E. S. Wing. 1999. *Zooarchaeology*. Cambridge: Cambridge University Press.

Ridington, R. 1982. Technology, world view, and adaptive strategy in a northern hunting society, *Canadian Review of Sociology and Anthropology* 19 (4):469–81.

Rindos, D. 1984. *The origins of agriculture: An evolutionary perspective*. New York: Academic Press.

——— 1989. Darwinism and its role in the explanation of domestication. In *Foraging and farming: The evolution of plant exploitation*. D. Harris and G. Hillman, eds. London: Unwin Hyman, pp. 29–39.

Rival, L. 1996. *Hijos del Sol. Padres del jaguar: Los Huaorani de ayer y hoy*. Quito: Biblioteca Abya-Yala.

——— 1998a. Trees, from symbols of life and regeneration to political artefacts. In *The social life of trees: Anthropological perspectives on tree symbolism*. L. Rivas, ed. Oxford: Berg Publishers, pp. 1–36.

——— 1998b. Domestication as a historical and symbolic process: Wild gardens and cultivated forests in the Ecuadorian Amazon. In *Advances in historical ecology*. W. Balée, ed. New York: Columbia University Press, pp. 232–50.

Rivet, P., and C. Testevin. 1920. Affinités du Makú et du Puinave, *Journal de la Société des Américanistes* 12:69–82.

Rodríguez, O., and J. Rodríguez. 1992. Los Nukak y los colonos: Contactos étnicos en el noroccidente del Guaviare. Paper presented at the 6to. Congreso Nacional de Antropología de Colombia, Symposium Pasado y Presente de los Cazadores Recolectores en América del Sur. Universidad de Los Andes, Santafé de Bogotá, Colombia.

Roosevelt, A. C. 1980. *Parmana: Prehistoric maize and manioc subsistence along the Amazon and Orinoco*. New York: Academic Press.

——— 1991. *Mount builders of the Amazon: Geophysical archaeology on Marajo Island, Brazil*. San Diego, CA: Academic Press.

——— 1998. Ancient and modern hunter-gatherers of Lowland South America: An evolutionary problem. In *Advances in historical ecology*. W. Balée, ed. New York: Columbia University Press, pp. 190–212.

Roosevelt, A. C, M. Lima da Costa, C. Lopes Machado, M. Michab, N. Mercier, H. Valladas, J. Feathers, W. Barnett, M. Imazio da Silveira, A. Henderson, J. Silva, B. Chernoff, D. S. Reese, J. A. Holman, N. Toth, and K. Schick. 1996. Paleoindian cave dwellers in the Amazon: The peopling of the Americas, *Science* 272:373–84.

Ross, E. B. 1978. Food taboos, diet and hunting strategy: The adaptation to animals in Amazon cultural ecology, *Current Anthropology* 19 (1):1–36.

———— 1980. Reply, *Current Anthropology* 21 (4):544–46.

Roux, V. 1985. *Le matériel de boyage: Étude ethnoarchéologique à Tichitt, Mauritanie.* Mémoire 58. Paris: Editions Recherches sur les Civilisations, ADPF.

Rowlands, M., and J. P. Warnier. 1993. The magical production of iron in the Cameroon Grassfields. In *The archaeology of Africa.* T. Shaw, ed. London: Routledge.

Rydén, S. 1941. *A study of the Siriono Indians.* Göteborg: Erlanders Boktryckeri Aktiebolag.

Salazar Gómez, O., I. Zarante, C. Barreto, D. Neira, and G. Naranjo. 1993. Los Nukak-Makú. Expedición a la "prehistoria": Informe preliminar, *América Negra* 5:115–19.

Sánchez B., E. 1998. Casos de protección de niños Nukak-Makú: Informe final de consultoría. Santafé de Bogotá.

Saunders, N. 1998. Architecture of symbolism: The feline image. In *Icons of power: Feline symbolism in the Americas.* N. J. Saunders, ed. London: Routledge. pp. 12–52.

Schiffer, M. B. 1976. *Behavioural archaeology.* New York: Academic Press.

———— 1978. Methodological issues in ethnoarchaeology. In *Explorations in ethnoarchaeology.* R. A. Gould, ed. Albuquerque: University of New Mexico Press, pp. 229–47.

———— 1985. Is there a "Pompeii" premise in archaeology?" *Journal of Anthropological Research* 41:18–41.

———— 1987. *Formation processes of the archaeological record.* Albuquerque: University of New Mexico Press.

———— 1995. *Behavioural archaeology: First principles.* Salt Lake City: University of Utah Press.

———— 1999. *The material life of human beings: Artifacts, behaviour and communication.* London: Routledge.

Schiffer, M., and J. M. Skibo. 1987. Theory and experiment in the study of technological change, *Current Anthropology* 28:595–622.

Schmitz, P. I. 1975. Projeto Paranaíba: Relatório prêvio, *Anuario de Divulgação Científica* 2:7–18. Brasil: Goiânia.

Schrire, C., ed. 1984. *Past and present in hunter-gatherer studies.* Orlando, FL: Academic Press.

Schultz, H. 1959. Ligeiras notas sôbre os Makú do Paraná Boá-Boá, *Revista do Museu Paulista. Nova Série* XI: 109–32. São Paulo.

Service, E. 1962. *Primitive social organization: An evolutionary perspective.* New York: Random House.

Shanks, M., and C. Tilley. 1987a. *Re-constructing archaeology.* Cambridge: Cambridge University Press.

———— 1987b. *Social theory and archaeology.* Cambridge: Polity Press.

Shipek, F. C. 1989. An example of intense plant husbandry: The Kumeyaay of southern California. In *Foraging and farming: The evolution of plant exploitation.* D. Harris and G. Hillman, eds. London: Unwin Hyman, pp. 159–70.

Shipman, P. 1981. *Life history of a fossil*. Cambridge, MA: Harvard University Press.

———— 1983. Early hominid lifestyle: Hunting and gathering or foraging and scavenging. In *Animals and archaeology 1: Hunters and their prey*. J. C. Brock and C. Grigson, eds. Oxford: Bar International Series 193, pp. 31–49.

Shott, M. 1989. On tool-class use lives and the formation of archaeological assemblages, *American Antiquity* 54 (1):9–30.

Silberbauer, G. 1981. *Hunter and habitat in the central Kalahari Desert*. New York: Cambridge University Press.

———— 1994. A sense of place. In *Key issues in hunter-gatherer research*. E. Burch, Jr., and J. Ellanna, eds. Oxford: Berg Publishers, pp. 119–46.

Sillar, B. 2000a. *Shaping culture: Making pots and constructing households. An Ethnoarchaeological study of pottery production, trade and use in the Andes*. Oxford: BAR International Series 883.

———— 2000b. Dung by preference: the choice of fuel as an example of how Andean pottery production is embedded within wider technical, social and economic practices, *Archaeometry* 41:43–60.

Silva, F. A. 2000. As tecnologías e seus significados: Um estudo da cerámica dos Asuriní do Xingu e da cestaria dos Kayapó-Xikrin sob uma perspectiva etnoarqueológica. Ph.D. dissertation. Departamento de Antropología de Filosofía e Ciências Humanas da Universidade de São Paulo. Brazil.

Silverwood-Cope, P. 1972. A contribution to the ethnography of the Colombian Makú. Unpublished Ph.D dissertation. Cambridge University, Department of Social Anthropology.

———— 1990. *Os Makú: Povo Caçador do Noroeste da Amazonia*. Brasilia: Coleçao Pensamiento Antropológico, Editorial Universidad de Brasilia.

Sinclair, A. 1995. The technique as a symbol in Late Glacial Europe, *World Archaeology* 27 (1):50–61.

Sofaer-Derevenki, J. 1994. Where are the children? Accessing children in the past, *Archaeological Review from Cambridge* 13 (2):7–20.

Sofaer-Derevenki, J., ed. 2000. *Children and material culture*. London: Routledge.

Solway, J., and R. B. Lee. 1990. Foragers genuine or spurious? Situating the Kalahari San in history, *Current Anthropology* 31:109–46.

Sotomayor, H., D. Mahecha, C. Franky, G. Cabrera, and M. L. Torres. 1998. La nutrición de los Nukak: Una sociedad Amazónica en proceso de contacto, *Maguaré* 13: 117–42.

Spaulding, A. C. 1953. Statistical techniques for the discovery of artifacts types, *American Antiquity* 18:305–13.

Speth, J. D. 1983. *Bison kills and bone counts*. Chicago: University of Chicago Press.

———— 1990. Seasonality, resource stress, and food sharing in so-called "egalitarian" foraging societies, *Journal of Anthropological Archaeology* 9:148–88.

Spier, R. 1970. *From the hand of man: Primitive and preindustrial technologies*. Boston: Houghton Mifflin.

Sponsel, L. E. 1986. Amazon ecology and adaptation, *Annual Review of Anthropology* 15:67–97.

Spruce, R. 1908. *Notes of a botanist on the Amazon and Andes*. London: MacMillan and Co.

Stahl, A. 1993. Concepts of time and approaches to analogical reasoning in historical perspective, *American Antiquity* 58:235–60.

Stahl, P. W. 2002. Paradigms in paradise: Revising standard Amazonian prehistory, *The Review of Archaeology* 23 (2):39–50.

Stahl, P., and Zeidler, J. 1990. Differential bone-refuse: Accumulation in food preparation and traffic areas on an early Ecuadorian house floor, *Latin American Antiquity* 1 (2):150–69.

Stearman, A. 1991. Making a living in the tropical forest: Yuqui foragers in the Bolivian Amazon, *Human Ecology* 19 (2):245–58.

Stein M., C. A. 1993. Hunter-gatherer social costs and nonviability of submarginal environments, *Journal of Anthropological Research* 49 (1):39–72.

Steele, D. G., and B. W. Baker. 1993. Multiple predation: A definitive human hunting strategy. In *From bones to behavior: Ethnoarchaeological and experimental contributions to the interpretation of faunal remains*. J. Hudson, ed. Carbondale, IL: Center for Archaeological Investigations. Southern Illinois University of Carbondale. Occasional Paper Nr. 31, pp. 9–37.

Stevenson, M. G. 1982. Toward an understanding of site abandonment behavior: Evidence from historic mining camps in the southwest Yukon, *Journal of Anthropological Archaeology* 2:237–65.

Steward, J. 1946–1950. *The handbook of South American Indians*. 6 Vols. Washington, DC: Bureau of American Ethnology.

——— 1948. Culture areas of the tropical forest. In *The handbook of South American Indians*. Vol. 3. Washington, DC: Bureau of American Ethnology, pp. 883–99.

Steward, J., and L. Faron. 1959. *Native people of South America*. New York: McGraw-Hill.

Stiles, D. 1992. The hunter-gatherer "Revisionist" Debate, *Anthropology Today* 8 (2): 13–17.

Storrie, R. 1999. Being human: Personhood, cosmology and subsistence for the Hotï of Venezuelan Guaina. Ph.D. dissertation. University of Manchester, United Kingdom.

Sutton, M. Q. 1995. Archaeological aspects of insect use, *Journal of Archaeological Method and Theory* 2 (3):253–98.

Taçon, P. 1991. The power of stone: Symbolic aspects of stone use and tool development in western Arnhem Land, Australia, *American Antiquity* 65:192–207.

——— 2004. Ochre, clay, stone and art: The symbolic importance of minerals as life-force among aboriginal peoples of northern and central Australia. In *Soils, stones and symbols*. N. Boivin and M. A. Owoc, eds. London: UCL Press, pp. 31–42.

Tambiah, S. J. 1969. Animals are good to think and good to prohibit, *Ethnology* 8: 423–57.

Tani, M. 1995. Beyond the identification of formation processes: Behavioral inference based on traces left by cultural formation processes, *Journal of Archaeological Method and Theory* 2 (3):231–52.

Tastevin, P.C. 1923. Les Makú du Japurá, *Journal de la Société del Américanistes de Paris* 15:99–108.

Terribilini, M., and M. Terribilini. 1961. Enquete chez des Indiens Makú du Caiari-Uaupes. Aoûy 1960, *Bulletin. Société Suisse des Américanistes* (SSA) 21:2–10.

Thomas, D. H., and D. Mayer. 1983. Behavioural faunal analysis of selected horizons. In *The archaeology of Monitor Valley 2: Gatecliff Shelter*. D. H. Thomas, ed. *Anthropological Papers of the American Museum of Natural History* 59 (1):353–90.

Thomas, J. 2000. Introduction. In *Interpretive archaeology: A reader*. J. Thomas, ed. London: Leicester University Press, pp. 1–18.

Tilley, C. 1999. *Metaphor and material culture*. Oxford: Routledge.

Tomka, S. A.1993. Site abandonment behaviour among transhumant agro-pastoralist: the effects of delayed curation on assemblages composition. In *Abandonment of settlement and regions*. C. M. Cameron and S. Tomka, eds. Cambridge: Cambridge University Press, pp. 11–24.

────── 2001. Up and down we move . . .: Factors conditioning agro-pastoral settlement organization in mountainous settings. In *Ethnoarchaeology of Andean South America: Contributions to archaeological method and theory*. L. Kuznar, ed. Ann Arbor, MI: International Monographs in Prehistory, Ethnoarchaeological Series 4, pp. 138–62.

Torrence, R. 1983. Time budgeting and hunter-gatherer technology. In *Hunter-gatherer economy in prehistory: A European perspective*. G. Bailey, ed. Cambridge: Cambridge University Press, pp. 11–22.

────── 1989. Re-tooling: Towards a behavioural theory of stone tools. In *Time, energy, and stone tools*. R. Torrence, ed. New York: Cambridge University Press, pp. 57–66.

Torres, W. 1994. Nukak: Aspectos etnográficos, *Revista Colombiana de Antropología* 31:197–234.

Toth, N., J. D. Clark, and G. Ligabue. 1992. The last stone ax makers, *Scientific American* 267 (1):88–93.

Towsend, P. K. 1990. On the possiblity/impossibily of tropical forest hunting and gathering, *American Anthropologist* 92:745–47.

Triana, G. 1987. *Introducción a la Colombia Amerindia*. Bogotá: Instituto Colombiano de Antropología, pp. 97–108.

Ucko, P. 1983. The politics of the indigenous minority, *Journal of Biosociological Science* 8:25–40.

────── 1985. Australian Aborigines and academic social anthropology. In *The future of farmer foragers*. C. Schrire and R. Gordon, eds. Cambridge: Cultural Survival Inc., pp. 63–73.

Useche, M. 1987. *Proceso colonial en el Alto Orinoco-Río Negro (Siglos XVI–XVIII)*. Bogotá: Finarco.

Valeri, V. 2000. *The forest of taboos*. Madison: The University of Wisconsin Press.

Van der Berghe, P. 1977. *Human family systems: An evolutionary view*. New York: Elsevier.

Van der Hammen, M. C. 1992. *El manejo del mundo: Naturaleza y sociedad entre los Yukuna de la Amazonía Colombiana*. Bogotá: Tropnebos, Colombia.

Vickers, W. 1989. *Los Sionas y Secoyas: Su adaptación al ambiente amazónico*. Quito: Ediciones Abya-Yala.

Vilera Diaz, D. 1985. Introducción morfológica de la lengua Hotï. Graduate Degree dissertation, Universidad Central de Caracas.

Viveiros de Castro, E. 1992. *From the enemy's point of view: Humanity and divinity in an Amazonian society*. Chicago: Chicago University Press.

────── 1996. Images of nature and society in Amazonian ethnology, *Annual Review of Anthropology* 25:179–200.

Watson, P. J. 1979. *Archaeological ethnography in western Iran*. Vicking Foundation Publications in Anthropology 57. Tucson: University of Arizona Press.

Wegner, R. 1931. *Zum Sonnentor durch altes Indianerland*. Darmstadt: Wittich.

Whiffen, T. 1915. *The North-West Amazons: Notes of some months spent among cannibal tribes*. New York: Duffield and Company.

White, T. E. 1952. Observation on the butchering techniques of some aboriginal people: 1, *American Antiquity* 17:337–38.

———— 1953. Observation on the butchering techniques of some aboriginal people: 2, *American Antiquity* 19 (2):160–64.

———— 1954. Observation on the butchering techniques of some aboriginal people: 3, 4, 5, and 6, *American Antiquity* 19:254–64.

Whitelaw, T. 1989. The social organization of space in hunter-gatherer communities: Some implications for social inference in archaeology. Ph.D. dissertation. University of Cambridge.

———— 1991. Some dimensions of variability in the social organization of community space among foragers. In *Ethnoarchaeological approaches to mobile campsites: Hunter-gatherer and pastoralist case studies*. C. S. Gamble and W. A. Boismier, eds. Ann Arbor, MI: International Monographs in Prehistory. Ethnoarchaeological Series 1, pp. 139–88.

Whitley, D. 1992. Prehistory and post-positivist science: A prolegomenon to cognitive archaeology, *Archaeological Method and Theory* 4:57–100.

———— 1998. *Reader in archaeological theory: Postprocessual and cognitive approaches*. London: Routledge.

Wiessner, P. 1983. Style and social information in Kalahari San projectile points, *American Antiquity* 48:253–76.

———— 1990. Is there a unity to style? In *The uses of style in archaeology*. M. W. Conkey and C. A. Hastorf, eds. Cambridge: Cambridge University Press, 105–12.

Wilbert, J., and K. Simoneau. 1992. *Folk literature of South American Indians*. Los Angeles: UCLA Latin American Center Publications, University of California.

Wilbert, J., and K. Simoneau, eds. 1991. *Folk literature of the Cuiva Indians*. Los Angeles: UCLA Latin American Center Publications, University of California.

Williams, E. 1994. Organización del espacio doméstico y producción cerámica en Huáncito, Michoacán. In *Contribuciones a la arqueología y etnohistoria del occidente de México* E. Williams, ed. Michoacán: El Colegio de Michoacán, pp. 189–225.

———— 1995. The spatial organization of pottery production in Huáncito, Michoacán, Mexico, *Papers from the Institute of Archaeology* 6:47–56.

Wilmsen, E. 1983. The ecology of illusion: Anthropological foraging in the Kalahari, *Reviews in Anthropology* 10 (1):9–20.

———— 1989. *Land filled with flies: A political economy of the Kalahari*. Chicago: Chicago University Press.

Winterhalder, B. 1987. The analysis of hunter-gatherer diets: Stalking an optimal foraging model. In *Food and evolution*. M. Harris and E. Ross, eds. Philadelphia: Temple University Press, pp. 311–39.

———— 2001. The behavioural ecology of hunter-gatherers. In *Hunter-gatherers: An interdisciplinary perspective*. C. Panter Brick, R. H. Layton, and P. Rowley Conwy, eds. Cambridge: Cambridge University Press, pp. 12–38.

Winterhalder, B., and E. Smith. 1992. *Evolutionary ecology and human behaviour*. New York: Aldine Press.

Wirpsa, L.1988. Un espíritu castigador persigue a los Nukak, *El Espectador* 1B–3B, Bogotá, 22 de Mayo.

Wirpsa, L., and H. Mondragón. 1988. Resettlement of Nukak Indians, Colombia, *Cultural Survival Quarterly* 12 (4):36–40.

Wobst, M. 1977. Stylistic behavior and information exchange. In *Papers for the director: Research essays in honor of James B. Griffin.* C. E. Cleland, ed. New York: Academic Press, pp. 317–42.

———— 1978. The archaeo-ethnography of hunter-gatherers or the tyranny of the ethnographic record in Archaeology, *American Antiquity* 42:303–09.

Woodburn, J. 1991. Hunters and gatherers and other people: A reexamination. In *Hunters and gatherers 1: History, evolution and social change.* T. Ingold, D. Riches, and J. Woodburn, eds. Oxford: Berg Publishers, pp. 31–64.

Wüst, I. 1975. A cerâmica carajá da Arauanã, *Anuario de Divulgação Científica* Año II (2):95–166. Goiânia, Brasil.

———— 1998. Continuities and discontinuities: Archaeology and ethnoarchaeology in the heart of the Eastern Bororo territory, Mato Grosso, Brazil, *Antiquity* 72:663–75.

Wüst, I., and C. Barreto 1999. The Ring Village of Central Brazil: A challenge for Amazonian archaeology, *Latin American Antiquity* 10:3–23.

Wylie, A. 1982. Analogy by any other name is just an analogy, *Journal of Anthropological Archaeology* 1 (4):382–401.

———— 1985. The reaction against analogy. In *Advances in archaeological method and theory.* Vol. 8. M. Schiffer, ed. Orlando, FL: Academic Press, pp. 63–111.

Yacobaccio, H. 1995. El aporte de la Etnoarqueología al conocimiento del registro arqueológico pastoril andino, *Actas del XIII Congreso Nacional de Arqueología Chilena, Hombre y Desierto* 9 (1):309–16. Antofagasta, Chile.

Yacobaccio, H., and C. M. Madero. 1994. Etnoarqueología de pastores surandinos: una herramienta para conocer el registro arqueológico, *Jornadas de Arqueología e Interdisciplina*: 203–36. Buenos Aires: CONICET-Programa de Estudios Prehistóricos.

———— 2001. Ethnoarchaeology of a pastoral settlement of the Andean Plateau: An investigation of archaeological scale. In *Ethnoarchaeology of Andean South America: Contributions to Archaeological method and theory.* L. Kuznar. Ann Arbor, MI: International Monographs in Prehistory, Ethnoarchaeological Series 4, pp. 84–96.

Yacobaccio, H., C. Madero, and M. Malmierca. 1998. *Etnoarqueología de pastores Surandinos.* Buenos Aires: Grupo Zooarqueología de Camélidos.

Yellen, J. E. 1977. *Archaeological approaches to the present.* New York: Academic Press.

———— 1991a. Small mammals: !Kung San utilization and the production of faunal assemblage, *Journal of Anthropological Archaeology* 10:1–26.

———— 1991b. Small mammals: Post-discard patterning of !Kung San faunal remains, *Journal of Anthropological Archaeology* 10:152–92.

Yost, J. 1981. People of the forest: The Waorani. In *Ecuador in the shadow of the volcanoes.* G. Ligabue, ed. Venice: Ediciones Libri Mundi, pp. 95–115.

Yunis, I., and M. Piñeros. Ms. Propuesta de investigación y atención en salud para la comunidad indígena Nukak. Santafé de Bogotá: Instituto Nacional de Salud. 1993.

Yunis, I., M. Piñeros, and J. P. Rueda. Ms. Informe del proyecto de investigación y atención en salud para la comunidad indígena Nukak. Santafé de Bogotá: Instituto Nacional de Salud. 1994.

Yunis, I., and J. P. Rueda. Ms. Demografía Nukak: Apunte iniciales sobre su nomadismo. Santafé de Bogotá: Instituto Nacional de Salud. 1995.

Zambrano, C. 1992. Los Nukak en Calamar: Encuentro posible de culturas distantes. In *Diversidad es riqueza*, 65–67. Santafé de Bogotá: Instituto Colombiano de Antropología.

——— 1994. El contacto con los Nukak de Guaviare, *Revista Colombiana de Antropología* 31:179–93.

Zarante, I., and O. Salazar Gómez. 1993. Los Nukak-Makú: Aproximación médica, *América Negra* 5:121–26.

Zeidler, J. 1984. Social space in Valdivia Society: Community patterning and domestic structure at Real Alto, 3,000–2,000 B.C. Unpublished Ph.D. dissertation. University of Illinois, Urbana-Champagne.

Zent, E. L., and S. Zent. 2002. Impactos ambientales generadores de biodiversidad: Conductas ecológicas de los Hotï de la Sierra Maigualida, Amazonas Venezolano, *Interciencia* 27 (1):3–10.

——— In Press. Amazonian Indians as ecological disturbance agents: The Hotï of the Sierra Maigualida, Venezuelan Amazon. In *Ethnobotany and conservation of biocultural diversity*. L. Maffi and T. Carlson, eds. New York: Botanical Garden Press.

Zent, S., E. L. Zent, and L. Martius. 2001. *Informe final del Proyecto Etnobotánica Cuantitativa de los indígenas Hotï de la Región Circum-Maigualida, Estados Amazonas y Bolivar, Venezuela.* Caraca: CONICIT.

Zimmermann Holt, J. 1996a. Beyond optimisation: Alternative ways of examining animal exploitation, *Zooarchaeology* 28 (1):89–109.

——— 1996b. In search of Hopewellian elites: Faunal remains from the Baehr site in the lower-central Illinois valley. Paper presented at the Society for American Archaeology 61st Annual Meeting Symposium. New Orleans, Louisiana.

SUBJECT AND NAME INDEX

PLANTS AND ANIMALS INDEX

About the Author

Gustavo G. Politis is a researcher at Consejo Nacional de Investigaciones Científicas y Técnicas (CONICET) of Argentina and professor at the Universidad Nacional del Centro de la Pcia. de Buenos Aires and Universidad Nacional de La Plata. His main research interests are the archaeology of the Southern Cone of South America and the ethnoarchaeology of the Amazon. He is author of two books and more than one hundred articles.